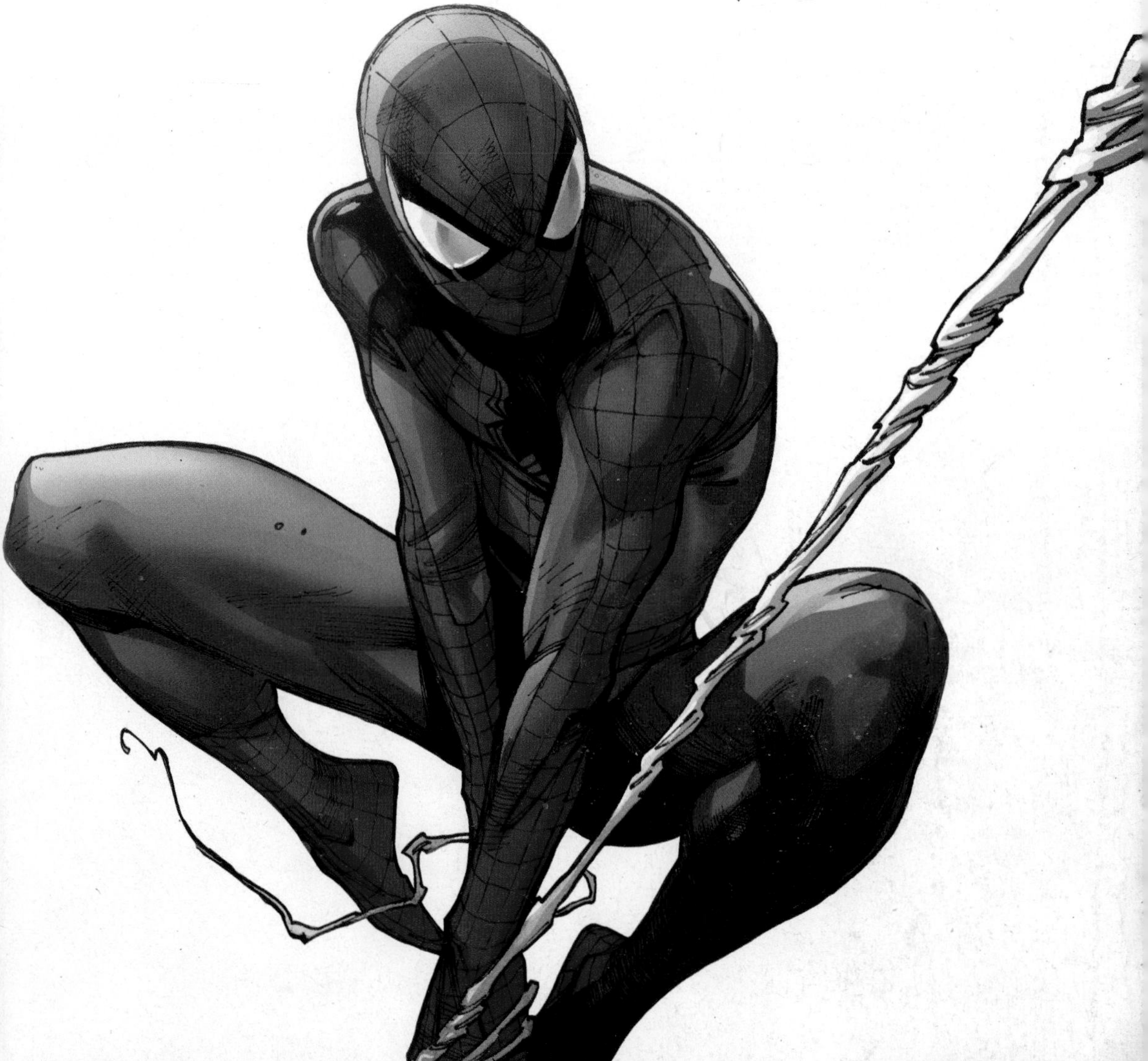

The AMAZING SPIDER-MAN

SPIDER-VERSE

Collection Editor: **Jennifer Grünwald**
Assistant Editor: **Sarah Brunstad**
Associate Managing Editor: **Alex Starbuck**
Editor, Special Projects: **Mark D. Beazley**
Senior Editor, Special Projects: **Jeff Youngquist**
SVP Print, Sales & Marketing: **David Gabriel**
Book Designer: **Jay Bowen**

Editor in Chief: **Axel Alonso**
Chief Creative Officer: **Joe Quesada**
Publisher: **Dan Buckley**
Executive Producer: **Alan Fine**

AMAZING SPIDER-MAN VOL. 3: SPIDER-VERSE. Contains material originally published in magazine form as AMAZING SPIDER-MAN #9-15. First printing 2015. ISBN# 978-0-7851-9234-3. Published by MARVEL WORLDWIDE, INC., a subsidiary of MARVEL ENTERTAINMENT, LLC. OFFICE OF PUBLICATION: 135 West 50th Street, New York, NY 10020. **Printed in the U.S.A.** ALAN FINE, President, Marvel Entertainment; DAN BUCKLEY, President, TV, Publishing and Brand Management; JOE QUESADA, Chief Creative Officer; TOM BREVOORT, SVP of Publishing; DAVID BOGART, SVP of Operations & Procurement, Publishing; C.B. CEBULSKI, VP of International Development & Brand Management; DAVID GABRIEL, SVP Print, Sales & Marketing; JIM O'KEEFE, VP of Operations & Logistics; DAN CARR, Executive Director of Publishing Technology; SUSAN CRESPI, Editorial Operations Manager; ALEX MORALES, Publishing Operations Manager; STAN LEE, Chairman Emeritus. For information regarding advertising in Marvel Comics or on Marvel.com, please contact Jonathan Rheingold, VP of Custom Solutions & Ad Sales, at jrheingold@marvel.com. For Marvel subscription inquiries, please call 800-217-9158. **Manufactured between 5/15/2015 and 6/22/2015 by R.R. DONNELLEY, INC., SALEM, VA, USA.**

10 9 8 7 6 5 4 3 2 1

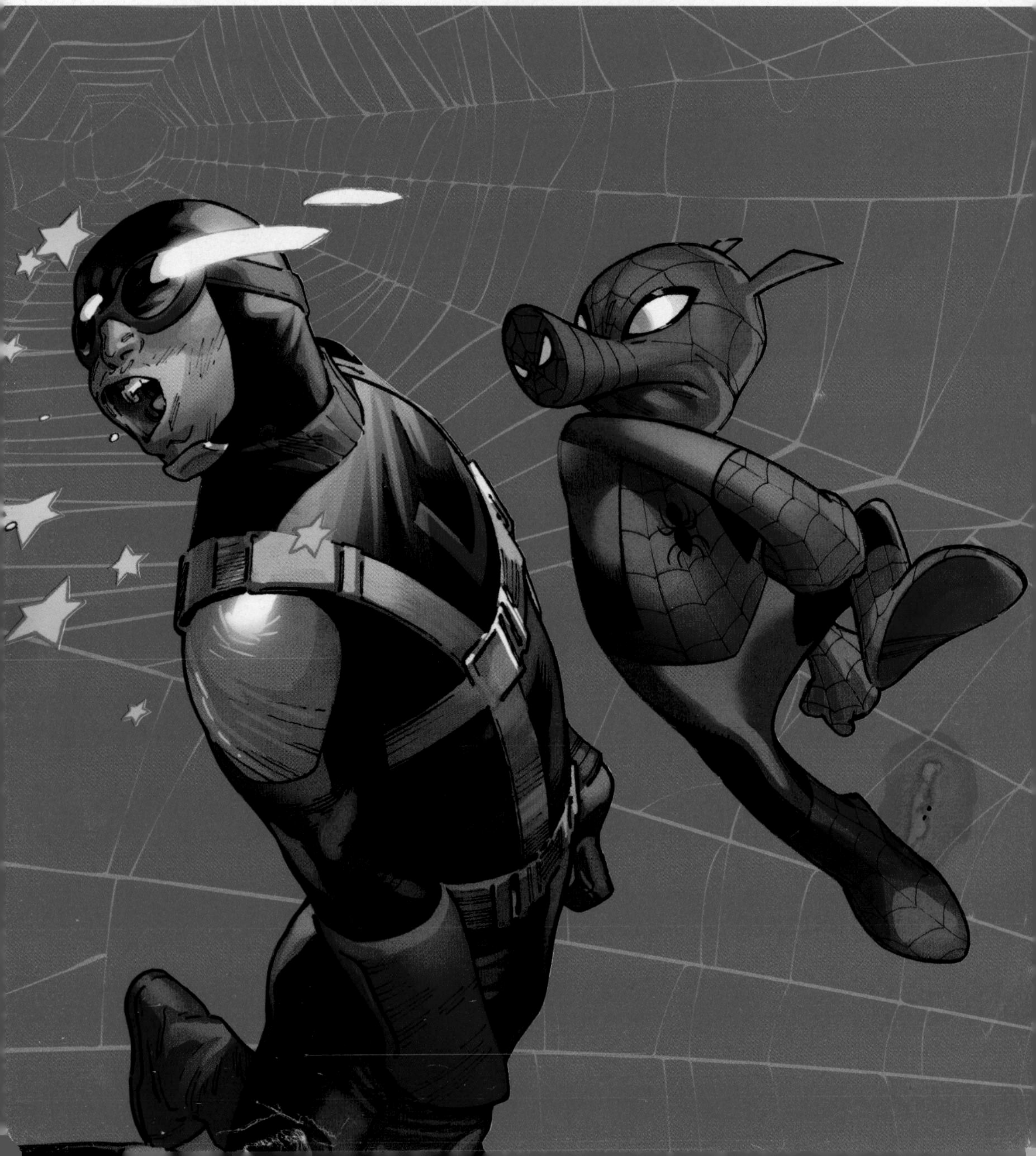

The AMAZING SPIDER-MAN

SPIDER-VERSE

WRITER:
DAN SLOTT

PENCILERS:
OLIVIER COIPEL
(#9-11 & #14)

& **GIUSEPPE CAMUNCOLI**
(#12-15)

INKERS:
OLIVIER COIPEL (#9-11),
CAM SMITH (#12-15)
& **WADE VON GRAWBADGER**
(#10, 11 & #14),
WITH **LIVESAY** (#11 & #14),
VICTOR OLAZABA (#11),
MARK MORALES (#11),
& **ROBERTO POGGI** (#15)

COLORIST:
JUSTIN PONSOR

LETTERERS: **CHRIS ELIOPOULOS**
WITH **VC'S TRAVIS LANHAM** (#11)

COVER ART: **OLIVIER COIPEL**
& **JUSTIN PONSOR** (#9-12),

**OLIVIER COIPEL,
WADE VON GRAWBADGER**
& **JUSTIN PONSOR** (#13)

AND **GIUSEPPE CAMUNCOLI,
CAM SMITH** & **JUSTIN PONSOR**
(#14-15)

"SPIDER-VERSE: THE FEAST"
WRITER: **DAN SLOTT**
PENCILER: **GIUSEPPE CAMUNCOLI**
INKER: **CAM SMITH**
COLORIST: **ANTONIO FABELA**
LETTERER: **VC'S TRAVIS LANHAM**

ASSISTANT EDITOR: **DEVIN LEWIS**
ASSOCIATE EDITOR: **ELLIE PYLE**
EDITOR: **NICK LOWE**

SPIDER-MAN CREATED BY STAN LEE & STEVE DITKO

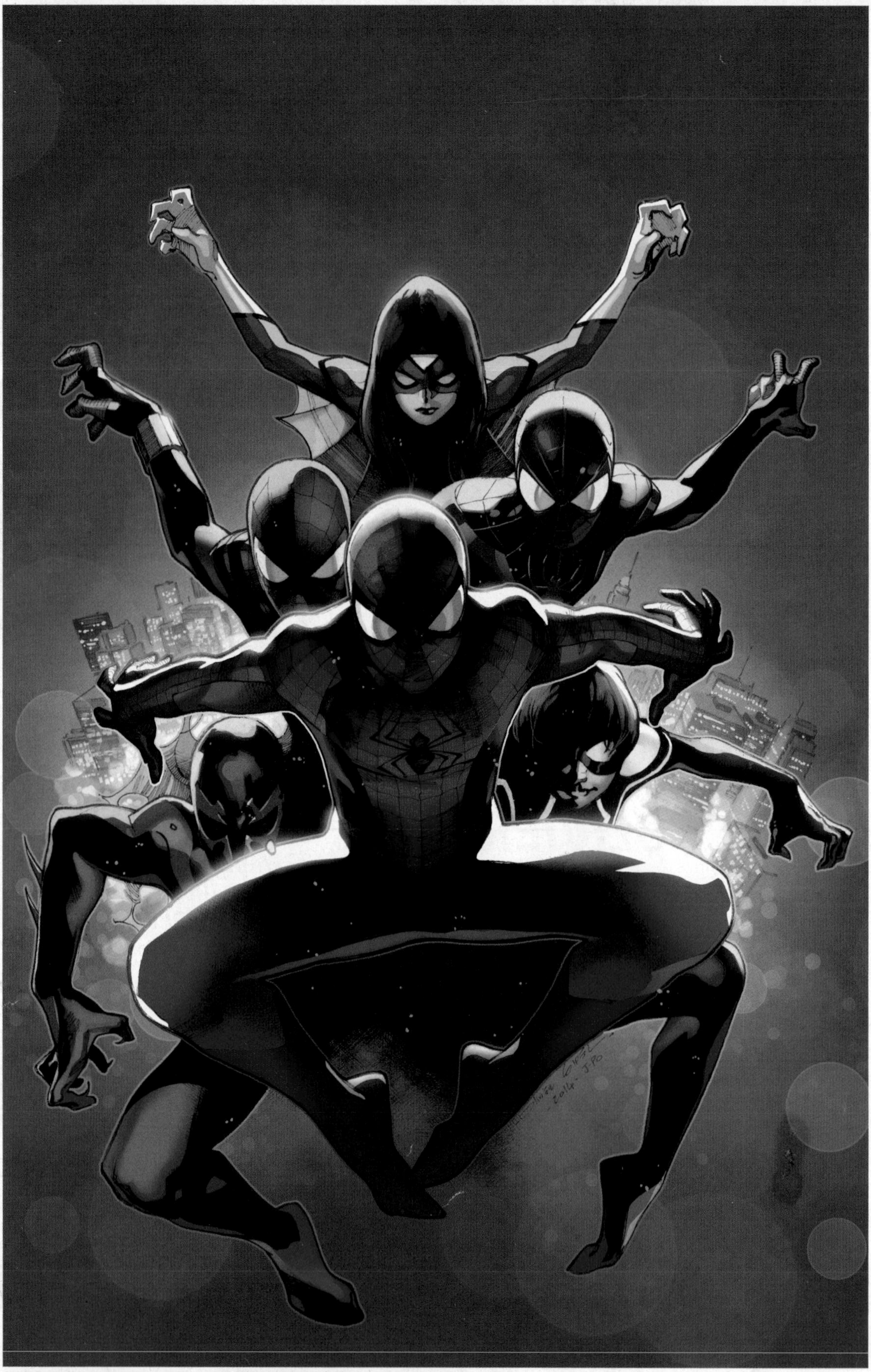

AMAZING SPIDER-MAN 9

SPIDER-VERSE, PART ONE: THE GATHERING

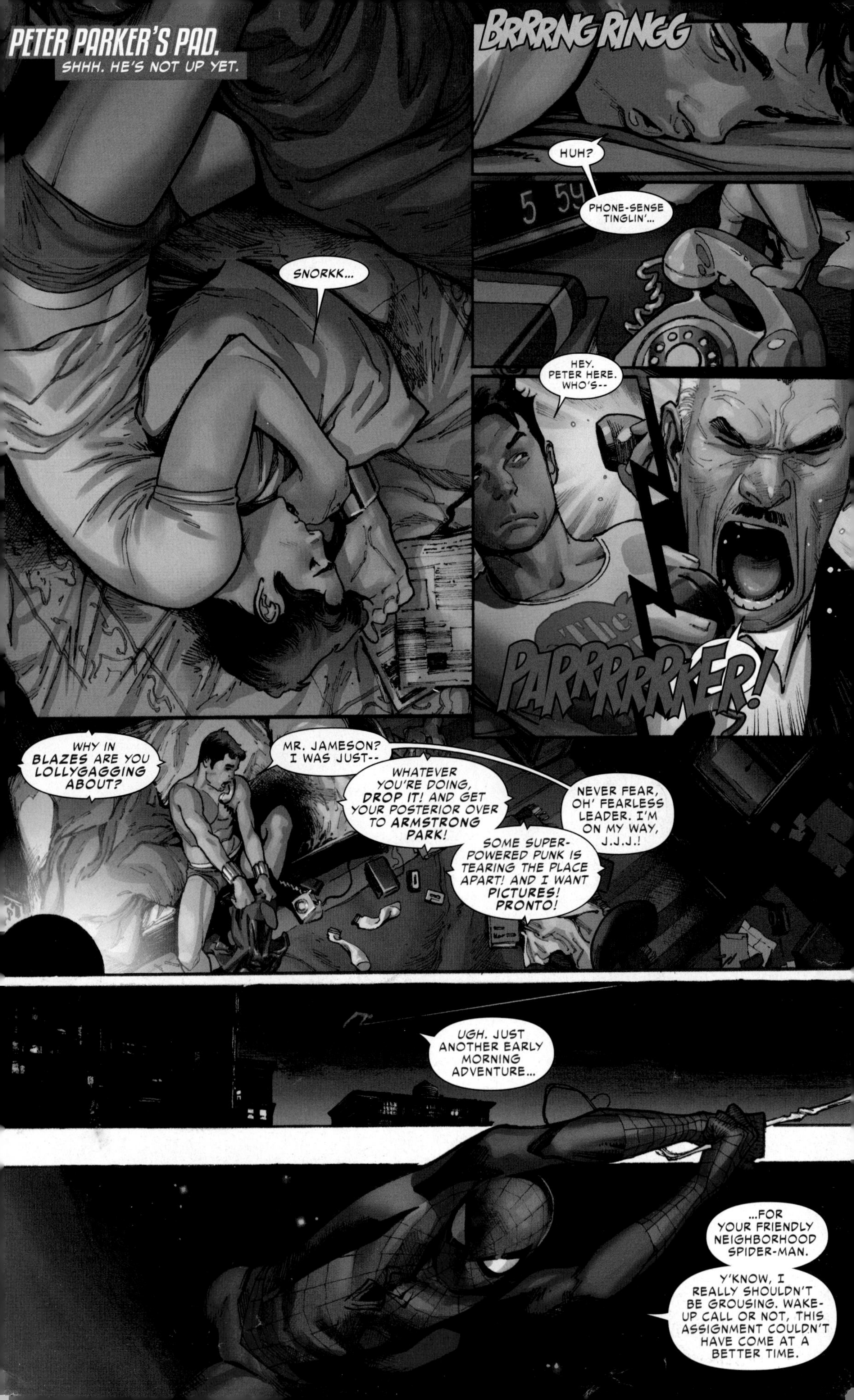
PETER PARKER'S PAD.
SHHH. HE'S NOT UP YET.
SNORKK...
BRRRNG RINGG
HUH?
PHONE-SENSE TINGLIN'...
HEY. PETER HERE. WHO'S--
PARRRRRRKER!
WHY IN BLAZES ARE YOU LOLLYGAGGING ABOUT?
MR. JAMESON? I WAS JUST--
WHATEVER YOU'RE DOING, DROP IT! AND GET YOUR POSTERIOR OVER TO ARMSTRONG PARK!
SOME SUPER-POWERED PUNK IS TEARING THE PLACE APART! AND I WANT PICTURES! PRONTO!
NEVER FEAR, OH' FEARLESS LEADER. I'M ON MY WAY, J.J.J.!
UGH. JUST ANOTHER EARLY MORNING ADVENTURE...
...FOR YOUR FRIENDLY NEIGHBORHOOD SPIDER-MAN.
Y'KNOW, I REALLY SHOULDN'T BE GROUSING. WAKE-UP CALL OR NOT, THIS ASSIGNMENT COULDN'T HAVE COME AT A BETTER TIME.

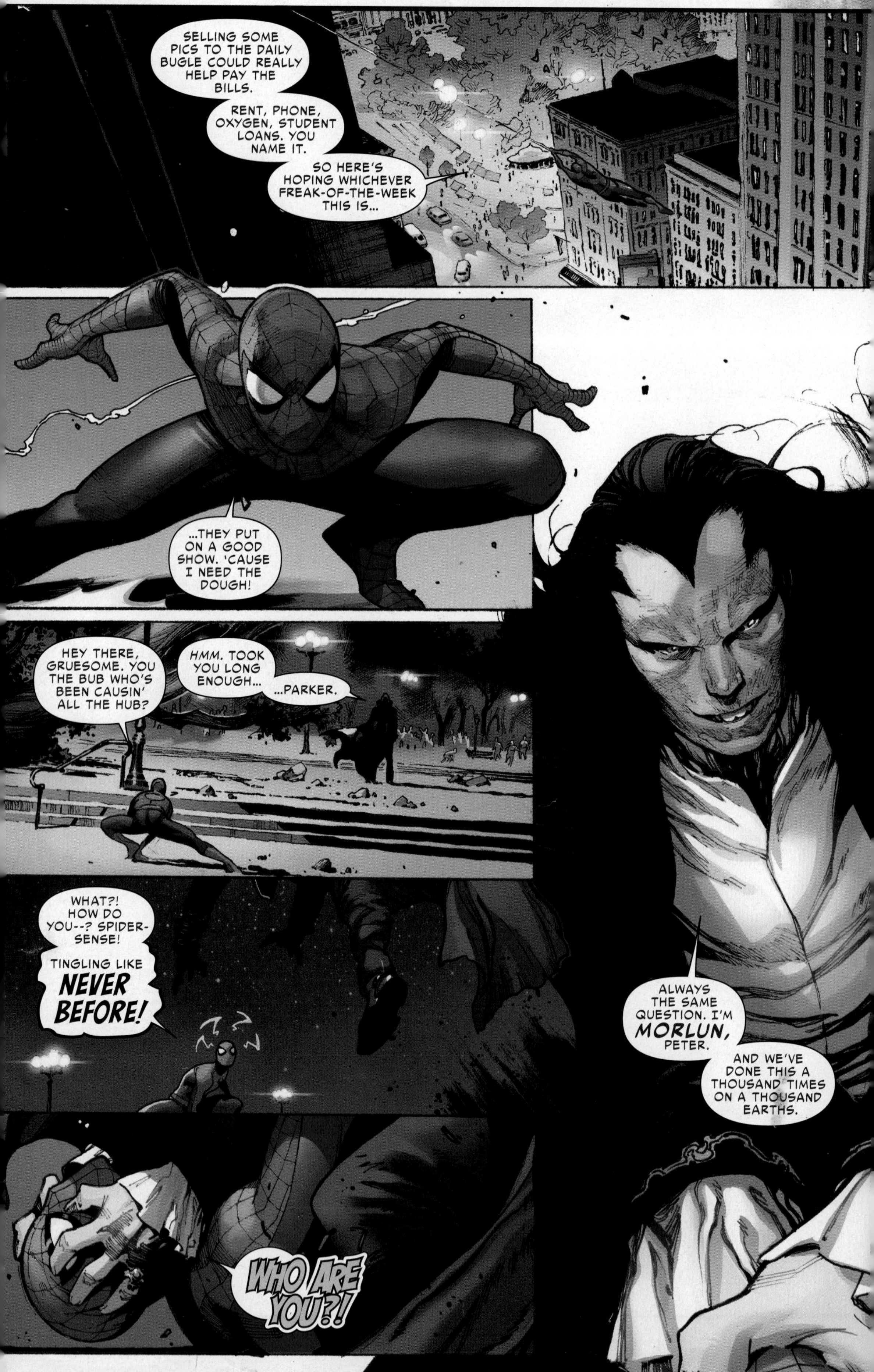
SELLING SOME PICS TO THE DAILY BUGLE COULD REALLY HELP PAY THE BILLS.
RENT, PHONE, OXYGEN, STUDENT LOANS. YOU NAME IT.
SO HERE'S HOPING WHICHEVER FREAK-OF-THE-WEEK THIS IS...
...THEY PUT ON A GOOD SHOW. 'CAUSE I NEED THE DOUGH!
HEY THERE, GRUESOME. YOU THE BUB WHO'S BEEN CAUSIN' ALL THE HUB?
HMM. TOOK YOU LONG ENOUGH...
...PARKER.
WHAT?! HOW DO YOU--? SPIDER-SENSE!
TINGLING LIKE NEVER BEFORE!
WHO ARE YOU?!
ALWAYS THE SAME QUESTION. I'M MORLUN, PETER.
AND WE'VE DONE THIS A THOUSAND TIMES ON A THOUSAND EARTHS.

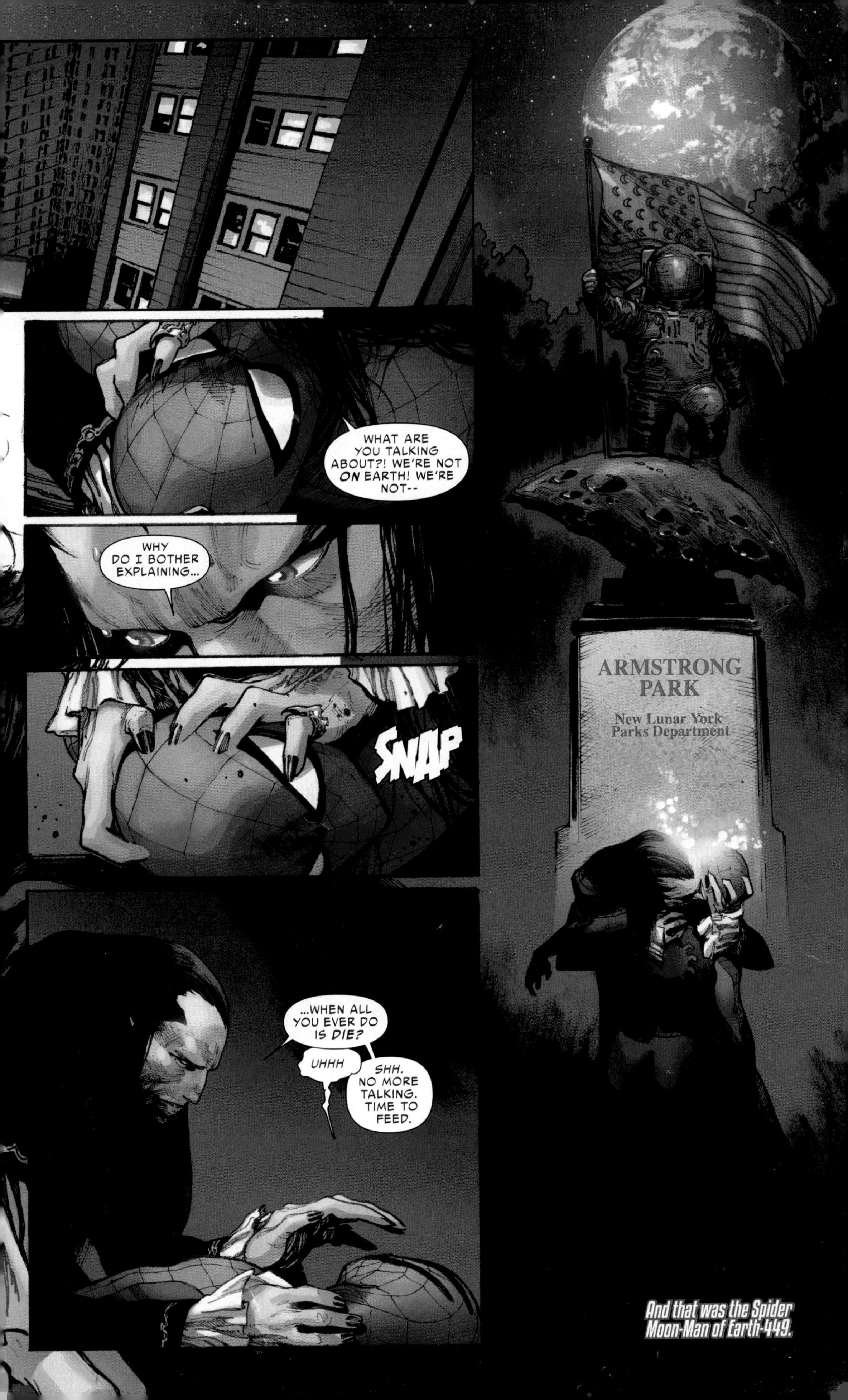
WHAT ARE YOU TALKING ABOUT?! WE'RE NOT ON EARTH! WE'RE NOT--
WHY DO I BOTHER EXPLAINING...
SNAP
...WHEN ALL YOU EVER DO IS DIE?
UHHH
SHH. NO MORE TALKING. TIME TO FEED.
ARMSTRONG PARK
New Lunar York Parks Department
And that was the Spider Moon-Man of Earth-449.

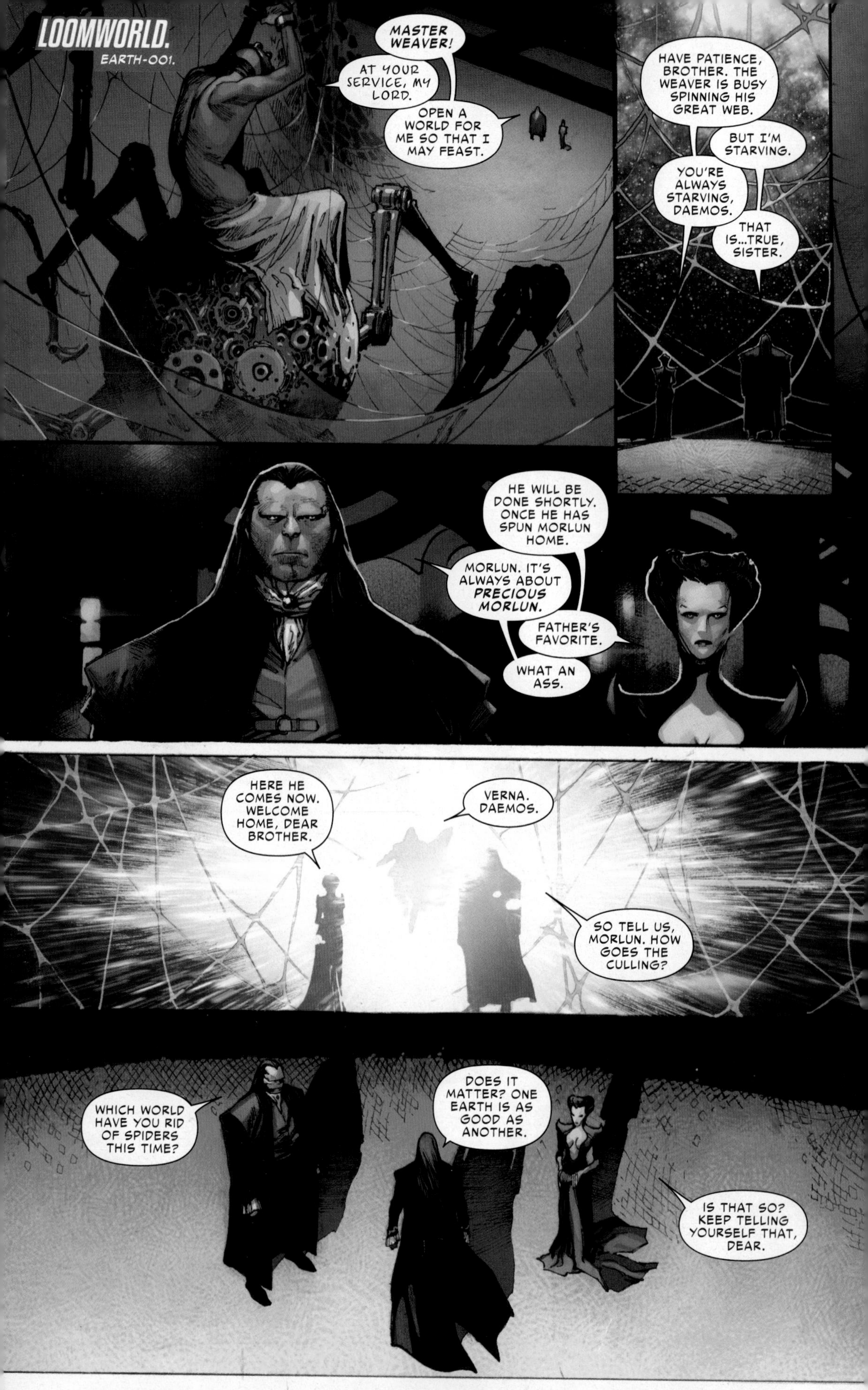
LOOMWORLD.
EARTH-001.
MASTER WEAVER!
AT YOUR SERVICE, MY LORD.
OPEN A WORLD FOR ME SO THAT I MAY FEAST.
HAVE PATIENCE, BROTHER. THE WEAVER IS BUSY SPINNING HIS GREAT WEB.
BUT I'M STARVING.
YOU'RE ALWAYS STARVING, DAEMOS.
THAT IS...TRUE, SISTER.
HE WILL BE DONE SHORTLY. ONCE HE HAS SPUN MORLUN HOME.
MORLUN. IT'S ALWAYS ABOUT PRECIOUS MORLUN.
FATHER'S FAVORITE.
WHAT AN ASS.
HERE HE COMES NOW. WELCOME HOME, DEAR BROTHER.
VERNA. DAEMOS.
SO TELL US, MORLUN. HOW GOES THE CULLING?
WHICH WORLD HAVE YOU RID OF SPIDERS THIS TIME?
DOES IT MATTER? ONE EARTH IS AS GOOD AS ANOTHER.
IS THAT SO? KEEP TELLING YOURSELF THAT, DEAR.

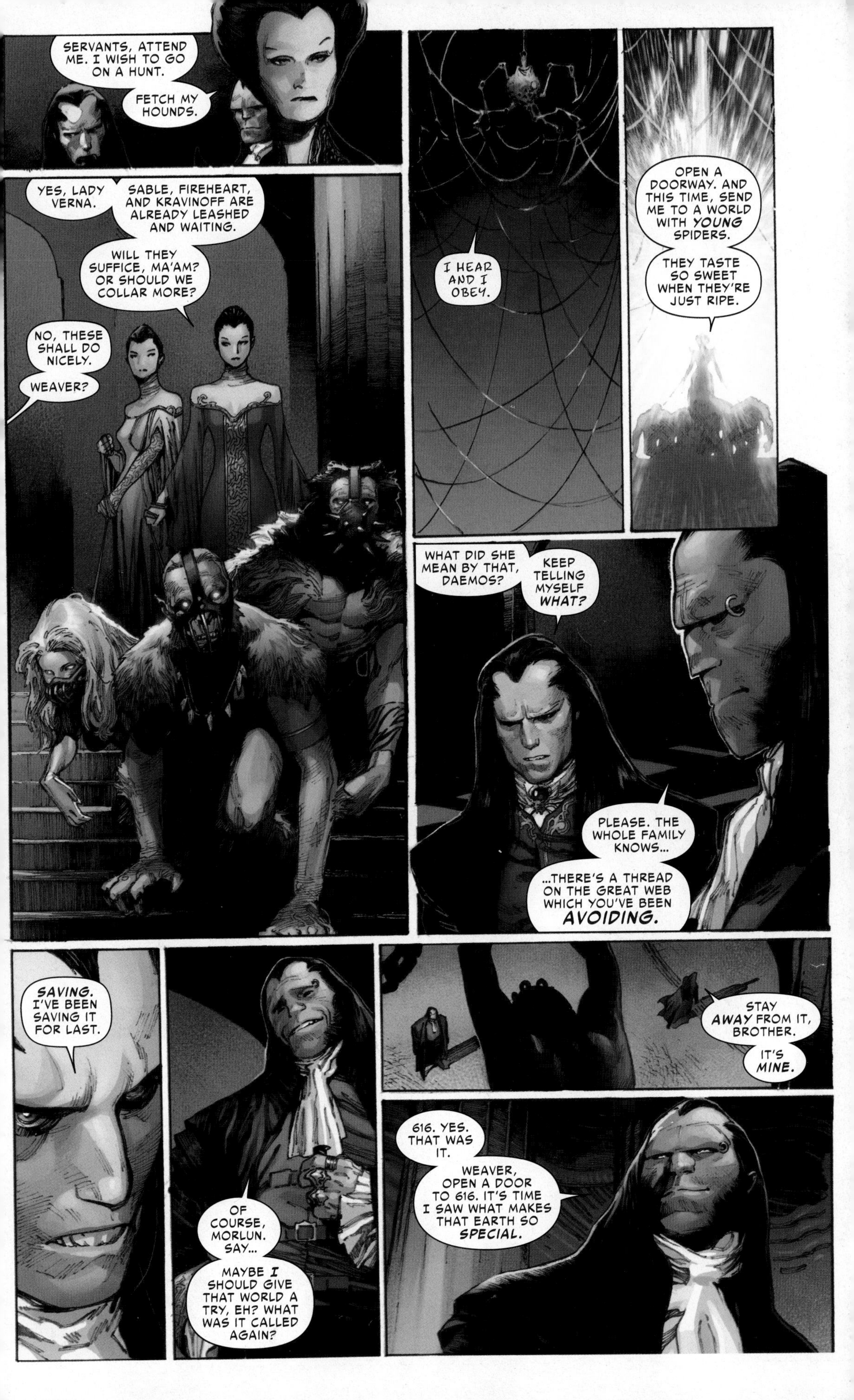
SERVANTS, ATTEND ME. I WISH TO GO ON A HUNT.
FETCH MY HOUNDS.
YES, LADY VERNA.
SABLE, FIREHEART, AND KRAVINOFF ARE ALREADY LEASHED AND WAITING.
WILL THEY SUFFICE, MA'AM? OR SHOULD WE COLLAR MORE?
NO, THESE SHALL DO NICELY.
WEAVER?
I HEAR AND I OBEY.
OPEN A DOORWAY. AND THIS TIME, SEND ME TO A WORLD WITH *YOUNG* SPIDERS.
THEY TASTE SO SWEET WHEN THEY'RE JUST RIPE.
WHAT DID SHE MEAN BY THAT, DAEMOS?
KEEP TELLING MYSELF *WHAT?*
PLEASE. THE WHOLE FAMILY KNOWS...
...THERE'S A THREAD ON THE GREAT WEB WHICH YOU'VE BEEN ***AVOIDING.***
SAVING. I'VE BEEN SAVING IT FOR LAST.
OF COURSE, MORLUN. SAY...
MAYBE *I* SHOULD GIVE THAT WORLD A TRY, EH? WHAT WAS IT CALLED AGAIN?
STAY *AWAY* FROM IT, BROTHER.
IT'S *MINE.*
616. YES. THAT WAS IT.
WEAVER, OPEN A DOOR TO 616. IT'S TIME I SAW WHAT MAKES THAT EARTH SO *SPECIAL.*

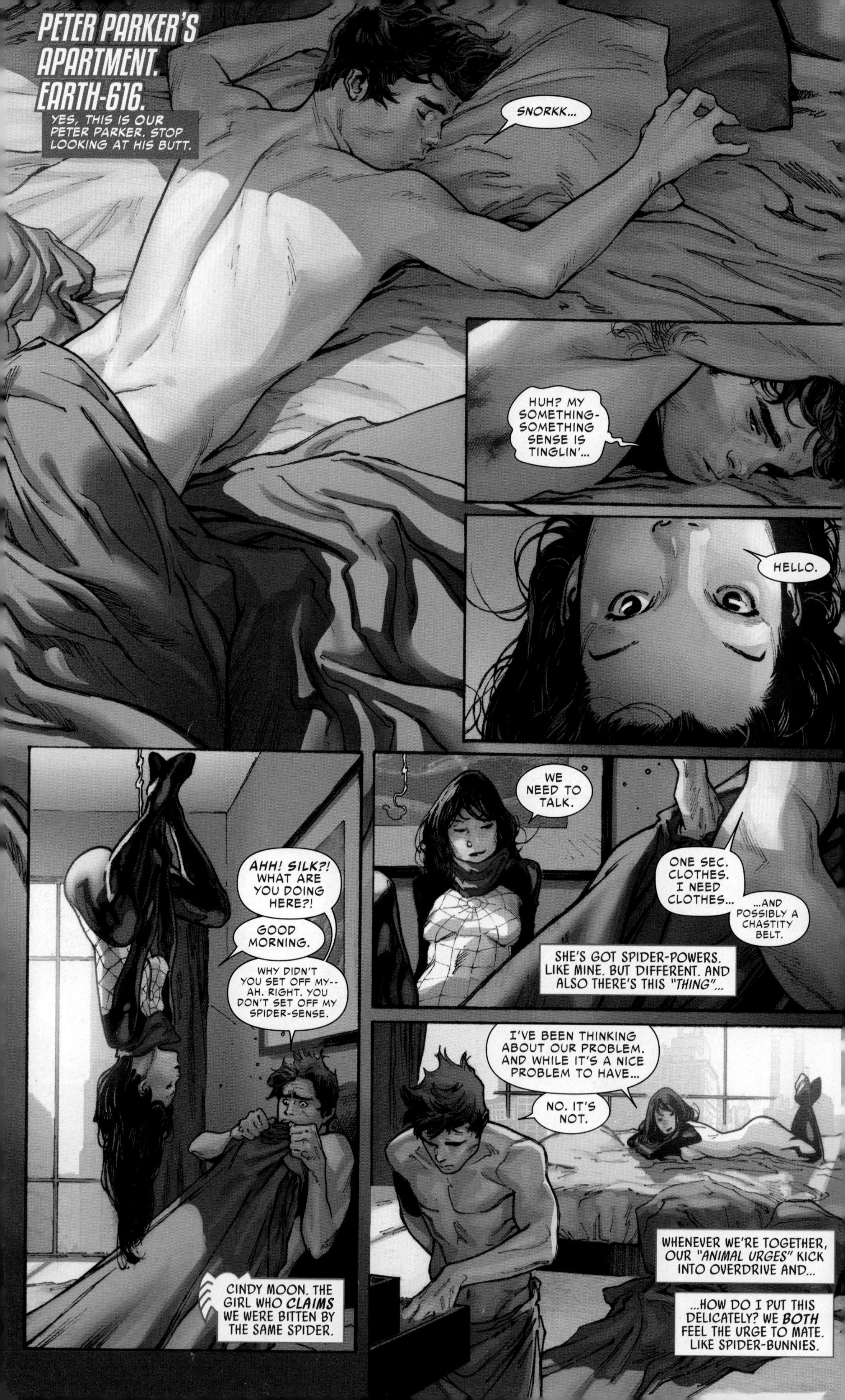
PETER PARKER'S APARTMENT. EARTH-616.
YES, THIS IS OUR PETER PARKER. STOP LOOKING AT HIS BUTT.
SNORKK...
HUH? MY SOMETHING-SOMETHING SENSE IS TINGLIN'...
HELLO.
AHH! SILK?! WHAT ARE YOU DOING HERE?!
GOOD MORNING.
WHY DIDN'T YOU SET OFF MY-- AH. RIGHT. YOU DON'T SET OFF MY SPIDER-SENSE.
CINDY MOON. THE GIRL WHO CLAIMS WE WERE BITTEN BY THE SAME SPIDER.
WE NEED TO TALK.
ONE SEC. CLOTHES. I NEED CLOTHES...
...AND POSSIBLY A CHASTITY BELT.
SHE'S GOT SPIDER-POWERS. LIKE MINE. BUT DIFFERENT. AND ALSO THERE'S THIS "THING"...
I'VE BEEN THINKING ABOUT OUR PROBLEM. AND WHILE IT'S A NICE PROBLEM TO HAVE...
NO. IT'S NOT.
WHENEVER WE'RE TOGETHER, OUR "ANIMAL URGES" KICK INTO OVERDRIVE AND...
...HOW DO I PUT THIS DELICATELY? WE BOTH FEEL THE URGE TO MATE. LIKE SPIDER-BUNNIES.

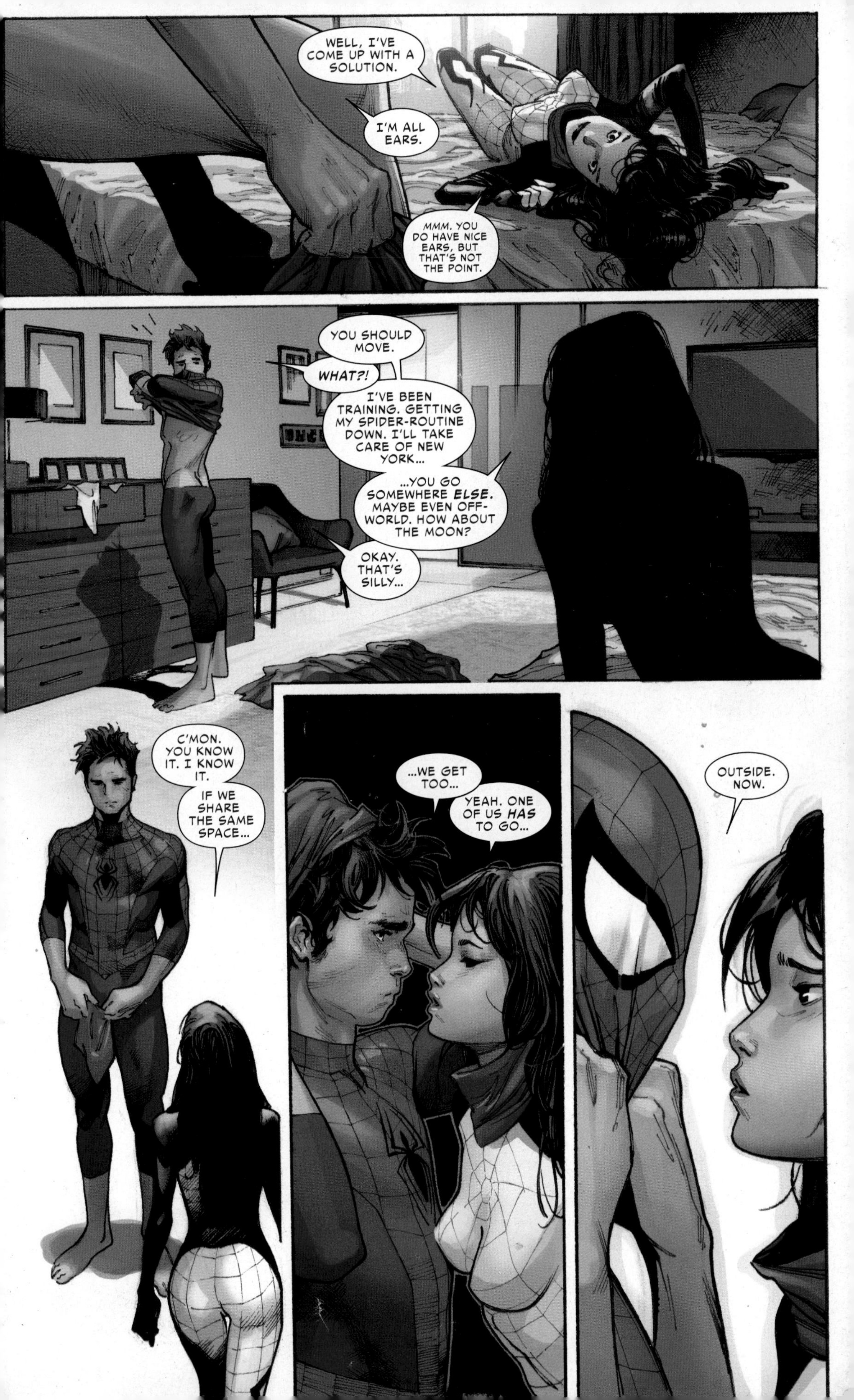

WELL, I'VE COME UP WITH A SOLUTION.
I'M ALL EARS.
MMM. YOU DO HAVE NICE EARS, BUT THAT'S NOT THE POINT.
YOU SHOULD MOVE.
WHAT?!
I'VE BEEN TRAINING. GETTING MY SPIDER-ROUTINE DOWN. I'LL TAKE CARE OF NEW YORK...
...YOU GO SOMEWHERE ELSE. MAYBE EVEN OFF-WORLD. HOW ABOUT THE MOON?
OKAY. THAT'S SILLY...
C'MON. YOU KNOW IT. I KNOW IT.
IF WE SHARE THE SAME SPACE...
...WE GET TOO...
YEAH. ONE OF US HAS TO GO...
OUTSIDE. NOW.

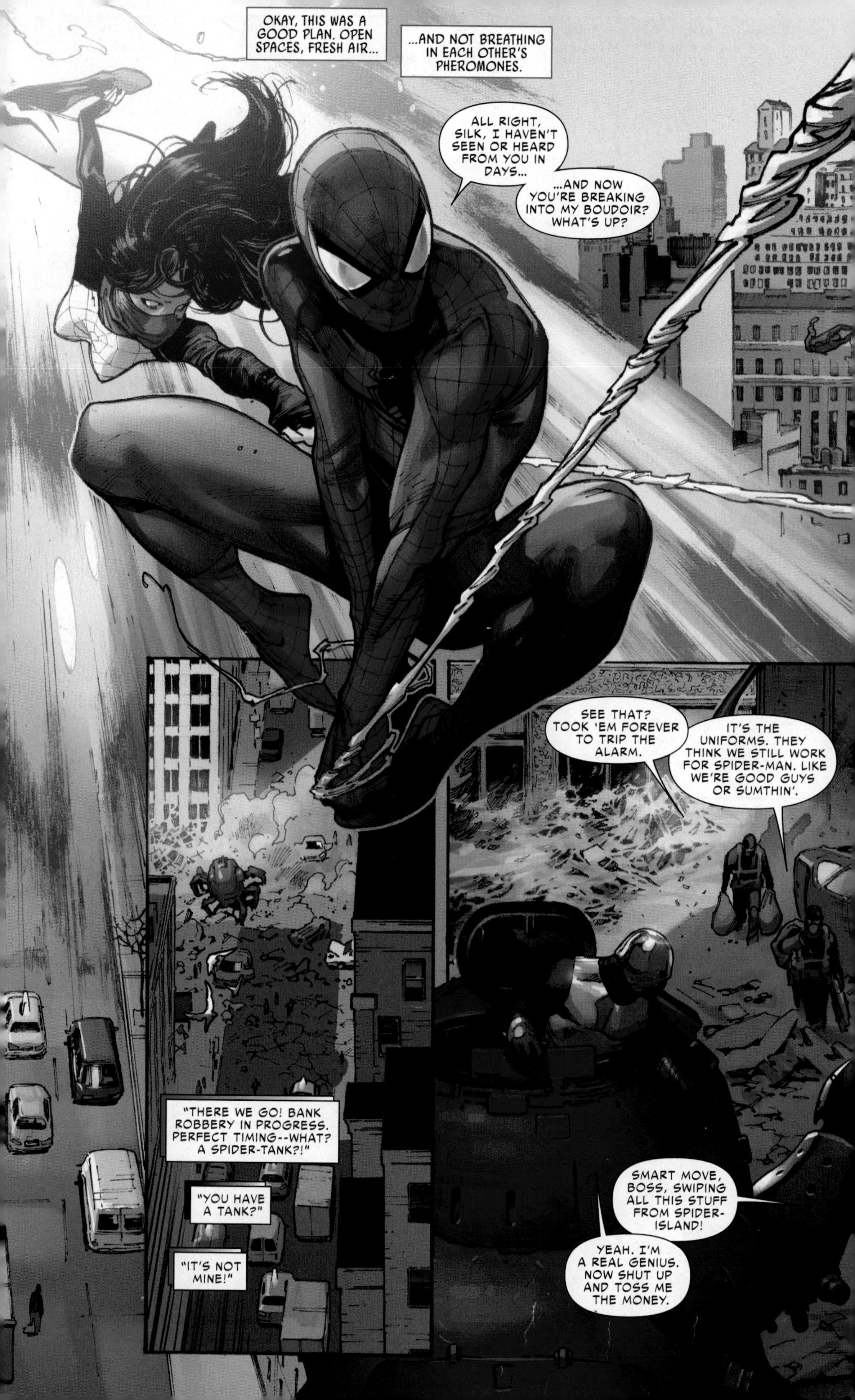
OKAY, THIS WAS A GOOD PLAN. OPEN SPACES, FRESH AIR...
...AND NOT BREATHING IN EACH OTHER'S PHEROMONES.
ALL RIGHT, SILK, I HAVEN'T SEEN OR HEARD FROM YOU IN DAYS...
...AND NOW YOU'RE BREAKING INTO MY BOUDOIR? WHAT'S UP?
SEE THAT? TOOK 'EM FOREVER TO TRIP THE ALARM.
IT'S THE UNIFORMS. THEY THINK WE STILL WORK FOR SPIDER-MAN. LIKE WE'RE GOOD GUYS OR SUMTHIN'.
"THERE WE GO! BANK ROBBERY IN PROGRESS. PERFECT TIMING--WHAT? A SPIDER-TANK?!"
"YOU HAVE A TANK?"
"IT'S NOT MINE!"
SMART MOVE, BOSS, SWIPING ALL THIS STUFF FROM SPIDER-ISLAND!
YEAH. I'M A REAL GENIUS. NOW SHUT UP AND TOSS ME THE MONEY.

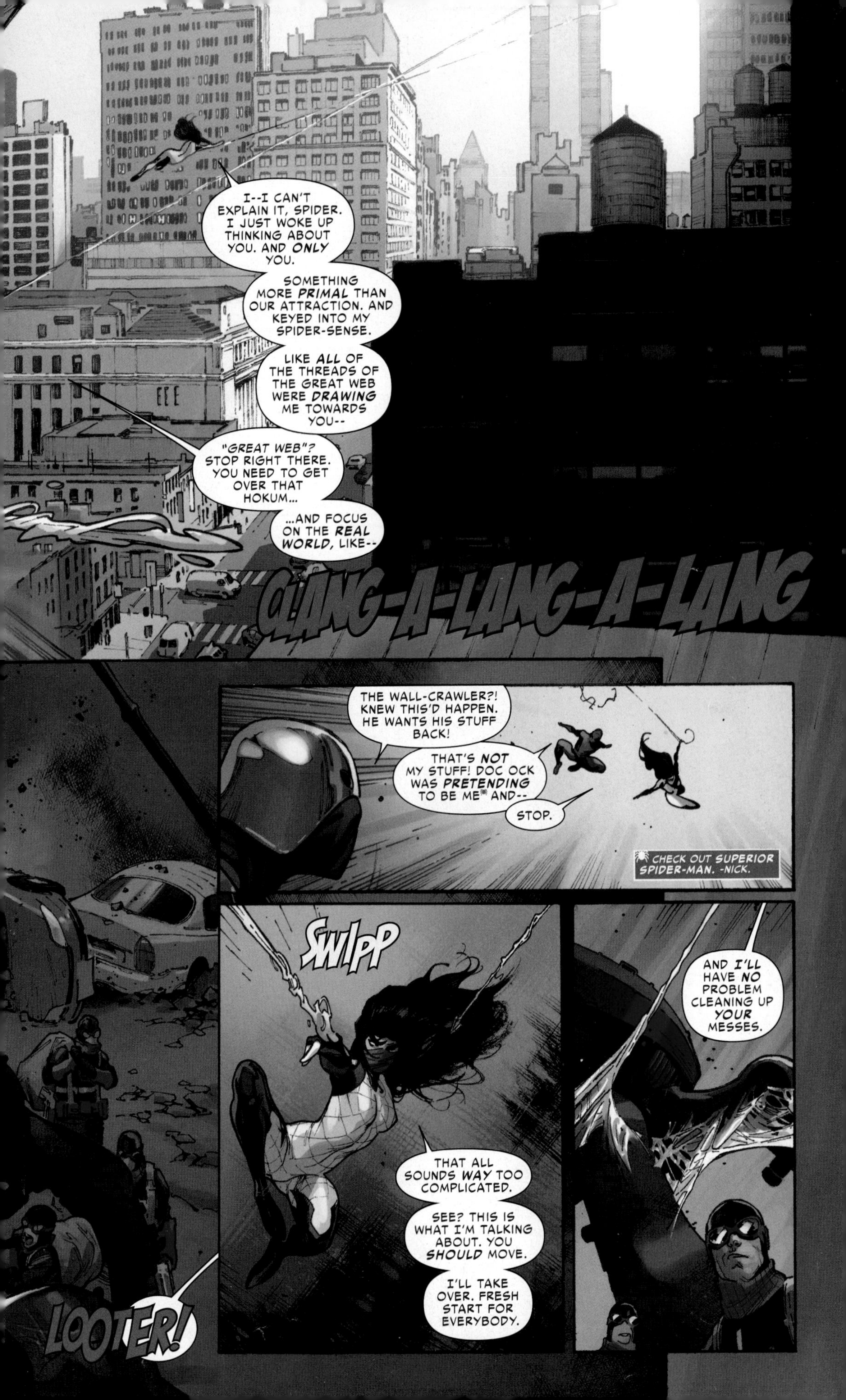
I--I CAN'T EXPLAIN IT, SPIDER. I JUST WOKE UP THINKING ABOUT YOU. AND ONLY YOU.
SOMETHING MORE PRIMAL THAN OUR ATTRACTION. AND KEYED INTO MY SPIDER-SENSE.
LIKE ALL OF THE THREADS OF THE GREAT WEB WERE DRAWING ME TOWARDS YOU--
"GREAT WEB"? STOP RIGHT THERE. YOU NEED TO GET OVER THAT HOKUM...
...AND FOCUS ON THE REAL WORLD, LIKE--
CLANG-A-LANG-A-LANG
THE WALL-CRAWLER?! KNEW THIS'D HAPPEN. HE WANTS HIS STUFF BACK!
THAT'S NOT MY STUFF! DOC OCK WAS PRETENDING TO BE ME* AND--
STOP.
*CHECK OUT SUPERIOR SPIDER-MAN. -NICK.
SWIPP
AND I'LL HAVE NO PROBLEM CLEANING UP YOUR MESSES.
THAT ALL SOUNDS WAY TOO COMPLICATED.
SEE? THIS IS WHAT I'M TALKING ABOUT. YOU SHOULD MOVE.
I'LL TAKE OVER. FRESH START FOR EVERYBODY.
LOOTER!

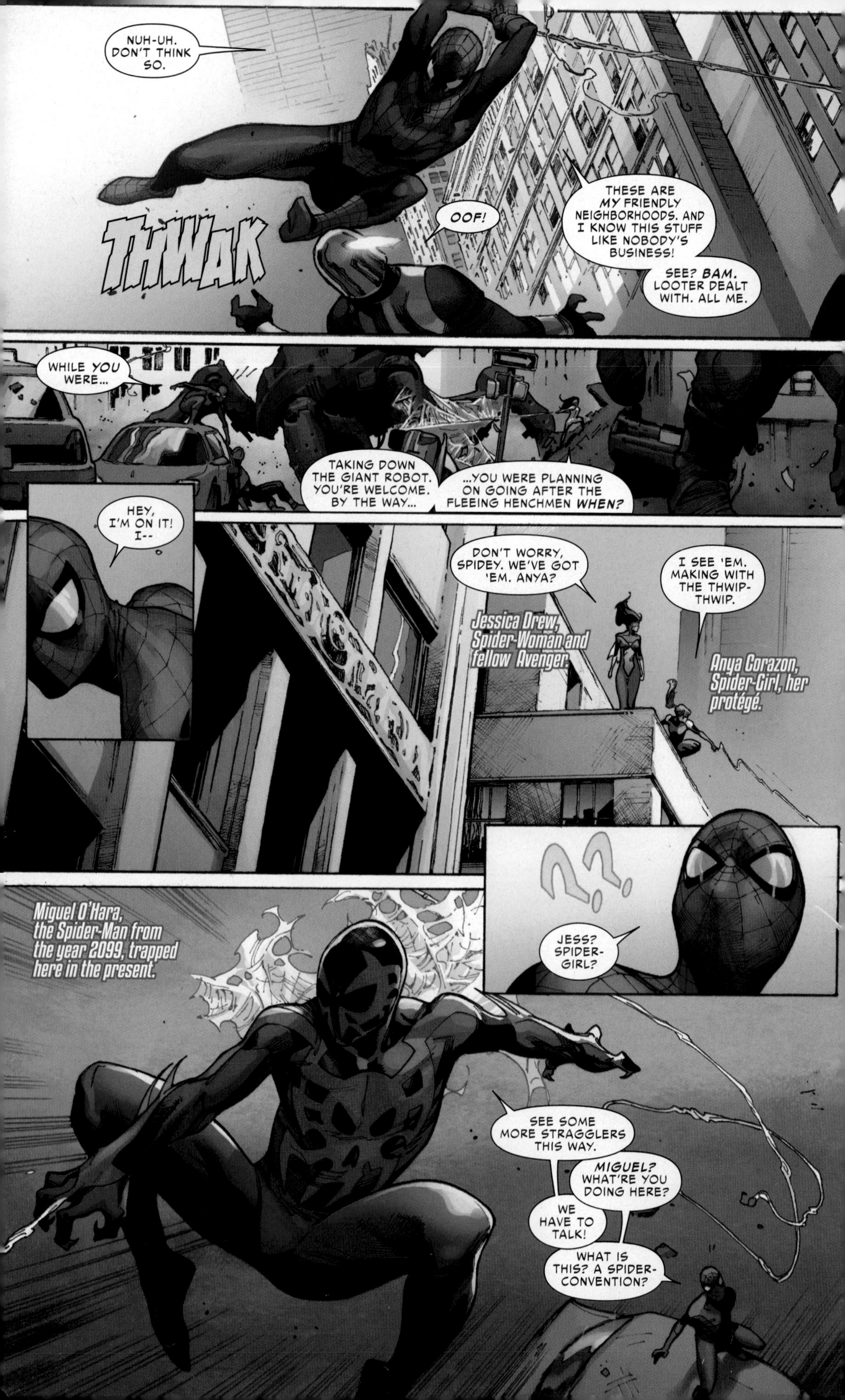
NUH-UH. DON'T THINK SO.
THWAK
OOF!
THESE ARE MY FRIENDLY NEIGHBORHOODS. AND I KNOW THIS STUFF LIKE NOBODY'S BUSINESS!
SEE? BAM. LOOTER DEALT WITH. ALL ME.
WHILE YOU WERE...
TAKING DOWN THE GIANT ROBOT. YOU'RE WELCOME. BY THE WAY...
...YOU WERE PLANNING ON GOING AFTER THE FLEEING HENCHMEN WHEN?
HEY, I'M ON IT! I--
DON'T WORRY, SPIDEY. WE'VE GOT 'EM. ANYA?
Jessica Drew, Spider-Woman and fellow Avenger.
I SEE 'EM. MAKING WITH THE THWIP-THWIP.
Anya Corazon, Spider-Girl, her protégé.
??
JESS? SPIDER-GIRL?
Miguel O'Hara, the Spider-Man from the year 2099, trapped here in the present.
SEE SOME MORE STRAGGLERS THIS WAY.
MIGUEL? WHAT'RE YOU DOING HERE?
WE HAVE TO TALK!
WHAT IS THIS? A SPIDER-CONVENTION?

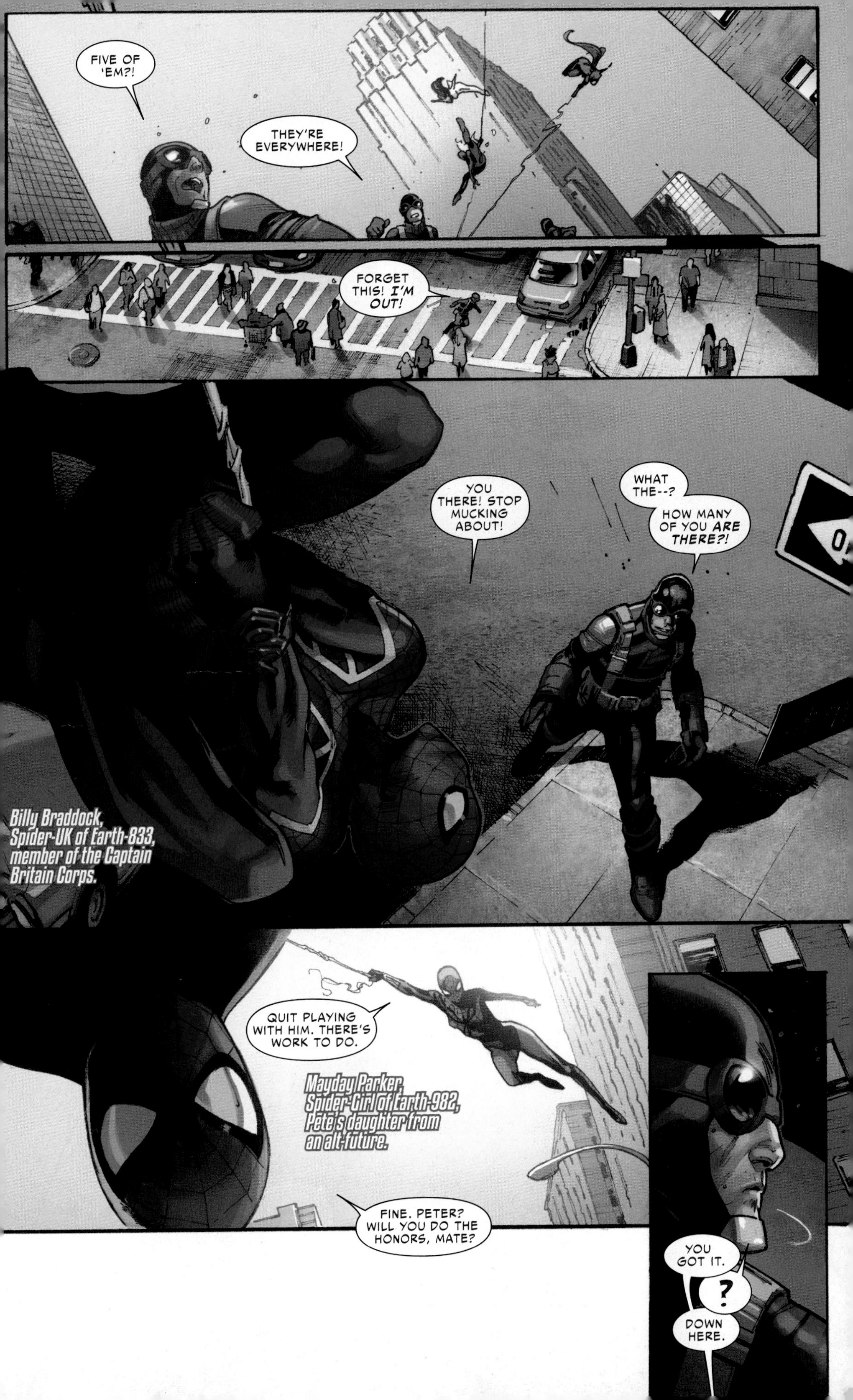
FIVE OF 'EM?!
THEY'RE EVERYWHERE!
FORGET THIS! I'M OUT!
YOU THERE! STOP MUCKING ABOUT!
WHAT THE--?
HOW MANY OF YOU ARE THERE?!
Billy Braddock, Spider-UK of Earth-833, member of the Captain Britain Corps.
QUIT PLAYING WITH HIM. THERE'S WORK TO DO.
Mayday Parker, Spider-Girl of Earth-982, Pete's daughter from an alt-future.
FINE. PETER? WILL YOU DO THE HONORS, MATE?
YOU GOT IT.
?
DOWN HERE.

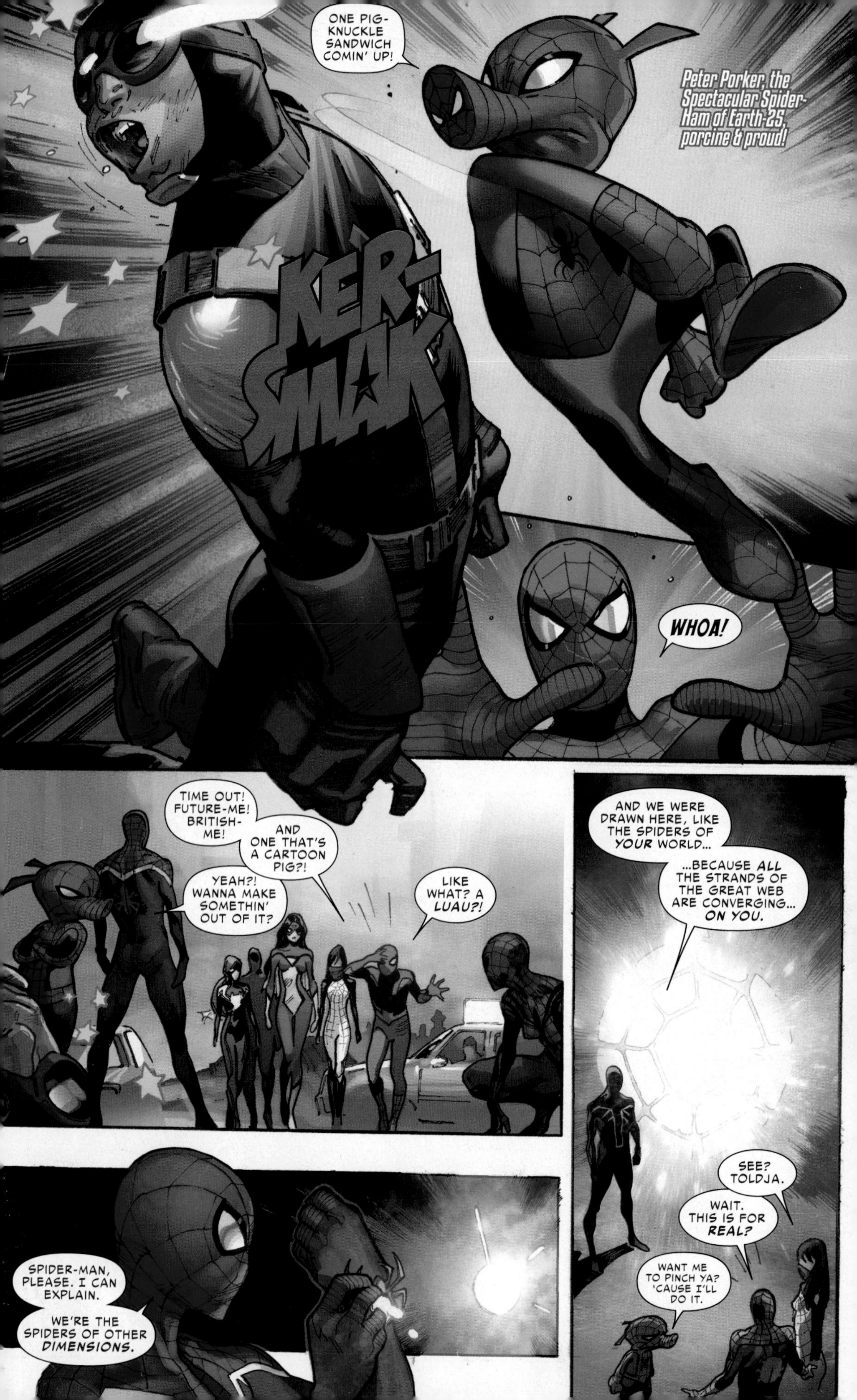
ONE PIG-KNUCKLE SANDWICH COMIN' UP!
Peter Porker, the Spectacular Spider-Ham of Earth-25, porcine & proud!
KER-SMAK
WHOA!
TIME OUT! FUTURE-ME! BRITISH-ME!
AND ONE THAT'S A CARTOON PIG?!
YEAH?! WANNA MAKE SOMETHIN' OUT OF IT?
LIKE WHAT? A LUAU?!
SPIDER-MAN, PLEASE. I CAN EXPLAIN.
WE'RE THE SPIDERS OF OTHER DIMENSIONS.
AND WE WERE DRAWN HERE, LIKE THE SPIDERS OF YOUR WORLD...
...BECAUSE ALL THE STRANDS OF THE GREAT WEB ARE CONVERGING... ON YOU.
SEE? TOLDJA.
WAIT. THIS IS FOR REAL?
WANT ME TO PINCH YA? 'CAUSE I'LL DO IT.

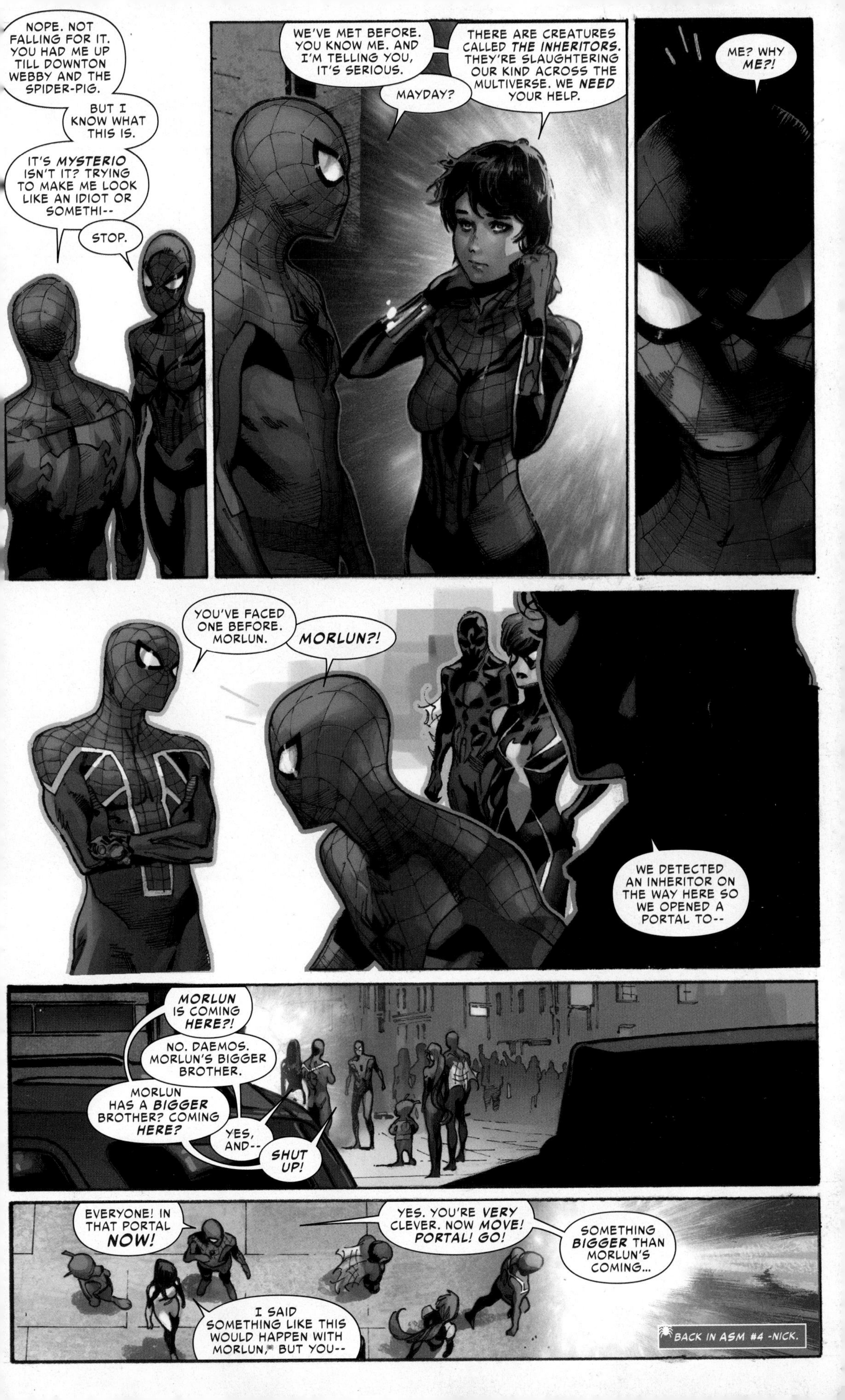

NOPE. NOT FALLING FOR IT. YOU HAD ME UP TILL DOWNTON WEBBY AND THE SPIDER-PIG.
BUT I KNOW WHAT THIS IS.
IT'S MYSTERIO ISN'T IT? TRYING TO MAKE ME LOOK LIKE AN IDIOT OR SOMETHI--
STOP.
WE'VE MET BEFORE. YOU KNOW ME. AND I'M TELLING YOU, IT'S SERIOUS.
MAYDAY?
THERE ARE CREATURES CALLED THE INHERITORS. THEY'RE SLAUGHTERING OUR KIND ACROSS THE MULTIVERSE. WE NEED YOUR HELP.
ME? WHY ME?!
YOU'VE FACED ONE BEFORE. MORLUN.
MORLUN?!
WE DETECTED AN INHERITOR ON THE WAY HERE SO WE OPENED A PORTAL TO--
MORLUN IS COMING HERE?!
NO. DAEMOS. MORLUN'S BIGGER BROTHER.
MORLUN HAS A BIGGER BROTHER? COMING HERE?
YES, AND--
SHUT UP!
EVERYONE! IN THAT PORTAL NOW!
YES. YOU'RE VERY CLEVER. NOW MOVE! PORTAL! GO!
SOMETHING BIGGER THAN MORLUN'S COMING...
I SAID SOMETHING LIKE THIS WOULD HAPPEN WITH MORLUN,* BUT YOU--
*BACK IN ASM #4 -NICK.

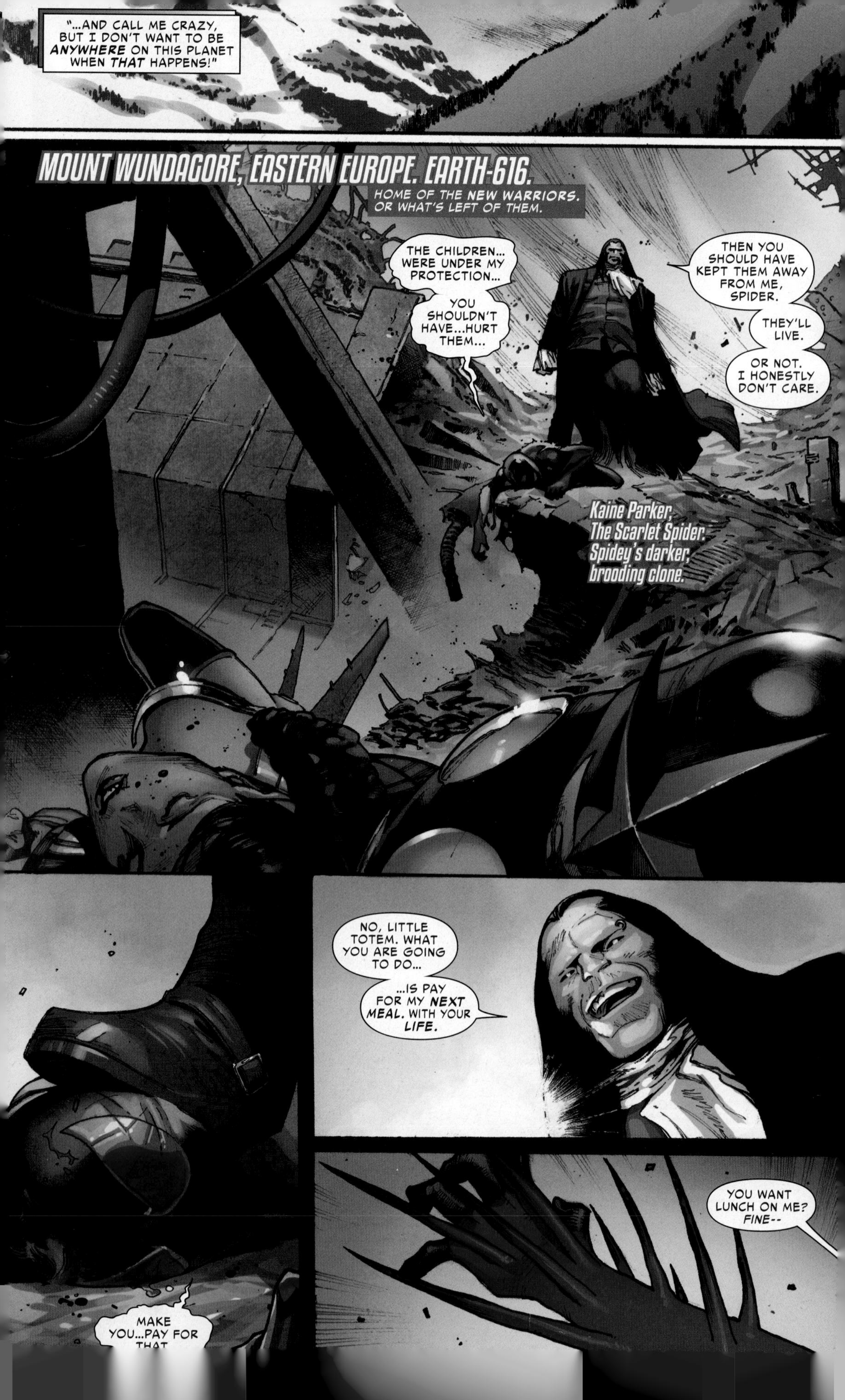
"...AND CALL ME CRAZY, BUT I DON'T WANT TO BE ANYWHERE ON THIS PLANET WHEN THAT HAPPENS!"
MOUNT WUNDAGORE, EASTERN EUROPE. EARTH-616.
HOME OF THE NEW WARRIORS. OR WHAT'S LEFT OF THEM.
THE CHILDREN... WERE UNDER MY PROTECTION...
YOU SHOULDN'T HAVE...HURT THEM...
THEN YOU SHOULD HAVE KEPT THEM AWAY FROM ME, SPIDER.
THEY'LL LIVE.
OR NOT. I HONESTLY DON'T CARE.
Kaine Parker, The Scarlet Spider. Spidey's darker, brooding clone.
NO, LITTLE TOTEM. WHAT YOU ARE GOING TO DO...
...IS PAY FOR MY NEXT MEAL. WITH YOUR LIFE.
YOU WANT LUNCH ON ME? FINE--
MAKE YOU...PAY FOR

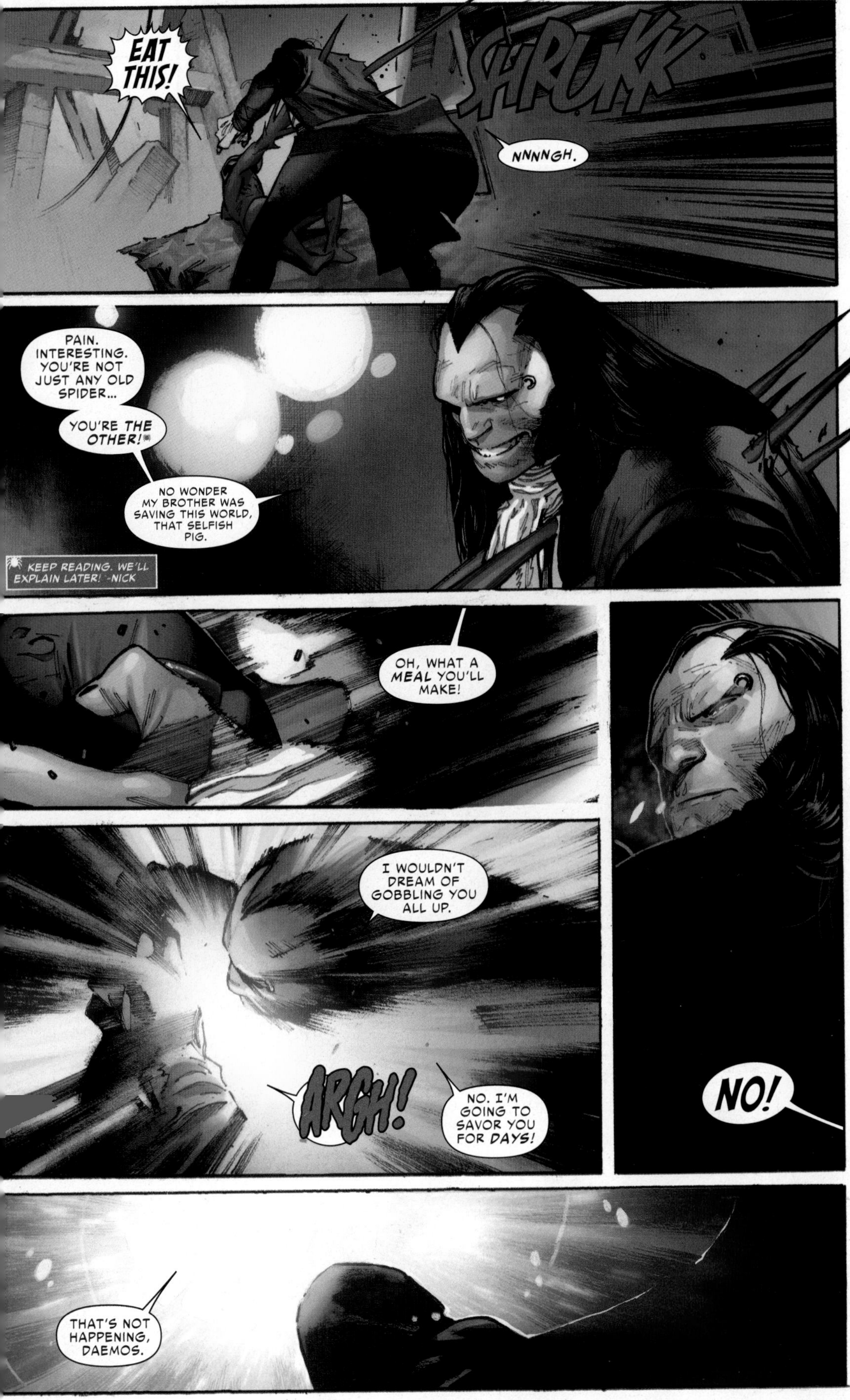

EAT THIS!
SHRUKK
NNNNGH.
PAIN. INTERESTING. YOU'RE NOT JUST ANY OLD SPIDER...
YOU'RE THE OTHER!
NO WONDER MY BROTHER WAS SAVING THIS WORLD, THAT SELFISH PIG.
KEEP READING. WE'LL EXPLAIN LATER! -NICK
OH, WHAT A MEAL YOU'LL MAKE!
I WOULDN'T DREAM OF GOBBLING YOU ALL UP.
ARGH!
NO. I'M GOING TO SAVOR YOU FOR DAYS!
NO!
THAT'S NOT HAPPENING, DAEMOS.

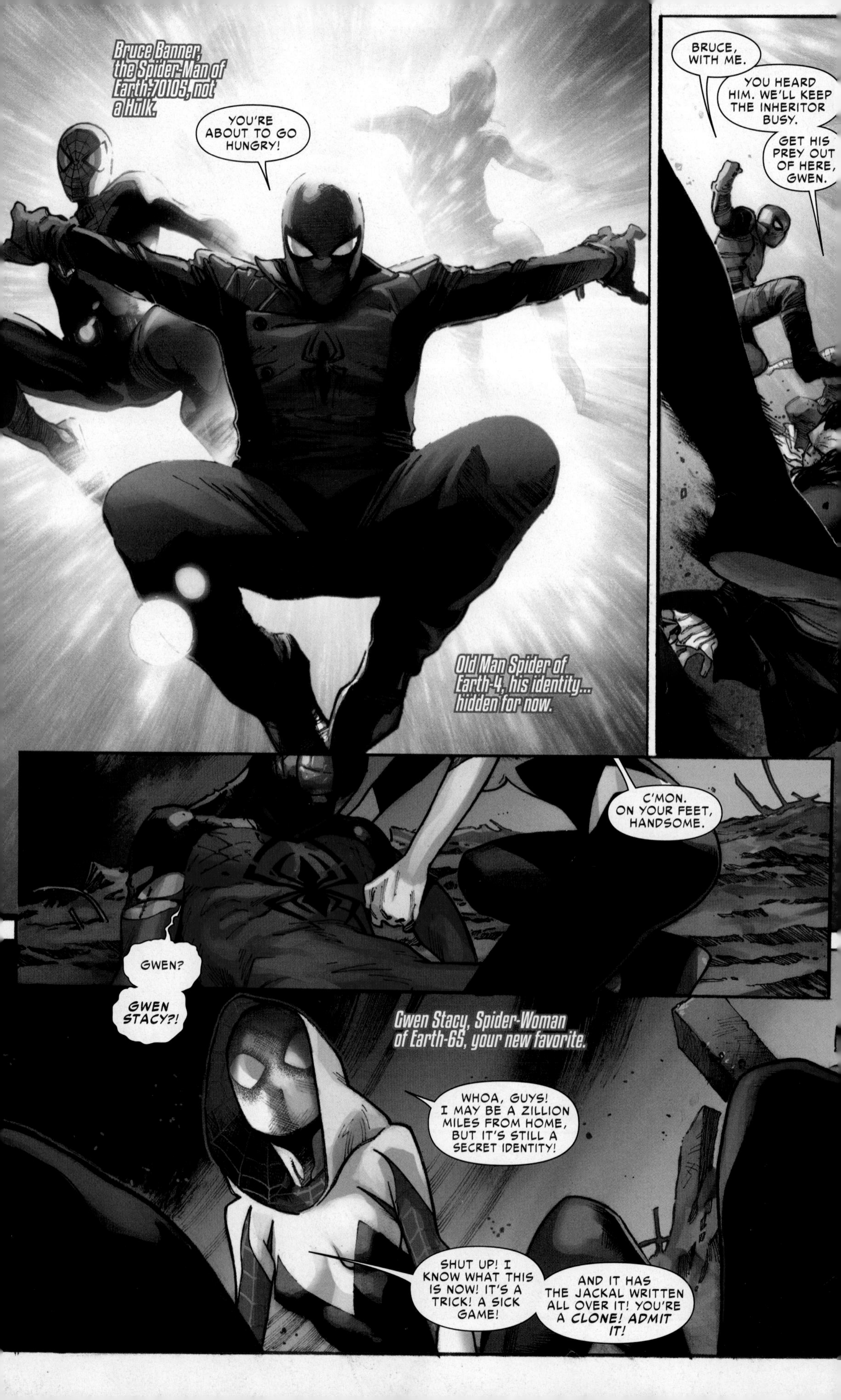
Bruce Banner, the Spider-Man of Earth-70105, not a Hulk.
YOU'RE ABOUT TO GO HUNGRY!
Old Man Spider of Earth-4, his identity... hidden for now.
BRUCE, WITH ME.
YOU HEARD HIM. WE'LL KEEP THE INHERITOR BUSY.
GET HIS PREY OUT OF HERE, GWEN.
C'MON. ON YOUR FEET, HANDSOME.
GWEN?
GWEN STACY?!
Gwen Stacy, Spider-Woman of Earth-65, your new favorite.
WHOA, GUYS! I MAY BE A ZILLION MILES FROM HOME, BUT IT'S STILL A SECRET IDENTITY!
SHUT UP! I KNOW WHAT THIS IS NOW! IT'S A TRICK! A SICK GAME!
AND IT HAS THE JACKAL WRITTEN ALL OVER IT! YOU'RE A CLONE! ADMIT IT!

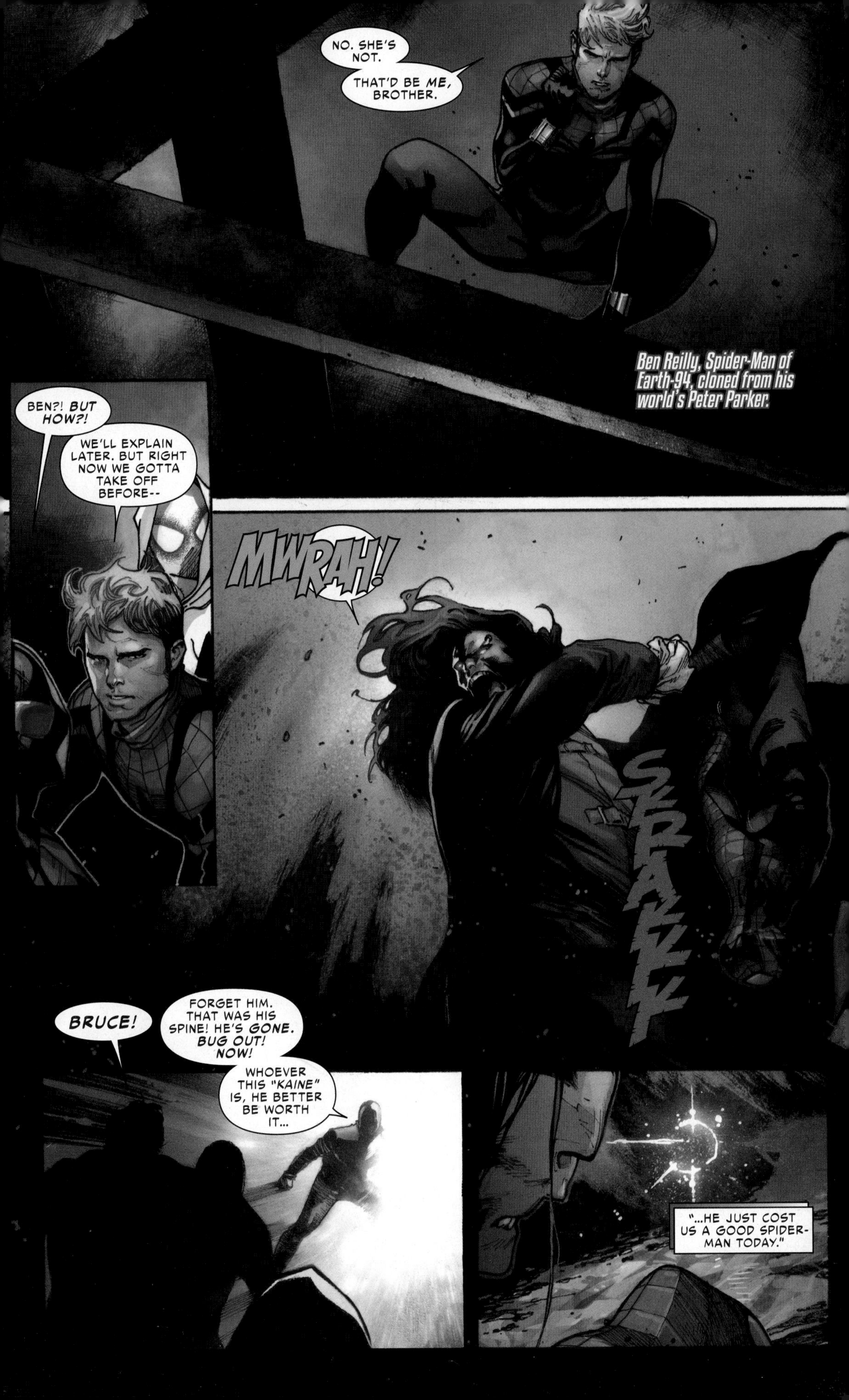

NO. SHE'S NOT.
THAT'D BE *ME*, BROTHER.
Ben Reilly, Spider-Man of Earth-94, cloned from his world's Peter Parker.
BEN?! *BUT HOW?!*
WE'LL EXPLAIN LATER. BUT RIGHT NOW WE GOTTA TAKE OFF BEFORE--
MWRAH!
SPRAKK
BRUCE!
FORGET HIM. THAT WAS HIS SPINE! HE'S *GONE*. *BUG OUT! NOW!*
WHOEVER THIS "*KAINE*" IS, HE BETTER BE WORTH IT...
"...HE JUST COST US A GOOD SPIDER-MAN TODAY."

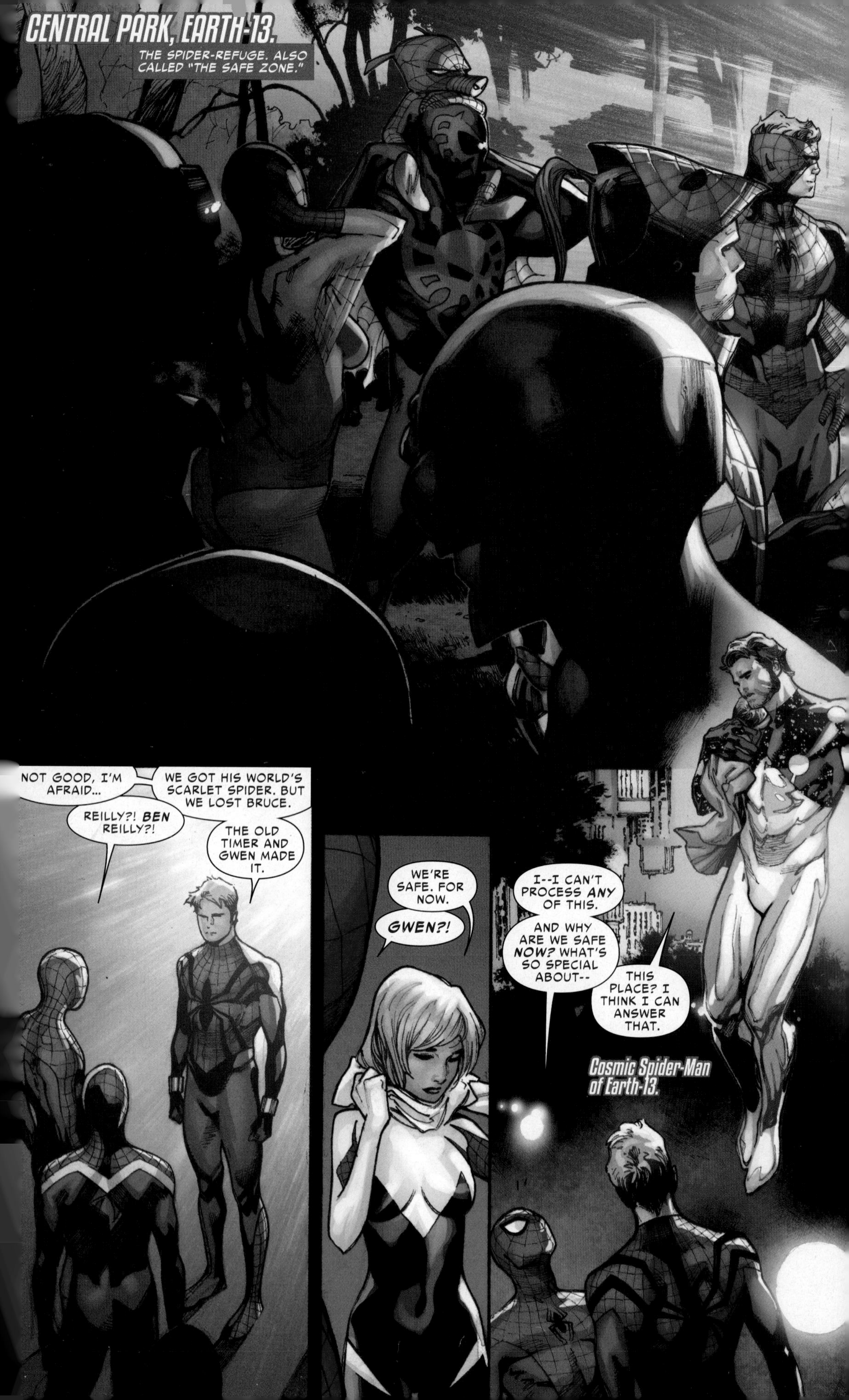
CENTRAL PARK, EARTH-13.
THE SPIDER-REFUGE. ALSO CALLED "THE SAFE ZONE."
NOT GOOD, I'M AFRAID...
WE GOT HIS WORLD'S SCARLET SPIDER. BUT WE LOST BRUCE.
REILLY?! BEN REILLY?!
THE OLD TIMER AND GWEN MADE IT.
WE'RE SAFE. FOR NOW.
GWEN?!
I--I CAN'T PROCESS ANY OF THIS.
AND WHY ARE WE SAFE NOW? WHAT'S SO SPECIAL ABOUT--
THIS PLACE? I THINK I CAN ANSWER THAT.
Cosmic Spider-Man of Earth-13.

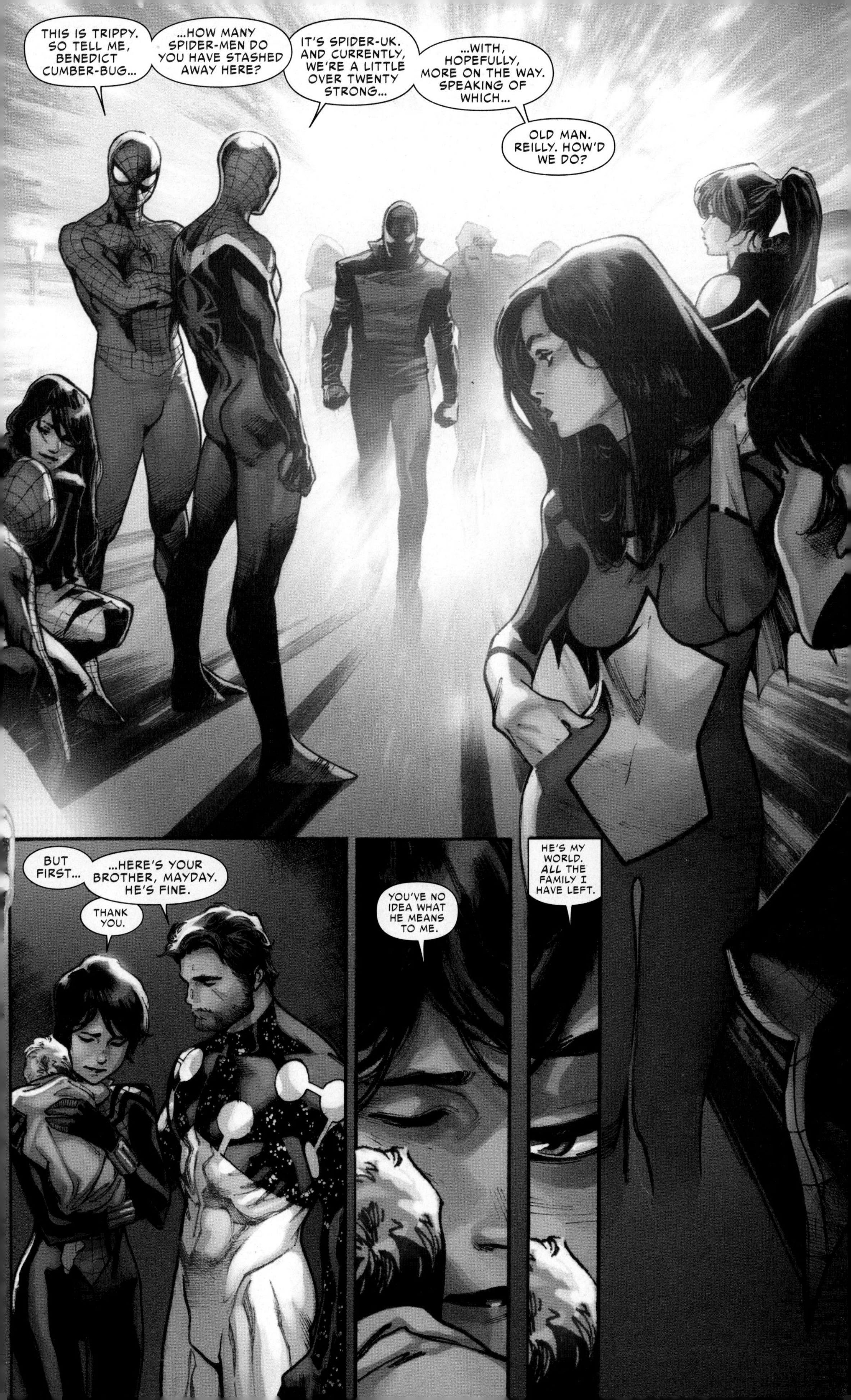
THIS IS TRIPPY. SO TELL ME, BENEDICT CUMBER-BUG...
...HOW MANY SPIDER-MEN DO YOU HAVE STASHED AWAY HERE?
IT'S SPIDER-UK. AND CURRENTLY, WE'RE A LITTLE OVER TWENTY STRONG...
...WITH, HOPEFULLY, MORE ON THE WAY. SPEAKING OF WHICH...
OLD MAN. REILLY. HOW'D WE DO?
BUT FIRST...
...HERE'S YOUR BROTHER, MAYDAY. HE'S FINE.
THANK YOU.
YOU'VE NO IDEA WHAT HE MEANS TO ME.
HE'S MY WORLD. ALL THE FAMILY I HAVE LEFT.

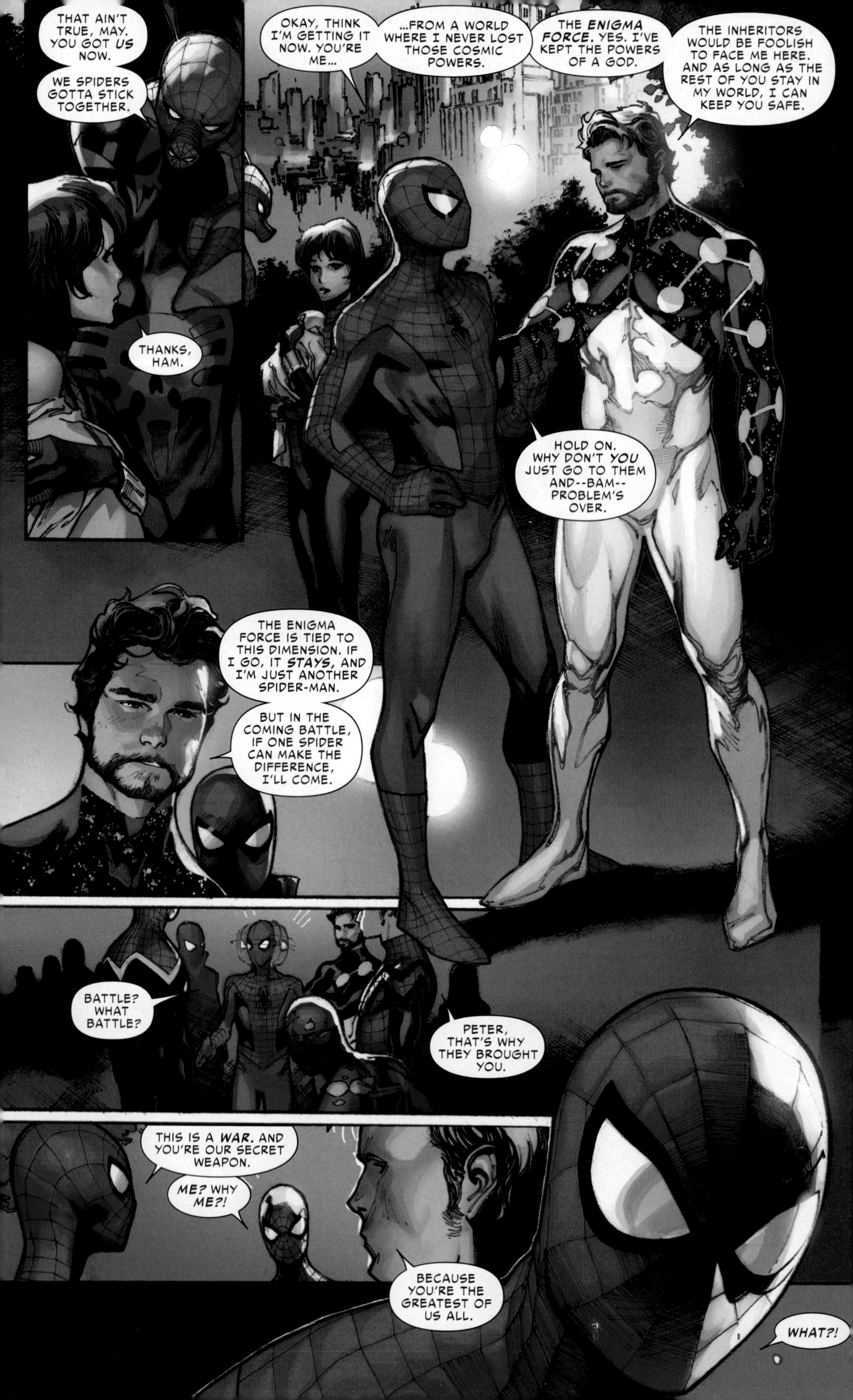
THAT AIN'T TRUE, MAY. YOU GOT *US* NOW.
WE SPIDERS GOTTA STICK TOGETHER.
THANKS, HAM.
OKAY, THINK I'M GETTING IT NOW. YOU'RE ME...
...FROM A WORLD WHERE I NEVER LOST THOSE COSMIC POWERS.
THE *ENIGMA FORCE.* YES. I'VE KEPT THE POWERS OF A GOD.
THE INHERITORS WOULD BE FOOLISH TO FACE ME HERE. AND AS LONG AS THE REST OF YOU STAY IN MY WORLD, I CAN KEEP YOU SAFE.
HOLD ON. WHY DON'T *YOU* JUST GO TO THEM AND--BAM--PROBLEM'S OVER.
THE ENIGMA FORCE IS TIED TO THIS DIMENSION. IF I GO, IT *STAYS,* AND I'M JUST ANOTHER SPIDER-MAN.
BUT IN THE COMING BATTLE, IF ONE SPIDER CAN MAKE THE DIFFERENCE, I'LL COME.
BATTLE? WHAT BATTLE?
PETER, THAT'S WHY THEY BROUGHT YOU.
THIS IS A *WAR.* AND YOU'RE OUR SECRET WEAPON.
ME? WHY *ME?!*
BECAUSE YOU'RE THE GREATEST OF US ALL.
WHAT?!

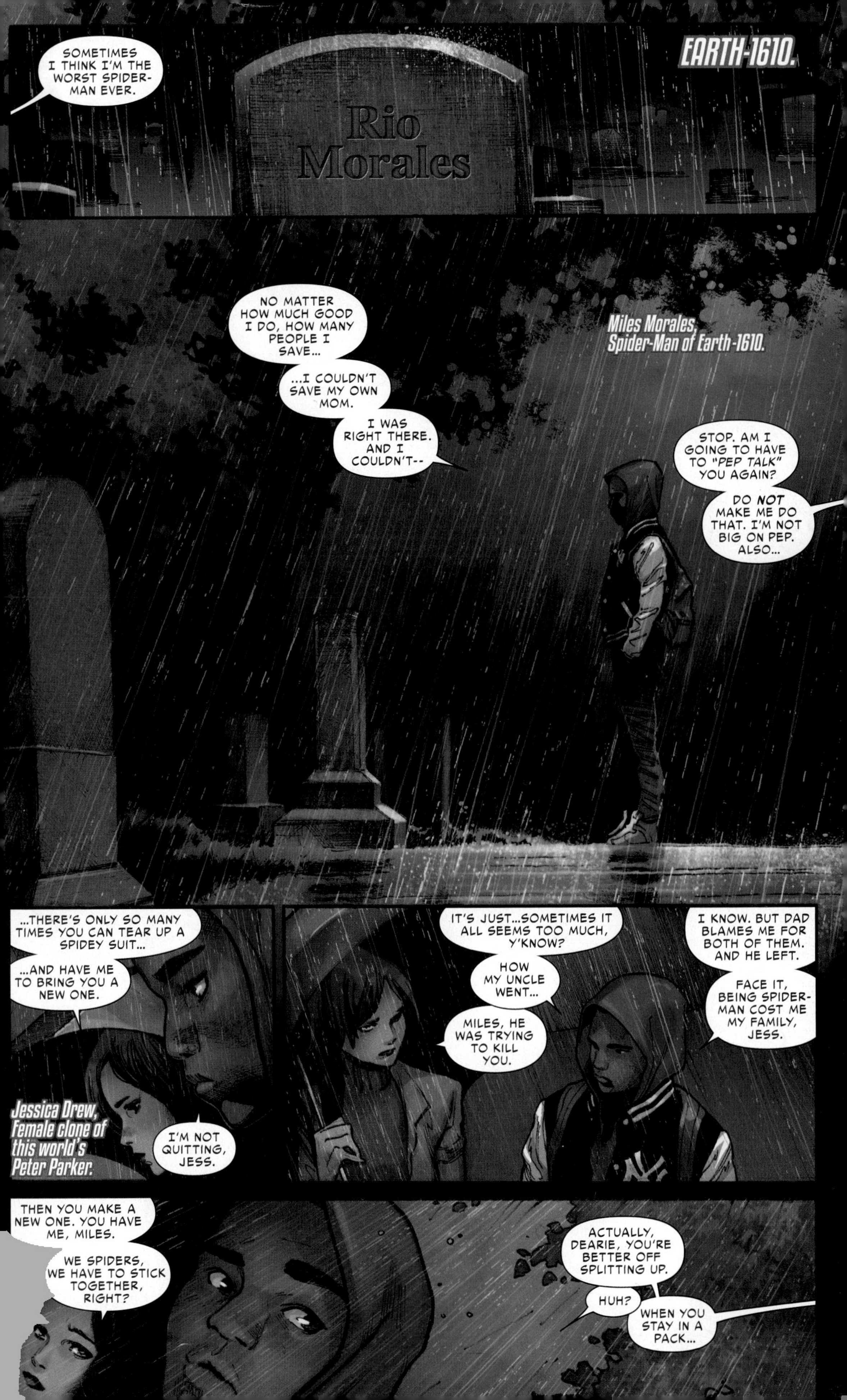

EARTH-1610.
SOMETIMES I THINK I'M THE WORST SPIDER-MAN EVER.
Rio Morales
NO MATTER HOW MUCH GOOD I DO, HOW MANY PEOPLE I SAVE...
...I COULDN'T SAVE MY OWN MOM.
I WAS RIGHT THERE. AND I COULDN'T--
Miles Morales, Spider-Man of Earth-1610.
STOP. AM I GOING TO HAVE TO "PEP TALK" YOU AGAIN?
DO NOT MAKE ME DO THAT. I'M NOT BIG ON PEP. ALSO...
...THERE'S ONLY SO MANY TIMES YOU CAN TEAR UP A SPIDEY SUIT...
...AND HAVE ME TO BRING YOU A NEW ONE.
Jessica Drew, Female clone of this world's Peter Parker.
I'M NOT QUITTING, JESS.
IT'S JUST...SOMETIMES IT ALL SEEMS TOO MUCH, Y'KNOW?
HOW MY UNCLE WENT...
MILES, HE WAS TRYING TO KILL YOU.
I KNOW. BUT DAD BLAMES ME FOR BOTH OF THEM. AND HE LEFT.
FACE IT, BEING SPIDER-MAN COST ME MY FAMILY, JESS.
THEN YOU MAKE A NEW ONE. YOU HAVE ME, MILES.
WE SPIDERS, WE HAVE TO STICK TOGETHER, RIGHT?
ACTUALLY, DEARIE, YOU'RE BETTER OFF SPLITTING UP.
HUH?
WHEN YOU STAY IN A PACK...

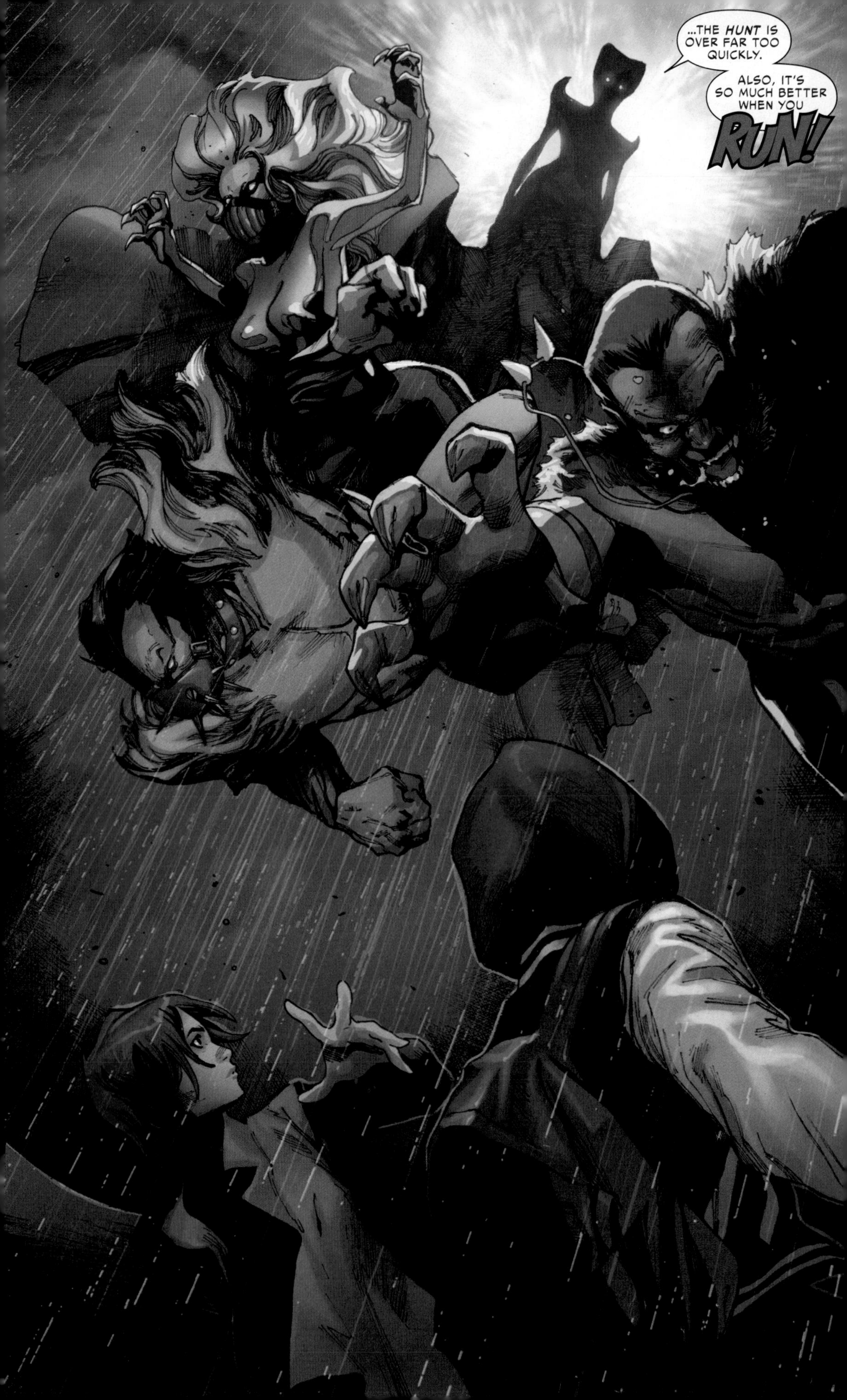
...THE *HUNT* IS OVER FAR TOO QUICKLY.
ALSO, IT'S SO MUCH BETTER WHEN YOU
RUN!

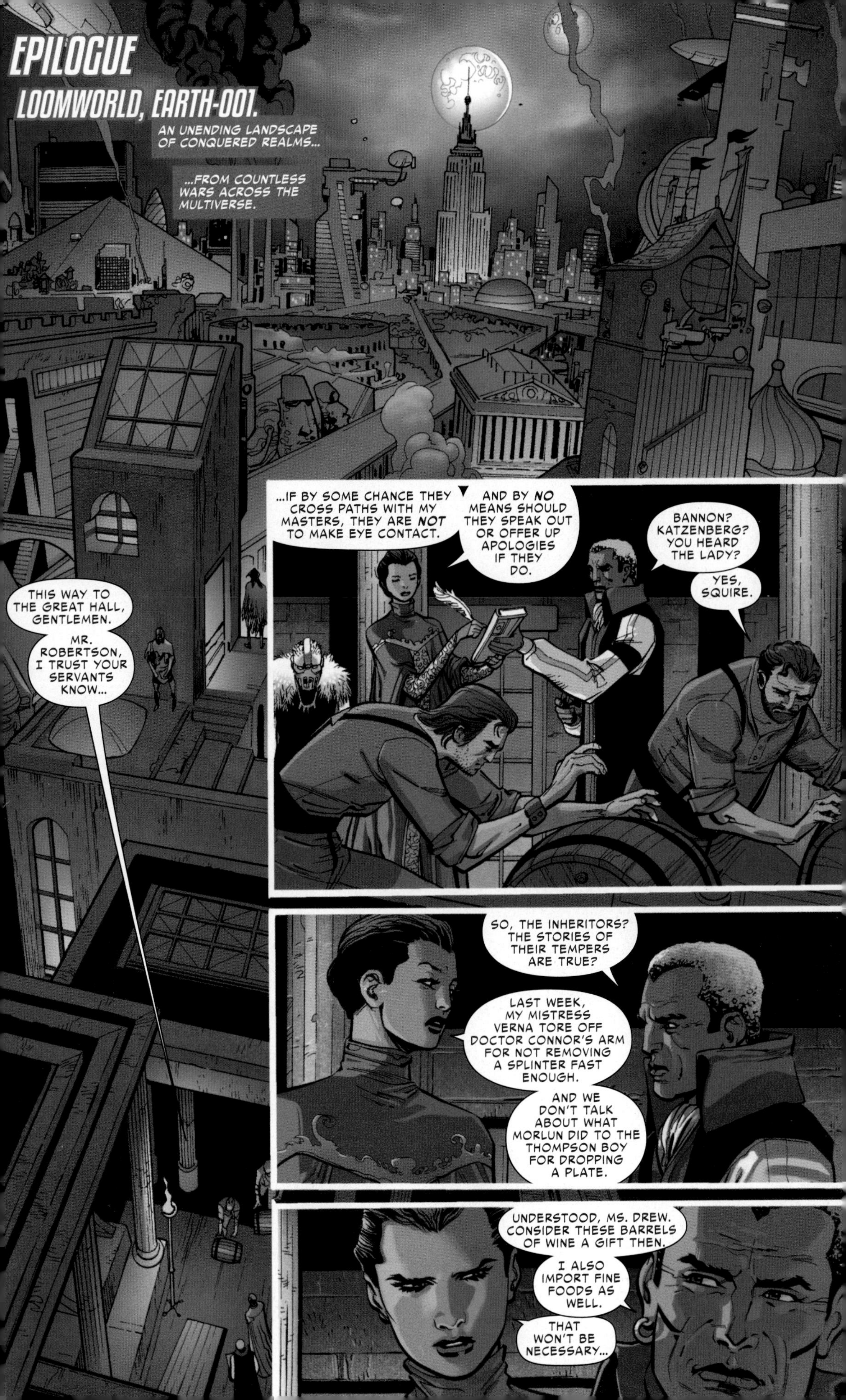
EPILOGUE
LOOMWORLD, EARTH-001.
AN UNENDING LANDSCAPE OF CONQUERED REALMS...
...FROM COUNTLESS WARS ACROSS THE MULTIVERSE.
THIS WAY TO THE GREAT HALL, GENTLEMEN.
MR. ROBERTSON, I TRUST YOUR SERVANTS KNOW...
...IF BY SOME CHANCE THEY CROSS PATHS WITH MY MASTERS, THEY ARE NOT TO MAKE EYE CONTACT.
AND BY NO MEANS SHOULD THEY SPEAK OUT OR OFFER UP APOLOGIES IF THEY DO.
BANNON? KATZENBERG? YOU HEARD THE LADY?
YES, SQUIRE.
SO, THE INHERITORS? THE STORIES OF THEIR TEMPERS ARE TRUE?
LAST WEEK, MY MISTRESS VERNA TORE OFF DOCTOR CONNOR'S ARM FOR NOT REMOVING A SPLINTER FAST ENOUGH.
AND WE DON'T TALK ABOUT WHAT MORLUN DID TO THE THOMPSON BOY FOR DROPPING A PLATE.
UNDERSTOOD, MS. DREW. CONSIDER THESE BARRELS OF WINE A GIFT THEN.
I ALSO IMPORT FINE FOODS AS WELL.
THAT WON'T BE NECESSARY...

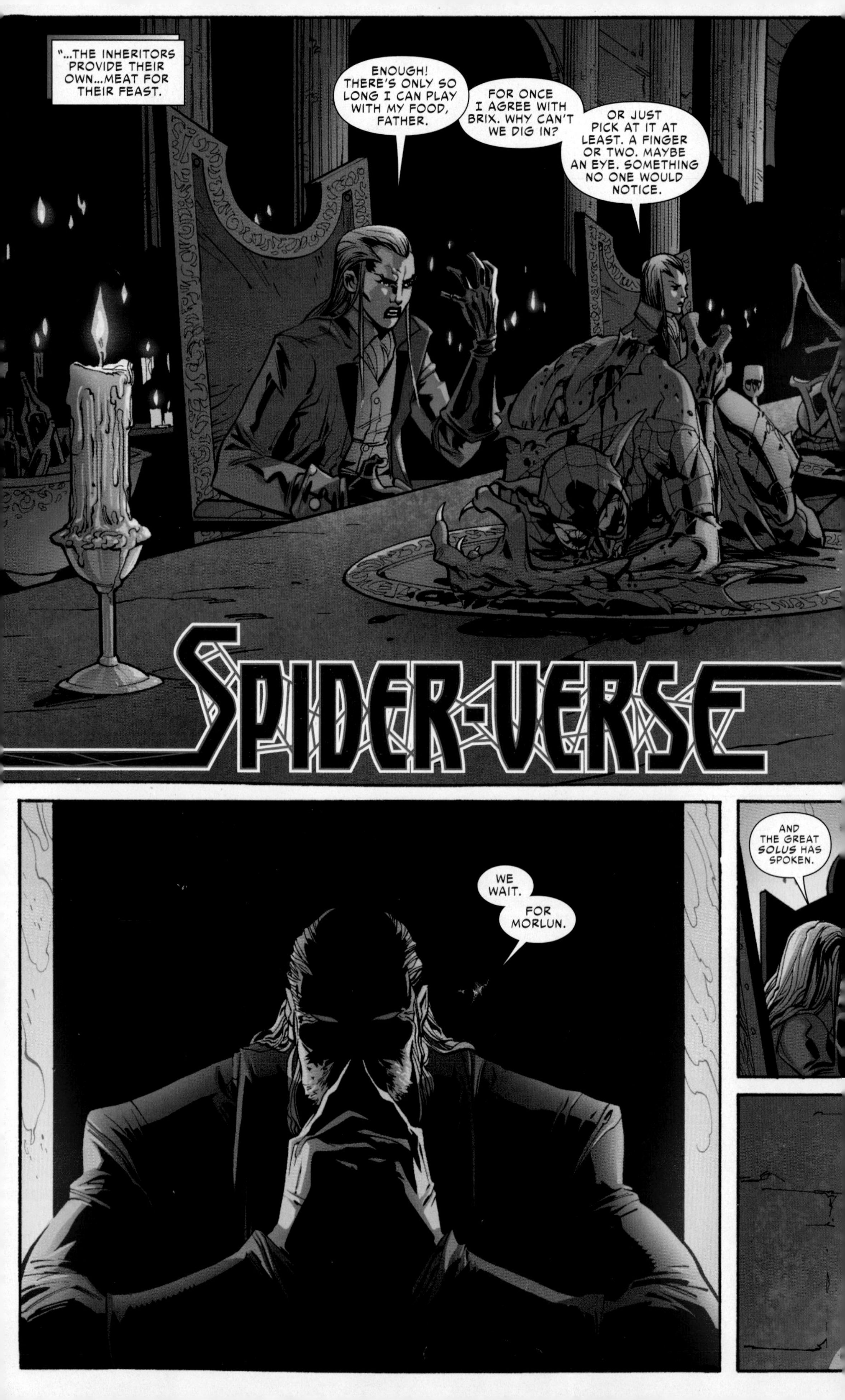
"...THE INHERITORS PROVIDE THEIR OWN...MEAT FOR THEIR FEAST.
ENOUGH! THERE'S ONLY SO LONG I CAN PLAY WITH MY FOOD, FATHER.
FOR ONCE I AGREE WITH BRIX. WHY CAN'T WE DIG IN?
OR JUST PICK AT IT AT LEAST. A FINGER OR TWO. MAYBE AN EYE. SOMETHING NO ONE WOULD NOTICE.
SPIDER-VERSE
WE WAIT.
FOR MORLUN.
AND THE GREAT SOLUS HAS SPOKEN.

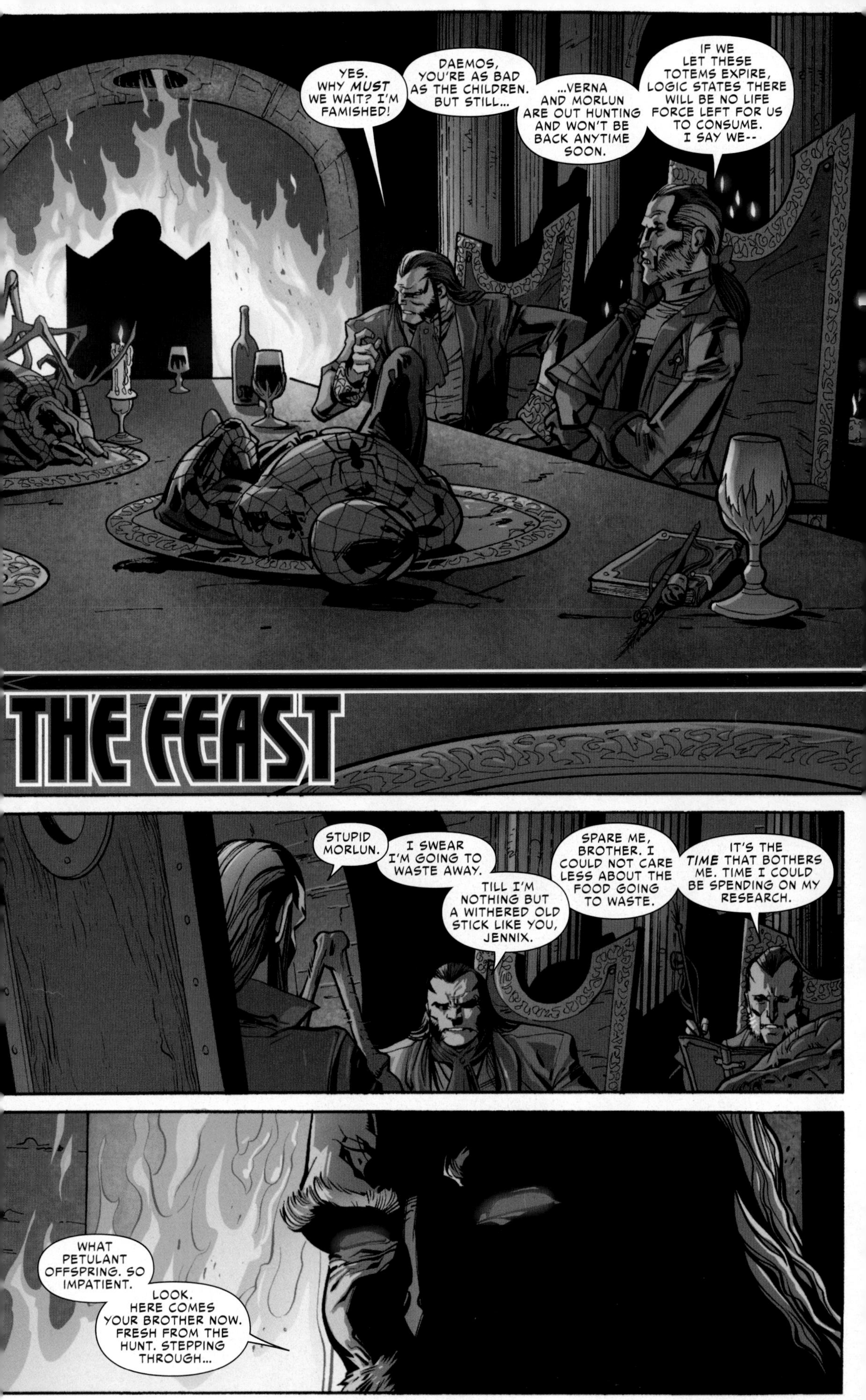
YES. WHY MUST WE WAIT? I'M FAMISHED!
DAEMOS, YOU'RE AS BAD AS THE CHILDREN. BUT STILL...
...VERNA AND MORLUN ARE OUT HUNTING AND WON'T BE BACK ANYTIME SOON.
IF WE LET THESE TOTEMS EXPIRE, LOGIC STATES THERE WILL BE NO LIFE FORCE LEFT FOR US TO CONSUME. I SAY WE--
THE FEAST
STUPID MORLUN.
I SWEAR I'M GOING TO WASTE AWAY.
TILL I'M NOTHING BUT A WITHERED OLD STICK LIKE YOU, JENNIX.
SPARE ME, BROTHER. I COULD NOT CARE LESS ABOUT THE FOOD GOING TO WASTE.
IT'S THE TIME THAT BOTHERS ME. TIME I COULD BE SPENDING ON MY RESEARCH.
WHAT PETULANT OFFSPRING. SO IMPATIENT.
LOOK. HERE COMES YOUR BROTHER NOW. FRESH FROM THE HUNT. STEPPING THROUGH...

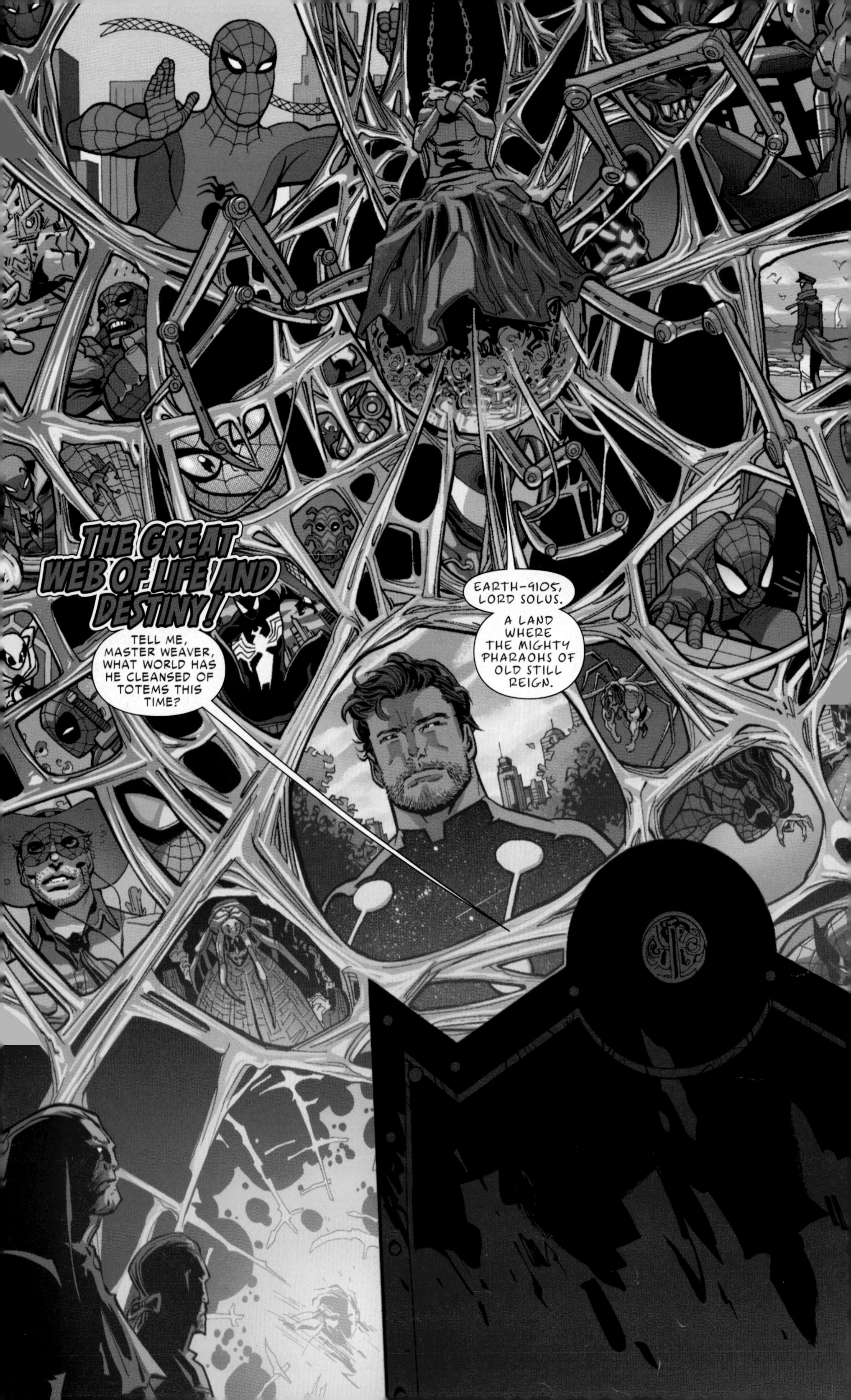
THE GREAT WEB OF LIFE AND DESTINY!
TELL ME, MASTER WEAVER, WHAT WORLD HAS HE CLEANSED OF TOTEMS THIS TIME?
EARTH-9105, LORD SOLUS.
A LAND WHERE THE MIGHTY PHARAOHS OF OLD STILL REIGN.

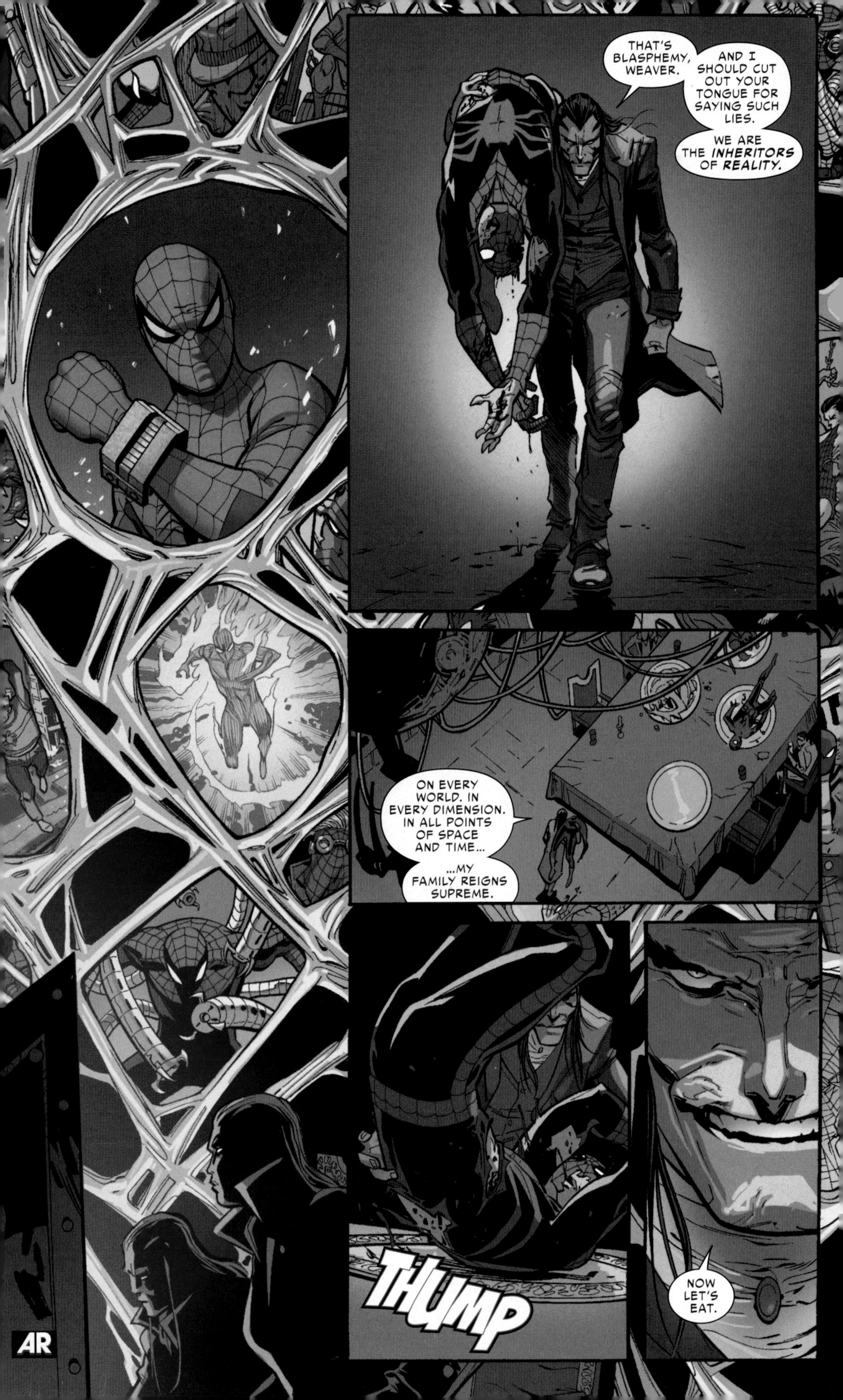
THAT'S BLASPHEMY, WEAVER.
AND I SHOULD CUT OUT YOUR TONGUE FOR SAYING SUCH LIES.
WE ARE THE *INHERITORS* OF *REALITY.*
ON EVERY WORLD. IN EVERY DIMENSION. IN ALL POINTS OF SPACE AND TIME...
...MY FAMILY REIGNS SUPREME.
THUMP
NOW LET'S EAT.
AR

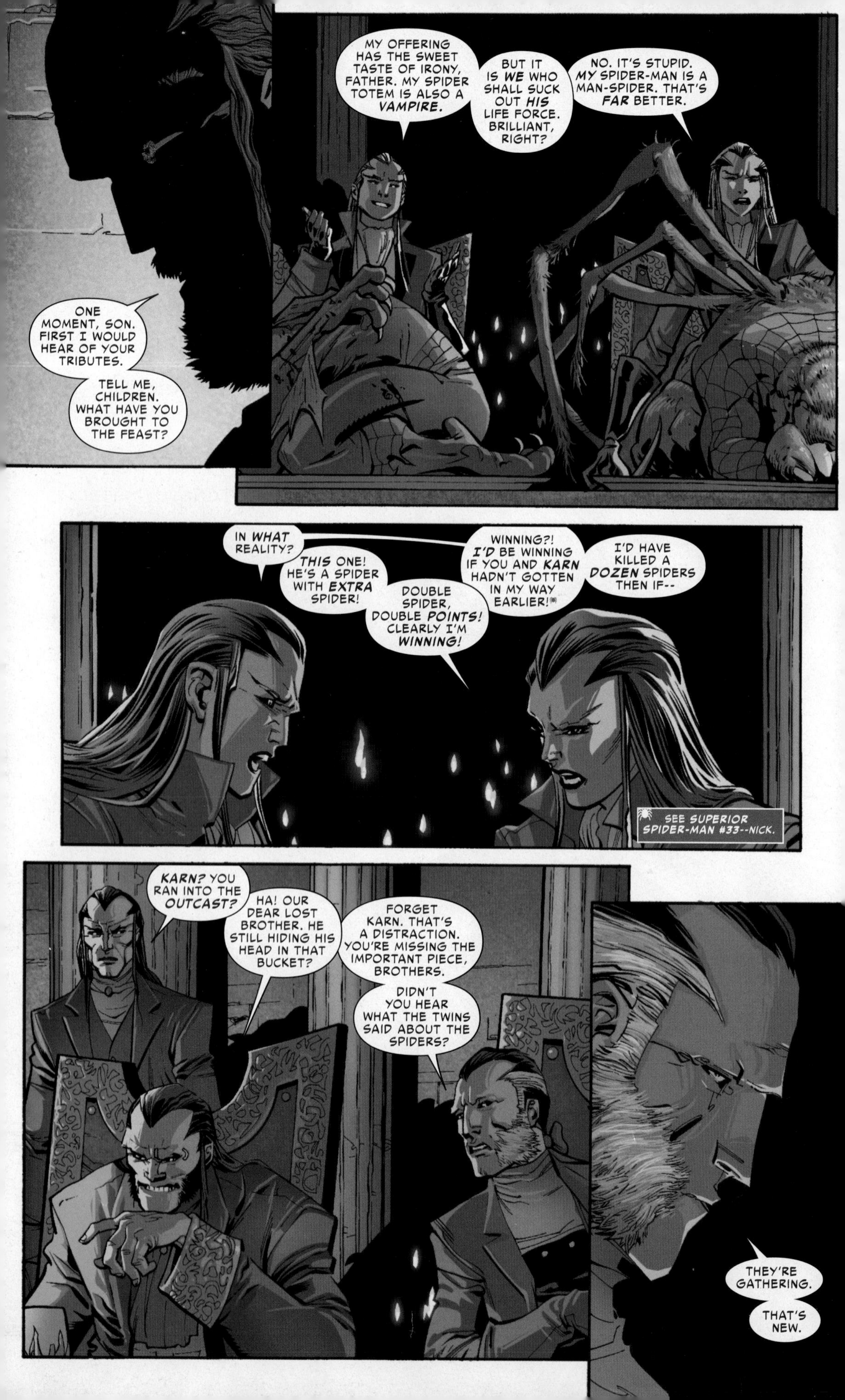
ONE MOMENT, SON. FIRST I WOULD HEAR OF YOUR TRIBUTES.
TELL ME, CHILDREN. WHAT HAVE YOU BROUGHT TO THE FEAST?
MY OFFERING HAS THE SWEET TASTE OF IRONY, FATHER. MY SPIDER TOTEM IS ALSO A VAMPIRE.
BUT IT IS WE WHO SHALL SUCK OUT HIS LIFE FORCE. BRILLIANT, RIGHT?
NO. IT'S STUPID. MY SPIDER-MAN IS A MAN-SPIDER. THAT'S FAR BETTER.
THIS ONE! HE'S A SPIDER WITH EXTRA SPIDER!
DOUBLE SPIDER, DOUBLE POINTS! CLEARLY I'M WINNING!
IN WHAT REALITY?
WINNING?! I'D BE WINNING IF YOU AND KARN HADN'T GOTTEN IN MY WAY EARLIER!
I'D HAVE KILLED A DOZEN SPIDERS THEN IF--
SEE SUPERIOR SPIDER-MAN #33--NICK.
KARN? YOU RAN INTO THE OUTCAST?
HA! OUR DEAR LOST BROTHER. HE STILL HIDING HIS HEAD IN THAT BUCKET?
FORGET KARN. THAT'S A DISTRACTION. YOU'RE MISSING THE IMPORTANT PIECE, BROTHERS.
DIDN'T YOU HEAR WHAT THE TWINS SAID ABOUT THE SPIDERS?
THEY'RE GATHERING.
THAT'S NEW.

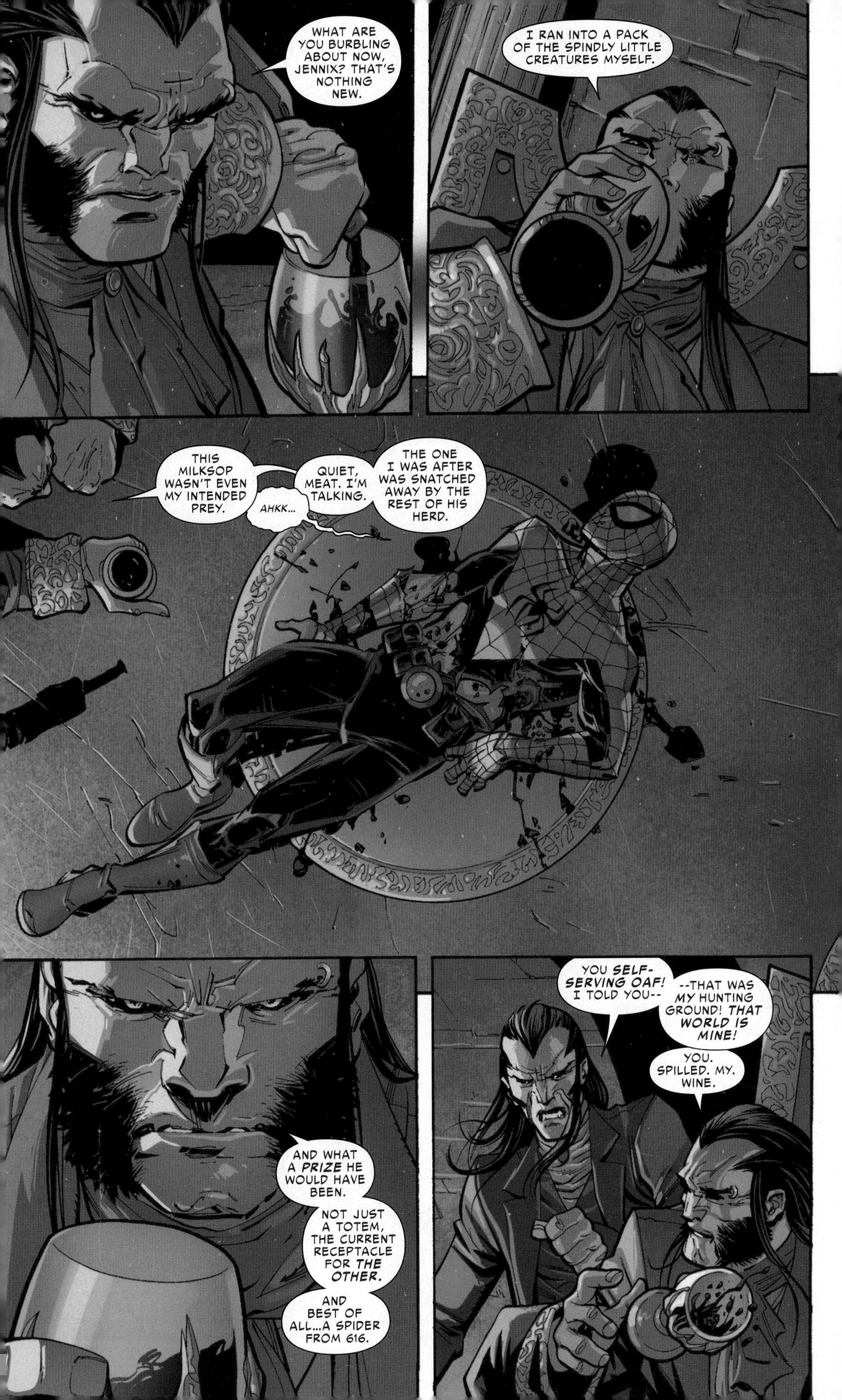

WHAT ARE YOU BURBLING ABOUT NOW, JENNIX? THAT'S NOTHING NEW.
I RAN INTO A PACK OF THE SPINDLY LITTLE CREATURES MYSELF.
THIS MILKSOP WASN'T EVEN MY INTENDED PREY.
AHKK...
QUIET, MEAT. I'M TALKING.
THE ONE I WAS AFTER WAS SNATCHED AWAY BY THE REST OF HIS HERD.
AND WHAT A PRIZE HE WOULD HAVE BEEN.
NOT JUST A TOTEM, THE CURRENT RECEPTACLE FOR THE OTHER.
AND BEST OF ALL...A SPIDER FROM 616.
YOU SELF-SERVING OAF! I TOLD YOU--
--THAT WAS MY HUNTING GROUND! THAT WORLD IS MINE!
YOU. SPILLED. MY. WINE.

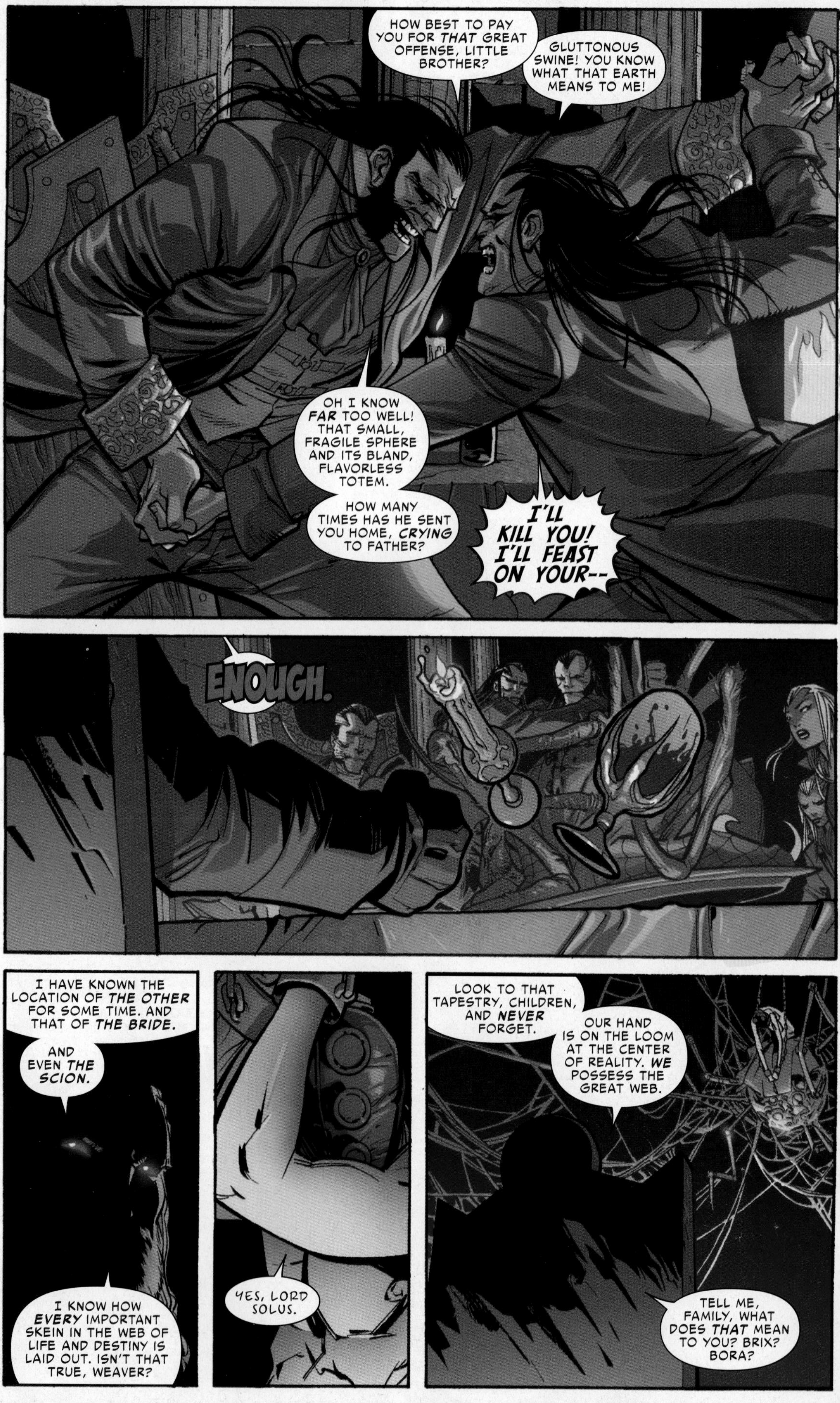

HOW BEST TO PAY YOU FOR THAT GREAT OFFENSE, LITTLE BROTHER?
GLUTTONOUS SWINE! YOU KNOW WHAT THAT EARTH MEANS TO ME!
OH I KNOW FAR TOO WELL! THAT SMALL, FRAGILE SPHERE AND ITS BLAND, FLAVORLESS TOTEM.
HOW MANY TIMES HAS HE SENT YOU HOME, CRYING TO FATHER?
I'LL KILL YOU! I'LL FEAST ON YOUR--
ENOUGH.
I HAVE KNOWN THE LOCATION OF THE OTHER FOR SOME TIME. AND THAT OF THE BRIDE.
AND EVEN THE SCION.
I KNOW HOW EVERY IMPORTANT SKEIN IN THE WEB OF LIFE AND DESTINY IS LAID OUT. ISN'T THAT TRUE, WEAVER?
YES, LORD SOLUS.
LOOK TO THAT TAPESTRY, CHILDREN, AND NEVER FORGET.
OUR HAND IS ON THE LOOM AT THE CENTER OF REALITY. WE POSSESS THE GREAT WEB.
TELL ME, FAMILY, WHAT DOES THAT MEAN TO YOU? BRIX? BORA?

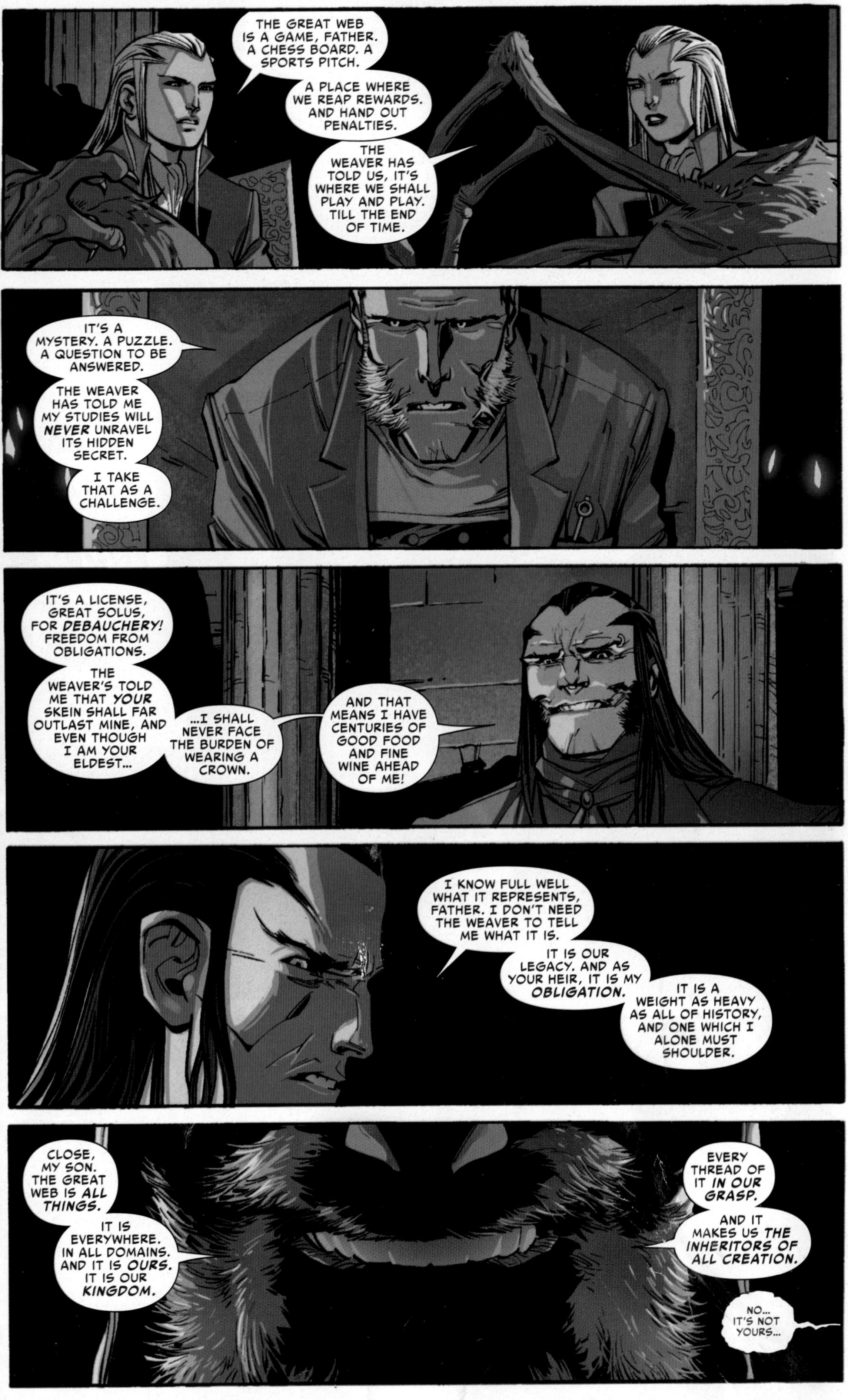
THE GREAT WEB IS A GAME, FATHER. A CHESS BOARD. A SPORTS PITCH.
A PLACE WHERE WE REAP REWARDS. AND HAND OUT PENALTIES.
THE WEAVER HAS TOLD US, IT'S WHERE WE SHALL PLAY AND PLAY. TILL THE END OF TIME.
IT'S A MYSTERY. A PUZZLE. A QUESTION TO BE ANSWERED.
THE WEAVER HAS TOLD ME MY STUDIES WILL NEVER UNRAVEL ITS HIDDEN SECRET.
I TAKE THAT AS A CHALLENGE.
IT'S A LICENSE, GREAT SOLUS, FOR DEBAUCHERY! FREEDOM FROM OBLIGATIONS.
THE WEAVER'S TOLD ME THAT YOUR SKEIN SHALL FAR OUTLAST MINE, AND EVEN THOUGH I AM YOUR ELDEST...
...I SHALL NEVER FACE THE BURDEN OF WEARING A CROWN.
AND THAT MEANS I HAVE CENTURIES OF GOOD FOOD AND FINE WINE AHEAD OF ME!
I KNOW FULL WELL WHAT IT REPRESENTS, FATHER. I DON'T NEED THE WEAVER TO TELL ME WHAT IT IS.
IT IS OUR LEGACY. AND AS YOUR HEIR, IT IS MY OBLIGATION.
IT IS A WEIGHT AS HEAVY AS ALL OF HISTORY, AND ONE WHICH I ALONE MUST SHOULDER.
CLOSE, MY SON. THE GREAT WEB IS ALL THINGS.
IT IS EVERYWHERE. IN ALL DOMAINS. AND IT IS OURS. IT IS OUR KINGDOM.
EVERY THREAD OF IT IN OUR GRASP.
AND IT MAKES US THE INHERITORS OF ALL CREATION.
NO... IT'S NOT YOURS...

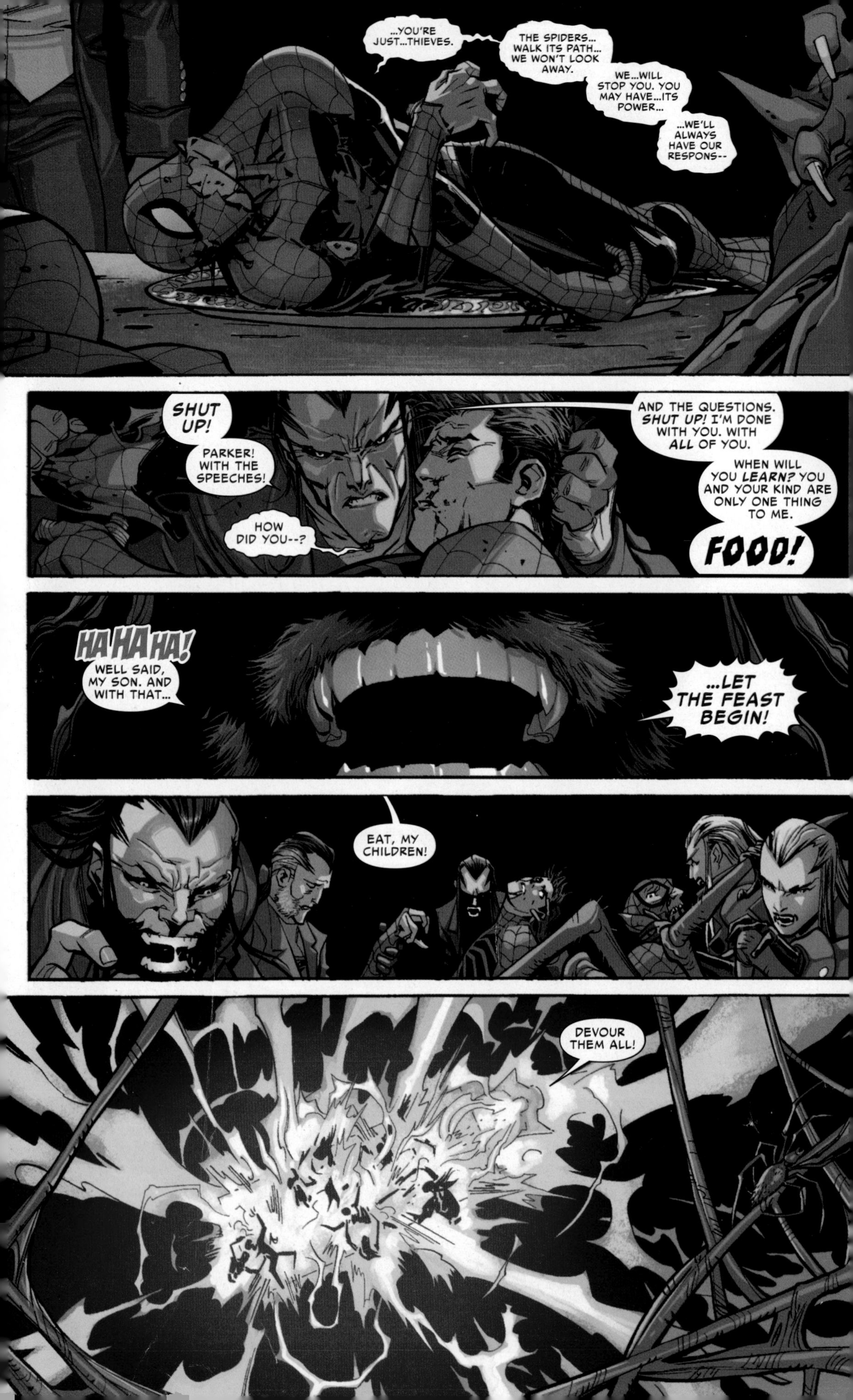
...YOU'RE JUST...THIEVES.
THE SPIDERS... WALK ITS PATH... WE WON'T LOOK AWAY.
WE...WILL STOP YOU. YOU MAY HAVE...ITS POWER...
...WE'LL ALWAYS HAVE OUR RESPONS--
SHUT UP!
PARKER! WITH THE SPEECHES!
HOW DID YOU--?
AND THE QUESTIONS. SHUT UP! I'M DONE WITH YOU. WITH ALL OF YOU.
WHEN WILL YOU LEARN? YOU AND YOUR KIND ARE ONLY ONE THING TO ME.
FOOD!
HAHAHA!
WELL SAID, MY SON. AND WITH THAT...
...LET THE FEAST BEGIN!
EAT, MY CHILDREN!
DEVOUR THEM ALL!

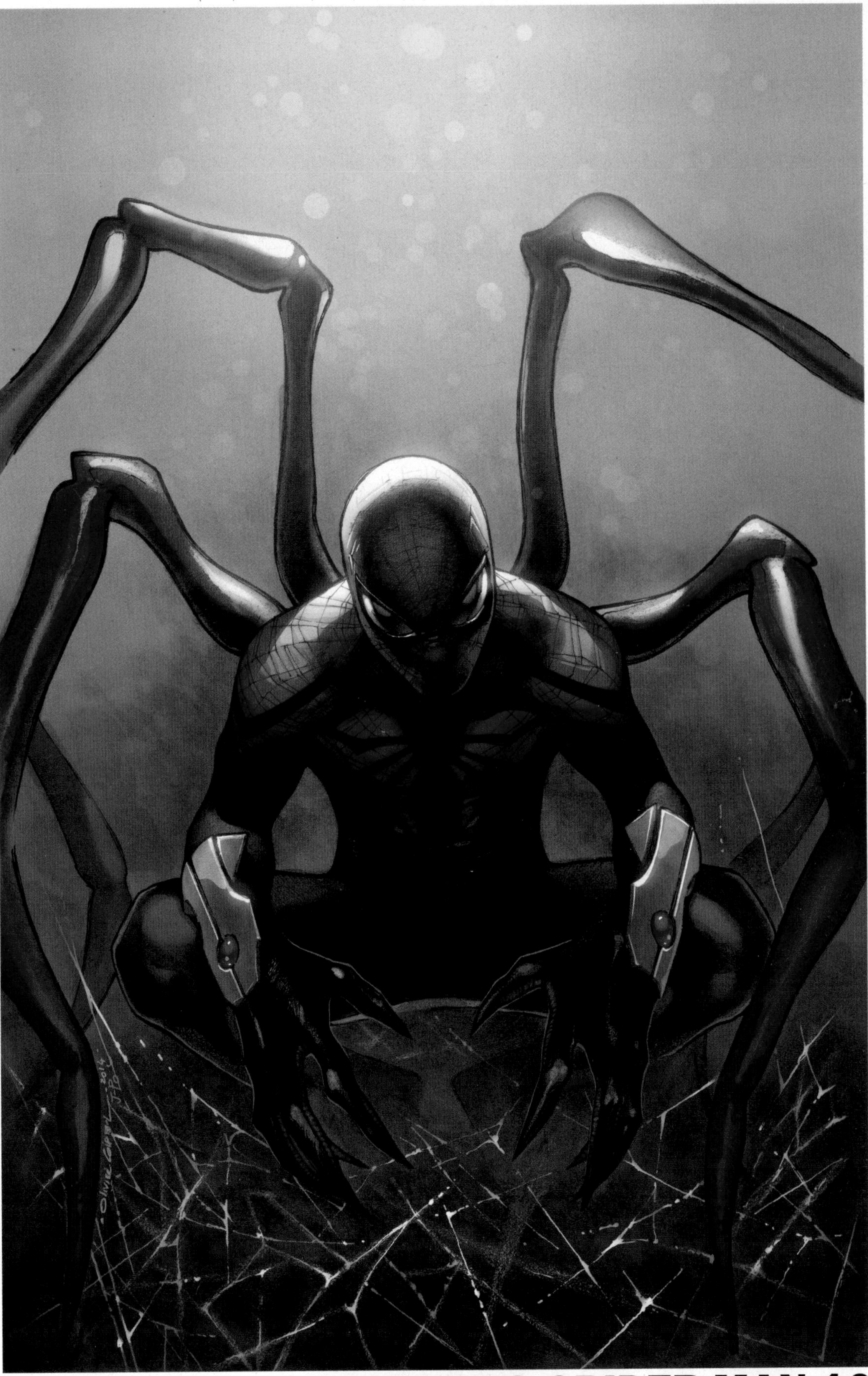

AMAZING SPIDER-MAN 10

SPIDER-VERSE, PART TWO: SUPERIOR FORCE

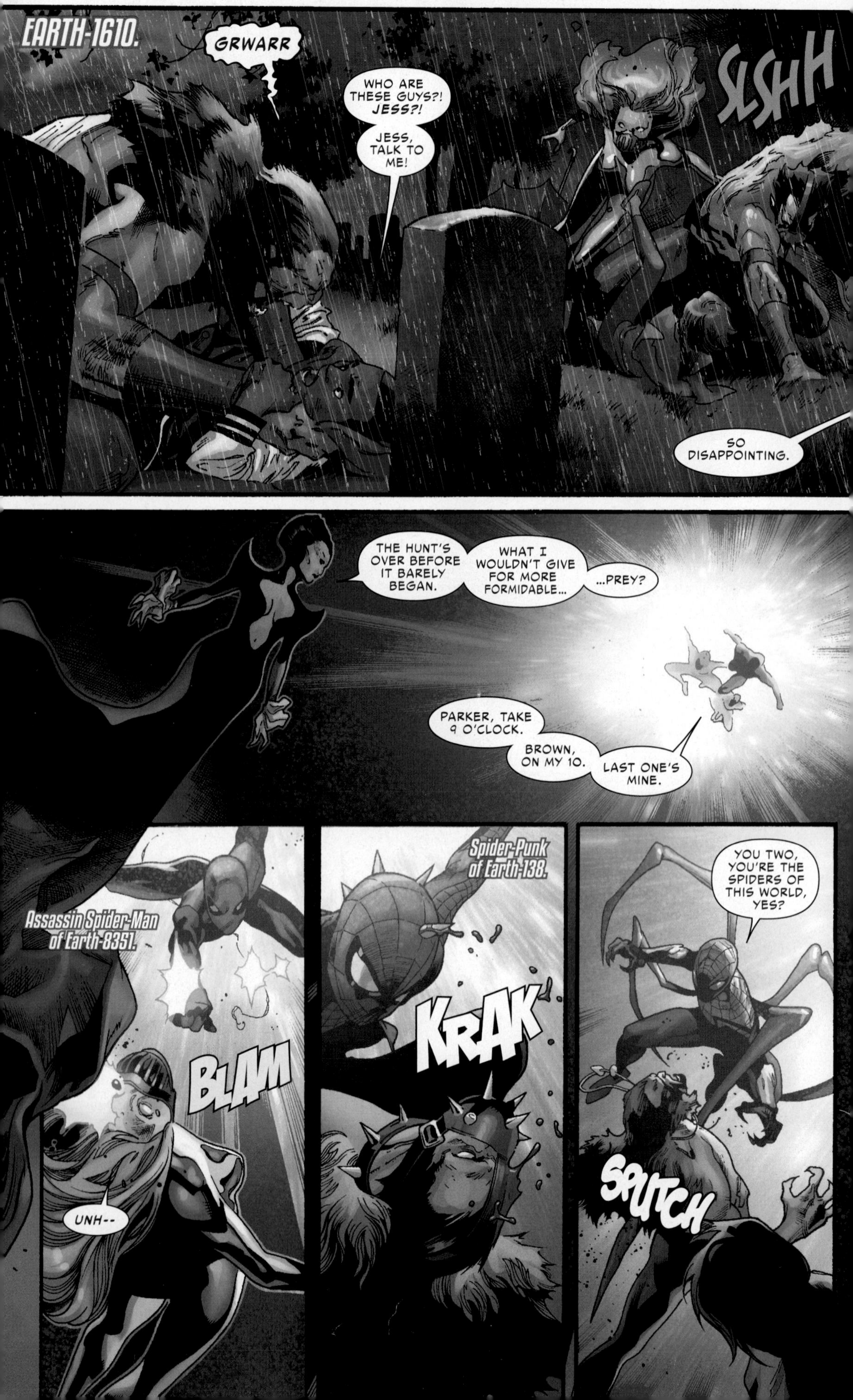

EARTH-1610.
GRWARR
WHO ARE THESE GUYS?! JESS?!
JESS, TALK TO ME!
SLSHH
SO DISAPPOINTING.
THE HUNT'S OVER BEFORE IT BARELY BEGAN.
WHAT I WOULDN'T GIVE FOR MORE FORMIDABLE...
...PREY?
PARKER, TAKE 9 O'CLOCK.
BROWN, ON MY 10.
LAST ONE'S MINE.
Assassin Spider-Man of Earth-8351.
BLAM
UNH--
Spider-Punk of Earth-138.
KRAK
YOU TWO, YOU'RE THE SPIDERS OF THIS WORLD, YES?
SPLUTCH

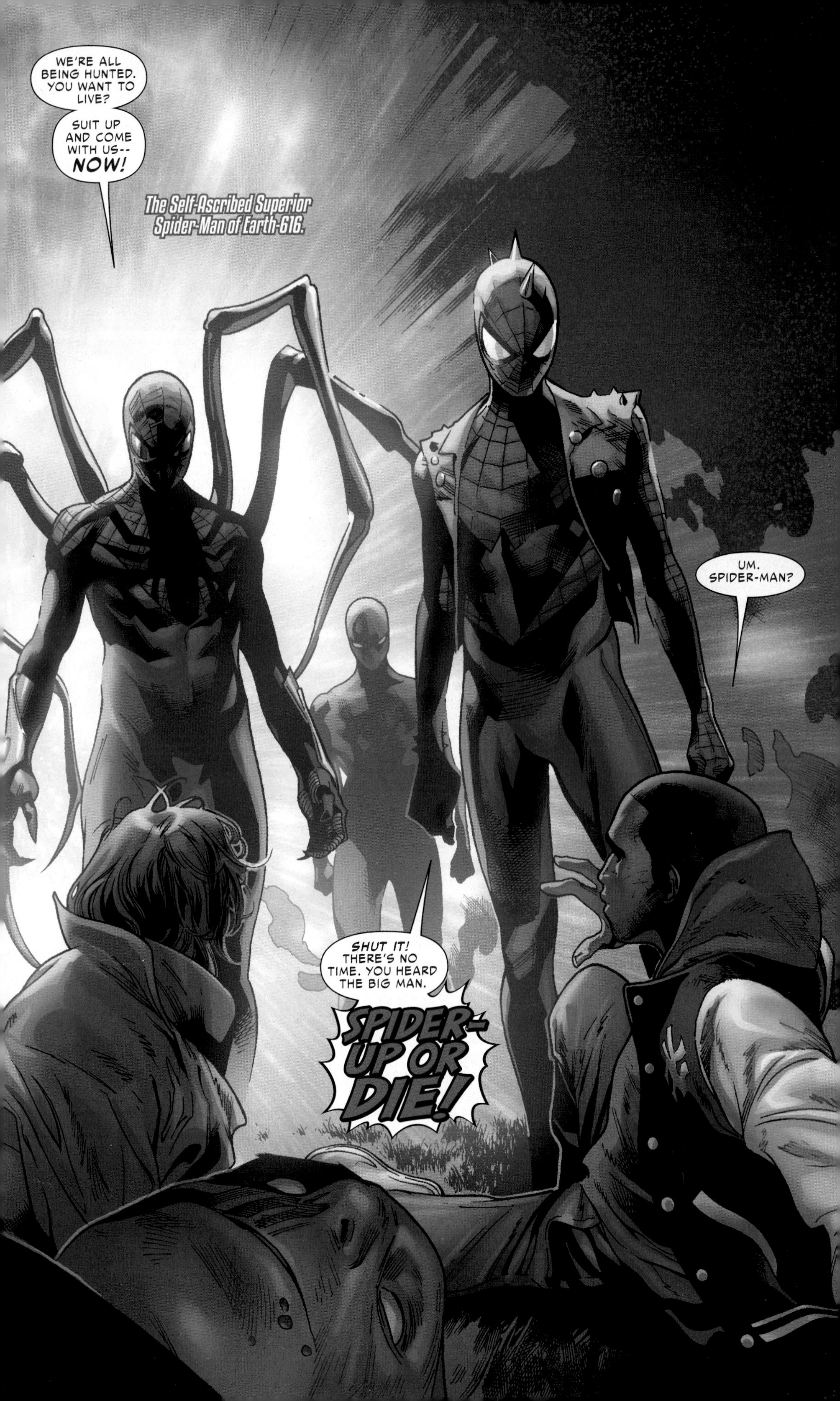
WE'RE ALL BEING HUNTED. YOU WANT TO LIVE?
SUIT UP AND COME WITH US-- NOW!
The Self-Ascribed Superior Spider-Man of Earth-616.
UM. SPIDER-MAN?
SHUT IT! THERE'S NO TIME. YOU HEARD THE BIG MAN.
SPIDER-UP OR DIE!

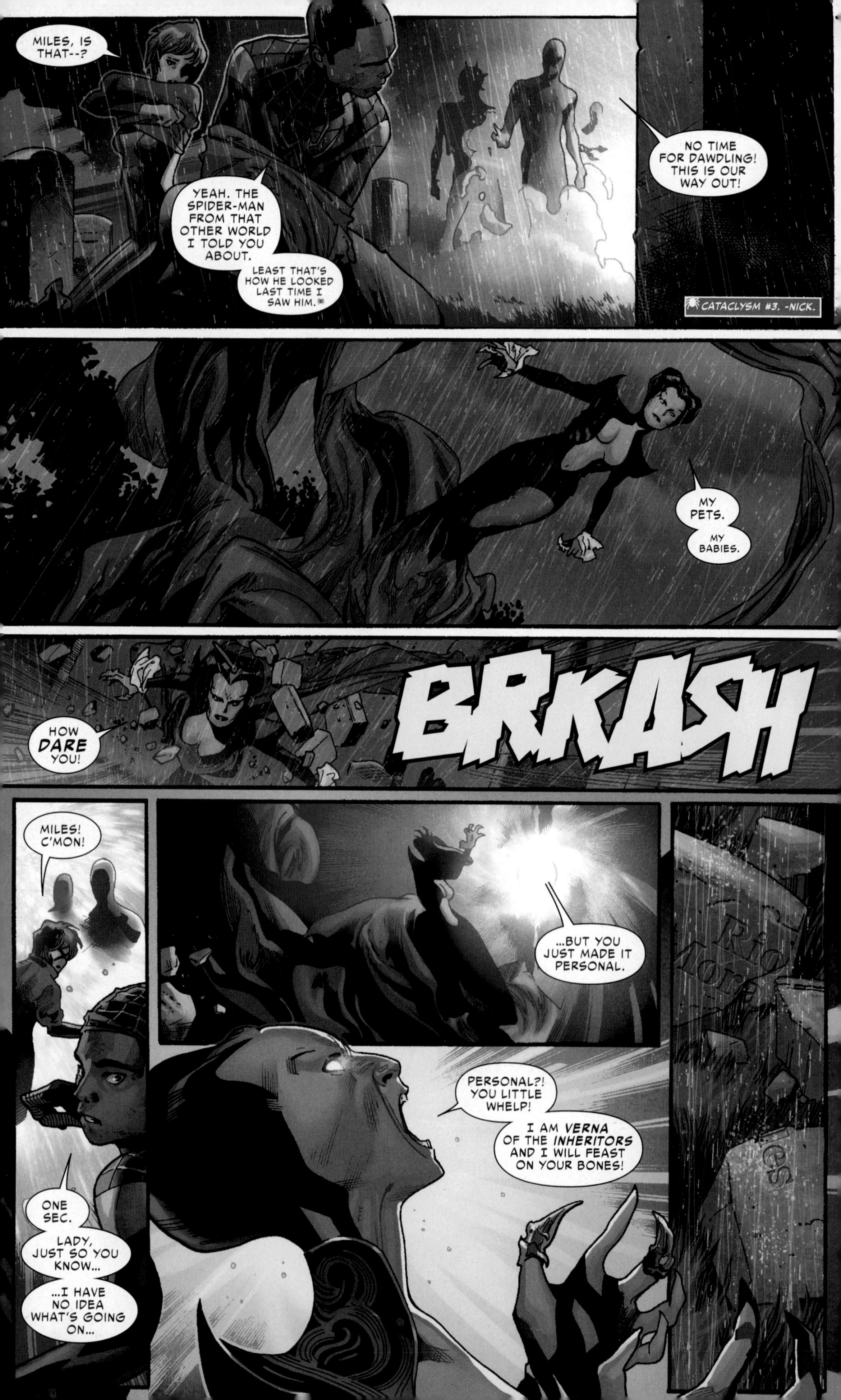
MILES, IS THAT--?
YEAH. THE SPIDER-MAN FROM THAT OTHER WORLD I TOLD YOU ABOUT.
LEAST THAT'S HOW HE LOOKED LAST TIME I SAW HIM.*
NO TIME FOR DAWDLING! THIS IS OUR WAY OUT!
*CATACLYSM #3. -NICK.
MY PETS.
MY BABIES.
HOW DARE YOU!
BRKASH
MILES! C'MON!
...BUT YOU JUST MADE IT PERSONAL.
PERSONAL?! YOU LITTLE WHELP!
I AM VERNA OF THE INHERITORS AND I WILL FEAST ON YOUR BONES!
ONE SEC.
LADY, JUST SO YOU KNOW...
...I HAVE NO IDEA WHAT'S GOING ON...

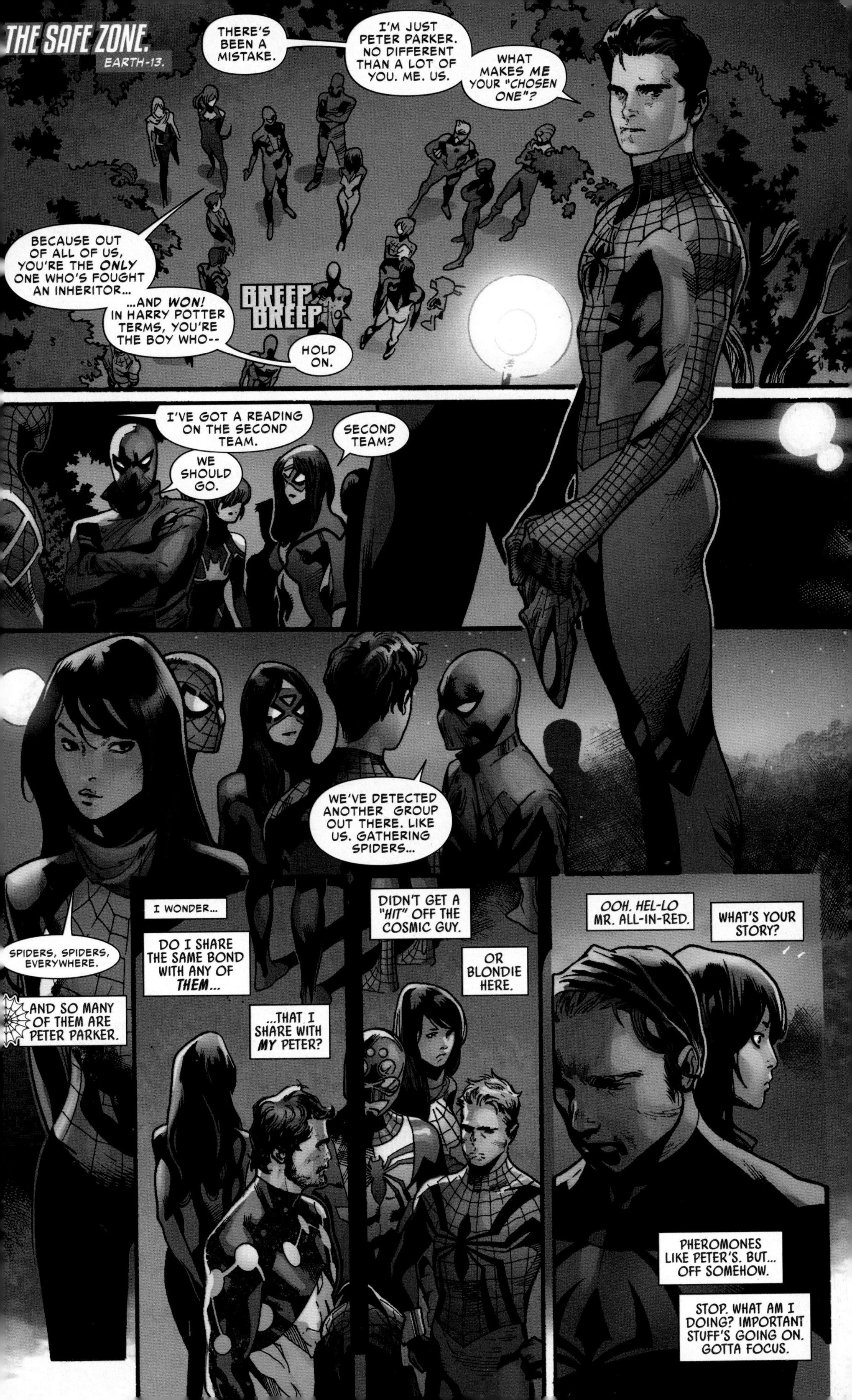
THE SAFE ZONE.
EARTH-13.
THERE'S BEEN A MISTAKE.
I'M JUST PETER PARKER. NO DIFFERENT THAN A LOT OF YOU. ME. US.
WHAT MAKES ME YOUR "CHOSEN ONE"?
BECAUSE OUT OF ALL OF US, YOU'RE THE ONLY ONE WHO'S FOUGHT AN INHERITOR...
...AND WON! IN HARRY POTTER TERMS, YOU'RE THE BOY WHO--
BREEP BREEP
HOLD ON.
I'VE GOT A READING ON THE SECOND TEAM.
WE SHOULD GO.
SECOND TEAM?
WE'VE DETECTED ANOTHER GROUP OUT THERE. LIKE US. GATHERING SPIDERS...
SPIDERS, SPIDERS, EVERYWHERE.
AND SO MANY OF THEM ARE PETER PARKER.
I WONDER...
DO I SHARE THE SAME BOND WITH ANY OF THEM...
...THAT I SHARE WITH MY PETER?
DIDN'T GET A "HIT" OFF THE COSMIC GUY.
OR BLONDIE HERE.
OOH. HEL-LO MR. ALL-IN-RED.
WHAT'S YOUR STORY?
PHEROMONES LIKE PETER'S. BUT... OFF SOMEHOW.
STOP. WHAT AM I DOING? IMPORTANT STUFF'S GOING ON. GOTTA FOCUS.

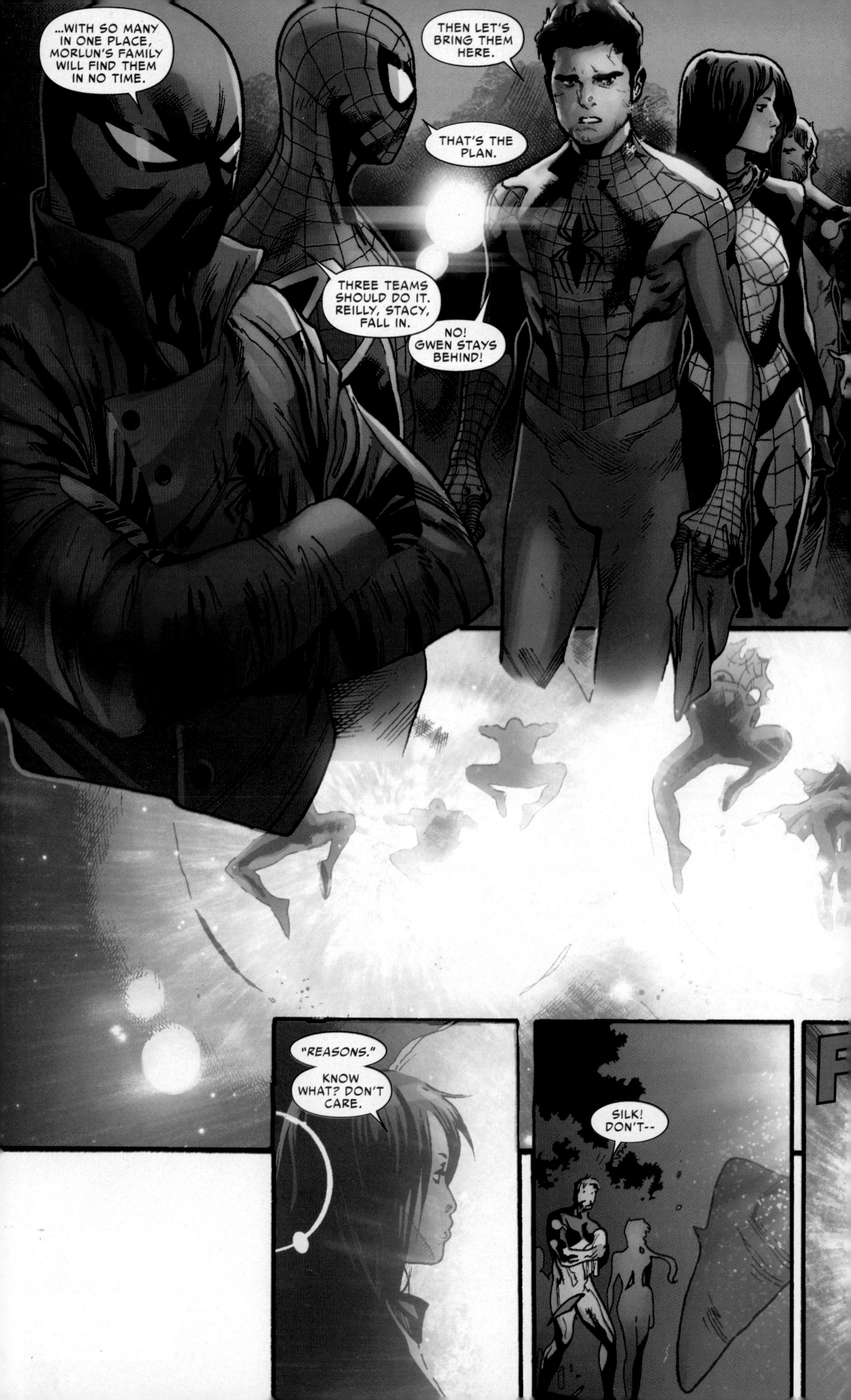
...WITH SO MANY IN ONE PLACE, MORLUN'S FAMILY WILL FIND THEM IN NO TIME.
THEN LET'S BRING THEM HERE.
THAT'S THE PLAN.
THREE TEAMS SHOULD DO IT. REILLY, STACY, FALL IN.
NO! GWEN STAYS BEHIND!
"REASONS."
KNOW WHAT? DON'T CARE.
SILK! DON'T--

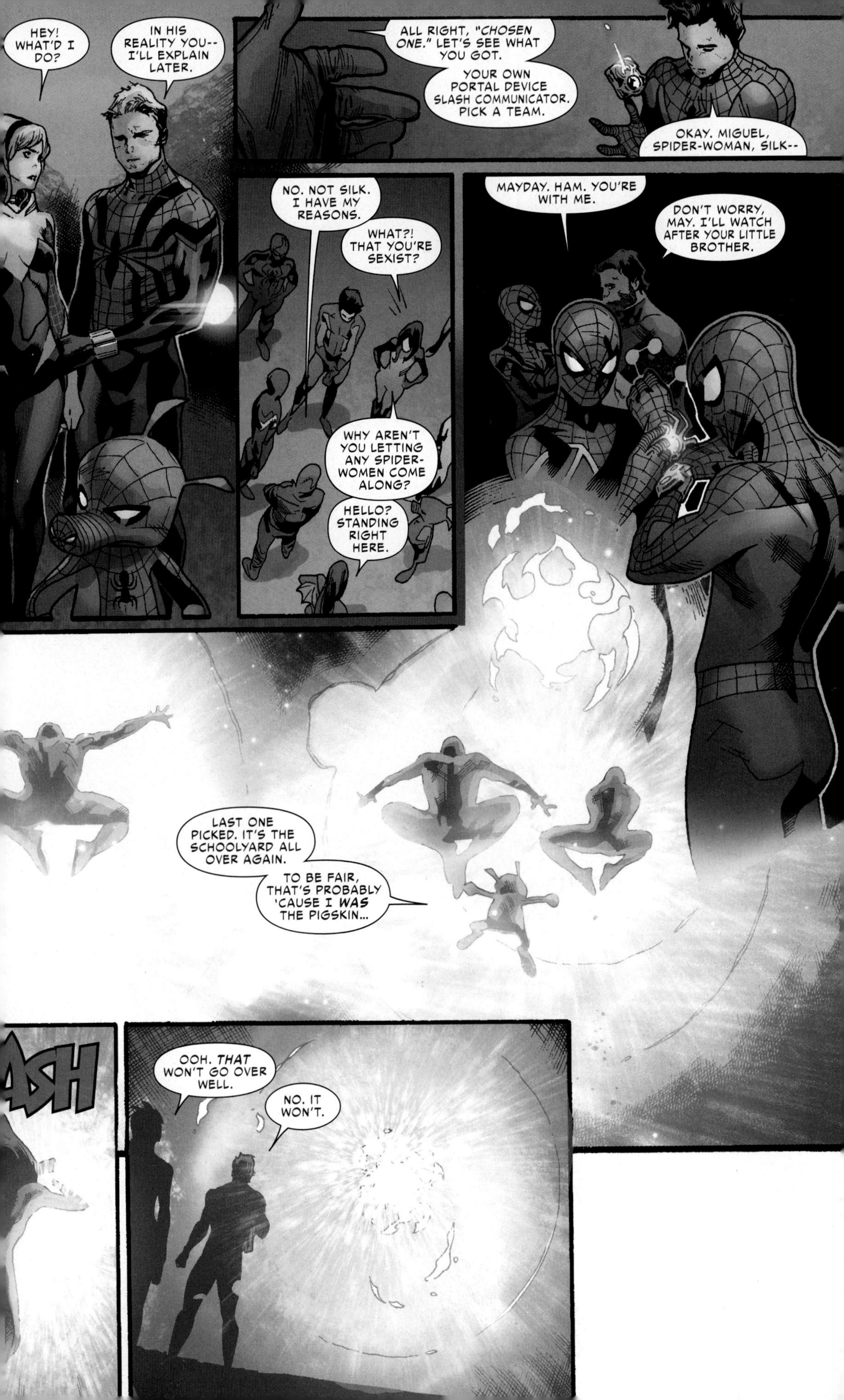
HEY! WHAT'D I DO?
IN HIS REALITY YOU-- I'LL EXPLAIN LATER.
ALL RIGHT, "CHOSEN ONE." LET'S SEE WHAT YOU GOT.
YOUR OWN PORTAL DEVICE SLASH COMMUNICATOR. PICK A TEAM.
OKAY. MIGUEL, SPIDER-WOMAN, SILK--
NO. NOT SILK. I HAVE MY REASONS.
WHAT?! THAT YOU'RE SEXIST?
WHY AREN'T YOU LETTING ANY SPIDER-WOMEN COME ALONG?
HELLO? STANDING RIGHT HERE.
MAYDAY. HAM. YOU'RE WITH ME.
DON'T WORRY, MAY. I'LL WATCH AFTER YOUR LITTLE BROTHER.
LAST ONE PICKED. IT'S THE SCHOOLYARD ALL OVER AGAIN.
TO BE FAIR, THAT'S PROBABLY 'CAUSE I WAS THE PIGSKIN...
ASH
OOH. THAT WON'T GO OVER WELL.
NO. IT WON'T.

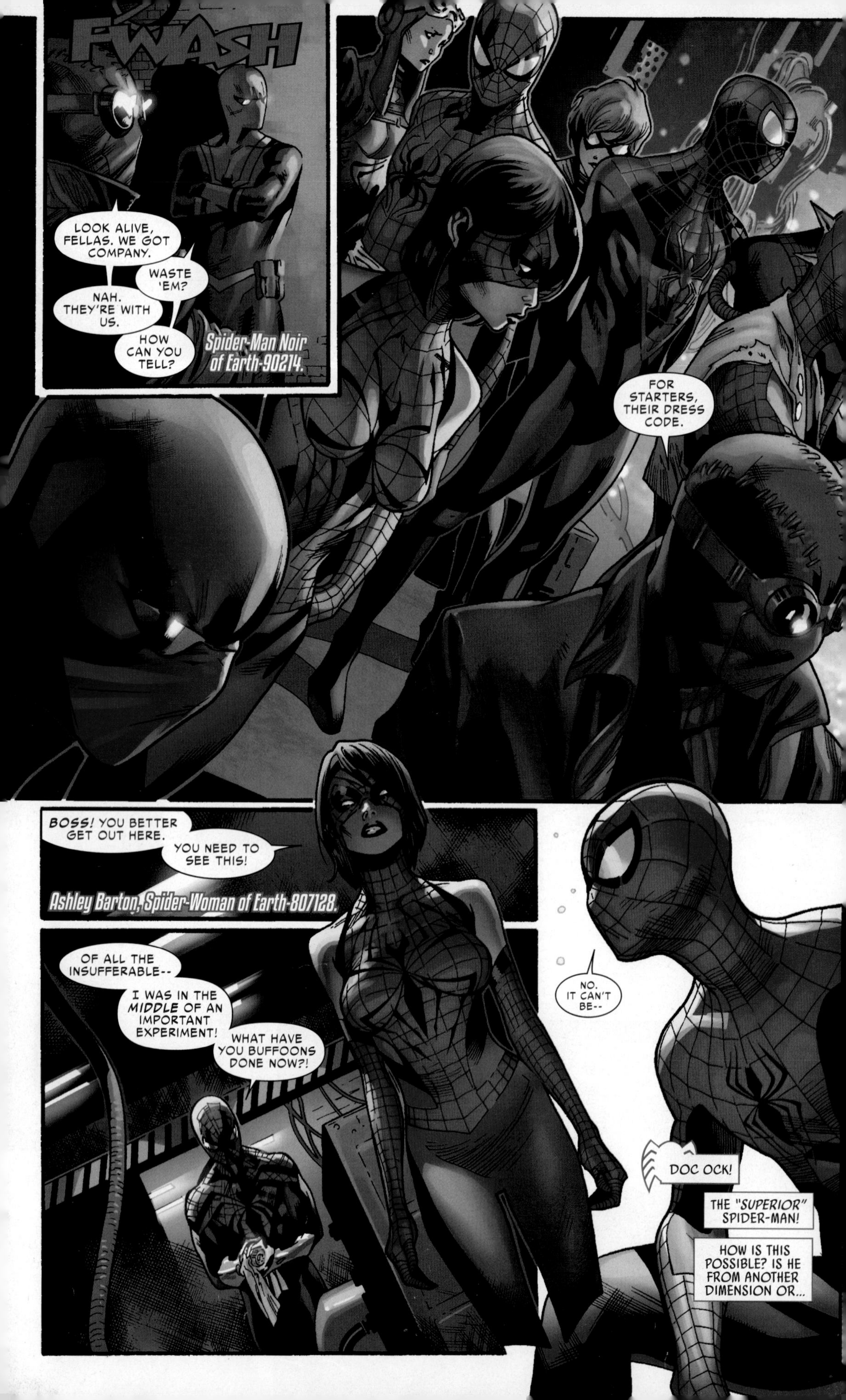
FWASH
LOOK ALIVE, FELLAS. WE GOT COMPANY.
WASTE 'EM?
NAH. THEY'RE WITH US.
HOW CAN YOU TELL?
Spider-Man Noir of Earth-90214.
FOR STARTERS, THEIR DRESS CODE.
BOSS! YOU BETTER GET OUT HERE.
YOU NEED TO SEE THIS!
Ashley Barton, Spider-Woman of Earth-807128.
OF ALL THE INSUFFERABLE--
I WAS IN THE MIDDLE OF AN IMPORTANT EXPERIMENT!
WHAT HAVE YOU BUFFOONS DONE NOW?!
NO. IT CAN'T BE--
DOC OCK!
THE "SUPERIOR" SPIDER-MAN!
HOW IS THIS POSSIBLE? IS HE FROM ANOTHER DIMENSION OR...

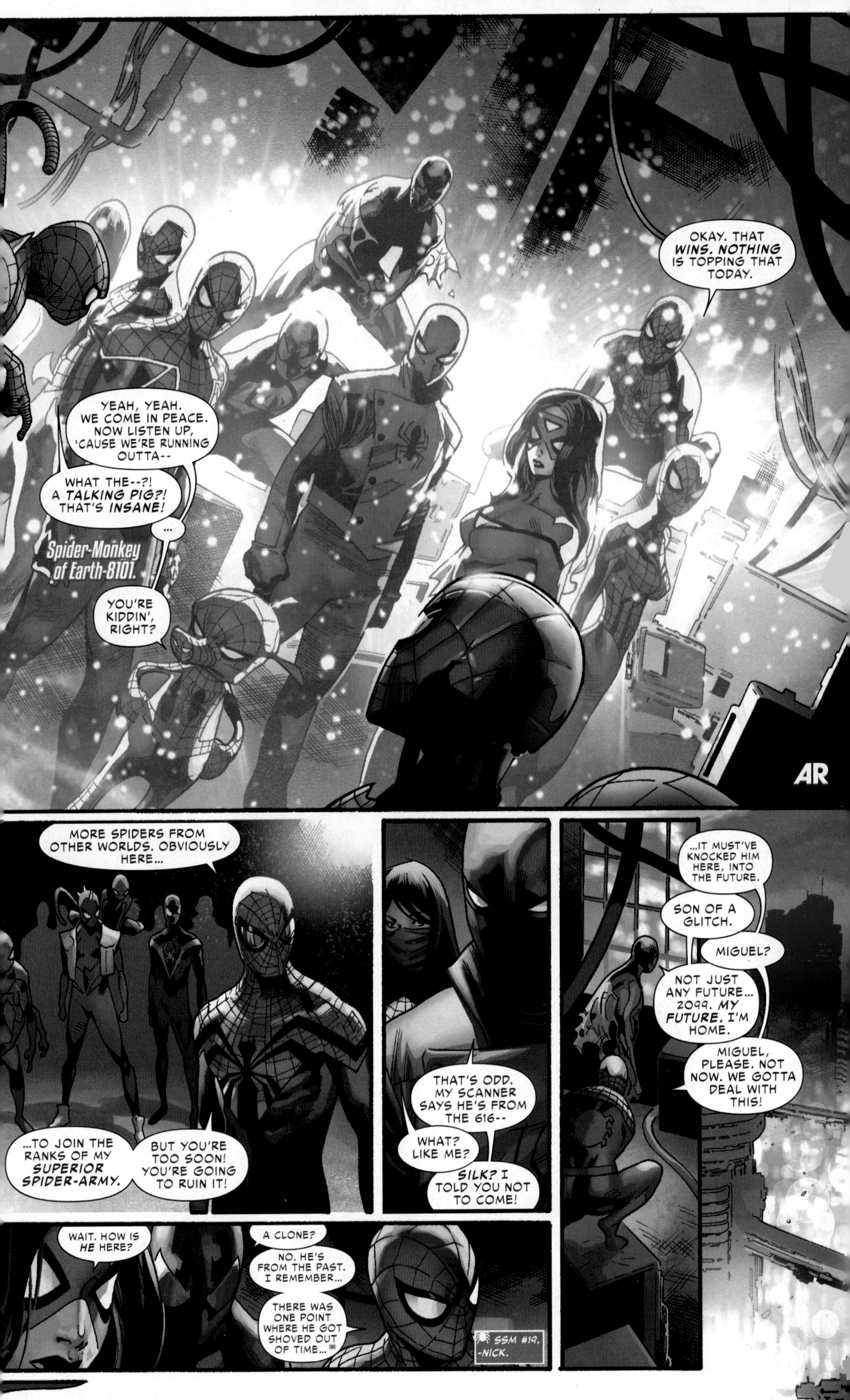
OKAY. THAT WINS. NOTHING IS TOPPING THAT TODAY.
YEAH, YEAH. WE COME IN PEACE. NOW LISTEN UP, 'CAUSE WE'RE RUNNING OUTTA--
WHAT THE--?! A TALKING PIG?! THAT'S INSANE!
...
Spider-Monkey of Earth-8101.
YOU'RE KIDDIN', RIGHT?
AR
MORE SPIDERS FROM OTHER WORLDS. OBVIOUSLY HERE...
...TO JOIN THE RANKS OF MY SUPERIOR SPIDER-ARMY.
BUT YOU'RE TOO SOON! YOU'RE GOING TO RUIN IT!
THAT'S ODD. MY SCANNER SAYS HE'S FROM THE 616--
WHAT? LIKE ME?
SILK? I TOLD YOU NOT TO COME!
...IT MUST'VE KNOCKED HIM HERE, INTO THE FUTURE.
SON OF A GLITCH.
MIGUEL?
NOT JUST ANY FUTURE... 2099. MY FUTURE. I'M HOME.
MIGUEL, PLEASE. NOT NOW. WE GOTTA DEAL WITH THIS!
WAIT. HOW IS HE HERE?
A CLONE?
NO. HE'S FROM THE PAST. I REMEMBER...
THERE WAS ONE POINT WHERE HE GOT SHOVED OUT OF TIME...
SSM #19. -NICK.

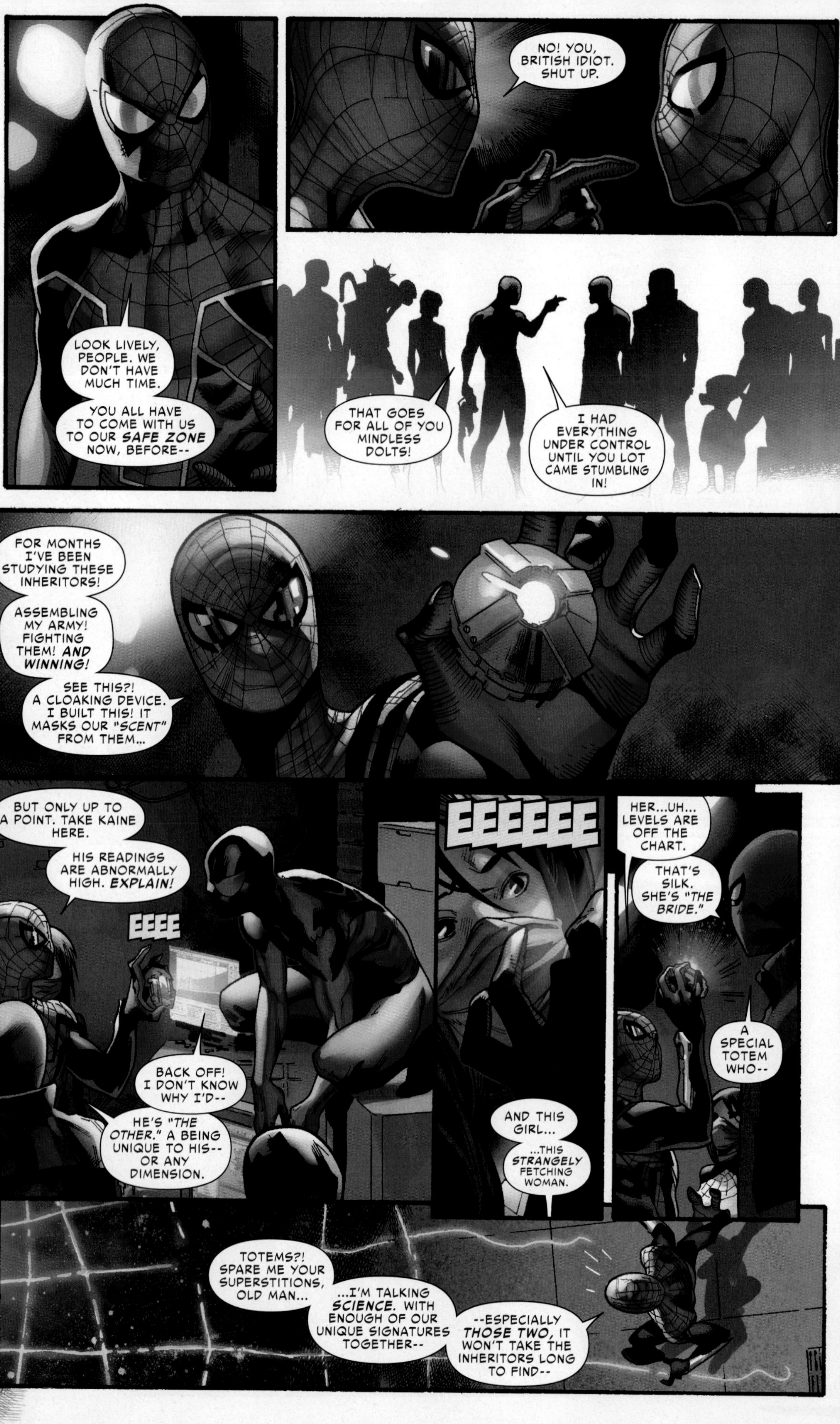

LOOK LIVELY, PEOPLE. WE DON'T HAVE MUCH TIME.
YOU ALL HAVE TO COME WITH US TO OUR SAFE ZONE NOW, BEFORE--
NO! YOU, BRITISH IDIOT. SHUT UP.
THAT GOES FOR ALL OF YOU MINDLESS DOLTS!
I HAD EVERYTHING UNDER CONTROL UNTIL YOU LOT CAME STUMBLING IN!
FOR MONTHS I'VE BEEN STUDYING THESE INHERITORS!
ASSEMBLING MY ARMY! FIGHTING THEM! AND WINNING!
SEE THIS?! A CLOAKING DEVICE. I BUILT THIS! IT MASKS OUR "SCENT" FROM THEM...
BUT ONLY UP TO A POINT. TAKE KAINE HERE.
HIS READINGS ARE ABNORMALLY HIGH. EXPLAIN!
EEEE
BACK OFF! I DON'T KNOW WHY I'D--
HE'S "THE OTHER." A BEING UNIQUE TO HIS-- OR ANY DIMENSION.
EEEEEE
AND THIS GIRL...
...THIS STRANGELY FETCHING WOMAN.
HER...UH... LEVELS ARE OFF THE CHART.
THAT'S SILK. SHE'S "THE BRIDE."
A SPECIAL TOTEM WHO--
TOTEMS?! SPARE ME YOUR SUPERSTITIONS, OLD MAN...
...I'M TALKING SCIENCE. WITH ENOUGH OF OUR UNIQUE SIGNATURES TOGETHER--
--ESPECIALLY THOSE TWO, IT WON'T TAKE THE INHERITORS LONG TO FIND--

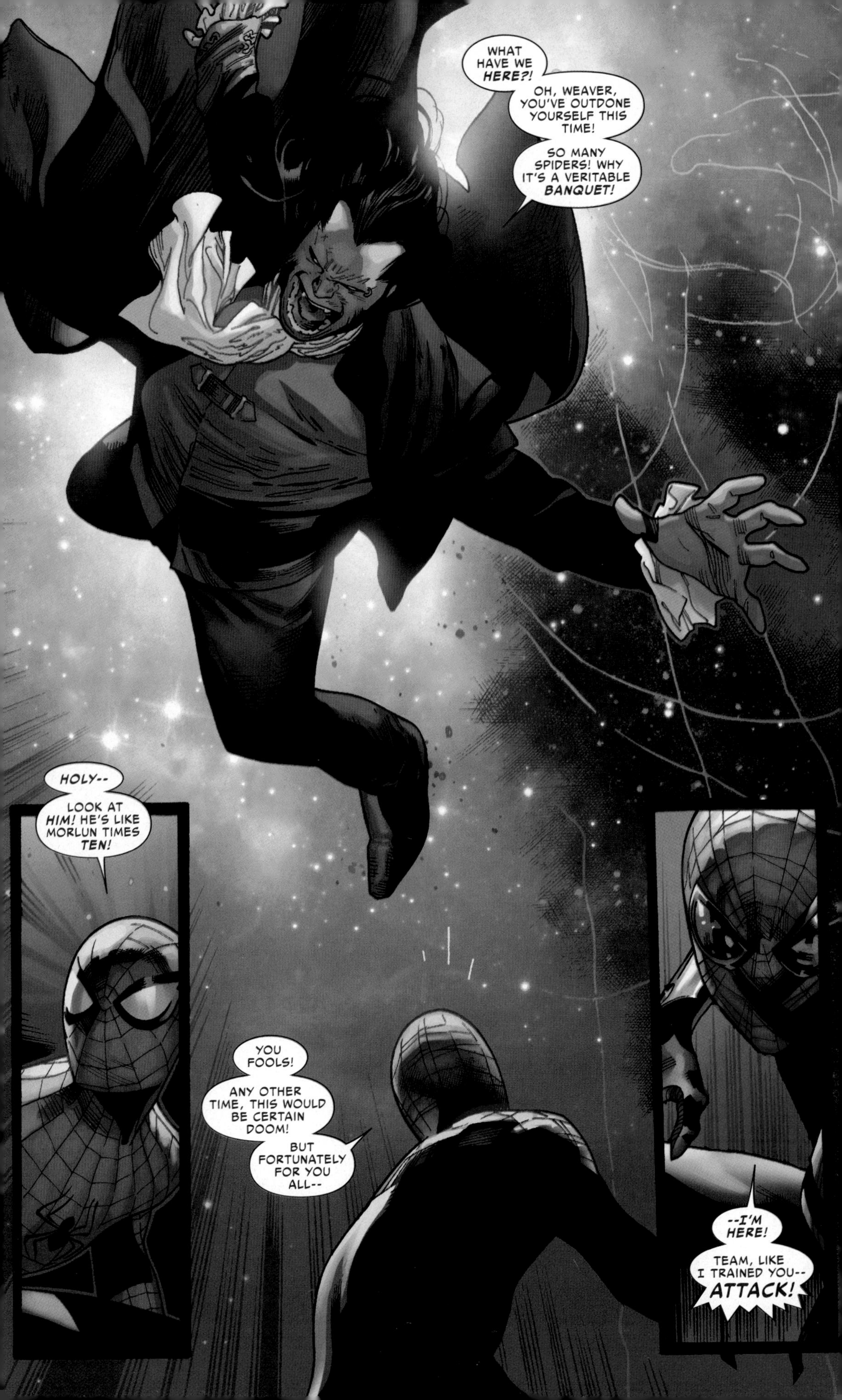
WHAT HAVE WE HERE?!
OH, WEAVER, YOU'VE OUTDONE YOURSELF THIS TIME!
SO MANY SPIDERS! WHY IT'S A VERITABLE BANQUET!
HOLY--
LOOK AT HIM! HE'S LIKE MORLUN TIMES TEN!
YOU FOOLS!
ANY OTHER TIME, THIS WOULD BE CERTAIN DOOM!
BUT FORTUNATELY FOR YOU ALL--
--I'M HERE!
TEAM, LIKE I TRAINED YOU-- ATTACK!

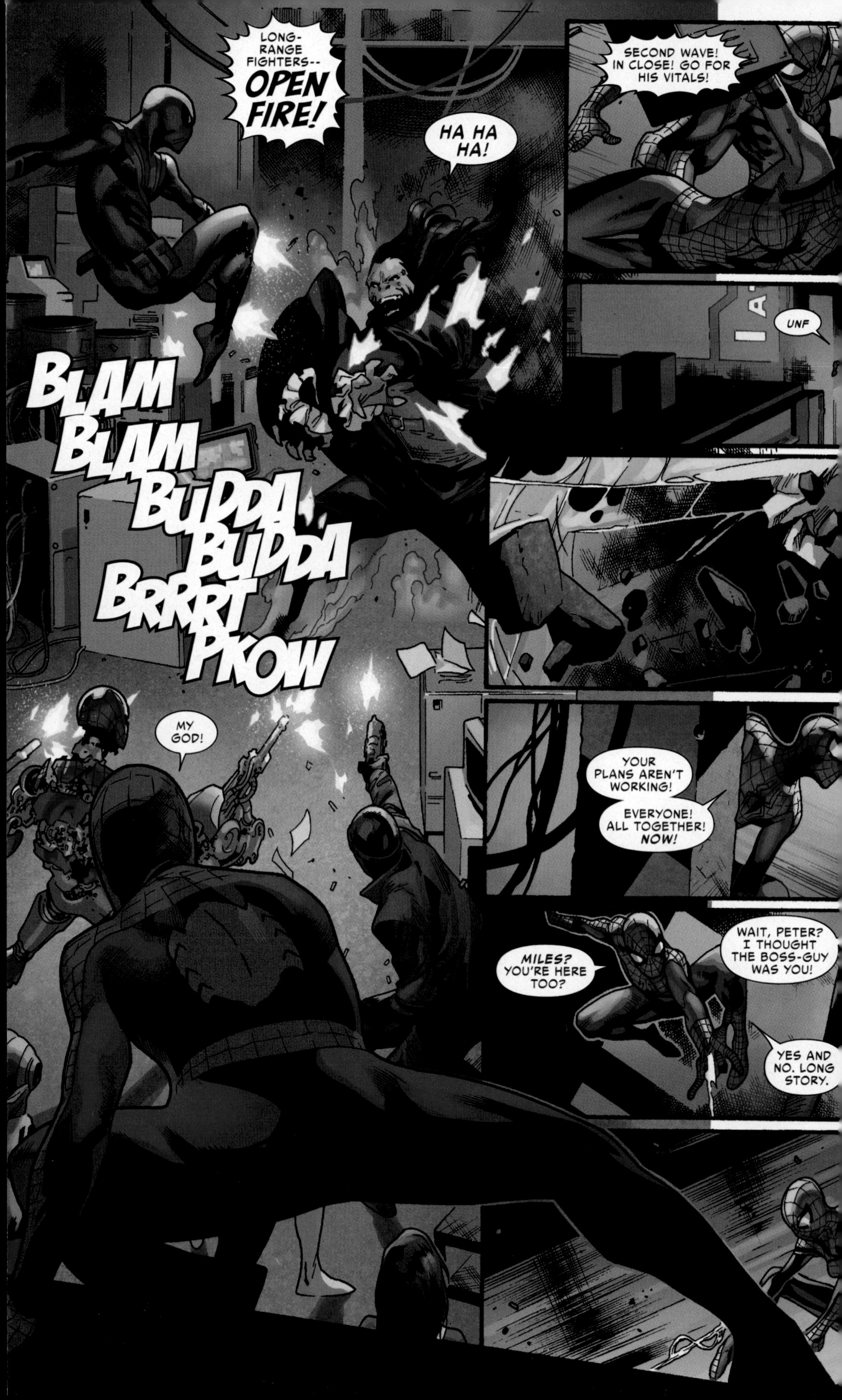
LONG-RANGE FIGHTERS-- OPEN FIRE!
HA HA HA!
SECOND WAVE! IN CLOSE! GO FOR HIS VITALS!
UNF
BLAM BLAM BUDDA BUDDA BRRRT PKOW
MY GOD!
YOUR PLANS AREN'T WORKING!
EVERYONE! ALL TOGETHER! NOW!
MILES? YOU'RE HERE TOO?
WAIT, PETER? I THOUGHT THE BOSS-GUY WAS YOU!
YES AND NO. LONG STORY.

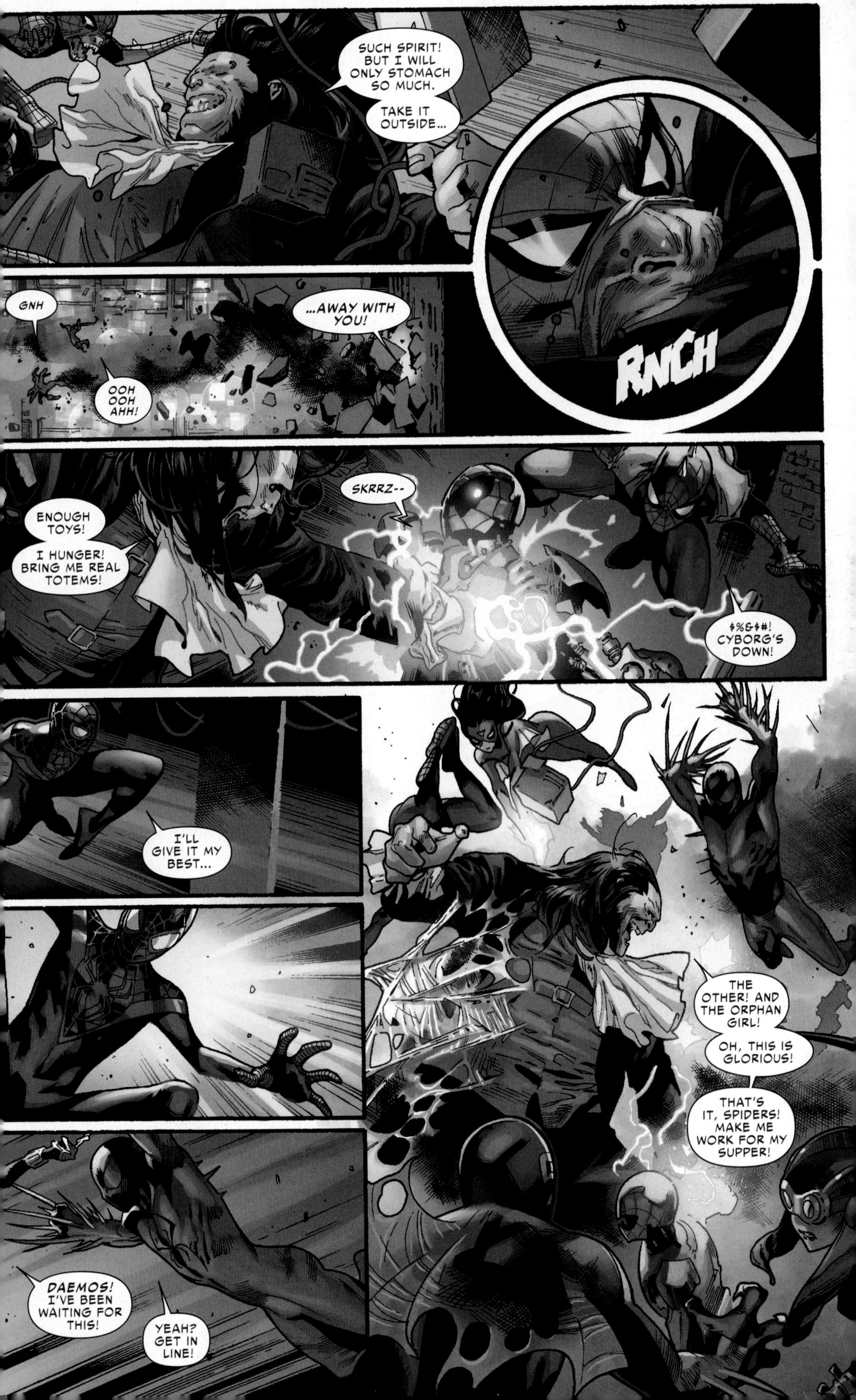
SUCH SPIRIT! BUT I WILL ONLY STOMACH SO MUCH.
TAKE IT OUTSIDE...
RNCH
GNH
...AWAY WITH YOU!
OOH OOH AHH!
SKRRZ--
ENOUGH TOYS!
I HUNGER! BRING ME REAL TOTEMS!
$%&$#! CYBORG'S DOWN!
I'LL GIVE IT MY BEST...
THE OTHER! AND THE ORPHAN GIRL!
OH, THIS IS GLORIOUS!
THAT'S IT, SPIDERS! MAKE ME WORK FOR MY SUPPER!
DAEMOS! I'VE BEEN WAITING FOR THIS!
YEAH? GET IN LINE!

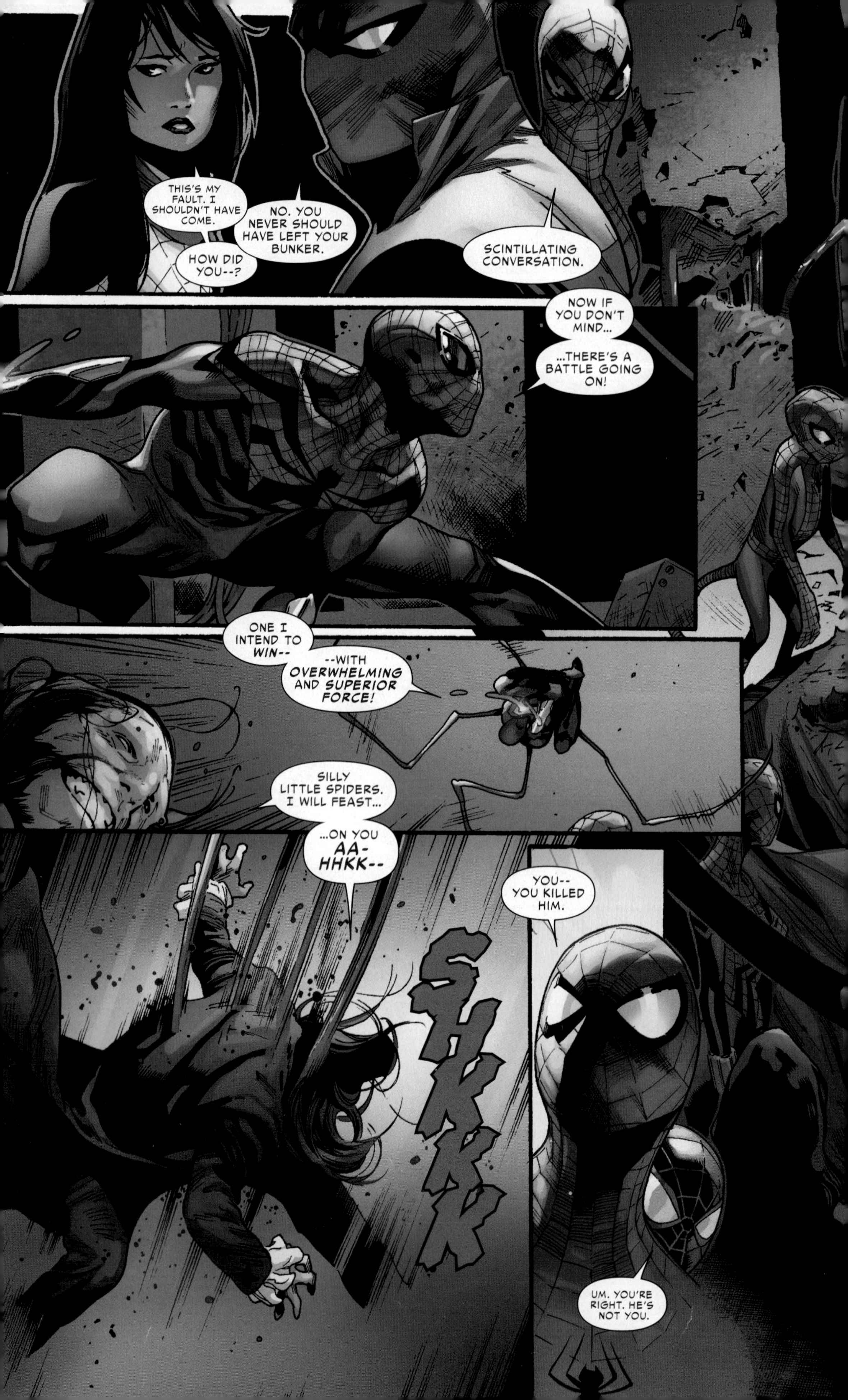
THIS'S MY FAULT. I SHOULDN'T HAVE COME.
HOW DID YOU--?
NO. YOU NEVER SHOULD HAVE LEFT YOUR BUNKER.
SCINTILLATING CONVERSATION.
NOW IF YOU DON'T MIND...
...THERE'S A BATTLE GOING ON!
ONE I INTEND TO WIN--
--WITH OVERWHELMING AND SUPERIOR FORCE!
SILLY LITTLE SPIDERS. I WILL FEAST...
...ON YOU AA-HHKK--
SHKK
YOU-- YOU KILLED HIM.
UM. YOU'RE RIGHT. HE'S NOT YOU.

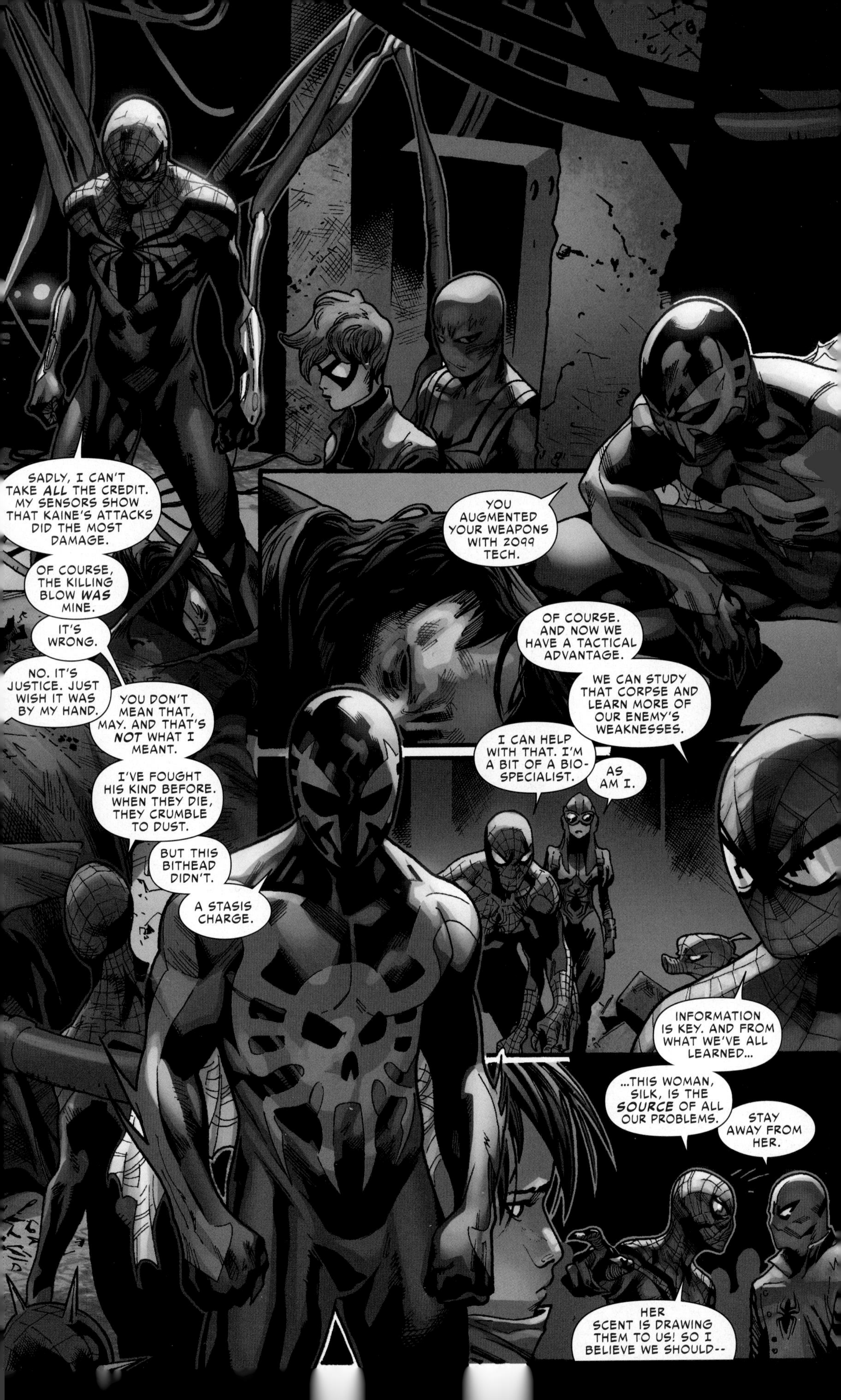

SADLY, I CAN'T TAKE ALL THE CREDIT. MY SENSORS SHOW THAT KAINE'S ATTACKS DID THE MOST DAMAGE.
OF COURSE, THE KILLING BLOW WAS MINE.
YOU AUGMENTED YOUR WEAPONS WITH 2099 TECH.
OF COURSE. AND NOW WE HAVE A TACTICAL ADVANTAGE.
WE CAN STUDY THAT CORPSE AND LEARN MORE OF OUR ENEMY'S WEAKNESSES.
I CAN HELP WITH THAT. I'M A BIT OF A BIO-SPECIALIST.
AS AM I.
IT'S WRONG.
NO. IT'S JUSTICE. JUST WISH IT WAS BY MY HAND.
YOU DON'T MEAN THAT, MAY. AND THAT'S NOT WHAT I MEANT.
I'VE FOUGHT HIS KIND BEFORE. WHEN THEY DIE, THEY CRUMBLE TO DUST.
BUT THIS BITHEAD DIDN'T.
A STASIS CHARGE.
INFORMATION IS KEY. AND FROM WHAT WE'VE ALL LEARNED...
...THIS WOMAN, SILK, IS THE SOURCE OF ALL OUR PROBLEMS.
STAY AWAY FROM HER.
HER SCENT IS DRAWING THEM TO US! SO I BELIEVE WE SHOULD--

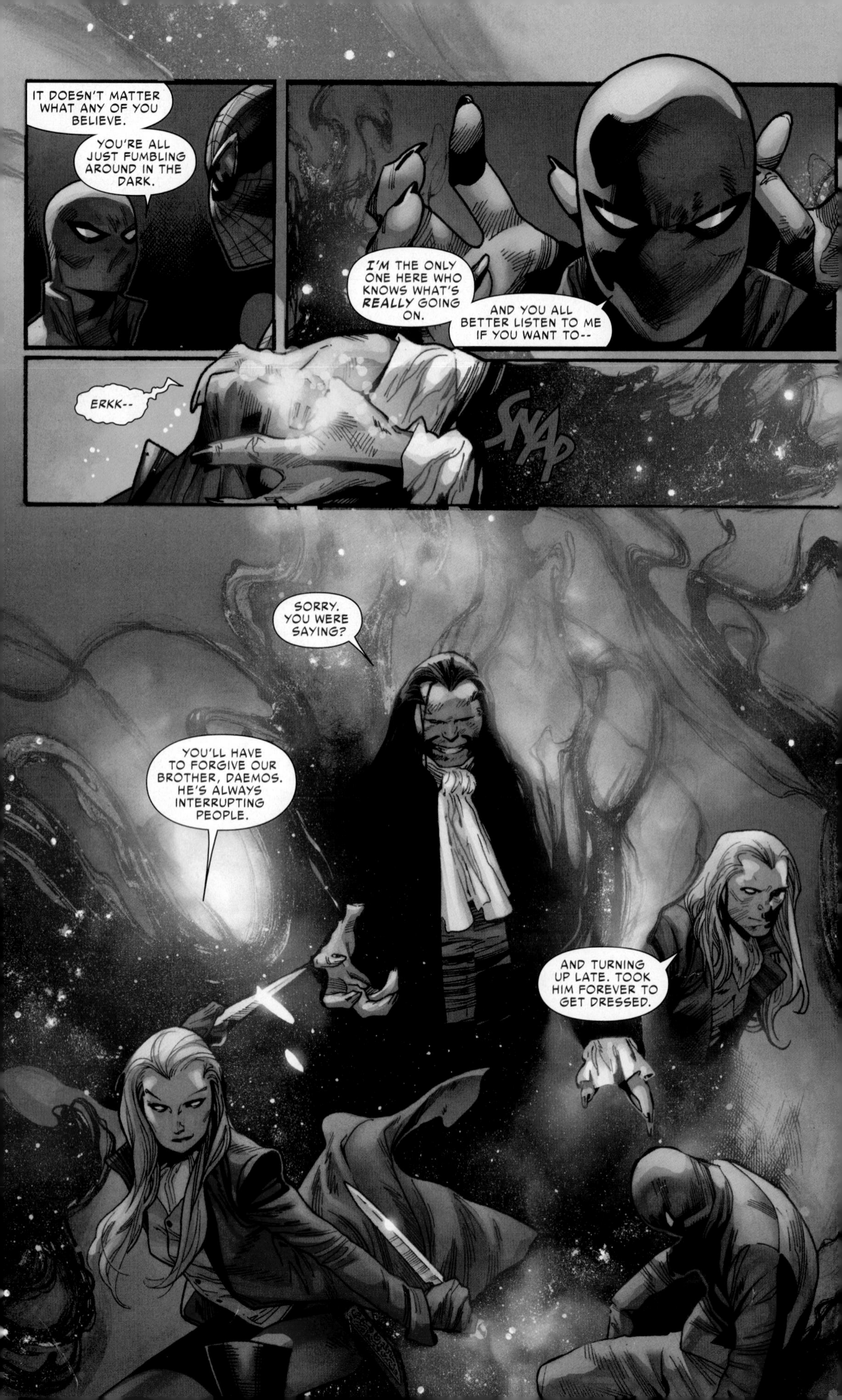
IT DOESN'T MATTER WHAT ANY OF YOU BELIEVE.
YOU'RE ALL JUST FUMBLING AROUND IN THE DARK.
I'M THE ONLY ONE HERE WHO KNOWS WHAT'S REALLY GOING ON.
AND YOU ALL BETTER LISTEN TO ME IF YOU WANT TO--
ERKK--
SNAP
SORRY. YOU WERE SAYING?
YOU'LL HAVE TO FORGIVE OUR BROTHER, DAEMOS. HE'S ALWAYS INTERRUPTING PEOPLE.
AND TURNING UP LATE. TOOK HIM FOREVER TO GET DRESSED.

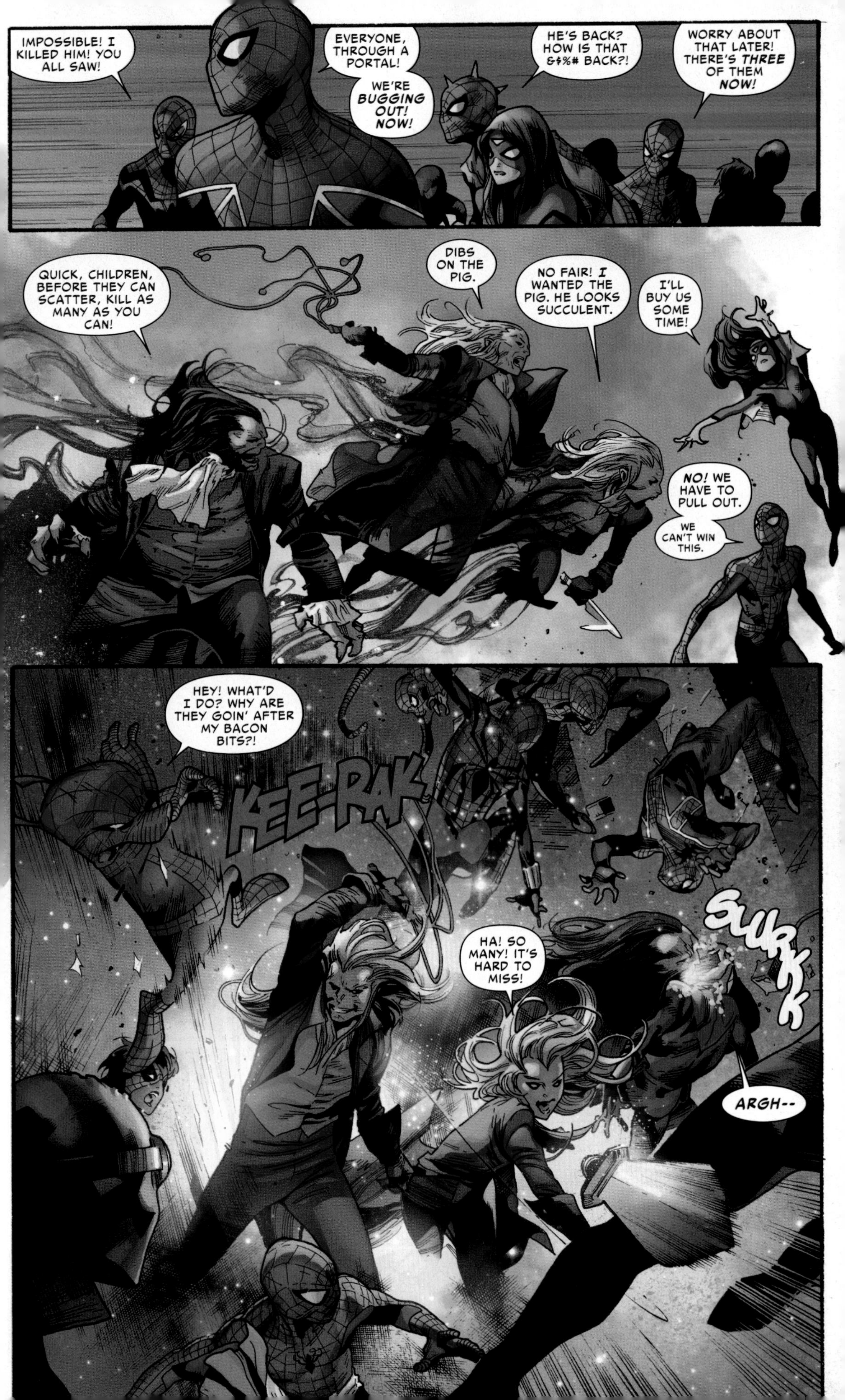
IMPOSSIBLE! I KILLED HIM! YOU ALL SAW!
EVERYONE, THROUGH A PORTAL!
WE'RE BUGGING OUT! NOW!
HE'S BACK? HOW IS THAT &$%# BACK?!
WORRY ABOUT THAT LATER! THERE'S THREE OF THEM NOW!
QUICK, CHILDREN, BEFORE THEY CAN SCATTER, KILL AS MANY AS YOU CAN!
DIBS ON THE PIG.
NO FAIR! I WANTED THE PIG. HE LOOKS SUCCULENT.
I'LL BUY US SOME TIME!
NO! WE HAVE TO PULL OUT.
WE CAN'T WIN THIS.
HEY! WHAT'D I DO? WHY ARE THEY GOIN' AFTER MY BACON BITS?!
KEE-RAK
HA! SO MANY! IT'S HARD TO MISS!
SHUNKK
ARGH--

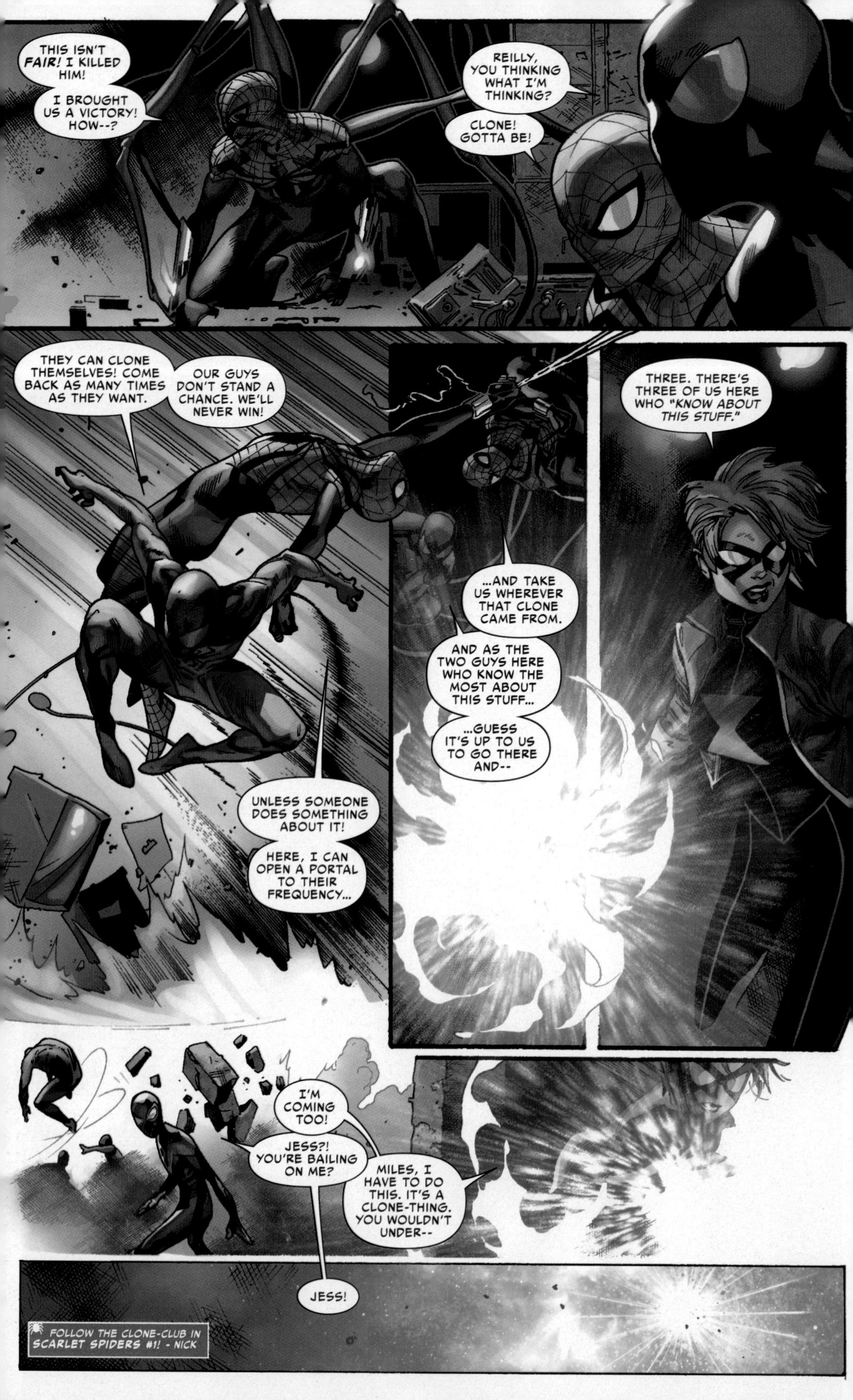

THIS ISN'T *FAIR!* I KILLED HIM!
I BROUGHT US A VICTORY! HOW--?
REILLY, YOU THINKING WHAT I'M THINKING?
CLONE! GOTTA BE!
THEY CAN CLONE THEMSELVES! COME BACK AS MANY TIMES AS THEY WANT.
OUR GUYS DON'T STAND A CHANCE. WE'LL NEVER WIN!
UNLESS SOMEONE DOES SOMETHING ABOUT IT!
HERE, I CAN OPEN A PORTAL TO THEIR FREQUENCY...
...AND TAKE US WHEREVER THAT CLONE CAME FROM.
AND AS THE TWO GUYS HERE WHO KNOW THE MOST ABOUT THIS STUFF...
...GUESS IT'S UP TO US TO GO THERE AND--
THREE. THERE'S THREE OF US HERE WHO *"KNOW ABOUT THIS STUFF."*
I'M COMING TOO!
JESS?! YOU'RE BAILING ON ME?
MILES, I HAVE TO DO THIS. IT'S A CLONE-THING. YOU WOULDN'T UNDER--
JESS!
FOLLOW THE CLONE-CLUB IN SCARLET SPIDERS #1! - NICK

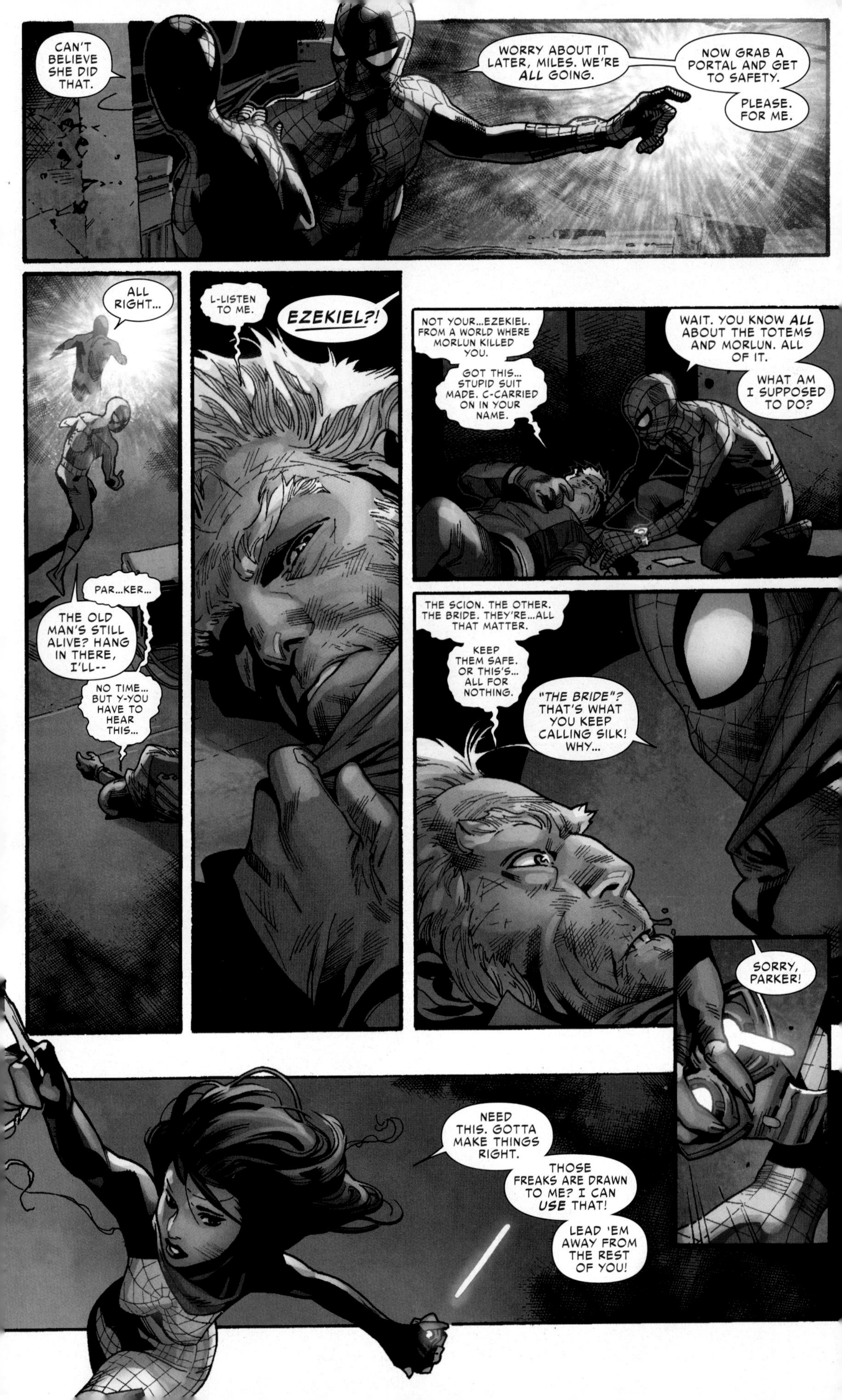

CAN'T BELIEVE SHE DID THAT.
WORRY ABOUT IT LATER, MILES. WE'RE ALL GOING.
NOW GRAB A PORTAL AND GET TO SAFETY.
PLEASE. FOR ME.
ALL RIGHT...
PAR...KER...
THE OLD MAN'S STILL ALIVE? HANG IN THERE, I'LL--
NO TIME... BUT Y-YOU HAVE TO HEAR THIS...
L-LISTEN TO ME.
EZEKIEL?!
NOT YOUR...EZEKIEL. FROM A WORLD WHERE MORLUN KILLED YOU.
GOT THIS... STUPID SUIT MADE. C-CARRIED ON IN YOUR NAME.
WAIT. YOU KNOW ALL ABOUT THE TOTEMS AND MORLUN. ALL OF IT.
WHAT AM I SUPPOSED TO DO?
THE SCION. THE OTHER. THE BRIDE. THEY'RE...ALL THAT MATTER.
KEEP THEM SAFE. OR THIS'S... ALL FOR NOTHING.
"THE BRIDE"? THAT'S WHAT YOU KEEP CALLING SILK! WHY...
SORRY, PARKER!
NEED THIS. GOTTA MAKE THINGS RIGHT.
THOSE FREAKS ARE DRAWN TO ME? I CAN USE THAT!
LEAD 'EM AWAY FROM THE REST OF YOU!

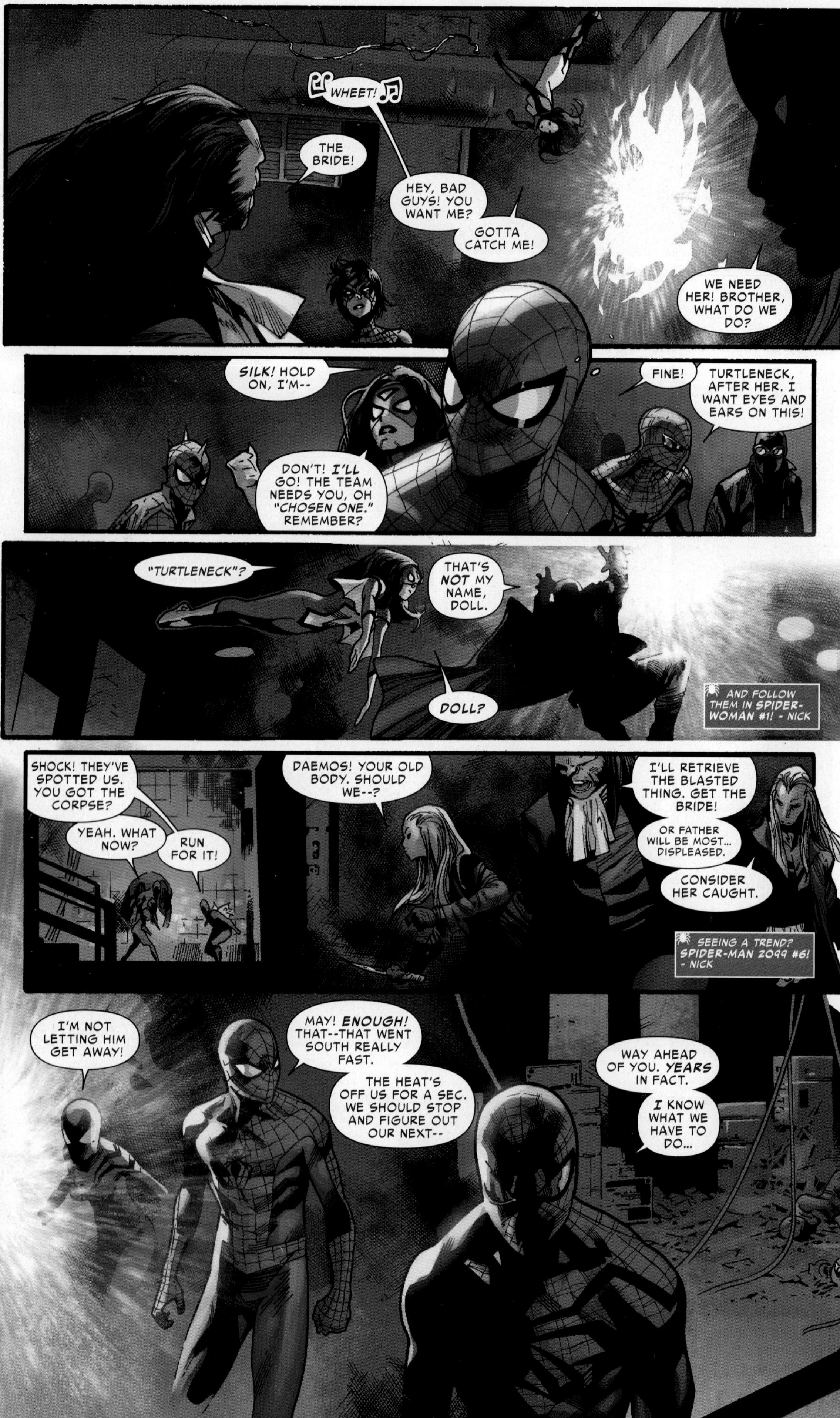
WHEET!
THE BRIDE!
HEY, BAD GUYS! YOU WANT ME?
GOTTA CATCH ME!
WE NEED HER! BROTHER, WHAT DO WE DO?
SILK! HOLD ON, I'M--
DON'T! I'LL GO! THE TEAM NEEDS YOU, OH "CHOSEN ONE." REMEMBER?
FINE!
TURTLENECK, AFTER HER. I WANT EYES AND EARS ON THIS!
"TURTLENECK"?
THAT'S NOT MY NAME, DOLL.
DOLL?
AND FOLLOW THEM IN SPIDER-WOMAN #1! - NICK
SHOCK! THEY'VE SPOTTED US. YOU GOT THE CORPSE?
YEAH. WHAT NOW?
RUN FOR IT!
DAEMOS! YOUR OLD BODY. SHOULD WE--?
I'LL RETRIEVE THE BLASTED THING. GET THE BRIDE!
OR FATHER WILL BE MOST... DISPLEASED.
CONSIDER HER CAUGHT.
SEEING A TREND? SPIDER-MAN 2099 #6! - NICK
I'M NOT LETTING HIM GET AWAY!
MAY! ENOUGH! THAT--THAT WENT SOUTH REALLY FAST.
THE HEAT'S OFF US FOR A SEC. WE SHOULD STOP AND FIGURE OUT OUR NEXT--
WAY AHEAD OF YOU. YEARS IN FACT.
I KNOW WHAT WE HAVE TO DO...

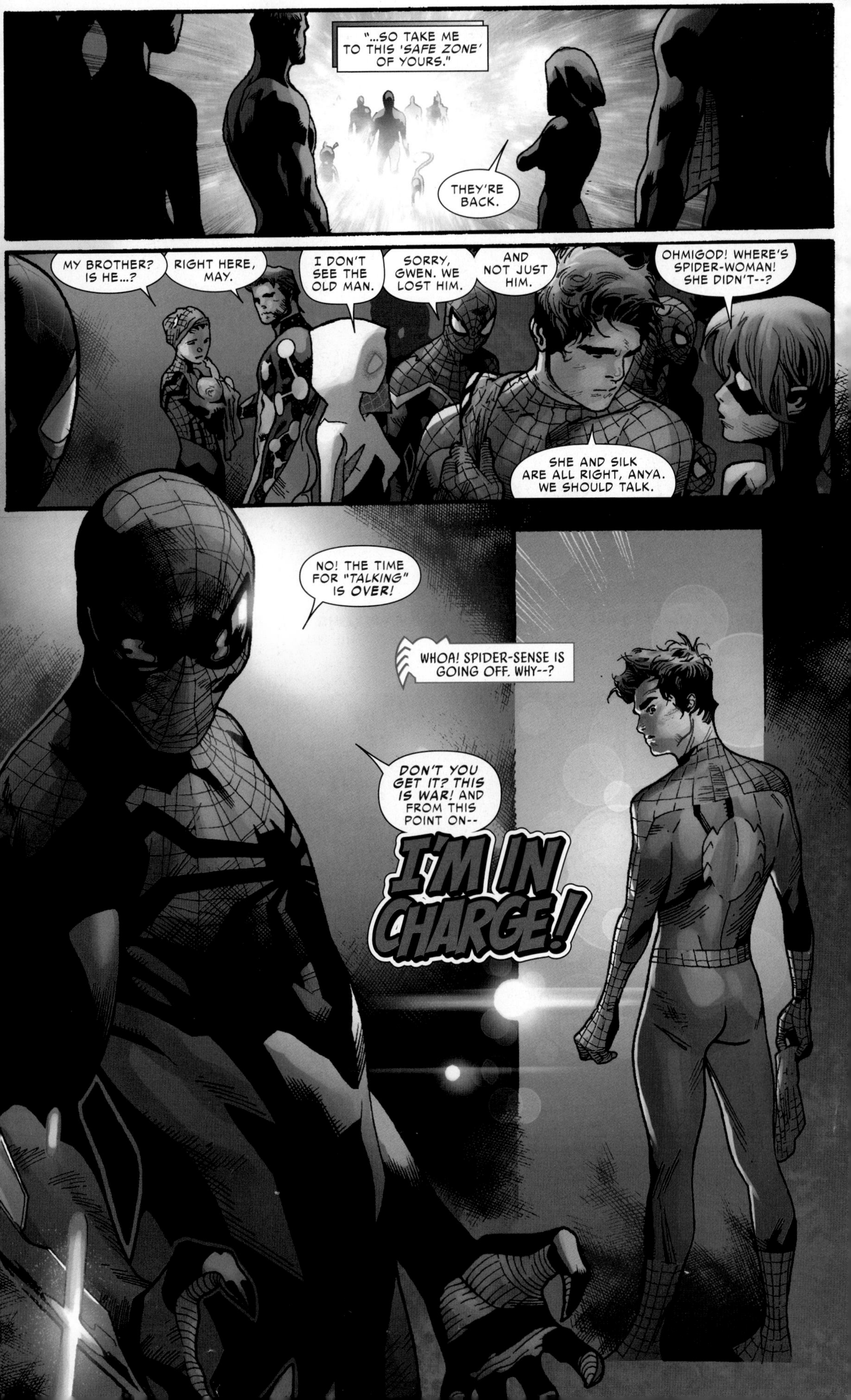
"...SO TAKE ME TO THIS 'SAFE ZONE' OF YOURS."
THEY'RE BACK.
MY BROTHER? IS HE...?
RIGHT HERE, MAY.
I DON'T SEE THE OLD MAN.
SORRY, GWEN. WE LOST HIM.
AND NOT JUST HIM.
OHMIGOD! WHERE'S SPIDER-WOMAN! SHE DIDN'T--?
SHE AND SILK ARE ALL RIGHT, ANYA. WE SHOULD TALK.
NO! THE TIME FOR "TALKING" IS OVER!
WHOA! SPIDER-SENSE IS GOING OFF. WHY--?
DON'T YOU GET IT? THIS IS WAR! AND FROM THIS POINT ON--
I'M IN CHARGE!

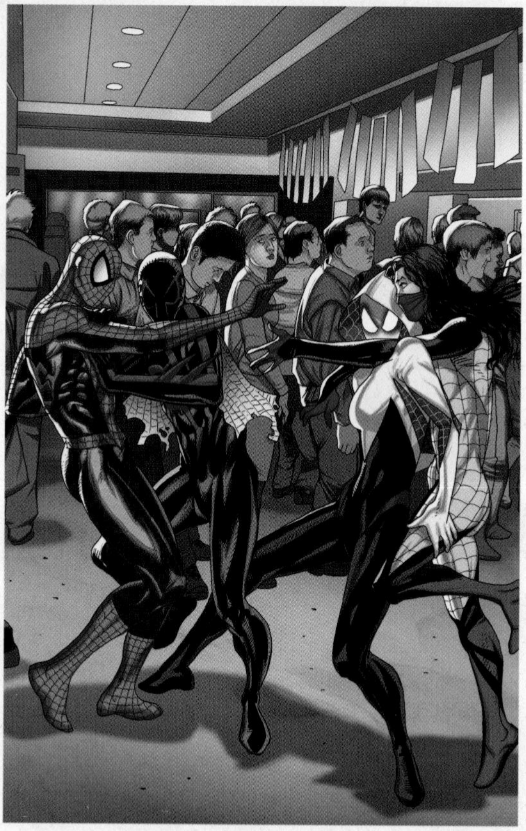

AMAZING SPIDER-MAN #13 WELCOME HOME VARIANT
BY SALVADOR LAROCCA & ISRAEL SILVA

Amazing Spider-Man

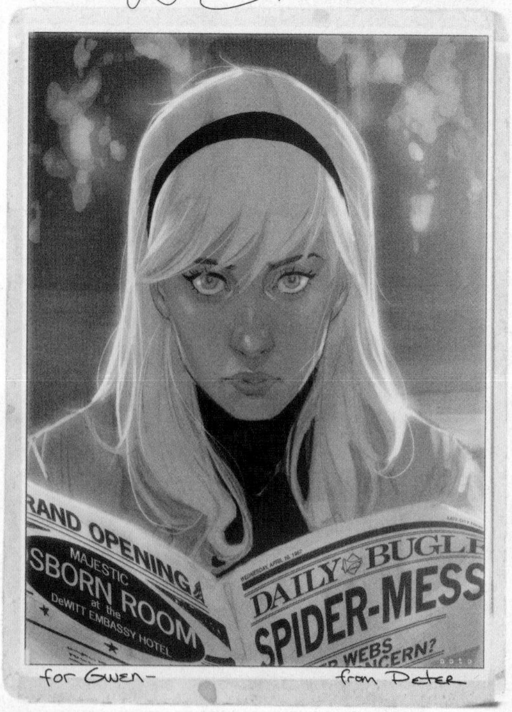
RAND OPENING
MAJESTIC
SBORN ROOM
at the
DeWITT EMBASSY HOTEL
DAILY BUGLE
SPIDER-MESS
for Gwen-
from Peter

AMAZING SPIDER-MAN #14 VARIANT
BY PHIL NOTO

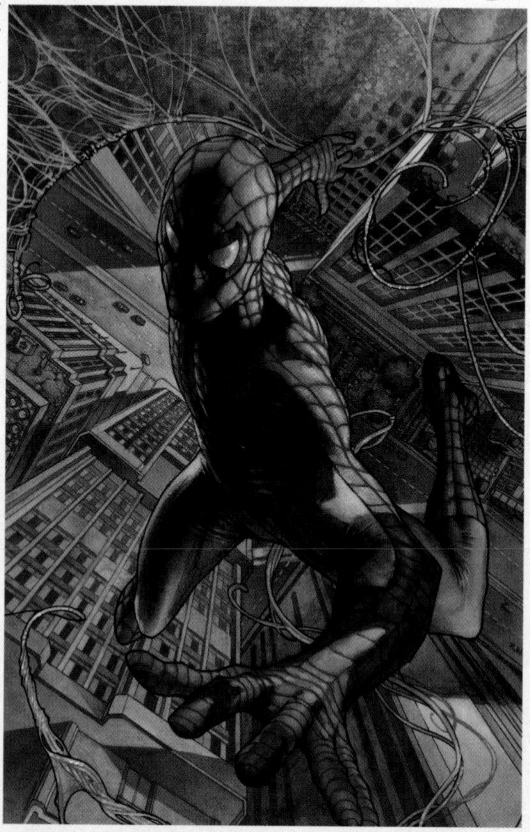

AMAZING SPIDER-MAN #15 VARIANT
BY SIMONE BIANCHI

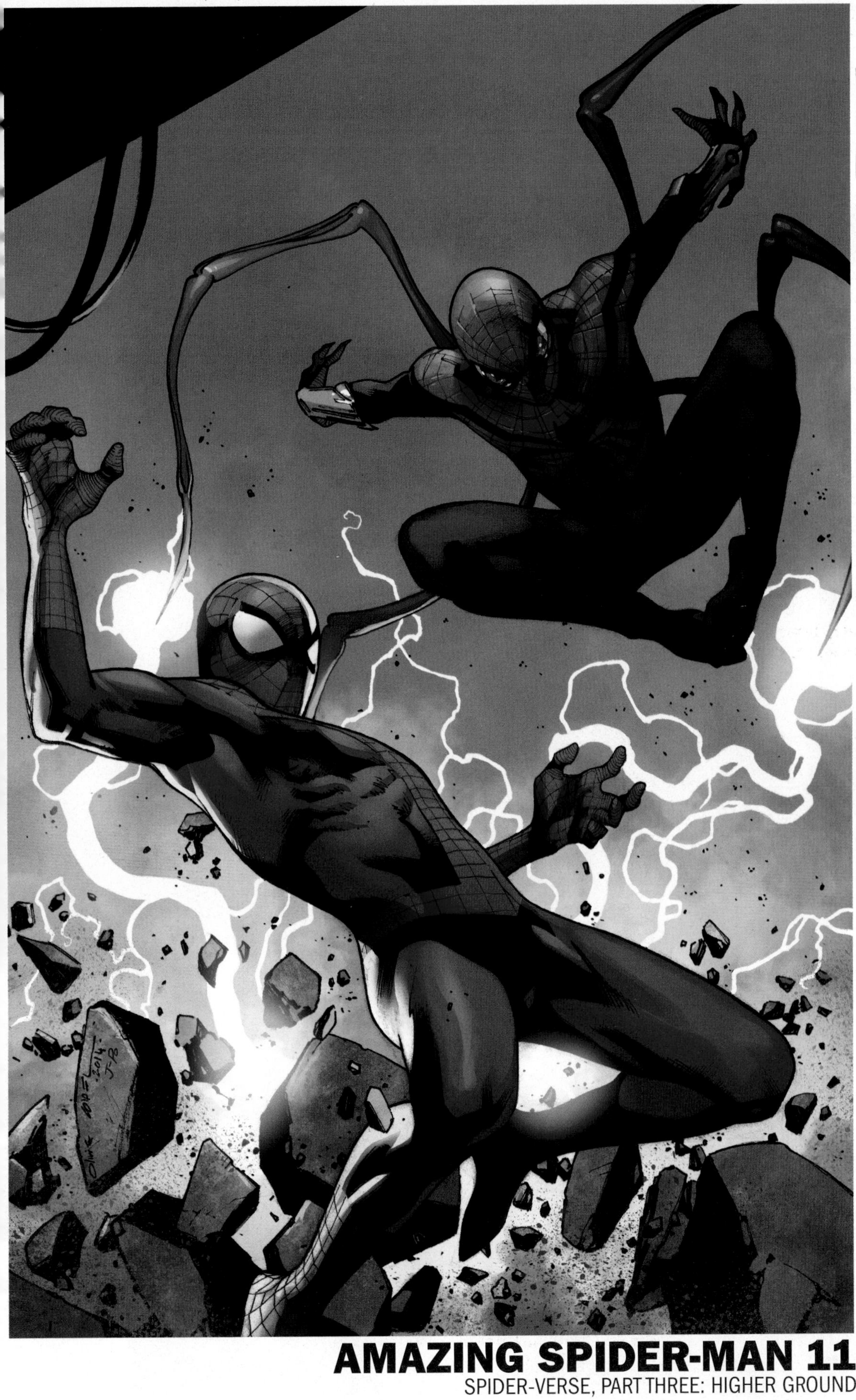

AMAZING SPIDER-MAN 11
SPIDER-VERSE, PART THREE: HIGHER GROUND

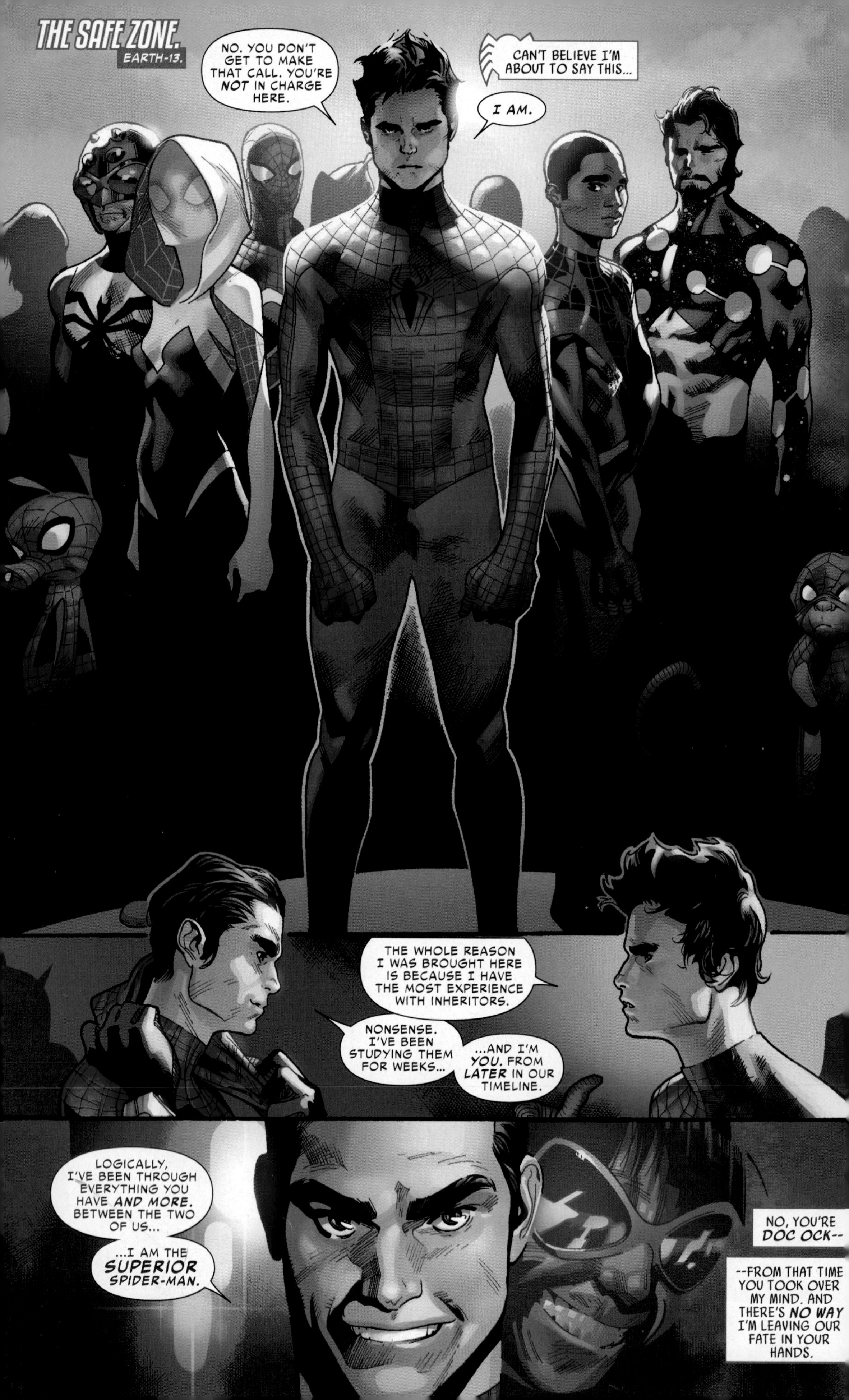
THE SAFE ZONE.
EARTH-13.
NO. YOU DON'T GET TO MAKE THAT CALL. YOU'RE NOT IN CHARGE HERE.
CAN'T BELIEVE I'M ABOUT TO SAY THIS...
I AM.
THE WHOLE REASON I WAS BROUGHT HERE IS BECAUSE I HAVE THE MOST EXPERIENCE WITH INHERITORS.
NONSENSE. I'VE BEEN STUDYING THEM FOR WEEKS...
...AND I'M YOU. FROM LATER IN OUR TIMELINE.
LOGICALLY, I'VE BEEN THROUGH EVERYTHING YOU HAVE AND MORE. BETWEEN THE TWO OF US...
...I AM THE SUPERIOR SPIDER-MAN.
NO, YOU'RE DOC OCK--
--FROM THAT TIME YOU TOOK OVER MY MIND. AND THERE'S NO WAY I'M LEAVING OUR FATE IN YOUR HANDS.

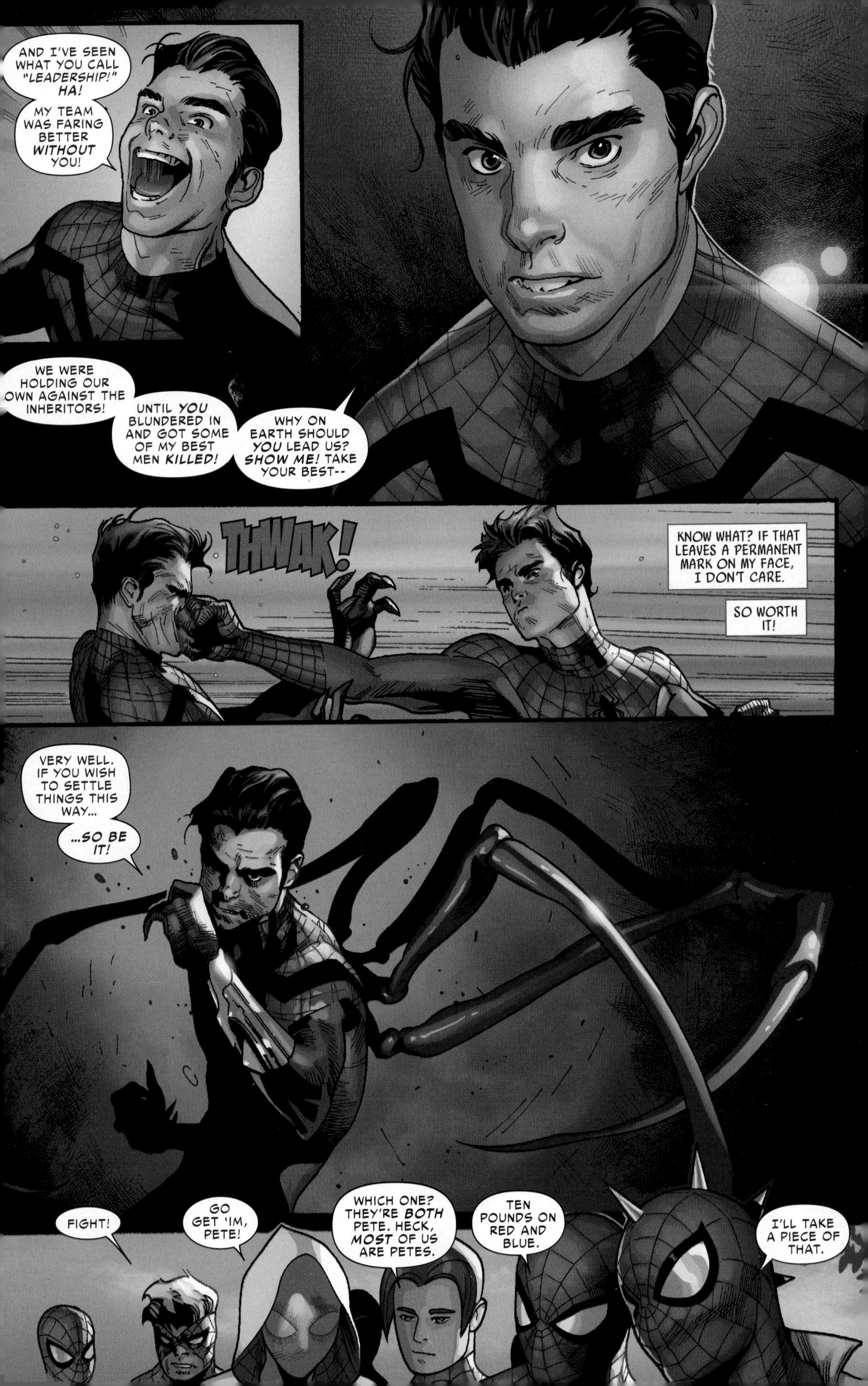
AND I'VE SEEN WHAT YOU CALL "LEADERSHIP!" HA!
MY TEAM WAS FARING BETTER WITHOUT YOU!
WE WERE HOLDING OUR OWN AGAINST THE INHERITORS!
UNTIL YOU BLUNDERED IN AND GOT SOME OF MY BEST MEN KILLED!
WHY ON EARTH SHOULD YOU LEAD US? SHOW ME! TAKE YOUR BEST--
THWAK!
KNOW WHAT? IF THAT LEAVES A PERMANENT MARK ON MY FACE, I DON'T CARE.
SO WORTH IT!
VERY WELL. IF YOU WISH TO SETTLE THINGS THIS WAY...
...SO BE IT!
FIGHT!
GO GET 'IM, PETE!
WHICH ONE? THEY'RE BOTH PETE. HECK, MOST OF US ARE PETES.
TEN POUNDS ON RED AND BLUE.
I'LL TAKE A PIECE OF THAT.

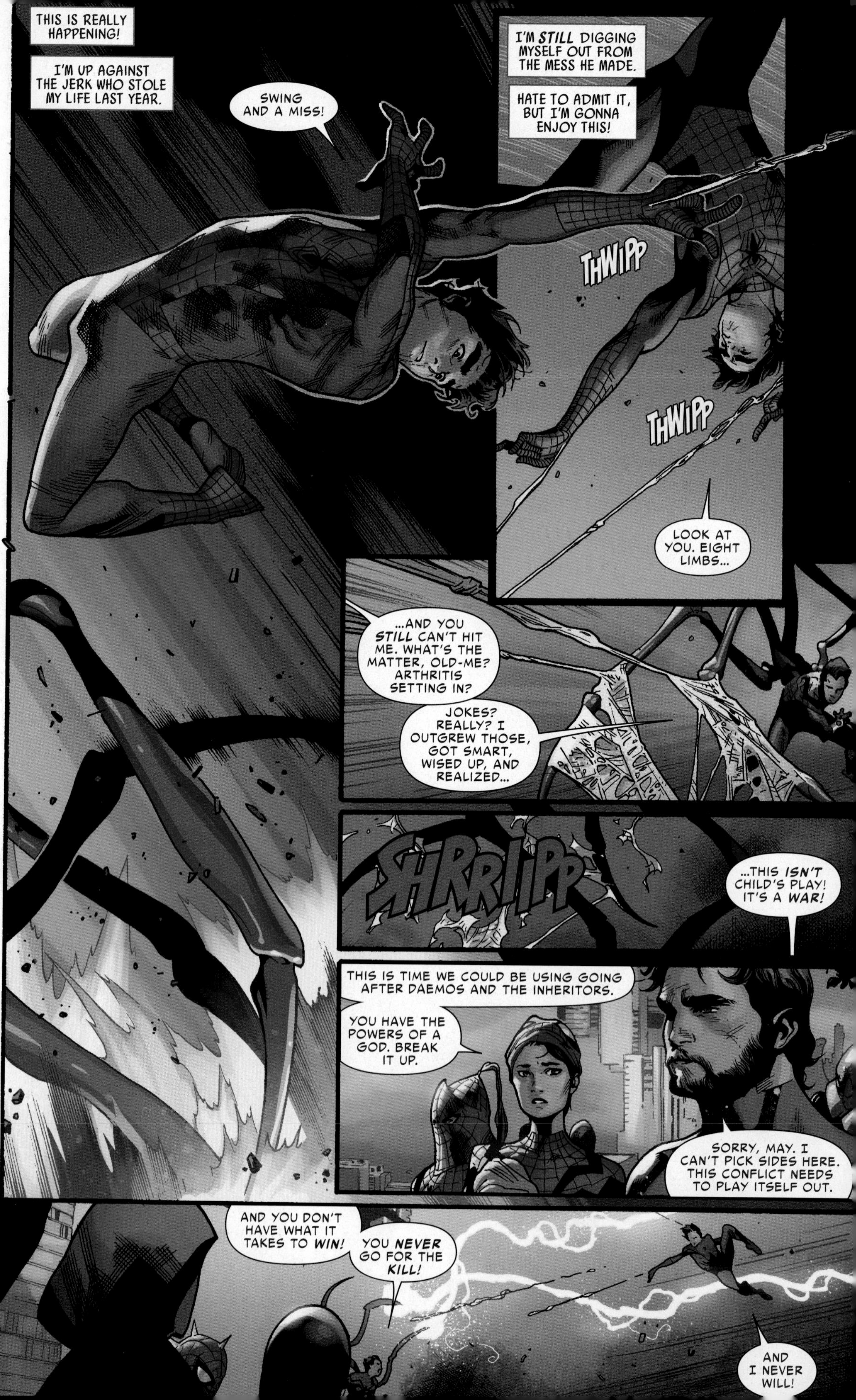
THIS IS REALLY HAPPENING!
I'M UP AGAINST THE JERK WHO STOLE MY LIFE LAST YEAR.
SWING AND A MISS!
I'M STILL DIGGING MYSELF OUT FROM THE MESS HE MADE.
HATE TO ADMIT IT, BUT I'M GONNA ENJOY THIS!
THWIPP
THWIPP
LOOK AT YOU. EIGHT LIMBS...
...AND YOU STILL CAN'T HIT ME. WHAT'S THE MATTER, OLD-ME? ARTHRITIS SETTING IN?
JOKES? REALLY? I OUTGREW THOSE, GOT SMART, WISED UP, AND REALIZED...
SHRRIPP
...THIS ISN'T CHILD'S PLAY! IT'S A WAR!
THIS IS TIME WE COULD BE USING GOING AFTER DAEMOS AND THE INHERITORS.
YOU HAVE THE POWERS OF A GOD. BREAK IT UP.
SORRY, MAY. I CAN'T PICK SIDES HERE. THIS CONFLICT NEEDS TO PLAY ITSELF OUT.
AND YOU DON'T HAVE WHAT IT TAKES TO WIN!
YOU NEVER GO FOR THE KILL!
AND I NEVER WILL!

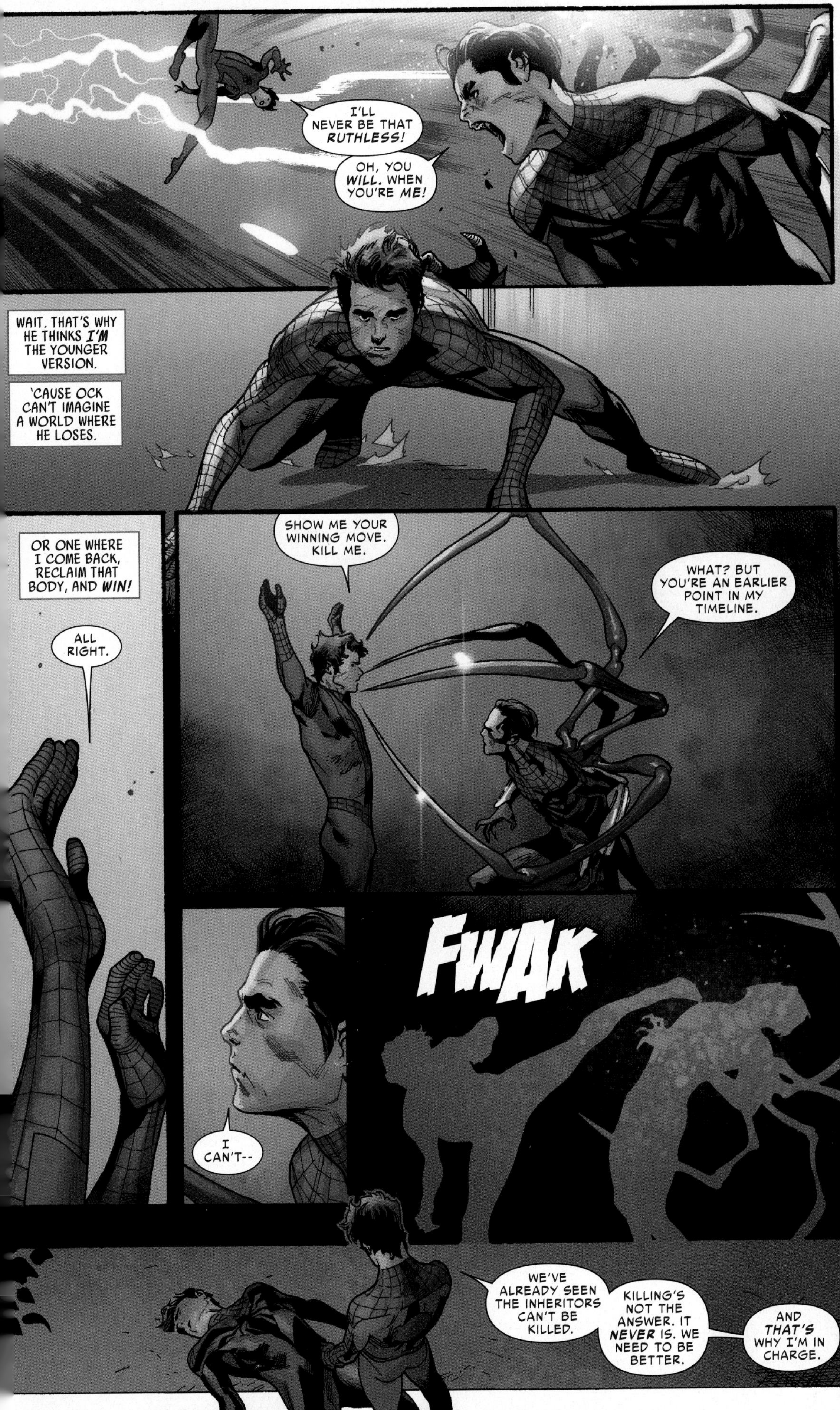
I'LL NEVER BE THAT RUTHLESS!
OH, YOU WILL. WHEN YOU'RE ME!
WAIT. THAT'S WHY HE THINKS I'M THE YOUNGER VERSION.
'CAUSE OCK CAN'T IMAGINE A WORLD WHERE HE LOSES.
OR ONE WHERE I COME BACK, RECLAIM THAT BODY, AND WIN!
ALL RIGHT.
SHOW ME YOUR WINNING MOVE. KILL ME.
WHAT? BUT YOU'RE AN EARLIER POINT IN MY TIMELINE.
I CAN'T--
FWAK
WE'VE ALREADY SEEN THE INHERITORS CAN'T BE KILLED.
KILLING'S NOT THE ANSWER. IT NEVER IS. WE NEED TO BE BETTER.
AND THAT'S WHY I'M IN CHARGE.

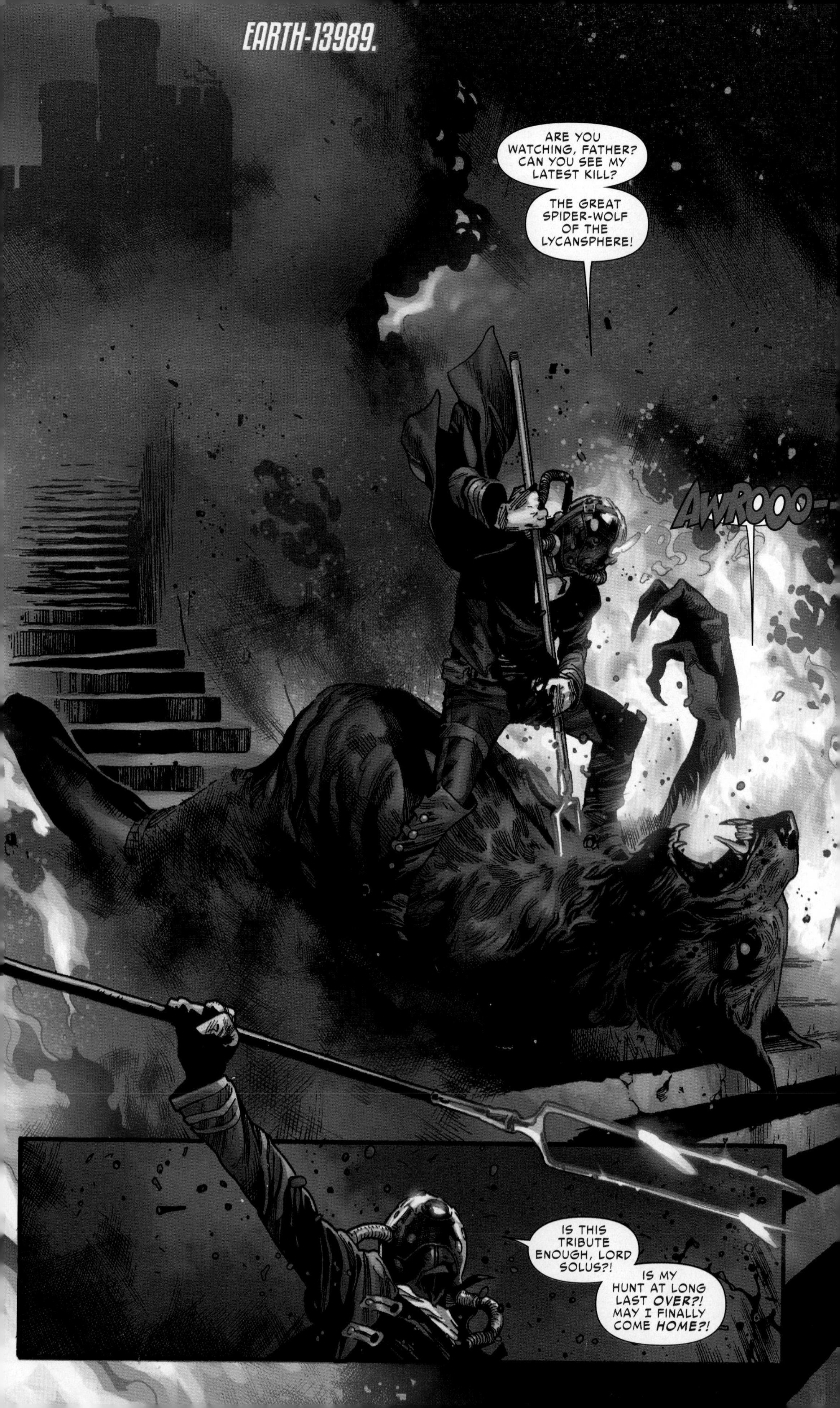
EARTH-13989.
ARE YOU WATCHING, FATHER? CAN YOU SEE MY LATEST KILL?
THE GREAT SPIDER-WOLF OF THE LYCANSPHERE!
AWROOO--
IS THIS TRIBUTE ENOUGH, LORD SOLUS?!
IS MY HUNT AT LONG LAST OVER?! MAY I FINALLY COME HOME?!

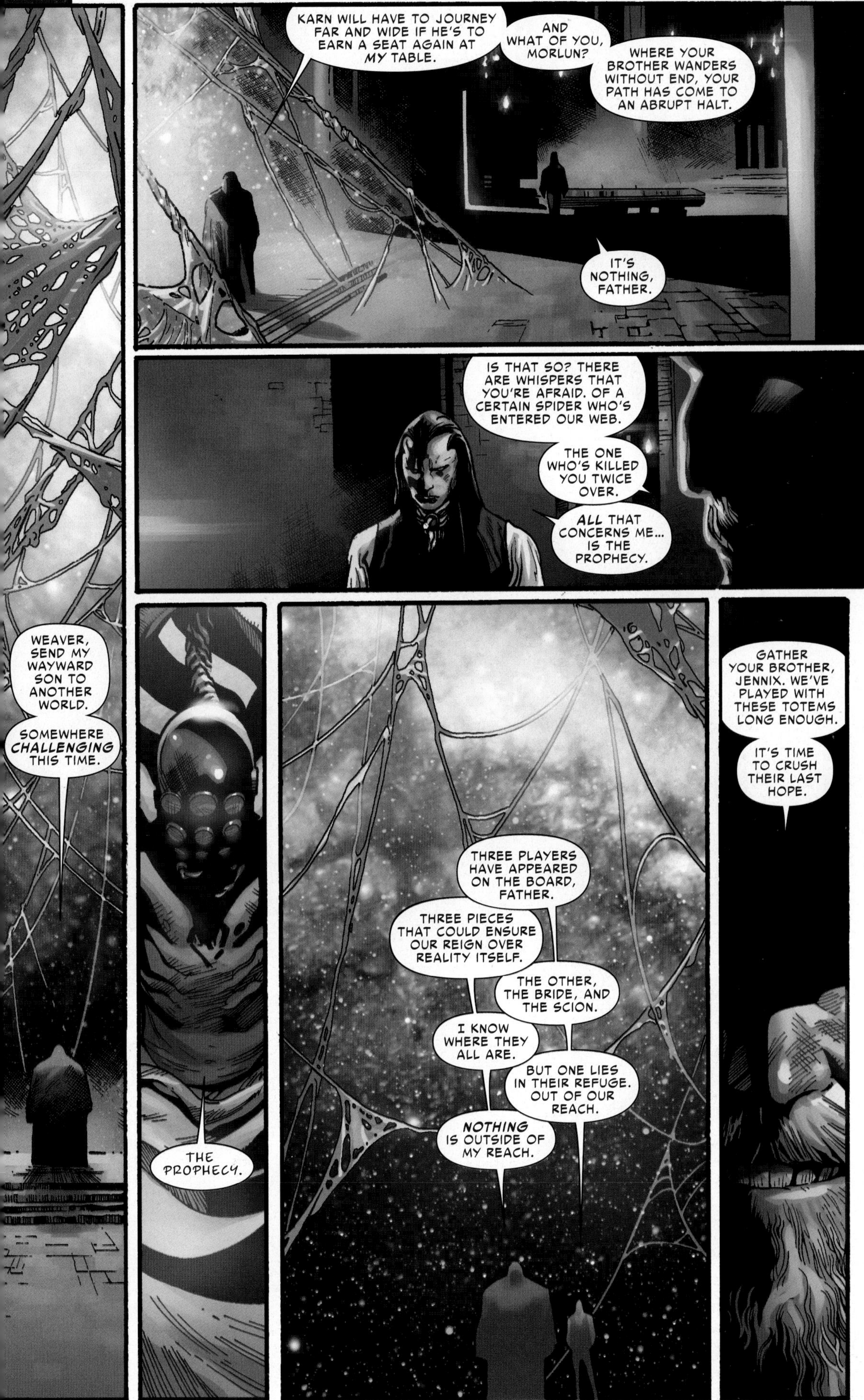
KARN WILL HAVE TO JOURNEY FAR AND WIDE IF HE'S TO EARN A SEAT AGAIN AT *MY* TABLE.
AND WHAT OF YOU, MORLUN?
WHERE YOUR BROTHER WANDERS WITHOUT END, YOUR PATH HAS COME TO AN ABRUPT HALT.
IT'S NOTHING, FATHER.
IS THAT SO? THERE ARE WHISPERS THAT YOU'RE AFRAID. OF A CERTAIN SPIDER WHO'S ENTERED OUR WEB.
THE ONE WHO'S KILLED YOU TWICE OVER.
ALL THAT CONCERNS ME... IS THE PROPHECY.
WEAVER, SEND MY WAYWARD SON TO ANOTHER WORLD.
SOMEWHERE *CHALLENGING* THIS TIME.
THE PROPHECY.
THREE PLAYERS HAVE APPEARED ON THE BOARD, FATHER.
THREE PIECES THAT COULD ENSURE OUR REIGN OVER REALITY ITSELF.
THE OTHER, THE BRIDE, AND THE SCION.
I KNOW WHERE THEY ALL ARE.
BUT ONE LIES IN THEIR REFUGE. OUT OF OUR REACH.
NOTHING IS OUTSIDE OF MY REACH.
GATHER YOUR BROTHER, JENNIX. WE'VE PLAYED WITH THESE TOTEMS LONG ENOUGH.
IT'S TIME TO CRUSH THEIR LAST HOPE.

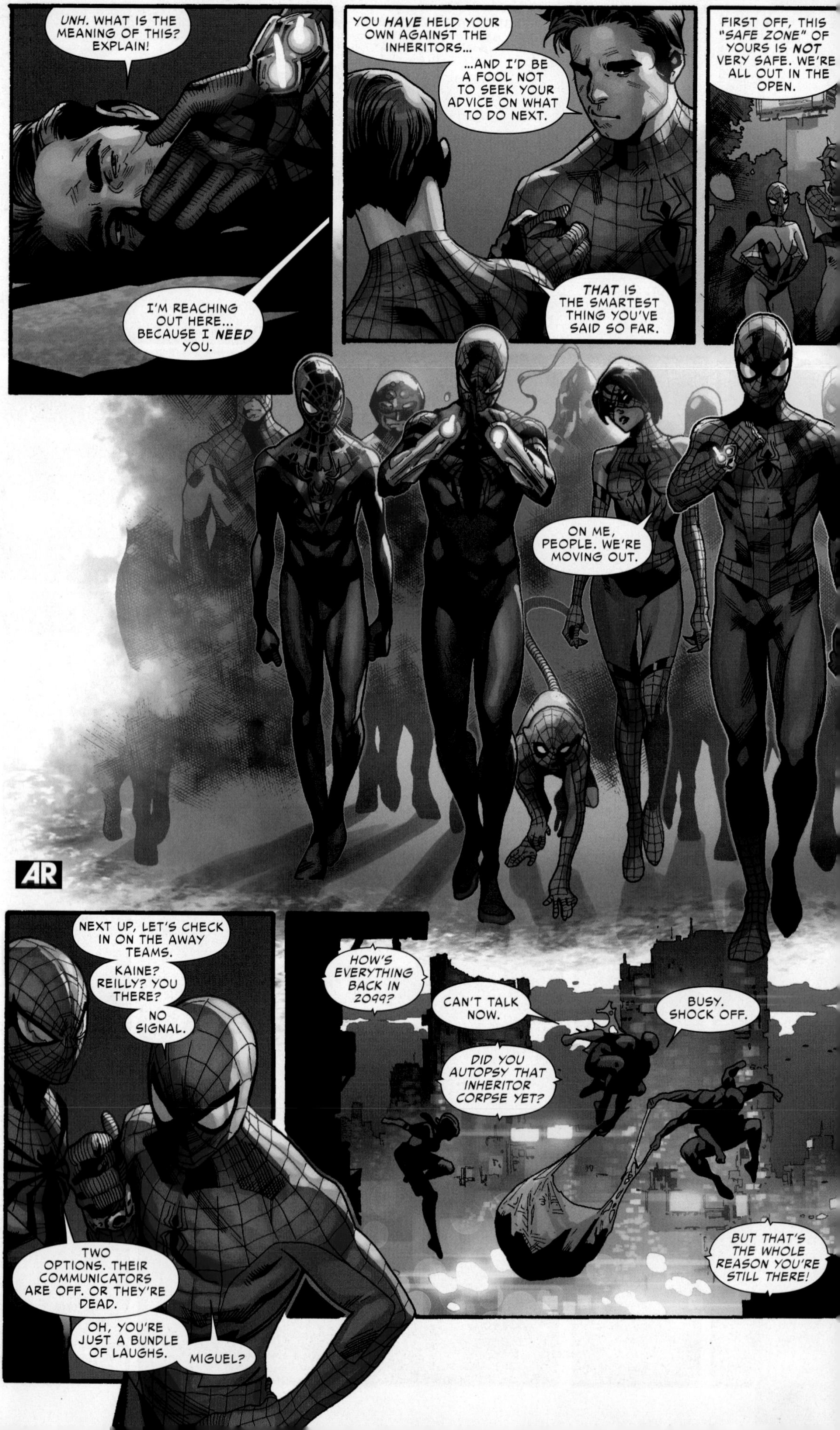
UNH. WHAT IS THE MEANING OF THIS? EXPLAIN!
I'M REACHING OUT HERE... BECAUSE I NEED YOU.
YOU HAVE HELD YOUR OWN AGAINST THE INHERITORS...
...AND I'D BE A FOOL NOT TO SEEK YOUR ADVICE ON WHAT TO DO NEXT.
THAT IS THE SMARTEST THING YOU'VE SAID SO FAR.
FIRST OFF, THIS "SAFE ZONE" OF YOURS IS NOT VERY SAFE. WE'RE ALL OUT IN THE OPEN.
ON ME, PEOPLE. WE'RE MOVING OUT.
AR
NEXT UP, LET'S CHECK IN ON THE AWAY TEAMS.
KAINE? REILLY? YOU THERE?
NO SIGNAL.
TWO OPTIONS. THEIR COMMUNICATORS ARE OFF. OR THEY'RE DEAD.
OH, YOU'RE JUST A BUNDLE OF LAUGHS.
MIGUEL?
HOW'S EVERYTHING BACK IN 2099?
CAN'T TALK NOW.
BUSY. SHOCK OFF.
DID YOU AUTOPSY THAT INHERITOR CORPSE YET?
BUT THAT'S THE WHOLE REASON YOU'RE STILL THERE!

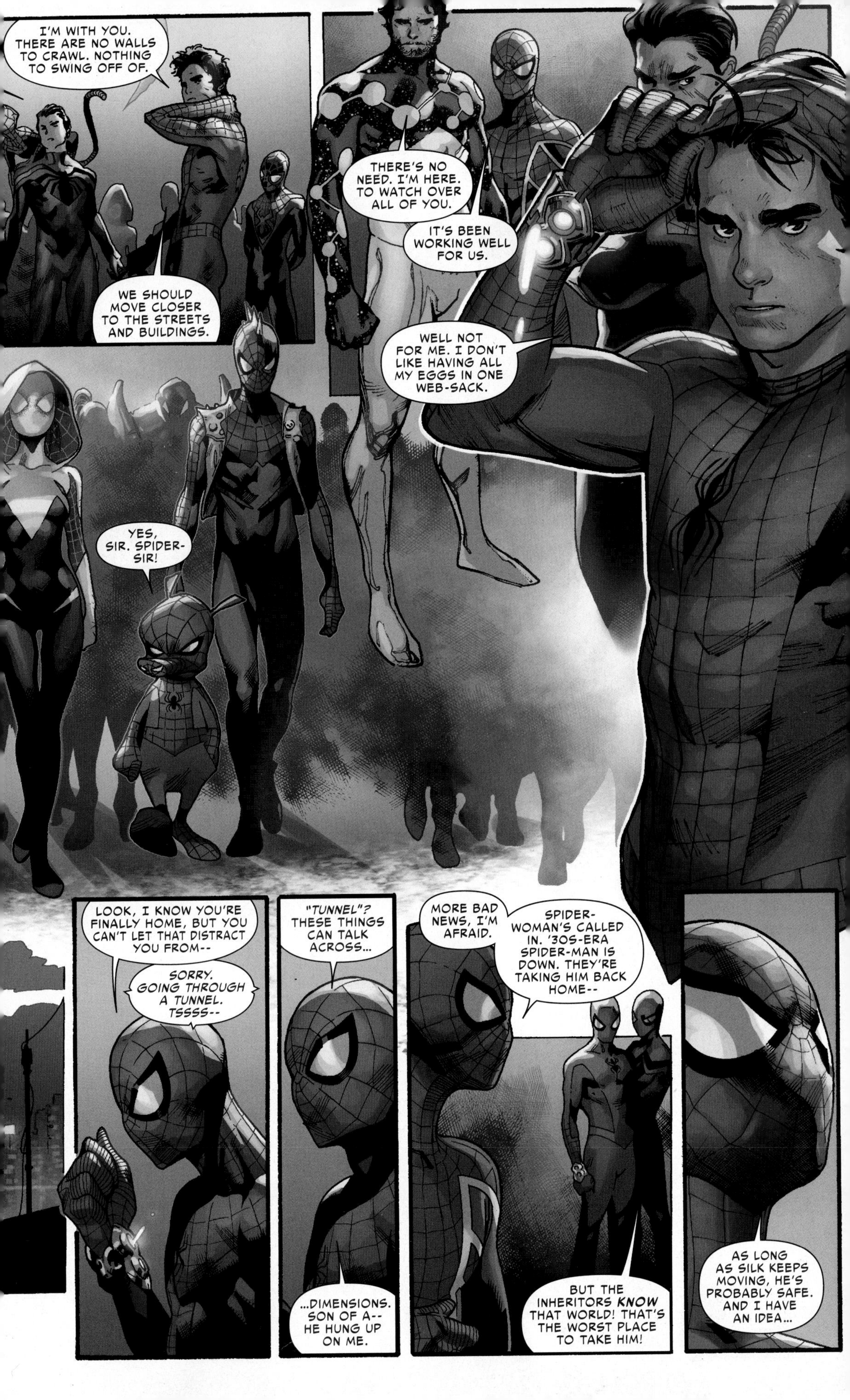
I'M WITH YOU. THERE ARE NO WALLS TO CRAWL. NOTHING TO SWING OFF OF.
WE SHOULD MOVE CLOSER TO THE STREETS AND BUILDINGS.
THERE'S NO NEED. I'M HERE. TO WATCH OVER ALL OF YOU.
IT'S BEEN WORKING WELL FOR US.
WELL NOT FOR ME. I DON'T LIKE HAVING ALL MY EGGS IN ONE WEB-SACK.
YES, SIR. SPIDER-SIR!
LOOK, I KNOW YOU'RE FINALLY HOME, BUT YOU CAN'T LET THAT DISTRACT YOU FROM--
SORRY. GOING THROUGH A TUNNEL. TSSSS--
"TUNNEL"? THESE THINGS CAN TALK ACROSS...
...DIMENSIONS. SON OF A-- HE HUNG UP ON ME.
MORE BAD NEWS, I'M AFRAID.
SPIDER-WOMAN'S CALLED IN. '30S-ERA SPIDER-MAN IS DOWN. THEY'RE TAKING HIM BACK HOME--
BUT THE INHERITORS KNOW THAT WORLD! THAT'S THE WORST PLACE TO TAKE HIM!
AS LONG AS SILK KEEPS MOVING, HE'S PROBABLY SAFE. AND I HAVE AN IDEA...

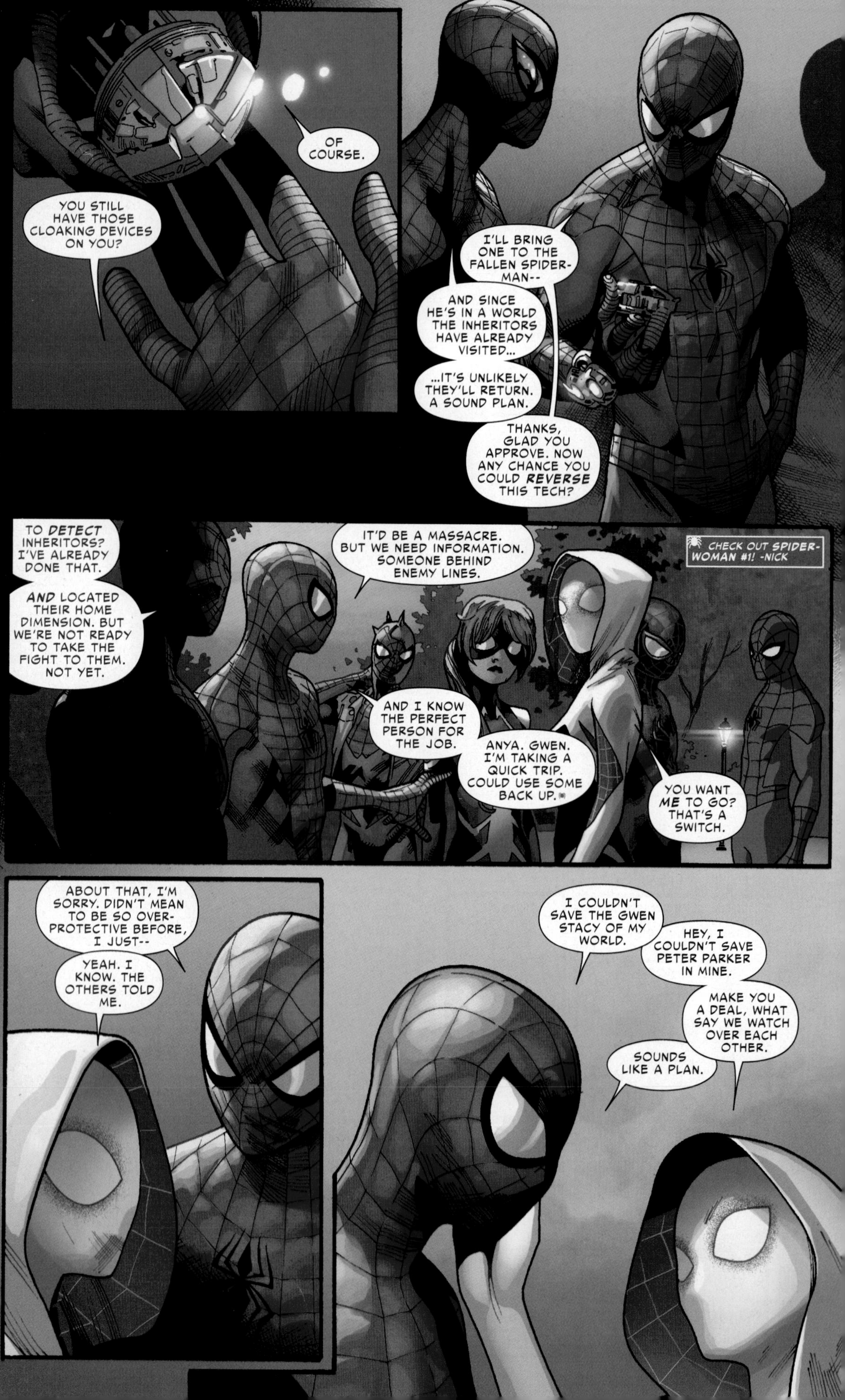
YOU STILL HAVE THOSE CLOAKING DEVICES ON YOU?
OF COURSE.
I'LL BRING ONE TO THE FALLEN SPIDER-MAN--
AND SINCE HE'S IN A WORLD THE INHERITORS HAVE ALREADY VISITED...
...IT'S UNLIKELY THEY'LL RETURN. A SOUND PLAN.
THANKS, GLAD YOU APPROVE. NOW ANY CHANCE YOU COULD REVERSE THIS TECH?
TO DETECT INHERITORS? I'VE ALREADY DONE THAT.
AND LOCATED THEIR HOME DIMENSION. BUT WE'RE NOT READY TO TAKE THE FIGHT TO THEM. NOT YET.
IT'D BE A MASSACRE. BUT WE NEED INFORMATION. SOMEONE BEHIND ENEMY LINES.
CHECK OUT SPIDER-WOMAN #1! -NICK
AND I KNOW THE PERFECT PERSON FOR THE JOB.
ANYA. GWEN. I'M TAKING A QUICK TRIP. COULD USE SOME BACK UP.
YOU WANT ME TO GO? THAT'S A SWITCH.
ABOUT THAT, I'M SORRY. DIDN'T MEAN TO BE SO OVER-PROTECTIVE BEFORE, I JUST--
YEAH. I KNOW. THE OTHERS TOLD ME.
I COULDN'T SAVE THE GWEN STACY OF MY WORLD.
HEY, I COULDN'T SAVE PETER PARKER IN MINE.
MAKE YOU A DEAL, WHAT SAY WE WATCH OVER EACH OTHER.
SOUNDS LIKE A PLAN.

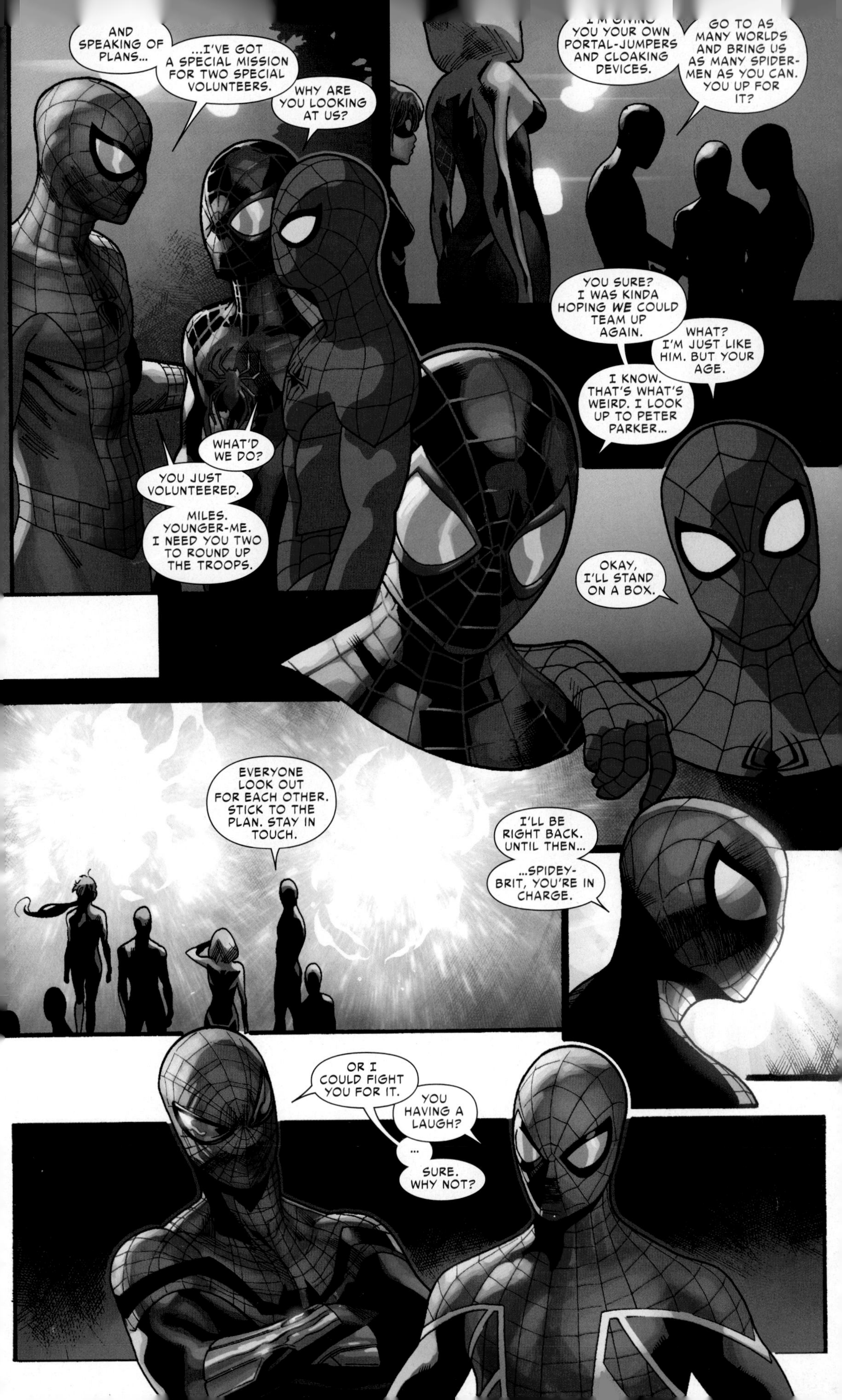

AND SPEAKING OF PLANS...
...I'VE GOT A SPECIAL MISSION FOR TWO SPECIAL VOLUNTEERS.
WHY ARE YOU LOOKING AT US?
WHAT'D WE DO?
YOU JUST VOLUNTEERED.
MILES. YOUNGER-ME. I NEED YOU TWO TO ROUND UP THE TROOPS.
YOU YOUR OWN PORTAL-JUMPERS AND CLOAKING DEVICES.
GO TO AS MANY WORLDS AND BRING US AS MANY SPIDER-MEN AS YOU CAN. YOU UP FOR IT?
YOU SURE? I WAS KINDA HOPING WE COULD TEAM UP AGAIN.
WHAT? I'M JUST LIKE HIM. BUT YOUR AGE.
I KNOW. THAT'S WHAT'S WEIRD. I LOOK UP TO PETER PARKER...
OKAY, I'LL STAND ON A BOX.
EVERYONE LOOK OUT FOR EACH OTHER. STICK TO THE PLAN. STAY IN TOUCH.
I'LL BE RIGHT BACK. UNTIL THEN...
...SPIDEY-BRIT, YOU'RE IN CHARGE.
OR I COULD FIGHT YOU FOR IT.
YOU HAVING A LAUGH?
...
SURE. WHY NOT?

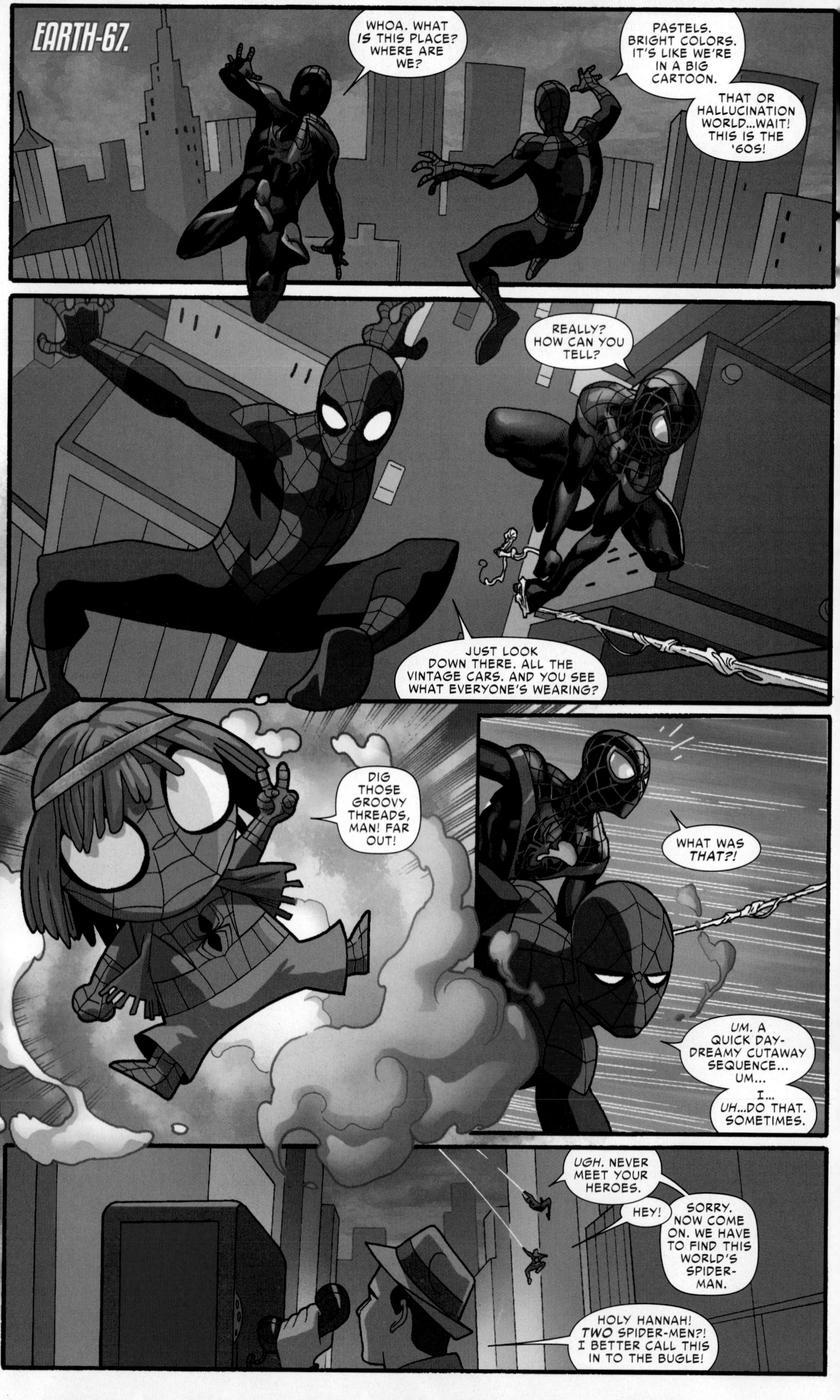

EARTH-67.
WHOA. WHAT IS THIS PLACE? WHERE ARE WE?
PASTELS. BRIGHT COLORS. IT'S LIKE WE'RE IN A BIG CARTOON.
THAT OR HALLUCINATION WORLD...WAIT! THIS IS THE '60S!
REALLY? HOW CAN YOU TELL?
JUST LOOK DOWN THERE. ALL THE VINTAGE CARS. AND YOU SEE WHAT EVERYONE'S WEARING?
DIG THOSE GROOVY THREADS, MAN! FAR OUT!
WHAT WAS THAT?!
UM. A QUICK DAY-DREAMY CUTAWAY SEQUENCE... UM... I... UH...DO THAT. SOMETIMES.
UGH. NEVER MEET YOUR HEROES.
HEY!
SORRY. NOW COME ON. WE HAVE TO FIND THIS WORLD'S SPIDER-MAN.
HOLY HANNAH! TWO SPIDER-MEN?! I BETTER CALL THIS IN TO THE BUGLE!

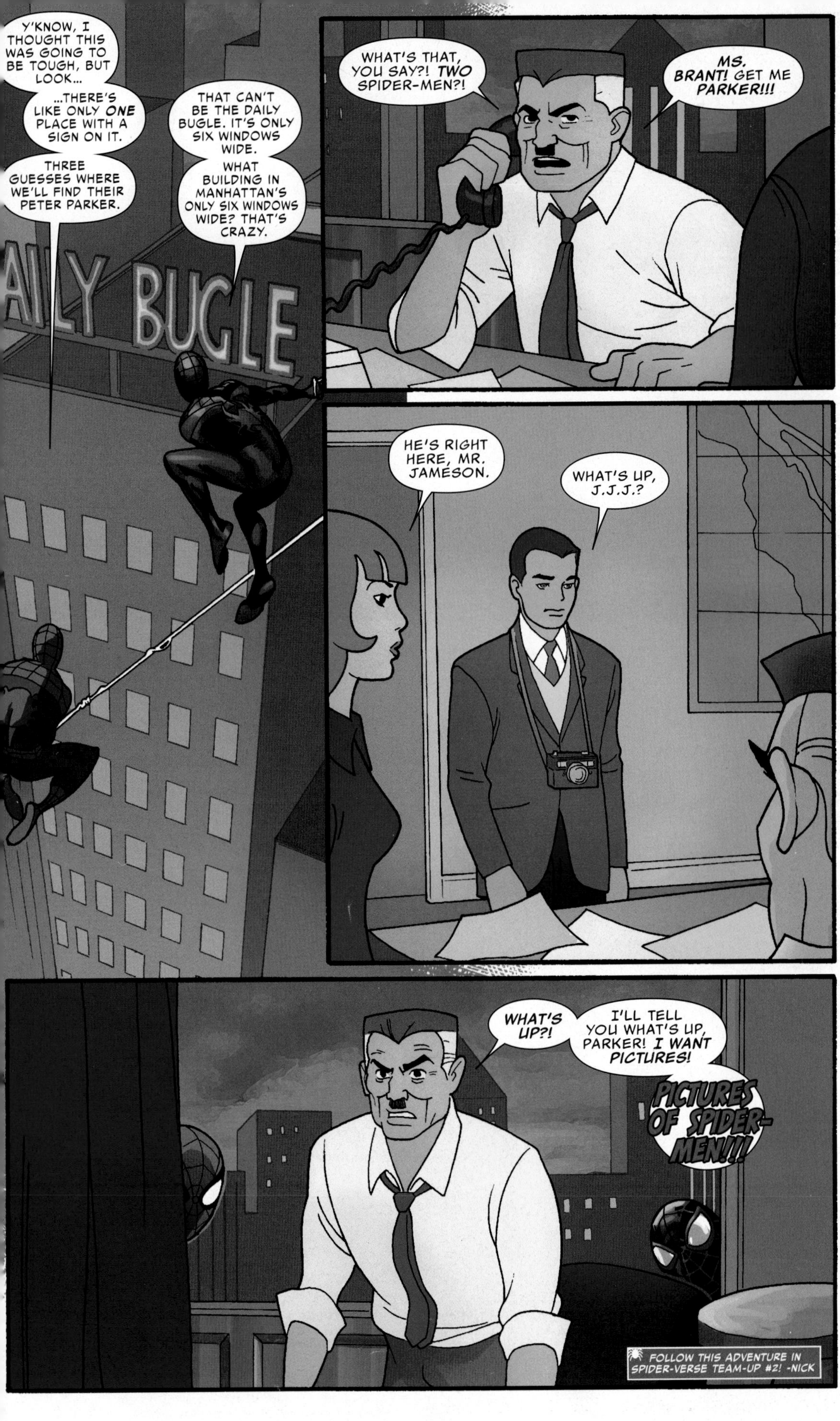

Y'KNOW, I THOUGHT THIS WAS GOING TO BE TOUGH, BUT LOOK...
...THERE'S LIKE ONLY *ONE* PLACE WITH A SIGN ON IT.
THREE GUESSES WHERE WE'LL FIND THEIR PETER PARKER.
THAT CAN'T BE THE DAILY BUGLE. IT'S ONLY SIX WINDOWS WIDE.
WHAT BUILDING IN MANHATTAN'S ONLY SIX WINDOWS WIDE? THAT'S CRAZY.
AILY BUGLE
WHAT'S THAT, YOU SAY?! *TWO* SPIDER-MEN?!
MS. BRANT! GET ME *PARKER!!!*
HE'S RIGHT HERE, MR. JAMESON.
WHAT'S UP, J.J.J.?
WHAT'S UP?!
I'LL TELL YOU WHAT'S UP, PARKER! *I WANT PICTURES!*
PICTURES OF SPIDER-MEN!?!
FOLLOW THIS ADVENTURE IN SPIDER-VERSE TEAM-UP #2! -NICK

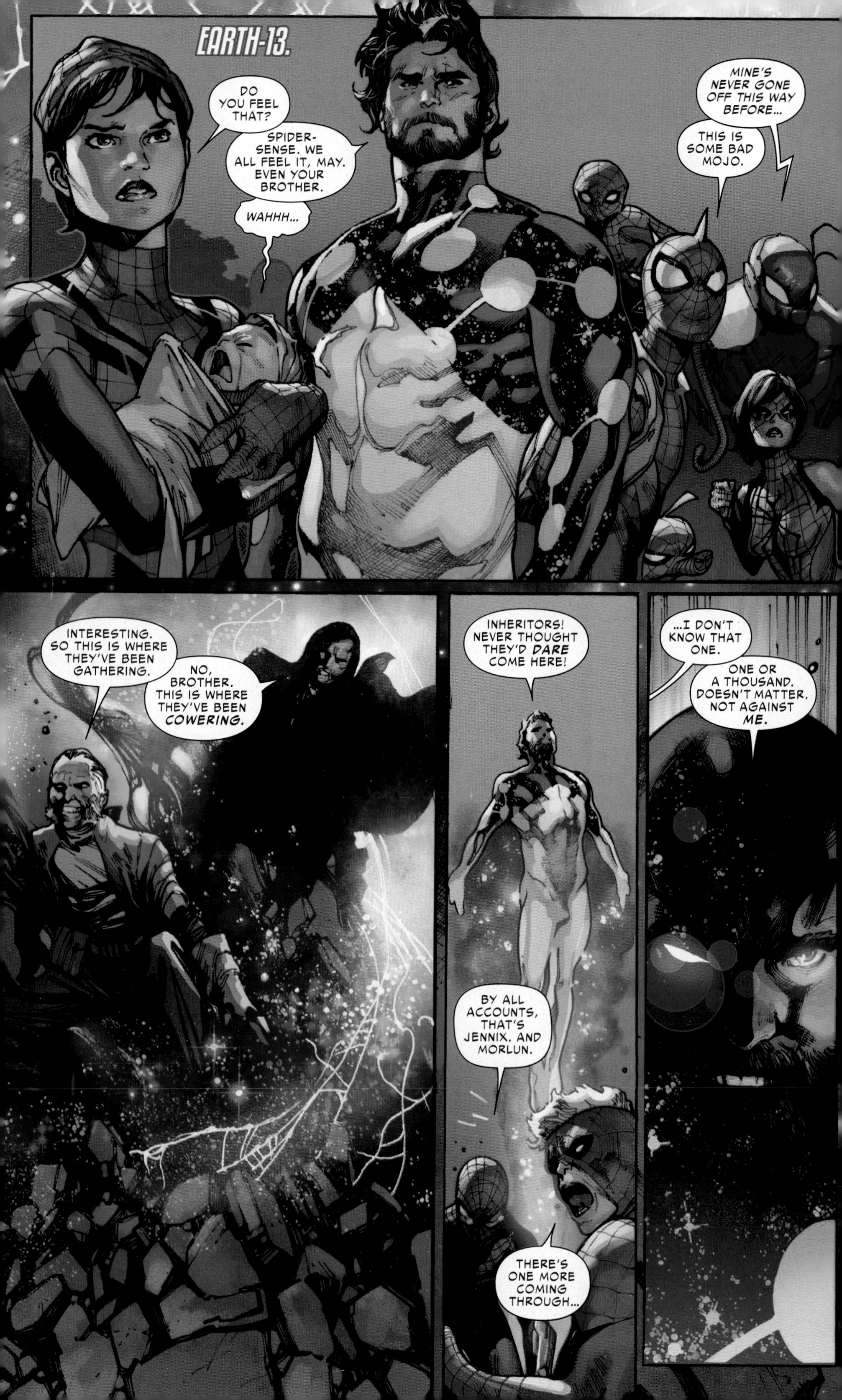
EARTH-13.
DO YOU FEEL THAT?
SPIDER-SENSE. WE ALL FEEL IT, MAY. EVEN YOUR BROTHER.
WAHHH...
MINE'S NEVER GONE OFF THIS WAY BEFORE...
THIS IS SOME BAD MOJO.
INTERESTING. SO THIS IS WHERE THEY'VE BEEN GATHERING.
NO, BROTHER. THIS IS WHERE THEY'VE BEEN COWERING.
INHERITORS! NEVER THOUGHT THEY'D DARE COME HERE!
BY ALL ACCOUNTS, THAT'S JENNIX. AND MORLUN.
THERE'S ONE MORE COMING THROUGH...
...I DON'T KNOW THAT ONE.
ONE OR A THOUSAND. DOESN'T MATTER. NOT AGAINST ME.

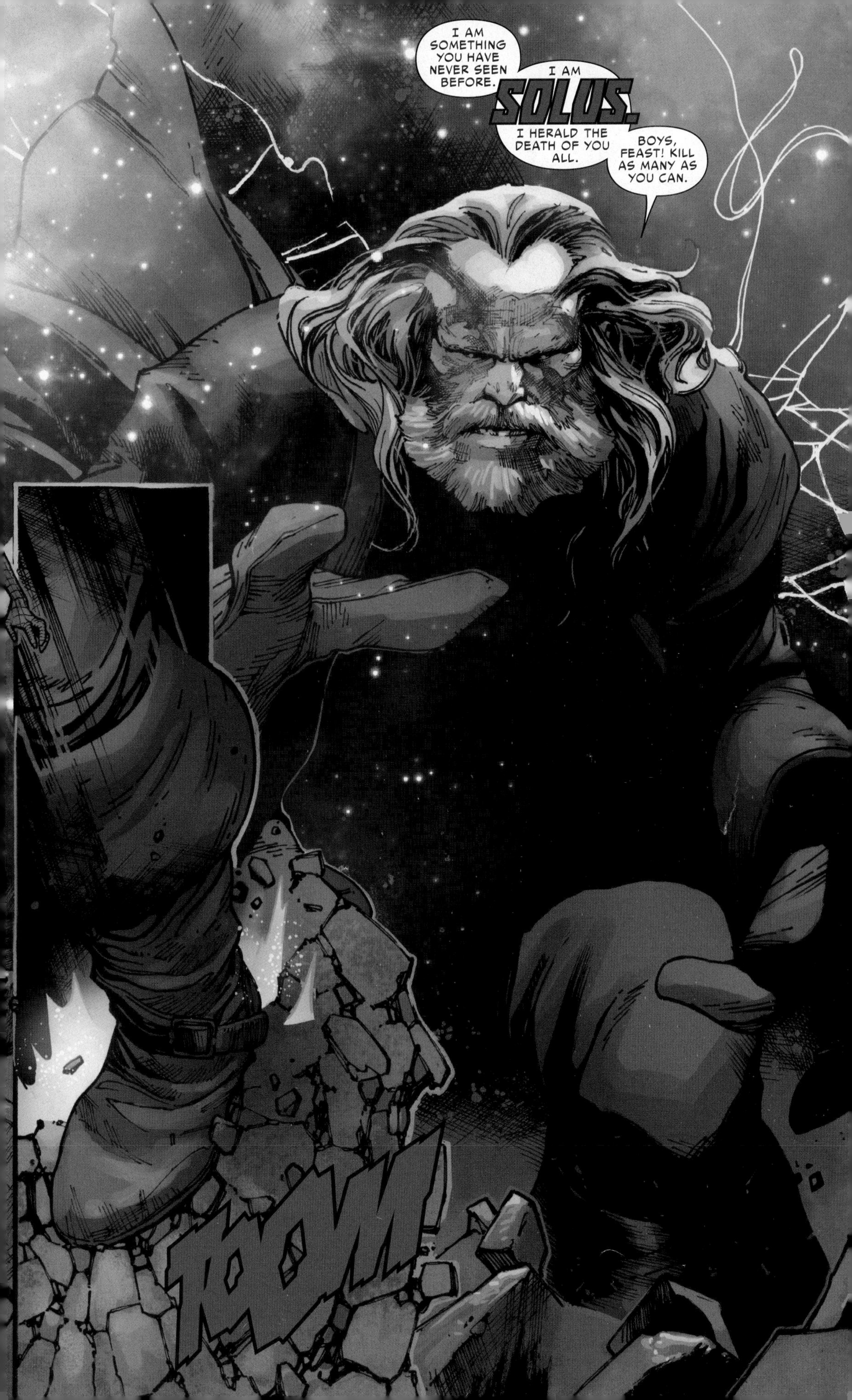
I AM SOMETHING YOU HAVE NEVER SEEN BEFORE.
I AM SOLUS.
I HERALD THE DEATH OF YOU ALL.
BOYS, FEAST! KILL AS MANY AS YOU CAN.
TOOM!

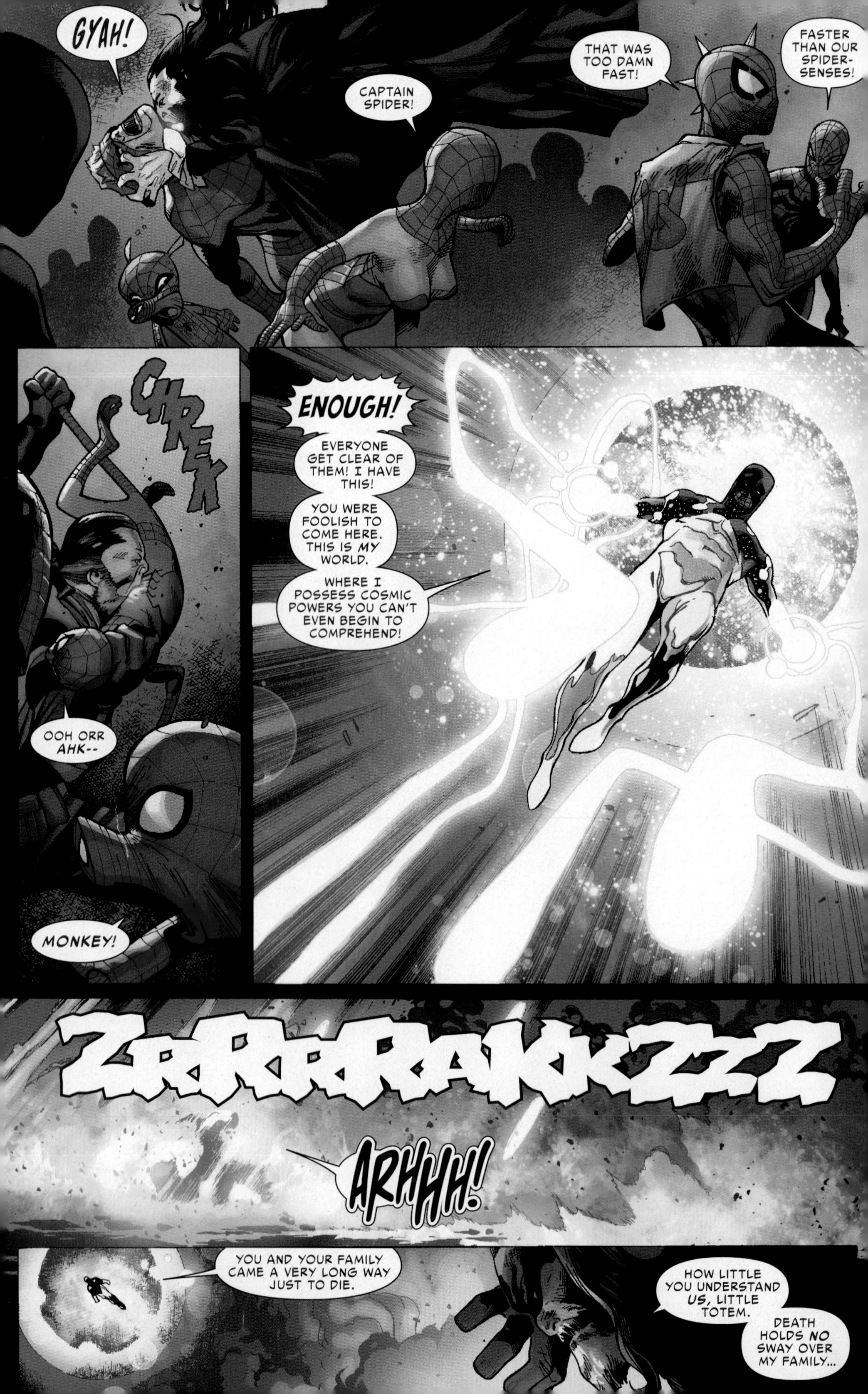
GYAH!
CAPTAIN SPIDER!
THAT WAS TOO DAMN FAST!
FASTER THAN OUR SPIDER-SENSES!
CHREK
OOH ORR AHK--
MONKEY!
ENOUGH!
EVERYONE GET CLEAR OF THEM! I HAVE THIS!
YOU WERE FOOLISH TO COME HERE. THIS IS MY WORLD.
WHERE I POSSESS COSMIC POWERS YOU CAN'T EVEN BEGIN TO COMPREHEND!
ZRRRRAKKZZZ
ARHHH!
YOU AND YOUR FAMILY CAME A VERY LONG WAY JUST TO DIE.
HOW LITTLE YOU UNDERSTAND US, LITTLE TOTEM.
DEATH HOLDS NO SWAY OVER MY FAMILY...

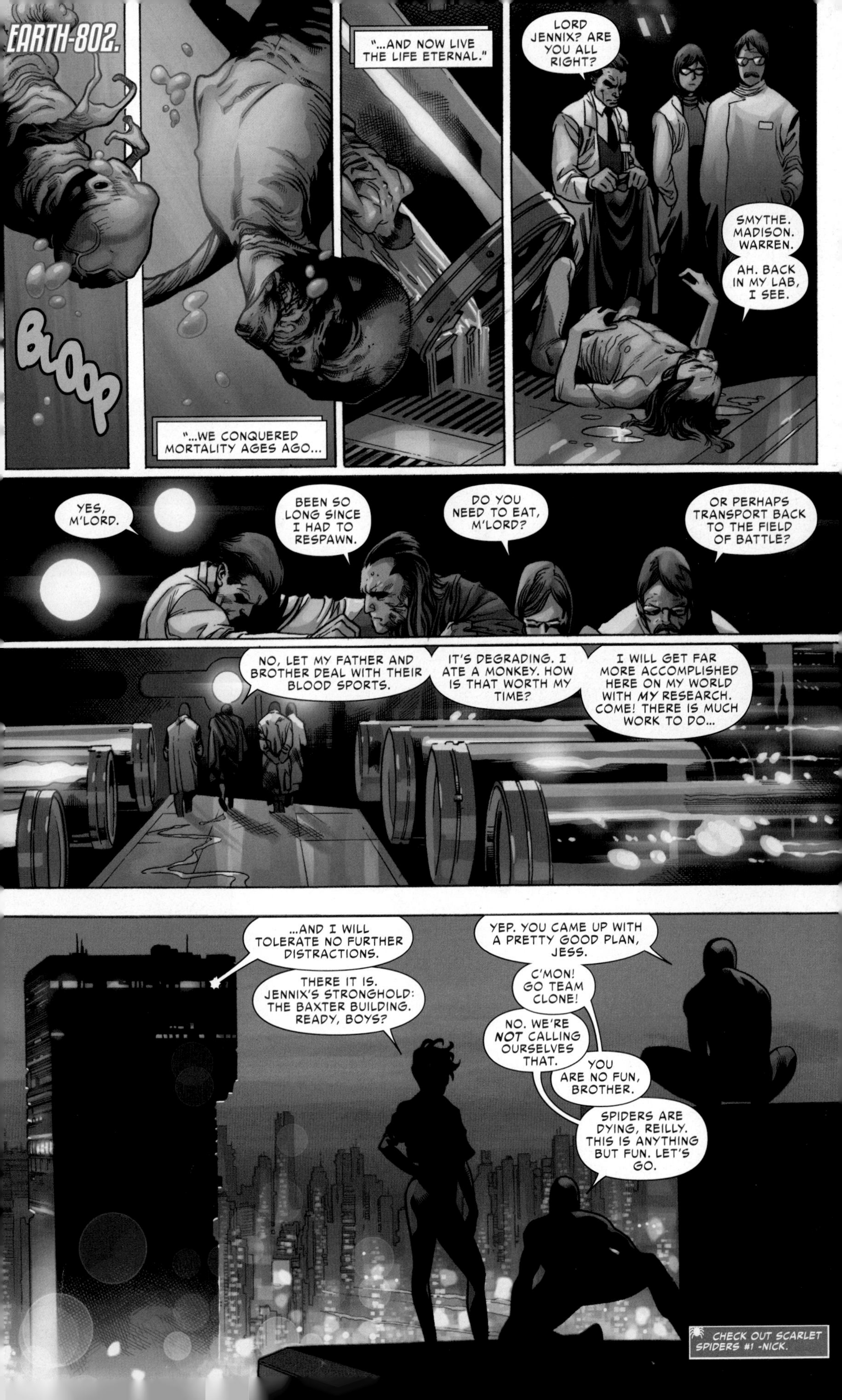
EARTH-802.
BLOOP
"...WE CONQUERED MORTALITY AGES AGO...
"...AND NOW LIVE THE LIFE ETERNAL."
LORD JENNIX? ARE YOU ALL RIGHT?
SMYTHE. MADISON. WARREN.
AH. BACK IN MY LAB, I SEE.
YES, M'LORD.
BEEN SO LONG SINCE I HAD TO RESPAWN.
DO YOU NEED TO EAT, M'LORD?
OR PERHAPS TRANSPORT BACK TO THE FIELD OF BATTLE?
NO, LET MY FATHER AND BROTHER DEAL WITH THEIR BLOOD SPORTS.
IT'S DEGRADING. I ATE A MONKEY. HOW IS THAT WORTH MY TIME?
I WILL GET FAR MORE ACCOMPLISHED HERE ON MY WORLD WITH MY RESEARCH. COME! THERE IS MUCH WORK TO DO...
...AND I WILL TOLERATE NO FURTHER DISTRACTIONS.
THERE IT IS. JENNIX'S STRONGHOLD: THE BAXTER BUILDING. READY, BOYS?
YEP. YOU CAME UP WITH A PRETTY GOOD PLAN, JESS.
C'MON! GO TEAM CLONE!
NO. WE'RE NOT CALLING OURSELVES THAT.
YOU ARE NO FUN, BROTHER.
SPIDERS ARE DYING, REILLY. THIS IS ANYTHING BUT FUN. LET'S GO.
CHECK OUT SCARLET SPIDERS #1 -NICK.

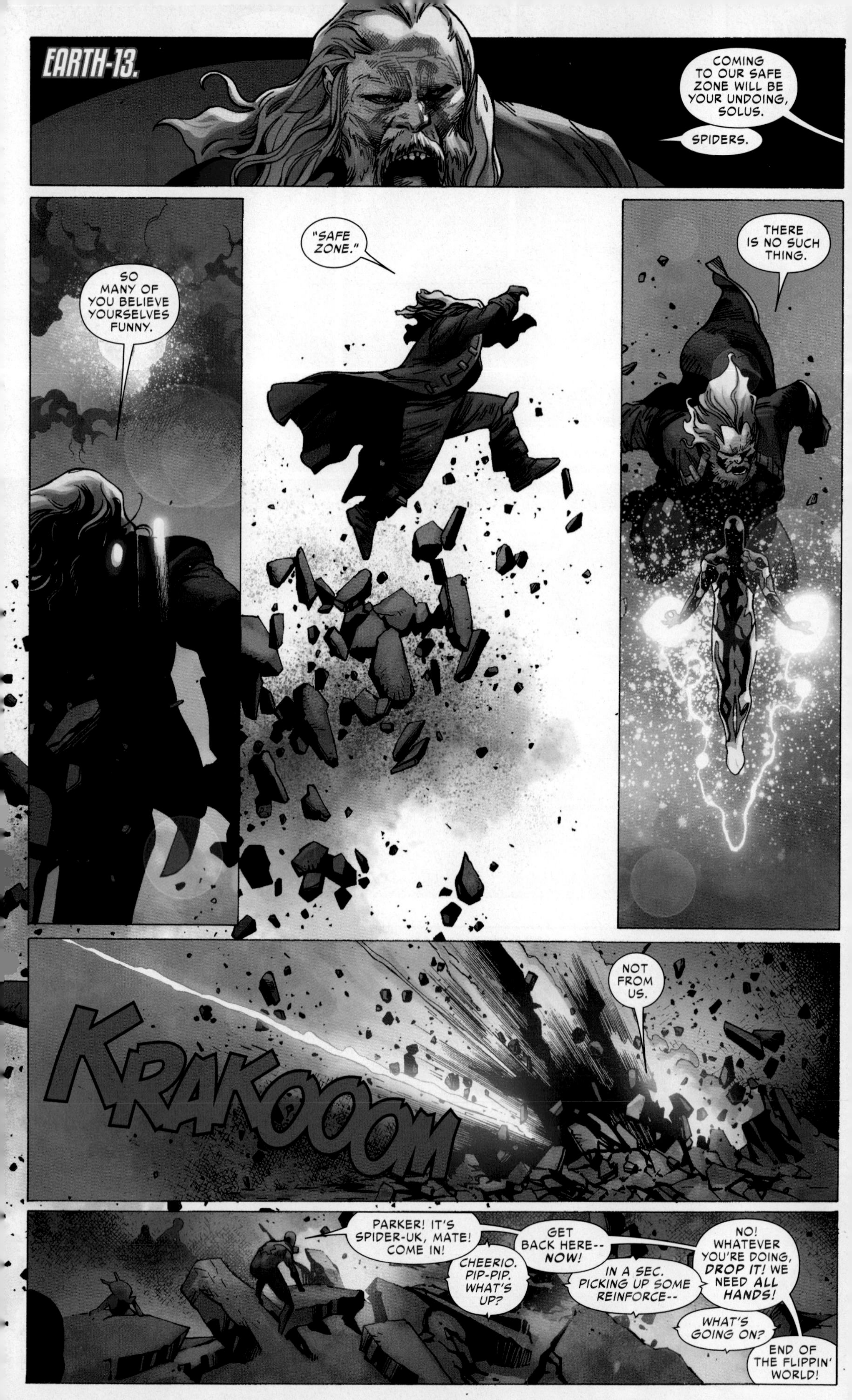
EARTH-13.
COMING TO OUR SAFE ZONE WILL BE YOUR UNDOING, SOLUS.
SPIDERS.
SO MANY OF YOU BELIEVE YOURSELVES FUNNY.
"SAFE ZONE."
THERE IS NO SUCH THING.
KRAKOOOM
NOT FROM US.
PARKER! IT'S SPIDER-UK, MATE! COME IN!
CHEERIO. PIP-PIP. WHAT'S UP?
GET BACK HERE-- NOW!
IN A SEC. PICKING UP SOME REINFORCE--
NO! WHATEVER YOU'RE DOING, DROP IT! WE NEED ALL HANDS!
WHAT'S GOING ON?
END OF THE FLIPPIN' WORLD!

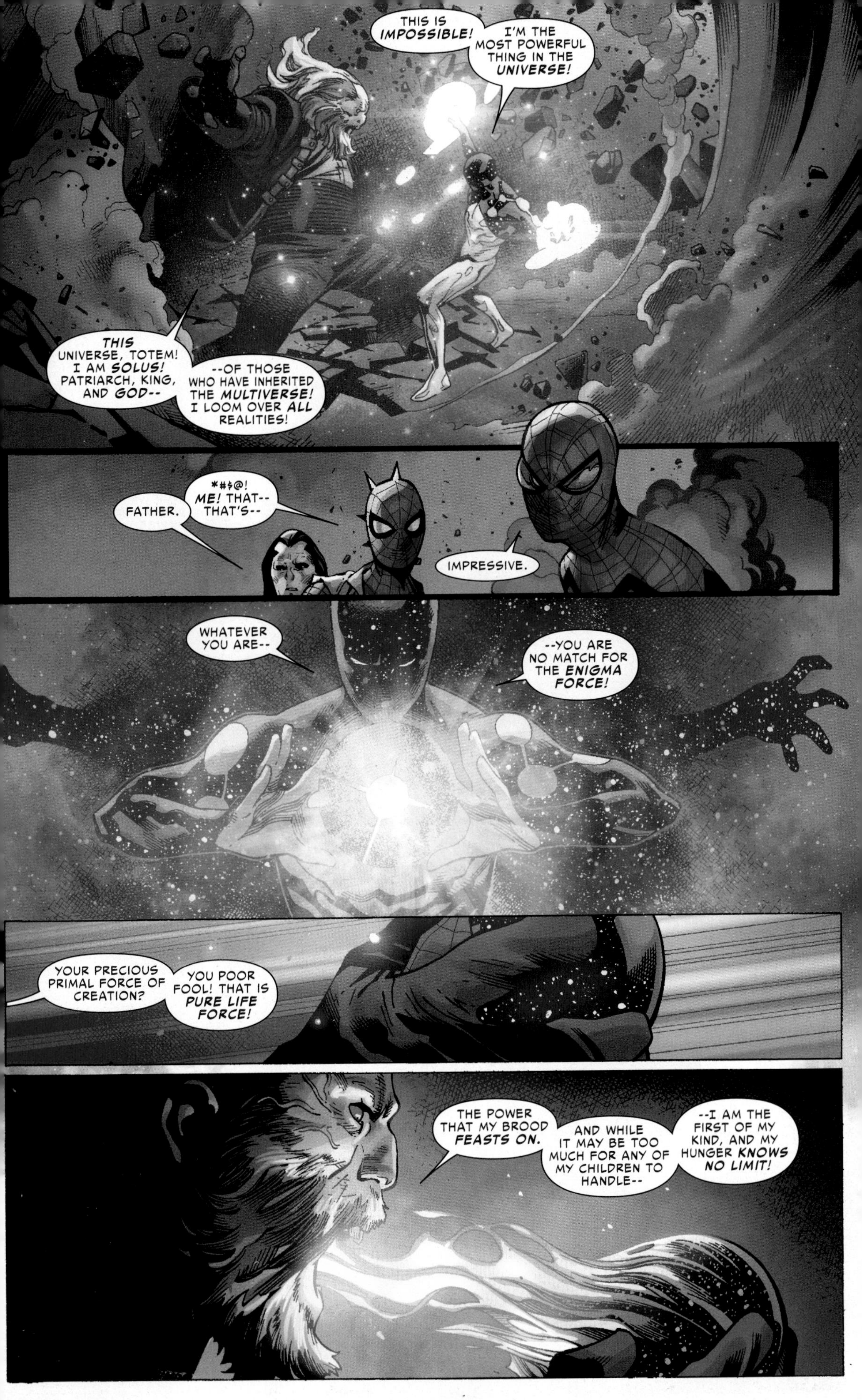
THIS IS IMPOSSIBLE!
I'M THE MOST POWERFUL THING IN THE UNIVERSE!
THIS UNIVERSE, TOTEM! I AM SOLUS! PATRIARCH, KING, AND GOD--
--OF THOSE WHO HAVE INHERITED THE MULTIVERSE! I LOOM OVER ALL REALITIES!
FATHER.
*#$@! ME! THAT-- THAT'S--
IMPRESSIVE.
WHATEVER YOU ARE--
--YOU ARE NO MATCH FOR THE ENIGMA FORCE!
YOUR PRECIOUS PRIMAL FORCE OF CREATION?
YOU POOR FOOL! THAT IS PURE LIFE FORCE!
THE POWER THAT MY BROOD FEASTS ON.
AND WHILE IT MAY BE TOO MUCH FOR ANY OF MY CHILDREN TO HANDLE--
--I AM THE FIRST OF MY KIND, AND MY HUNGER KNOWS NO LIMIT!

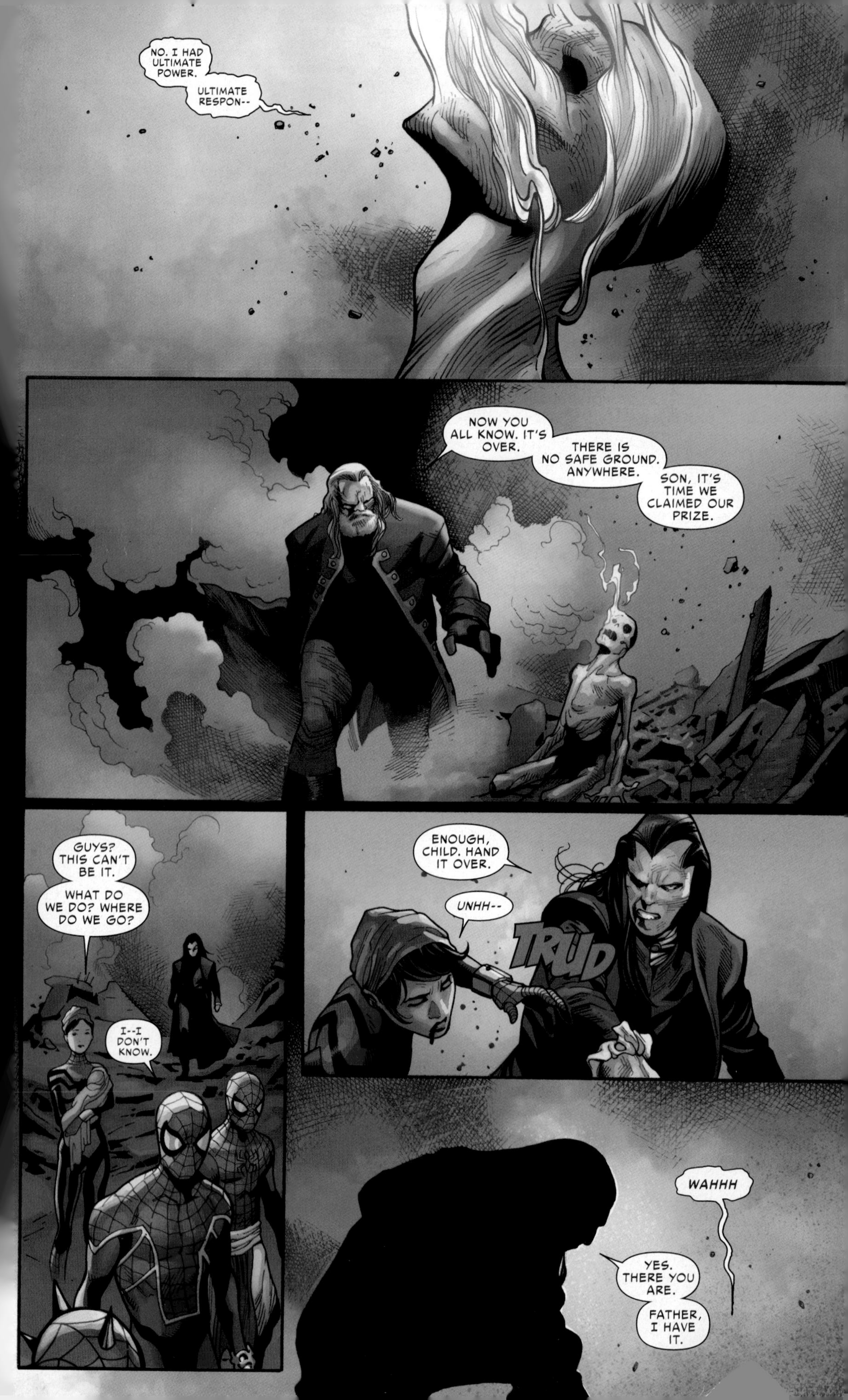

NO. I HAD ULTIMATE POWER.
ULTIMATE RESPON--
NOW YOU ALL KNOW. IT'S OVER.
THERE IS NO SAFE GROUND. ANYWHERE.
SON, IT'S TIME WE CLAIMED OUR PRIZE.
GUYS? THIS CAN'T BE IT.
WHAT DO WE DO? WHERE DO WE GO?
I--I DON'T KNOW.
ENOUGH, CHILD. HAND IT OVER.
UNHH--
TRUD
WAHHH
YES. THERE YOU ARE.
FATHER, I HAVE IT.

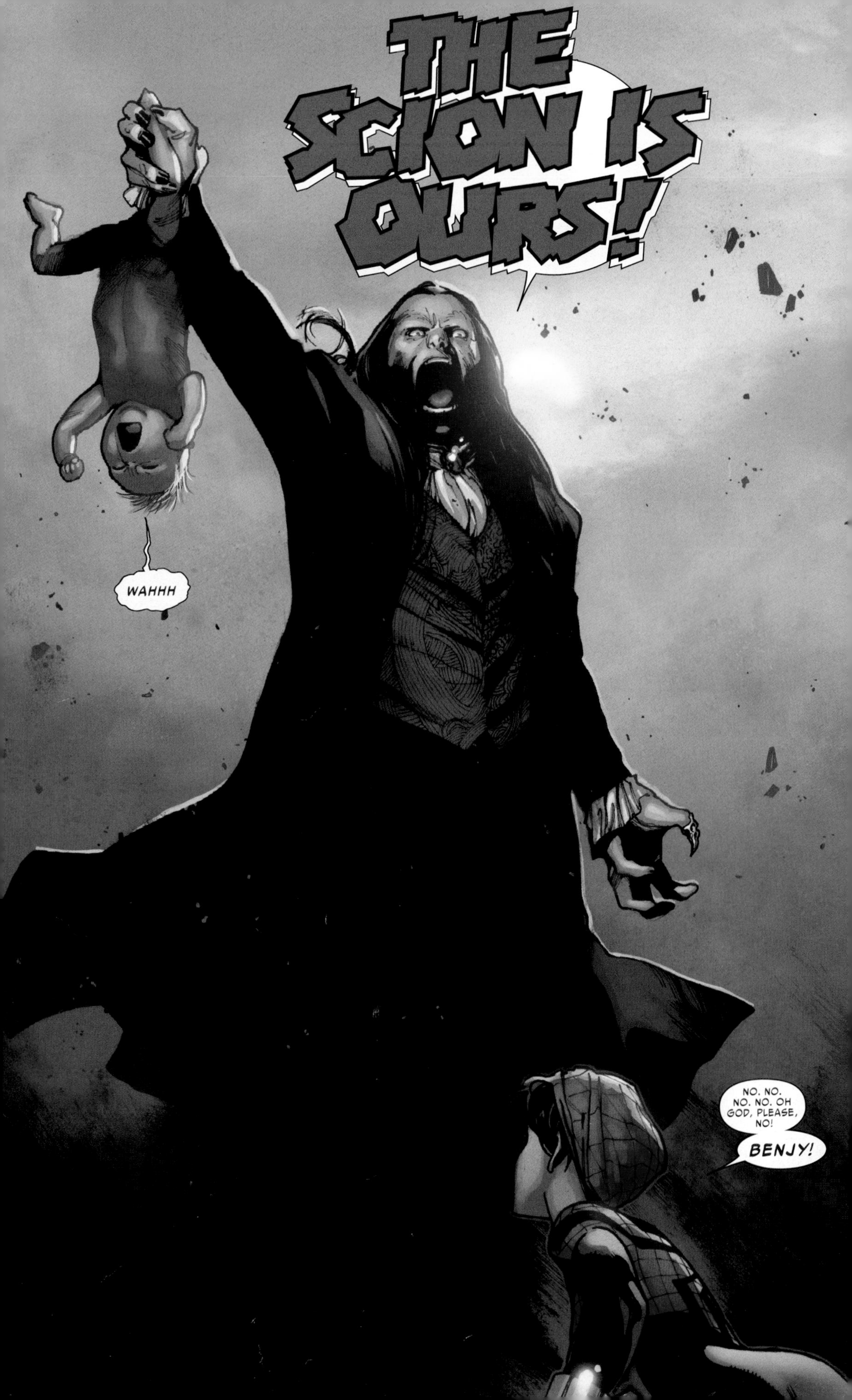
THE SCION IS OURS!
WAHHH
NO. NO. NO. NO. OH GOD, PLEASE, NO!
BENJY!

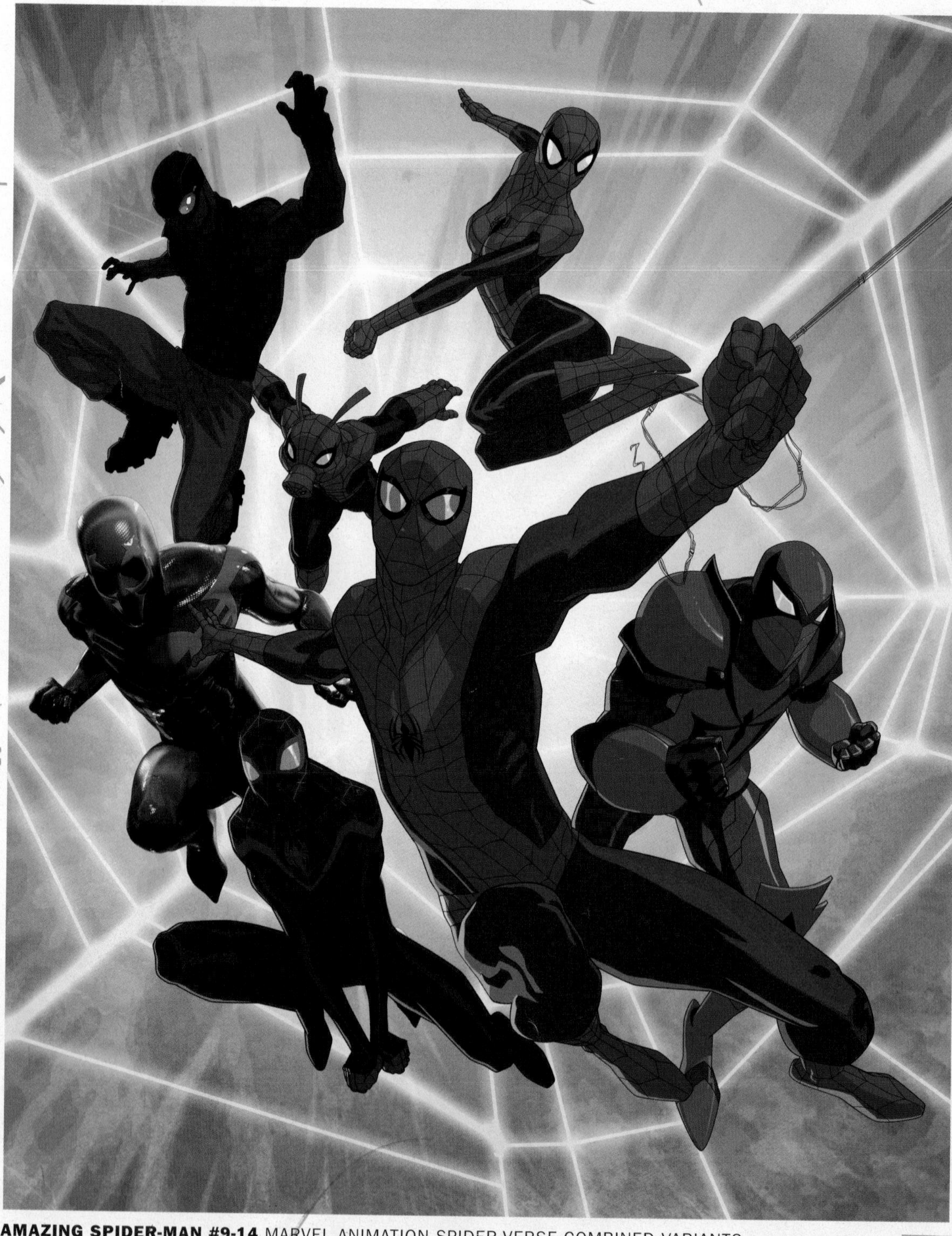

AMAZING SPIDER-MAN #9-14 MARVEL ANIMATION SPIDER-VERSE COMBINED VARIANTS
BY JEFF WAMESTER

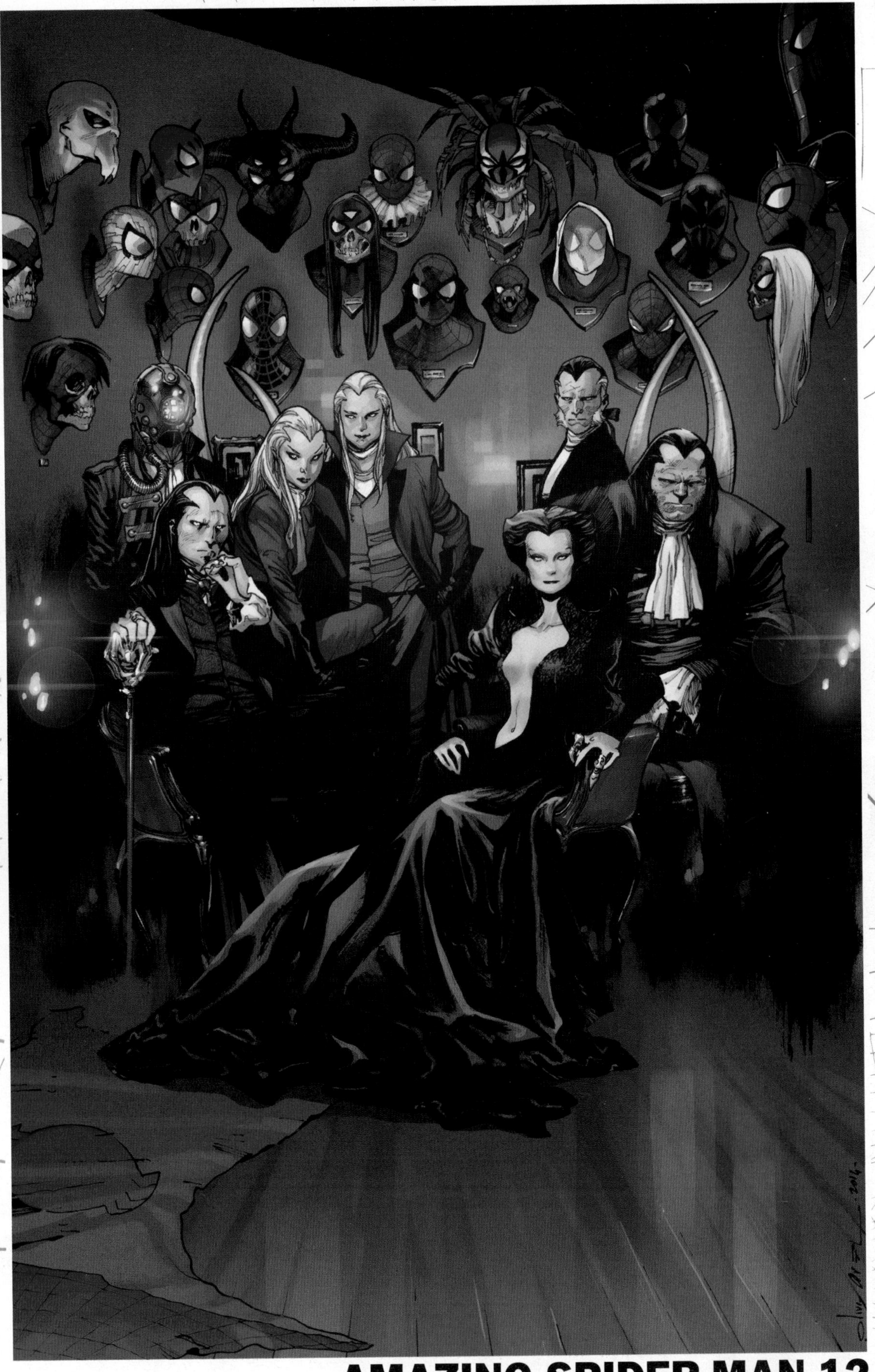

AMAZING SPIDER-MAN 12
SPIDER-VERSE, PART FOUR: ANYWHERE BUT HERE

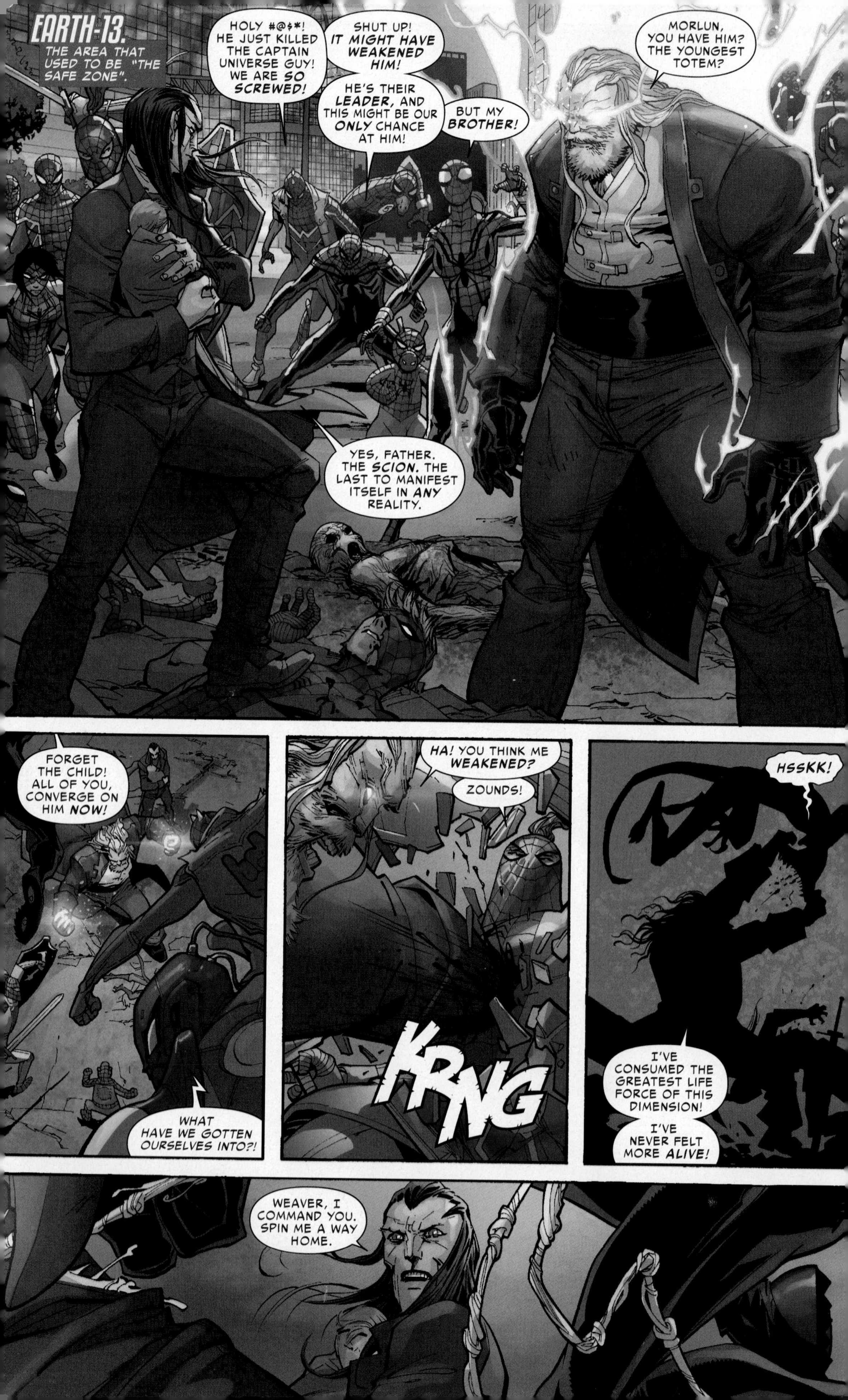
EARTH-13.
THE AREA THAT USED TO BE "THE SAFE ZONE".
HOLY #@$*! HE JUST KILLED THE CAPTAIN UNIVERSE GUY! WE ARE SO SCREWED!
SHUT UP! IT MIGHT HAVE WEAKENED HIM!
HE'S THEIR LEADER, AND THIS MIGHT BE OUR ONLY CHANCE AT HIM!
BUT MY BROTHER!
MORLUN, YOU HAVE HIM? THE YOUNGEST TOTEM?
YES, FATHER. THE SCION. THE LAST TO MANIFEST ITSELF IN ANY REALITY.
FORGET THE CHILD! ALL OF YOU, CONVERGE ON HIM NOW!
WHAT HAVE WE GOTTEN OURSELVES INTO?!
HA! YOU THINK ME WEAKENED?
ZOUNDS!
KRNG
HSSKK!
I'VE CONSUMED THE GREATEST LIFE FORCE OF THIS DIMENSION!
I'VE NEVER FELT MORE ALIVE!
WEAVER, I COMMAND YOU. SPIN ME A WAY HOME.

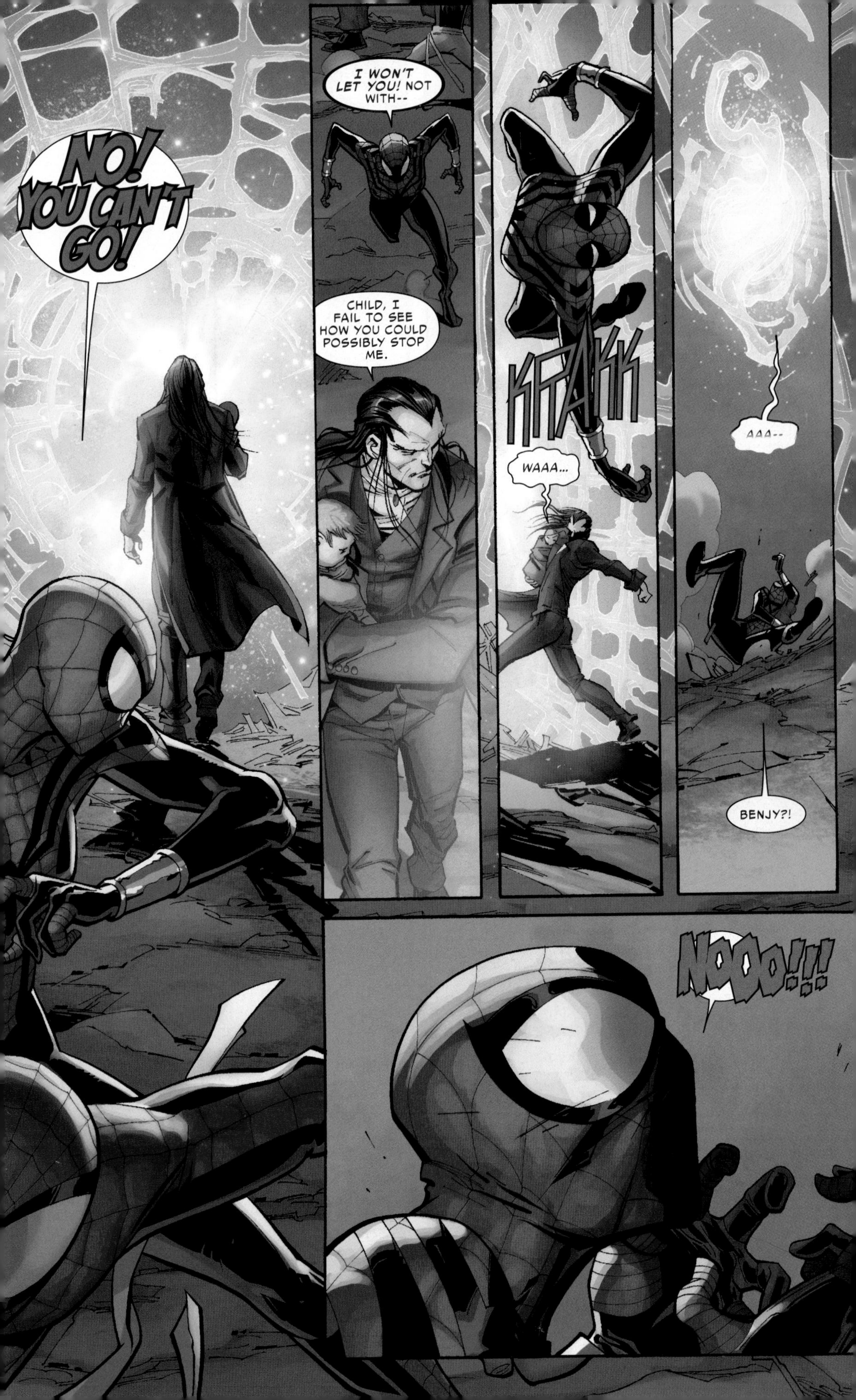
NO! YOU CAN'T GO!
I WON'T LET YOU! NOT WITH--
CHILD, I FAIL TO SEE HOW YOU COULD POSSIBLY STOP ME.
KRAKK
WAAA...
AAA--
BENJY?!
NOOO!!!

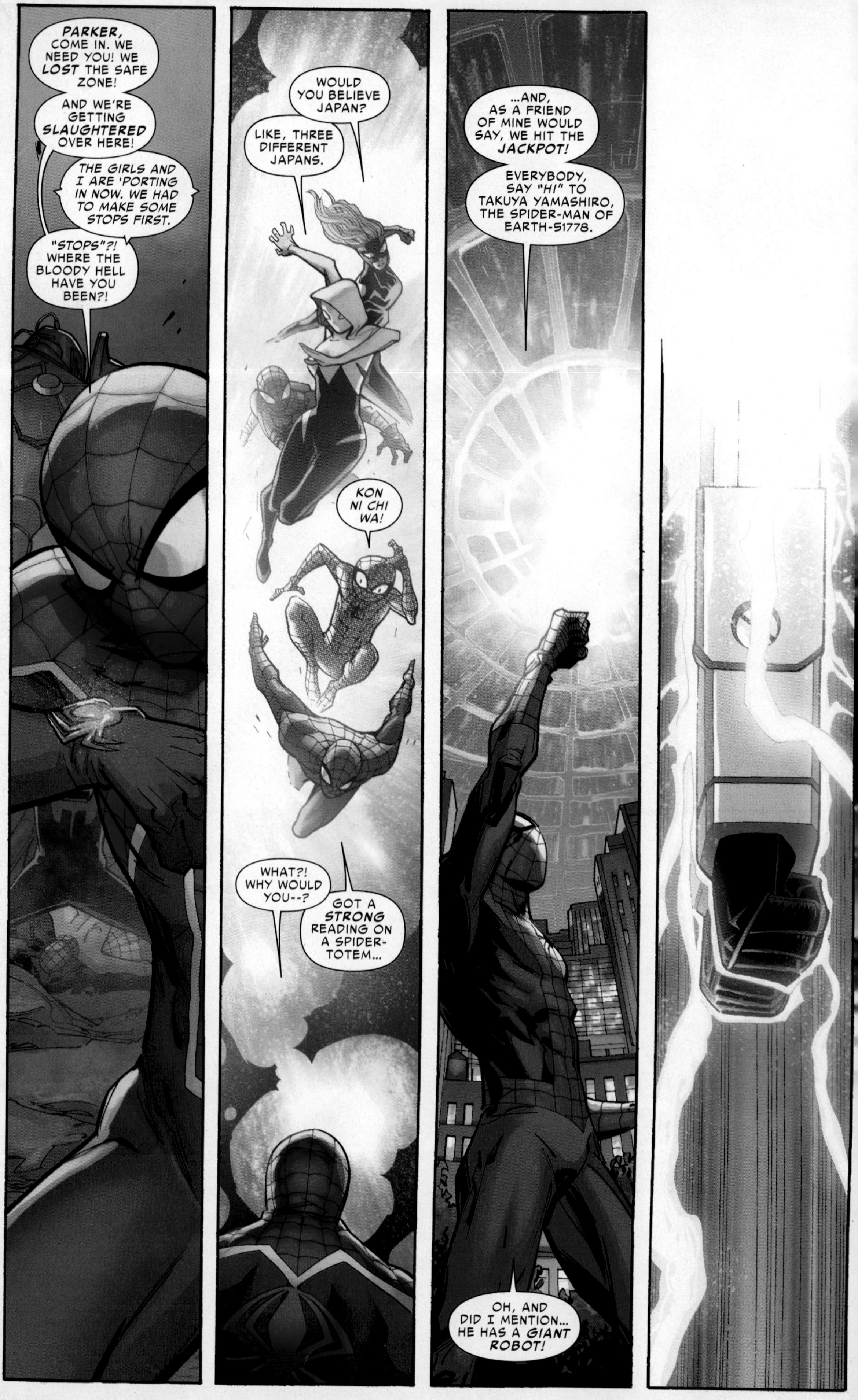
PARKER, COME IN. WE NEED YOU! WE LOST THE SAFE ZONE!
AND WE'RE GETTING SLAUGHTERED OVER HERE!
THE GIRLS AND I ARE 'PORTING IN NOW. WE HAD TO MAKE SOME STOPS FIRST.
"STOPS"?! WHERE THE BLOODY HELL HAVE YOU BEEN?!
WOULD YOU BELIEVE JAPAN?
LIKE, THREE DIFFERENT JAPANS.
KON NI CHI WA!
WHAT?! WHY WOULD YOU--?
GOT A STRONG READING ON A SPIDER-TOTEM...
...AND, AS A FRIEND OF MINE WOULD SAY, WE HIT THE JACKPOT!
EVERYBODY, SAY "HI" TO TAKUYA YAMASHIRO, THE SPIDER-MAN OF EARTH-51778.
OH, AND DID I MENTION... HE HAS A GIANT ROBOT!

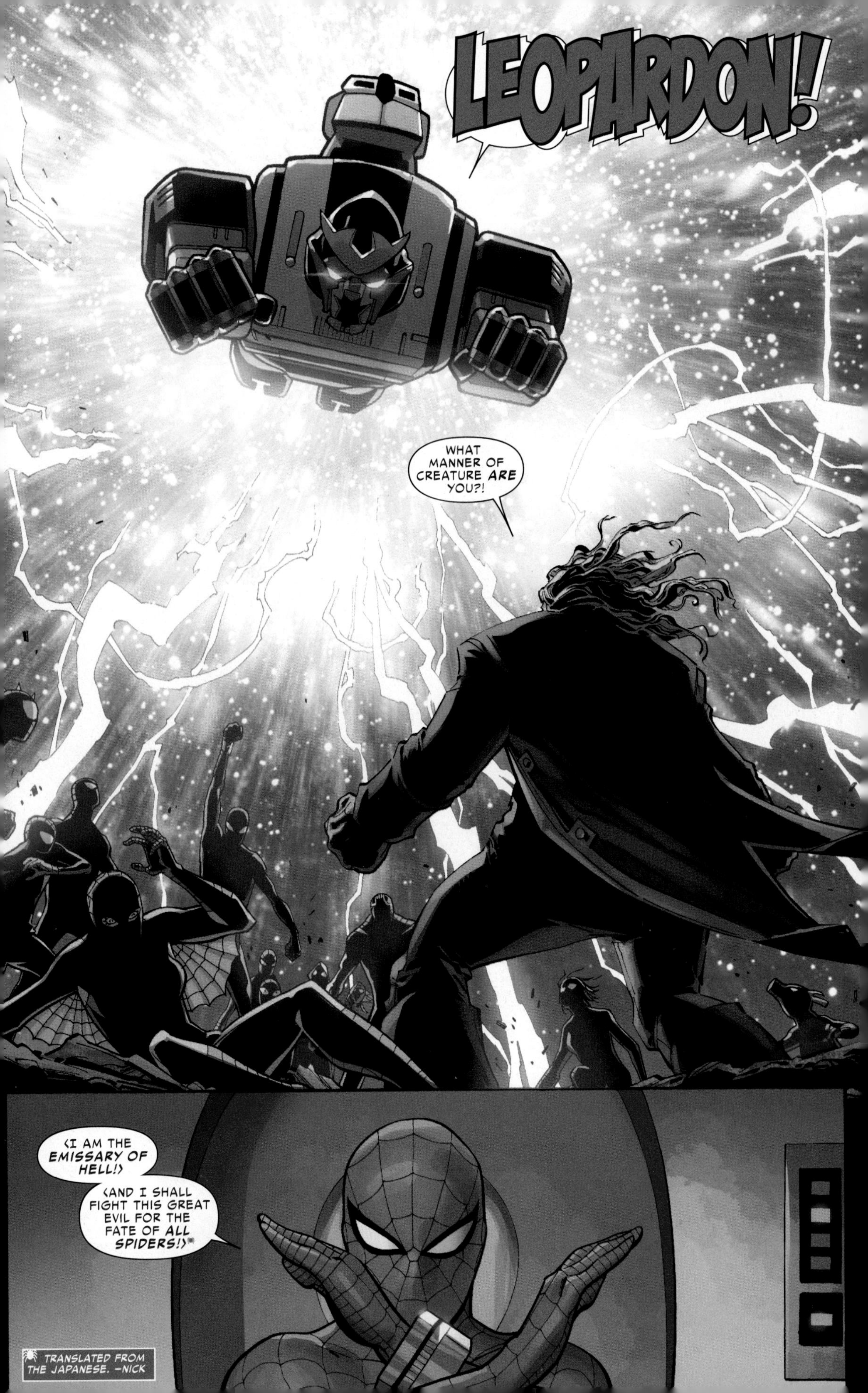
LEOPARDON!
WHAT MANNER OF CREATURE ARE YOU?!
‹I AM THE EMISSARY OF HELL!›
‹AND I SHALL FIGHT THIS GREAT EVIL FOR THE FATE OF ALL SPIDERS!›*
*TRANSLATED FROM THE JAPANESE. –NICK

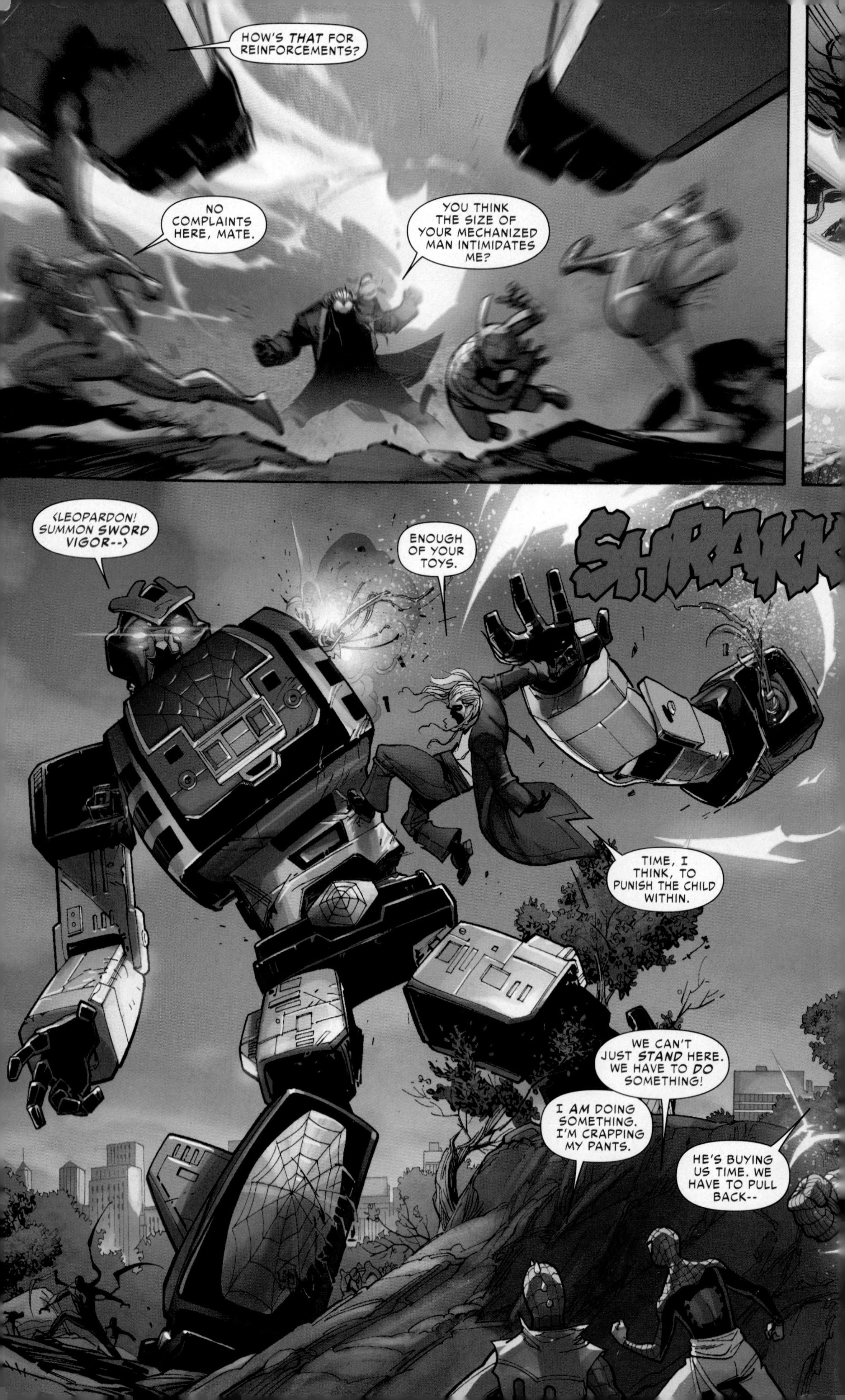
HOW'S THAT FOR REINFORCEMENTS?
NO COMPLAINTS HERE, MATE.
YOU THINK THE SIZE OF YOUR MECHANIZED MAN INTIMIDATES ME?
<LEOPARDON! SUMMON SWORD VIGOR-->
ENOUGH OF YOUR TOYS.
SHRAKK
TIME, I THINK, TO PUNISH THE CHILD WITHIN.
WE CAN'T JUST STAND HERE. WE HAVE TO DO SOMETHING!
I AM DOING SOMETHING. I'M CRAPPING MY PANTS.
HE'S BUYING US TIME. WE HAVE TO PULL BACK--

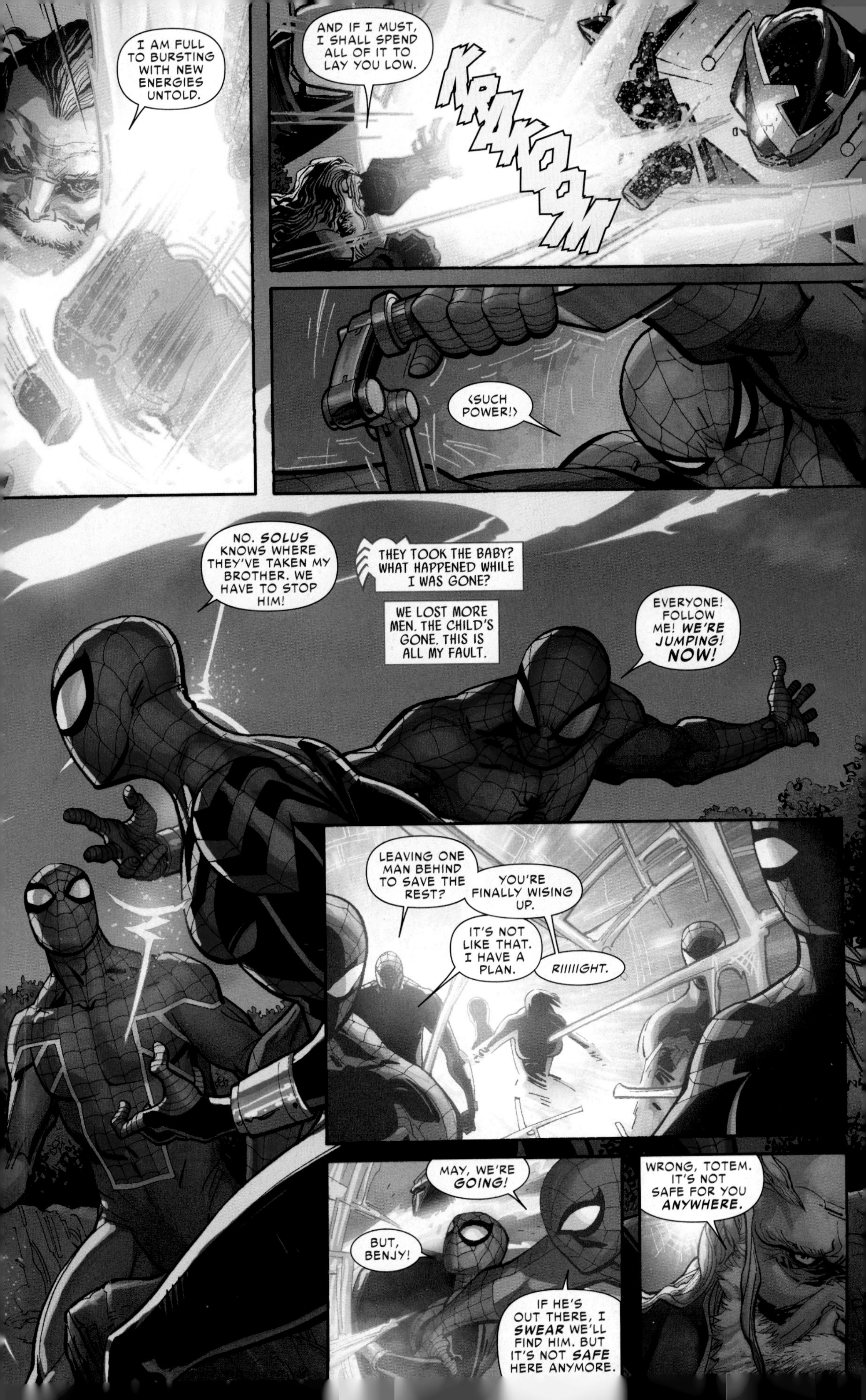
I AM FULL TO BURSTING WITH NEW ENERGIES UNTOLD.
AND IF I MUST, I SHALL SPEND ALL OF IT TO LAY YOU LOW.
KRAKOOM
‹SUCH POWER!›
NO. SOLUS KNOWS WHERE THEY'VE TAKEN MY BROTHER. WE HAVE TO STOP HIM!
THEY TOOK THE BABY? WHAT HAPPENED WHILE I WAS GONE?
WE LOST MORE MEN. THE CHILD'S GONE. THIS IS ALL MY FAULT.
EVERYONE! FOLLOW ME! WE'RE JUMPING! NOW!
LEAVING ONE MAN BEHIND TO SAVE THE REST?
YOU'RE FINALLY WISING UP.
IT'S NOT LIKE THAT. I HAVE A PLAN.
RIIIIIGHT.
MAY, WE'RE GOING!
BUT, BENJY!
IF HE'S OUT THERE, I SWEAR WE'LL FIND HIM. BUT IT'S NOT SAFE HERE ANYMORE.
WRONG, TOTEM. IT'S NOT SAFE FOR YOU ANYWHERE.

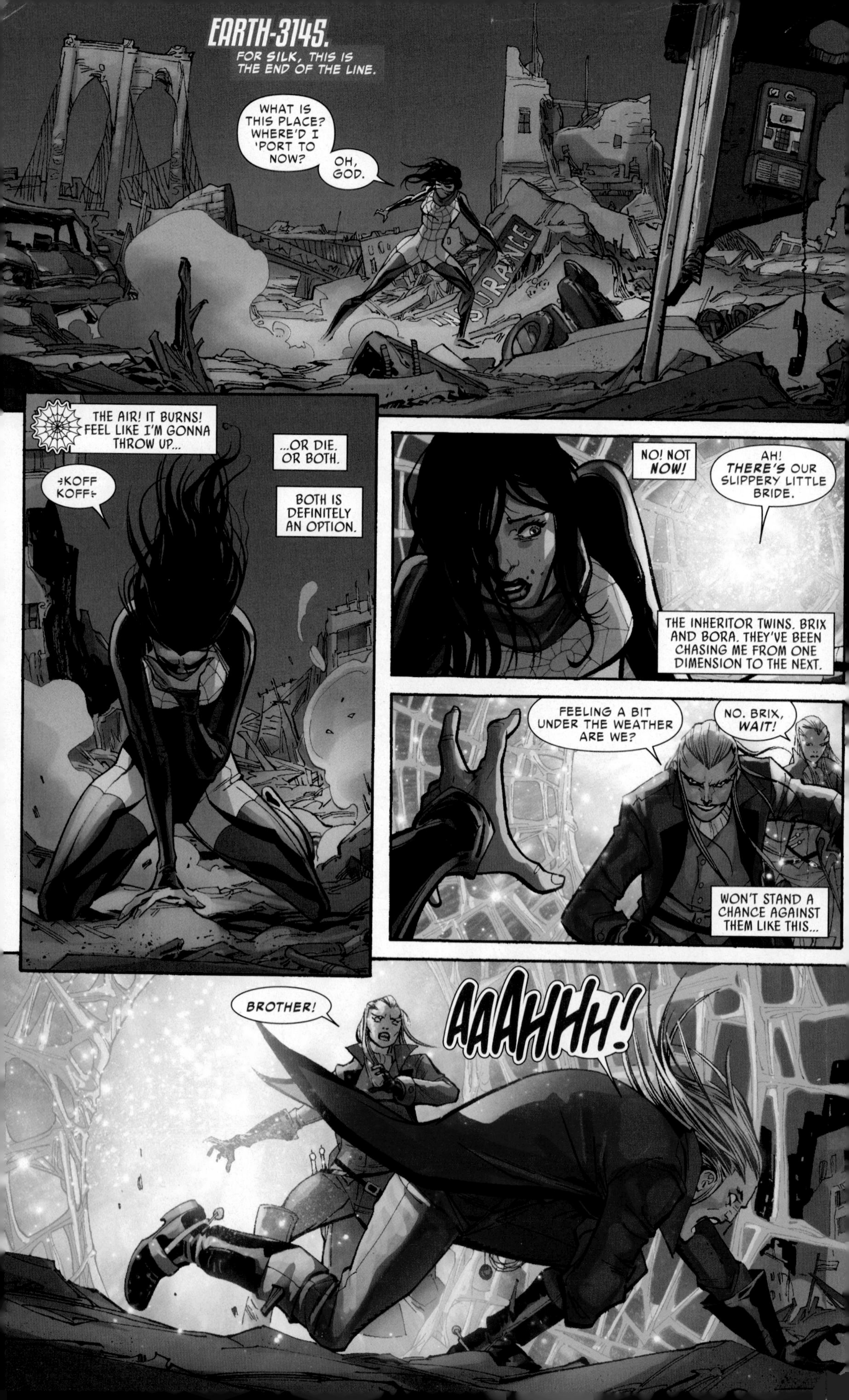
EARTH-3145.
FOR SILK, THIS IS THE END OF THE LINE.
WHAT IS THIS PLACE? WHERE'D I 'PORT TO NOW?
OH, GOD.
THE AIR! IT BURNS! FEEL LIKE I'M GONNA THROW UP...
...OR DIE. OR BOTH.
BOTH IS DEFINITELY AN OPTION.
KOFF KOFF
NO! NOT NOW!
AH! THERE'S OUR SLIPPERY LITTLE BRIDE.
THE INHERITOR TWINS. BRIX AND BORA. THEY'VE BEEN CHASING ME FROM ONE DIMENSION TO THE NEXT.
FEELING A BIT UNDER THE WEATHER ARE WE?
NO. BRIX, WAIT!
WON'T STAND A CHANCE AGAINST THEM LIKE THIS...
BROTHER!
AAAHHH!

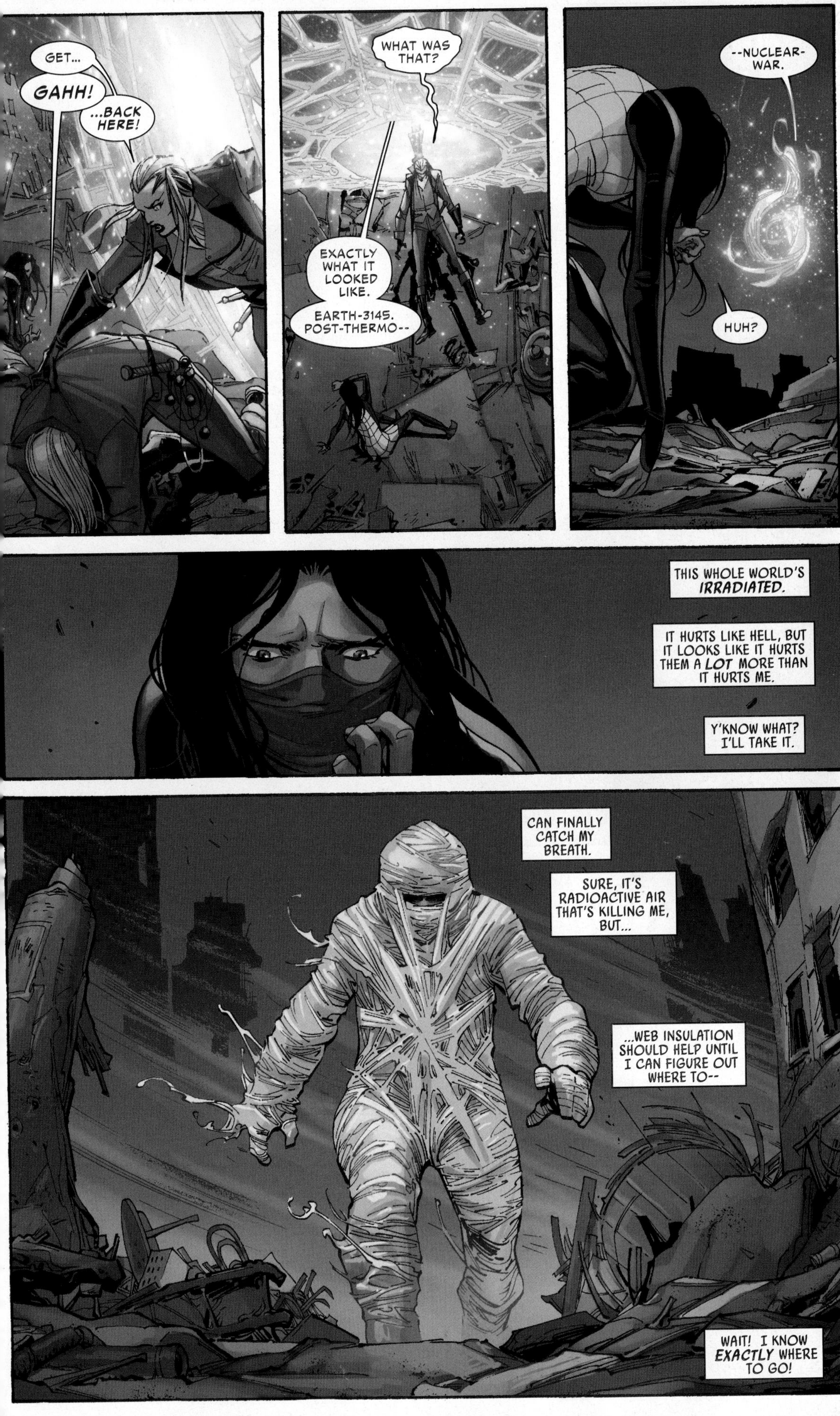
GET...
GAHH!
...BACK HERE!
WHAT WAS THAT?
EXACTLY WHAT IT LOOKED LIKE.
EARTH-3145. POST-THERMO--
--NUCLEAR-WAR.
HUH?
THIS WHOLE WORLD'S IRRADIATED.
IT HURTS LIKE HELL, BUT IT LOOKS LIKE IT HURTS THEM A LOT MORE THAN IT HURTS ME.
Y'KNOW WHAT? I'LL TAKE IT.
CAN FINALLY CATCH MY BREATH.
SURE, IT'S RADIOACTIVE AIR THAT'S KILLING ME, BUT...
...WEB INSULATION SHOULD HELP UNTIL I CAN FIGURE OUT WHERE TO--
WAIT! I KNOW EXACTLY WHERE TO GO!

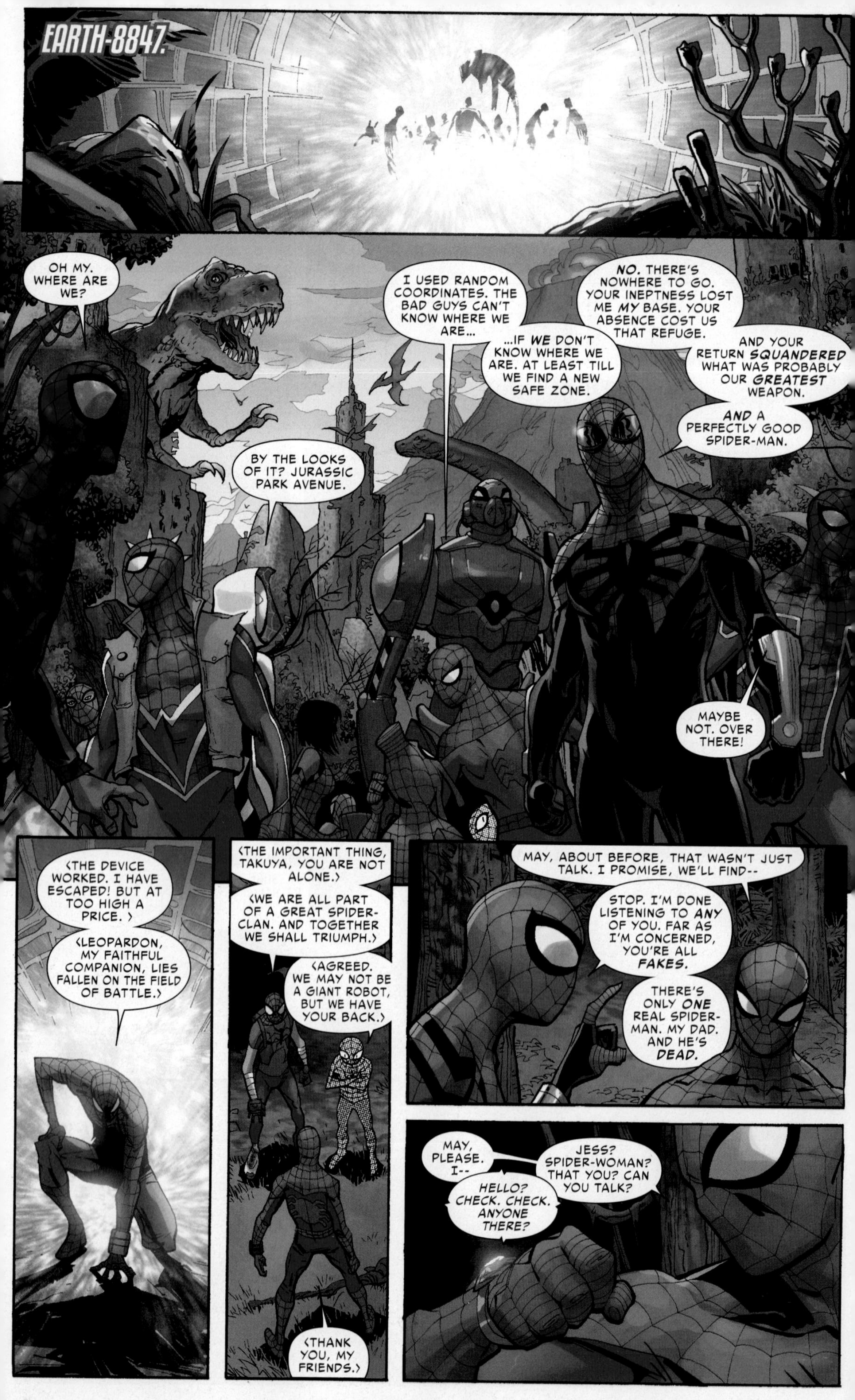
EARTH-8847.
OH MY. WHERE ARE WE?
BY THE LOOKS OF IT? JURASSIC PARK AVENUE.
I USED RANDOM COORDINATES. THE BAD GUYS CAN'T KNOW WHERE WE ARE...
...IF WE DON'T KNOW WHERE WE ARE. AT LEAST TILL WE FIND A NEW SAFE ZONE.
NO. THERE'S NOWHERE TO GO. YOUR INEPTNESS LOST ME MY BASE. YOUR ABSENCE COST US THAT REFUGE.
AND YOUR RETURN SQUANDERED WHAT WAS PROBABLY OUR GREATEST WEAPON.
AND A PERFECTLY GOOD SPIDER-MAN.
MAYBE NOT. OVER THERE!
‹THE DEVICE WORKED. I HAVE ESCAPED! BUT AT TOO HIGH A PRICE. ›
‹LEOPARDON, MY FAITHFUL COMPANION, LIES FALLEN ON THE FIELD OF BATTLE.›
‹THE IMPORTANT THING, TAKUYA, YOU ARE NOT ALONE.›
‹WE ARE ALL PART OF A GREAT SPIDER-CLAN. AND TOGETHER WE SHALL TRIUMPH.›
‹AGREED. WE MAY NOT BE A GIANT ROBOT, BUT WE HAVE YOUR BACK.›
‹THANK YOU, MY FRIENDS.›
MAY, ABOUT BEFORE, THAT WASN'T JUST TALK. I PROMISE, WE'LL FIND--
STOP. I'M DONE LISTENING TO ANY OF YOU. FAR AS I'M CONCERNED, YOU'RE ALL FAKES.
THERE'S ONLY ONE REAL SPIDER-MAN. MY DAD. AND HE'S DEAD.
MAY, PLEASE. I--
JESS? SPIDER-WOMAN? THAT YOU? CAN YOU TALK?
HELLO? CHECK. CHECK. ANYONE THERE?

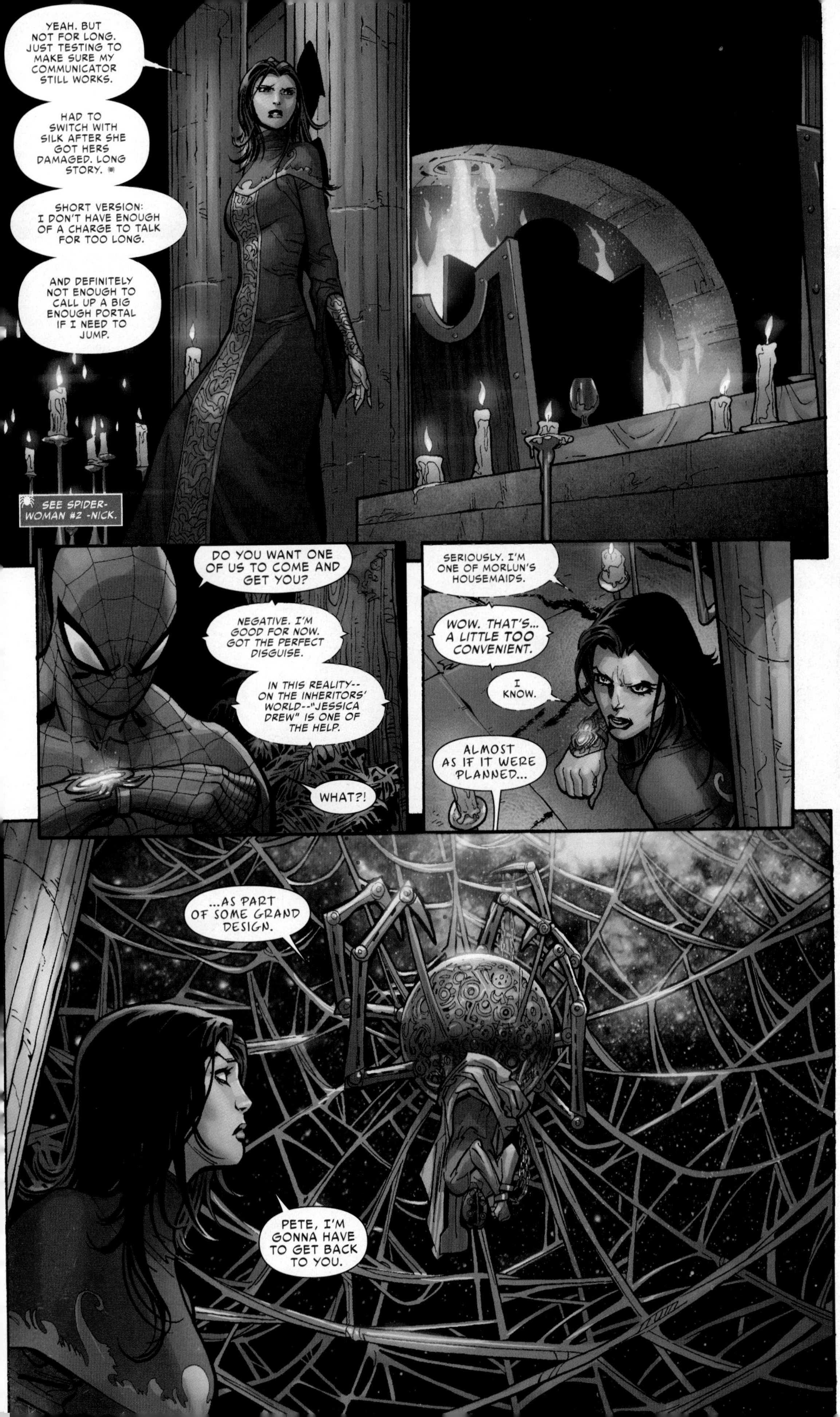
YEAH. BUT NOT FOR LONG. JUST TESTING TO MAKE SURE MY COMMUNICATOR STILL WORKS.
HAD TO SWITCH WITH SILK AFTER SHE GOT HERS DAMAGED. LONG STORY.
SHORT VERSION: I DON'T HAVE ENOUGH OF A CHARGE TO TALK FOR TOO LONG.
AND DEFINITELY NOT ENOUGH TO CALL UP A BIG ENOUGH PORTAL IF I NEED TO JUMP.
SEE SPIDER-WOMAN #2 -NICK.
DO YOU WANT ONE OF US TO COME AND GET YOU?
NEGATIVE. I'M GOOD FOR NOW. GOT THE PERFECT DISGUISE.
IN THIS REALITY-- ON THE INHERITORS' WORLD--"JESSICA DREW" IS ONE OF THE HELP.
WHAT?!
SERIOUSLY. I'M ONE OF MORLUN'S HOUSEMAIDS.
WOW. THAT'S... A LITTLE TOO CONVENIENT.
I KNOW.
ALMOST AS IF IT WERE PLANNED...
...AS PART OF SOME GRAND DESIGN.
PETE, I'M GONNA HAVE TO GET BACK TO YOU.

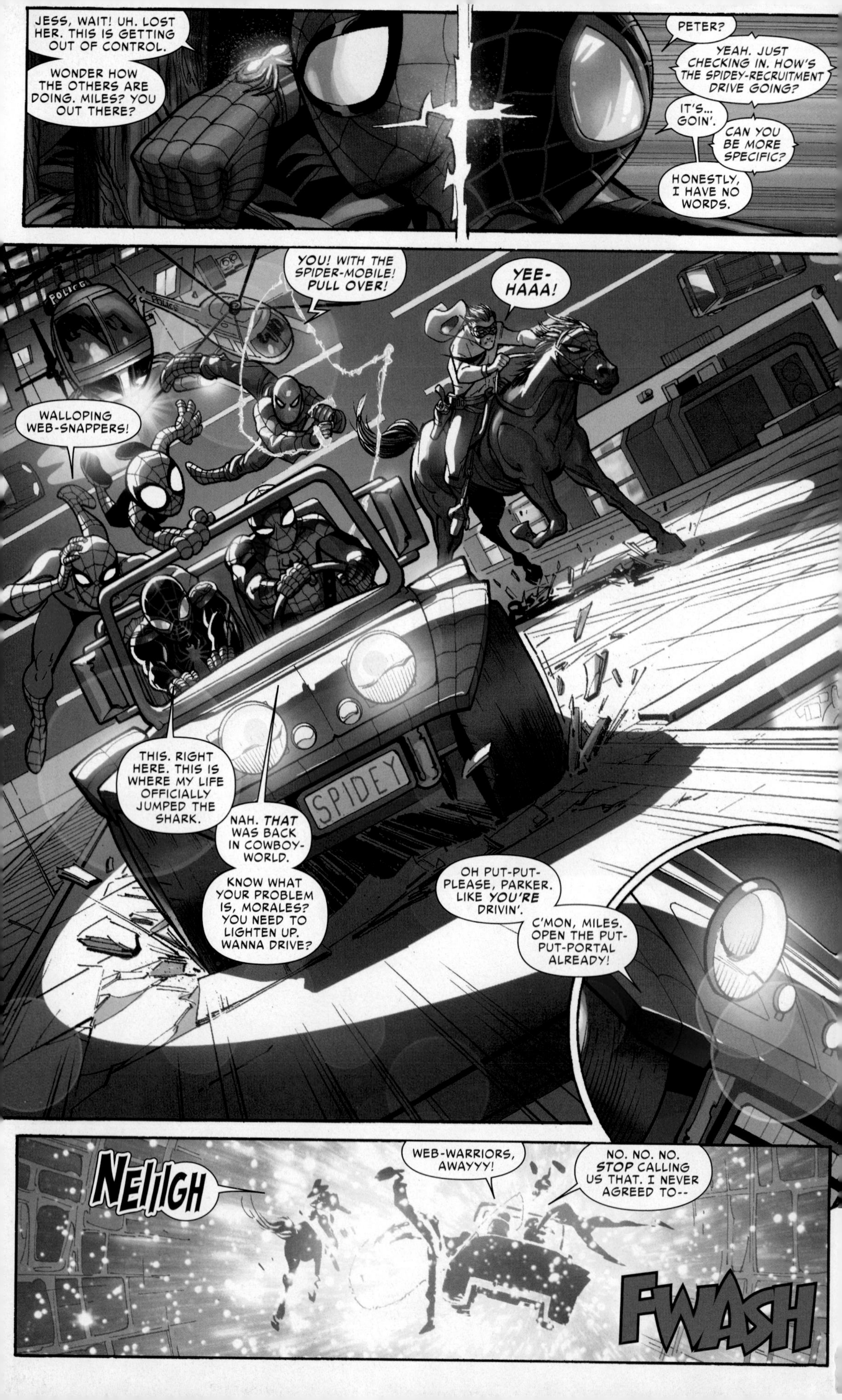

JESS, WAIT! UH. LOST HER. THIS IS GETTING OUT OF CONTROL.
WONDER HOW THE OTHERS ARE DOING. MILES? YOU OUT THERE?
PETER?
YEAH. JUST CHECKING IN. HOW'S THE SPIDEY-RECRUITMENT DRIVE GOING?
IT'S... GOIN'.
CAN YOU BE MORE SPECIFIC?
HONESTLY, I HAVE NO WORDS.
YOU! WITH THE SPIDER-MOBILE! PULL OVER!
YEE-HAAA!
WALLOPING WEB-SNAPPERS!
THIS. RIGHT HERE. THIS IS WHERE MY LIFE OFFICIALLY JUMPED THE SHARK.
NAH. THAT WAS BACK IN COWBOY-WORLD.
KNOW WHAT YOUR PROBLEM IS, MORALES? YOU NEED TO LIGHTEN UP. WANNA DRIVE?
OH PUT-PUT-PLEASE, PARKER. LIKE YOU'RE DRIVIN'.
C'MON, MILES. OPEN THE PUT-PUT-PORTAL ALREADY!
SPIDEY
NEIIIGH
WEB-WARRIORS, AWAYYY!
NO. NO. NO. STOP CALLING US THAT. I NEVER AGREED TO--
FWASH

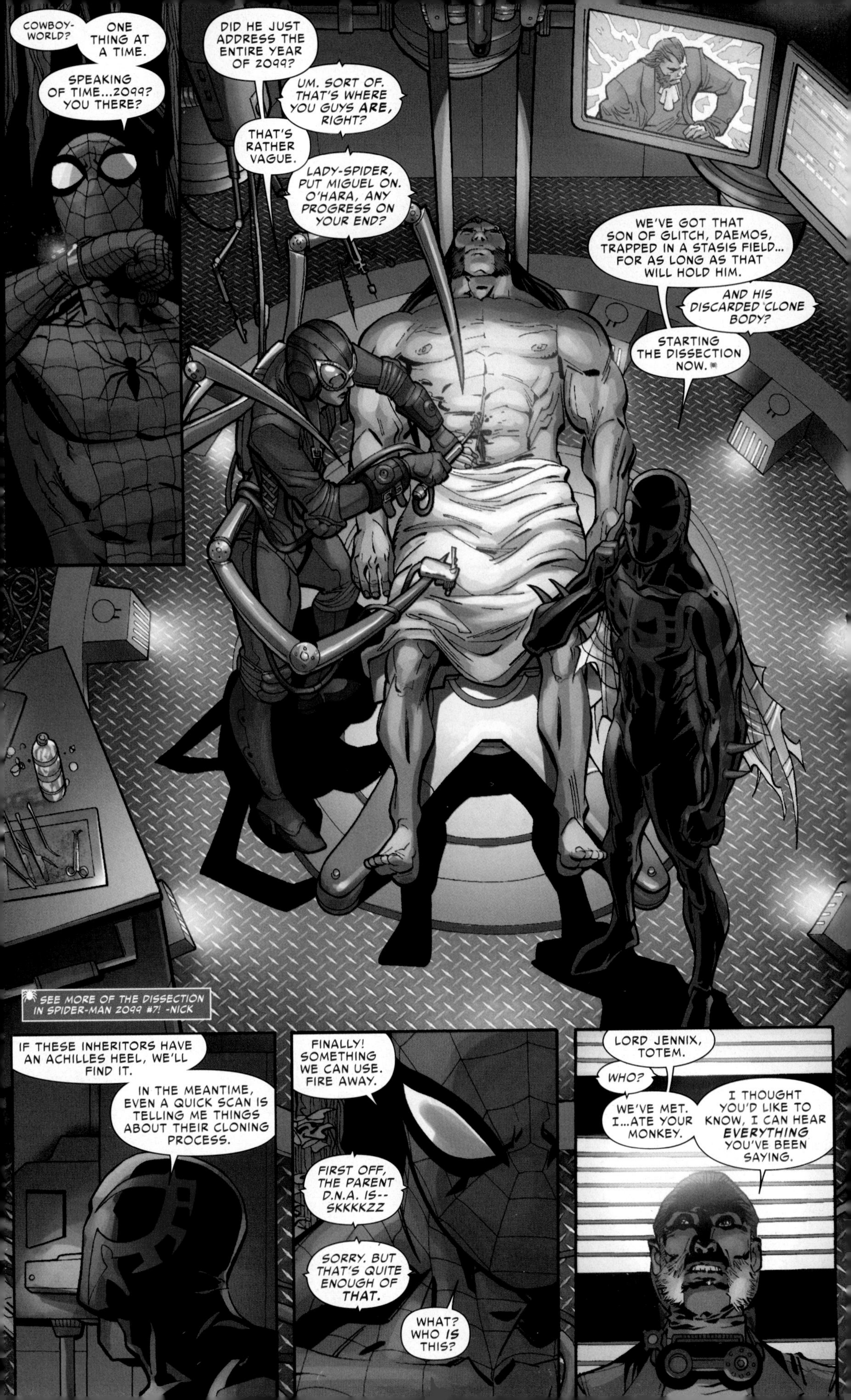
COWBOY-WORLD?
ONE THING AT A TIME.
SPEAKING OF TIME...2099? YOU THERE?
DID HE JUST ADDRESS THE ENTIRE YEAR OF 2099?
UM. SORT OF. THAT'S WHERE YOU GUYS ARE, RIGHT?
THAT'S RATHER VAGUE.
LADY-SPIDER, PUT MIGUEL ON. O'HARA, ANY PROGRESS ON YOUR END?
WE'VE GOT THAT SON OF GLITCH, DAEMOS, TRAPPED IN A STASIS FIELD... FOR AS LONG AS THAT WILL HOLD HIM.
AND HIS DISCARDED CLONE BODY?
STARTING THE DISSECTION NOW.
SEE MORE OF THE DISSECTION IN SPIDER-MAN 2099 #7! -NICK
IF THESE INHERITORS HAVE AN ACHILLES HEEL, WE'LL FIND IT.
IN THE MEANTIME, EVEN A QUICK SCAN IS TELLING ME THINGS ABOUT THEIR CLONING PROCESS.
FINALLY! SOMETHING WE CAN USE. FIRE AWAY.
FIRST OFF, THE PARENT D.N.A. IS-- SKKKKZZ
SORRY. BUT THAT'S QUITE ENOUGH OF THAT.
WHAT? WHO IS THIS?
LORD JENNIX, TOTEM.
WHO?
WE'VE MET. I...ATE YOUR MONKEY.
I THOUGHT YOU'D LIKE TO KNOW, I CAN HEAR EVERYTHING YOU'VE BEEN SAYING.

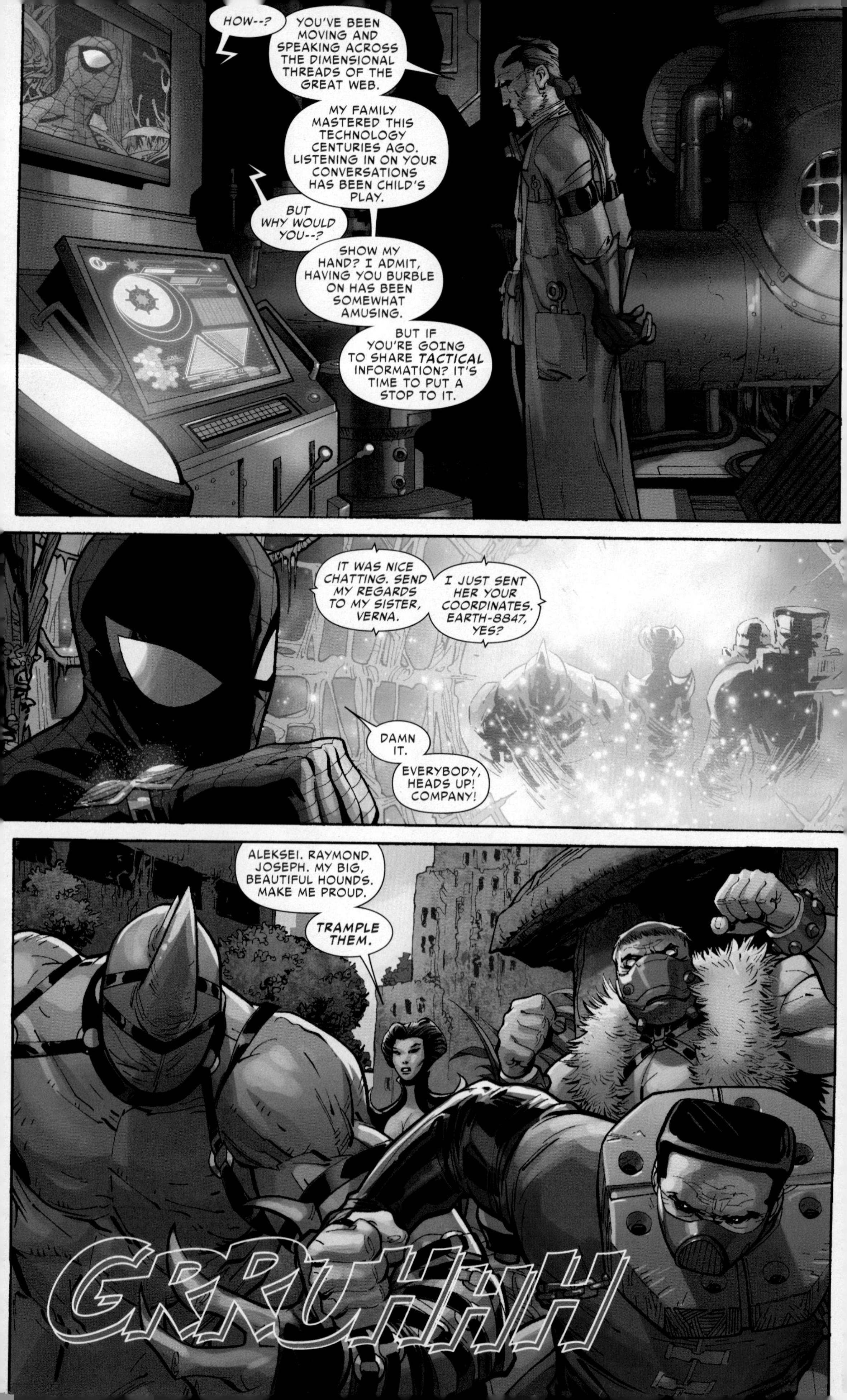
HOW--?
YOU'VE BEEN MOVING AND SPEAKING ACROSS THE DIMENSIONAL THREADS OF THE GREAT WEB.
MY FAMILY MASTERED THIS TECHNOLOGY CENTURIES AGO. LISTENING IN ON YOUR CONVERSATIONS HAS BEEN CHILD'S PLAY.
BUT WHY WOULD YOU--?
SHOW MY HAND? I ADMIT, HAVING YOU BURBLE ON HAS BEEN SOMEWHAT AMUSING.
BUT IF YOU'RE GOING TO SHARE *TACTICAL* INFORMATION? IT'S TIME TO PUT A STOP TO IT.
IT WAS NICE CHATTING. SEND MY REGARDS TO MY SISTER, VERNA.
I JUST SENT HER YOUR COORDINATES. EARTH-8847, YES?
DAMN IT.
EVERYBODY, HEADS UP! COMPANY!
ALEKSEI. RAYMOND. JOSEPH. MY BIG, BEAUTIFUL HOUNDS. MAKE ME PROUD.
TRAMPLE THEM.
GRUHHH

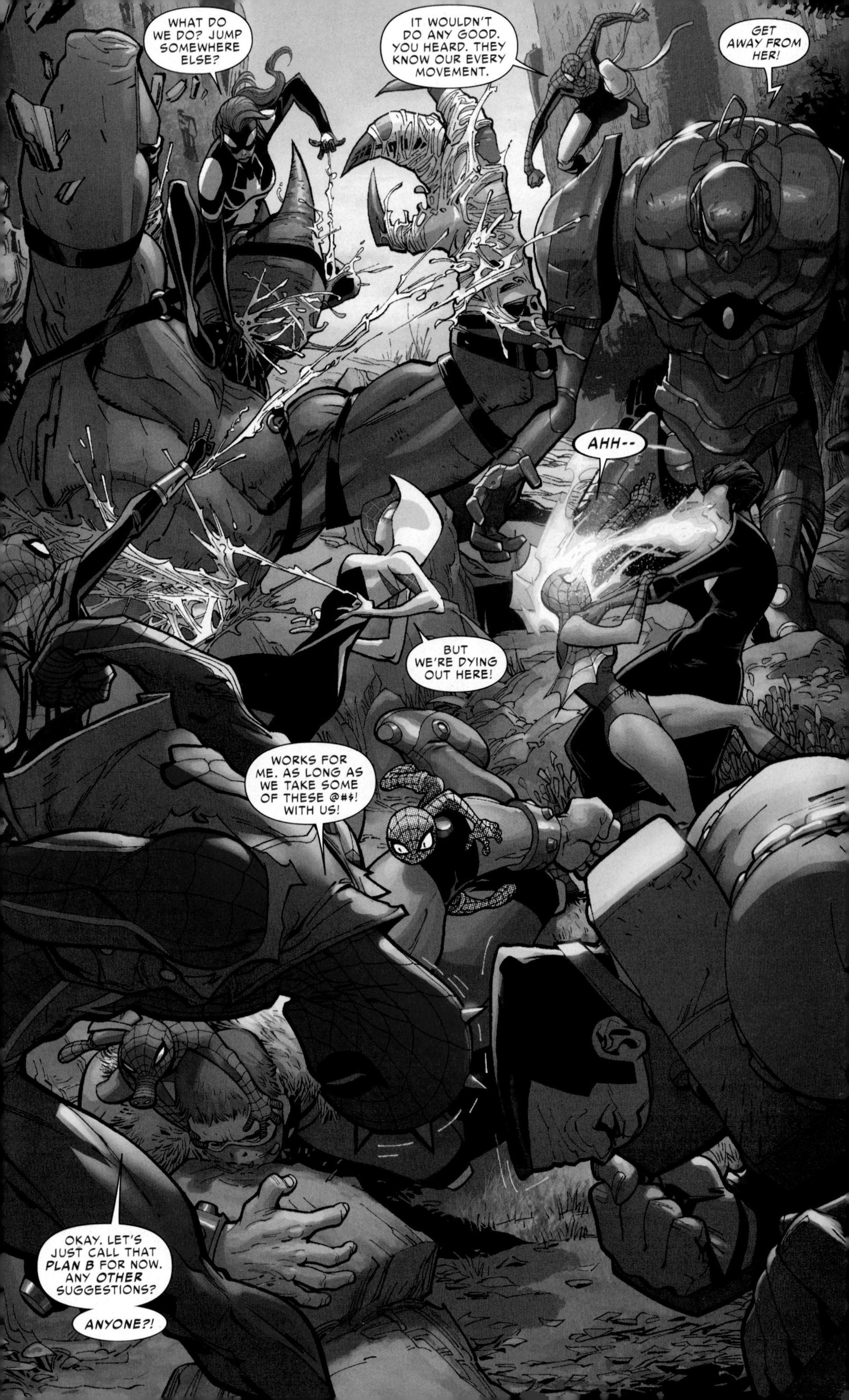
WHAT DO WE DO? JUMP SOMEWHERE ELSE?
IT WOULDN'T DO ANY GOOD. YOU HEARD. THEY KNOW OUR EVERY MOVEMENT.
GET AWAY FROM HER!
AHH--
BUT WE'RE DYING OUT HERE!
WORKS FOR ME. AS LONG AS WE TAKE SOME OF THESE @#$! WITH US!
OKAY. LET'S JUST CALL THAT *PLAN B* FOR NOW. ANY *OTHER* SUGGESTIONS?
ANYONE?!

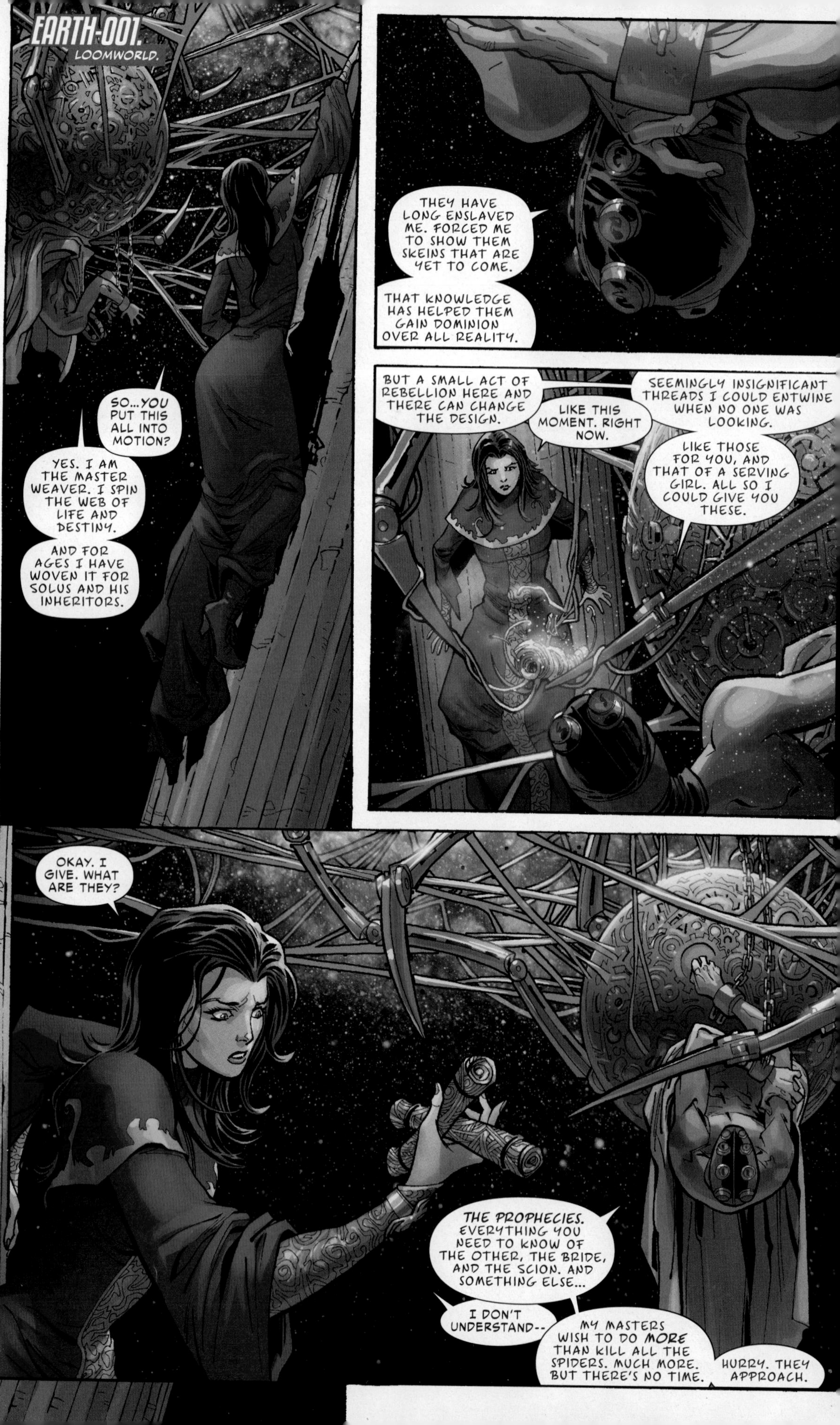
EARTH-001.
LOOMWORLD.
THEY HAVE LONG ENSLAVED ME. FORCED ME TO SHOW THEM SKEINS THAT ARE YET TO COME.
THAT KNOWLEDGE HAS HELPED THEM GAIN DOMINION OVER ALL REALITY.
SO...YOU PUT THIS ALL INTO MOTION?
YES. I AM THE MASTER WEAVER. I SPIN THE WEB OF LIFE AND DESTINY.
AND FOR AGES I HAVE WOVEN IT FOR SOLUS AND HIS INHERITORS.
BUT A SMALL ACT OF REBELLION HERE AND THERE CAN CHANGE THE DESIGN.
SEEMINGLY INSIGNIFICANT THREADS I COULD ENTWINE WHEN NO ONE WAS LOOKING.
LIKE THIS MOMENT. RIGHT NOW.
LIKE THOSE FOR YOU, AND THAT OF A SERVING GIRL. ALL SO I COULD GIVE YOU THESE.
OKAY. I GIVE. WHAT ARE THEY?
THE PROPHECIES. EVERYTHING YOU NEED TO KNOW OF THE OTHER, THE BRIDE, AND THE SCION. AND SOMETHING ELSE...
I DON'T UNDERSTAND--
MY MASTERS WISH TO DO MORE THAN KILL ALL THE SPIDERS. MUCH MORE. BUT THERE'S NO TIME.
HURRY. THEY APPROACH.

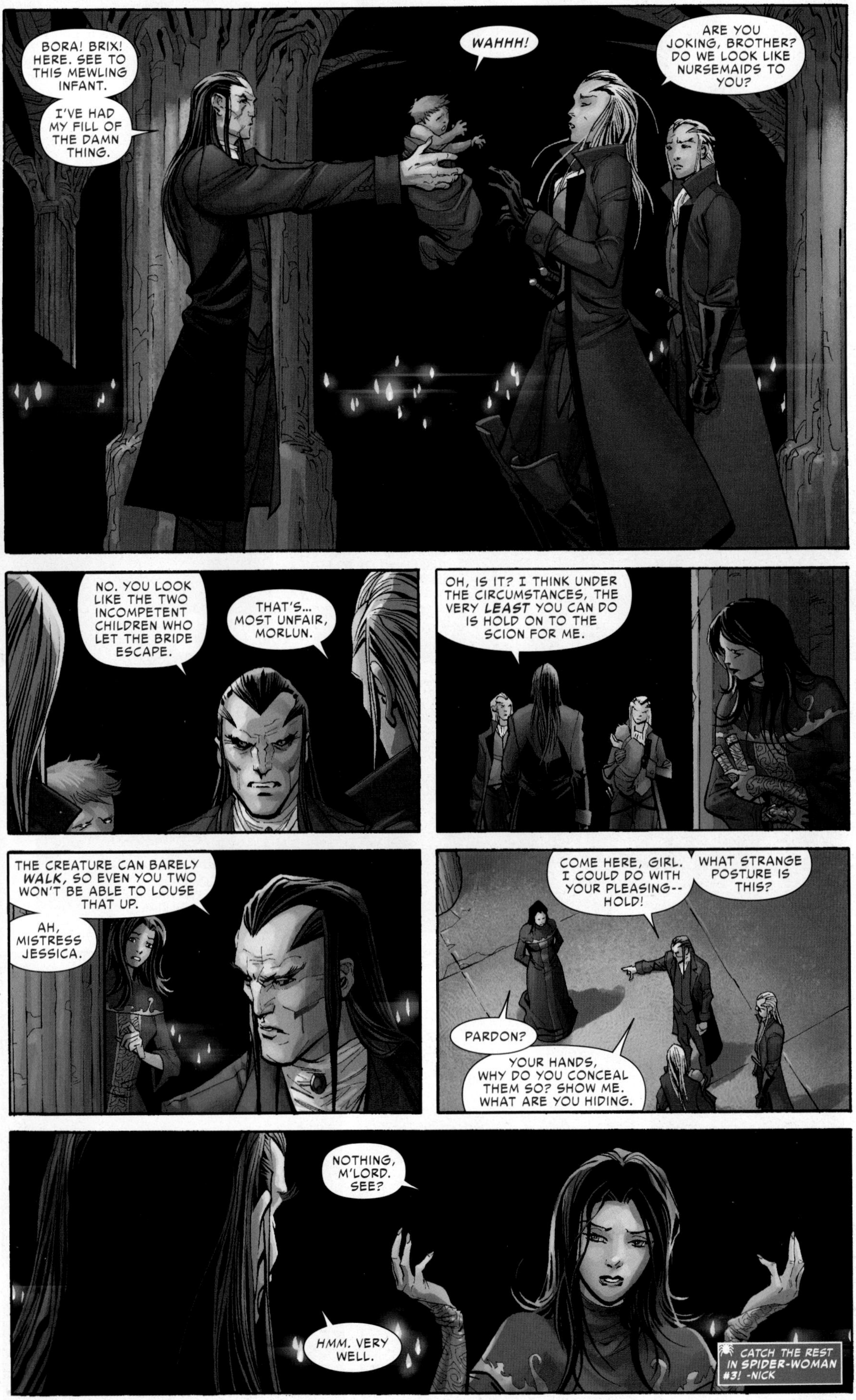
BORA! BRIX! HERE. SEE TO THIS MEWLING INFANT.
I'VE HAD MY FILL OF THE DAMN THING.
WAHHH!
ARE YOU JOKING, BROTHER? DO WE LOOK LIKE NURSEMAIDS TO YOU?
NO. YOU LOOK LIKE THE TWO INCOMPETENT CHILDREN WHO LET THE BRIDE ESCAPE.
THAT'S... MOST UNFAIR, MORLUN.
OH, IS IT? I THINK UNDER THE CIRCUMSTANCES, THE VERY LEAST YOU CAN DO IS HOLD ON TO THE SCION FOR ME.
THE CREATURE CAN BARELY WALK, SO EVEN YOU TWO WON'T BE ABLE TO LOUSE THAT UP.
AH, MISTRESS JESSICA.
COME HERE, GIRL. I COULD DO WITH YOUR PLEASING--HOLD!
WHAT STRANGE POSTURE IS THIS?
PARDON?
YOUR HANDS, WHY DO YOU CONCEAL THEM SO? SHOW ME. WHAT ARE YOU HIDING.
NOTHING, M'LORD. SEE?
HMM. VERY WELL.
CATCH THE REST IN SPIDER-WOMAN #3! -NICK

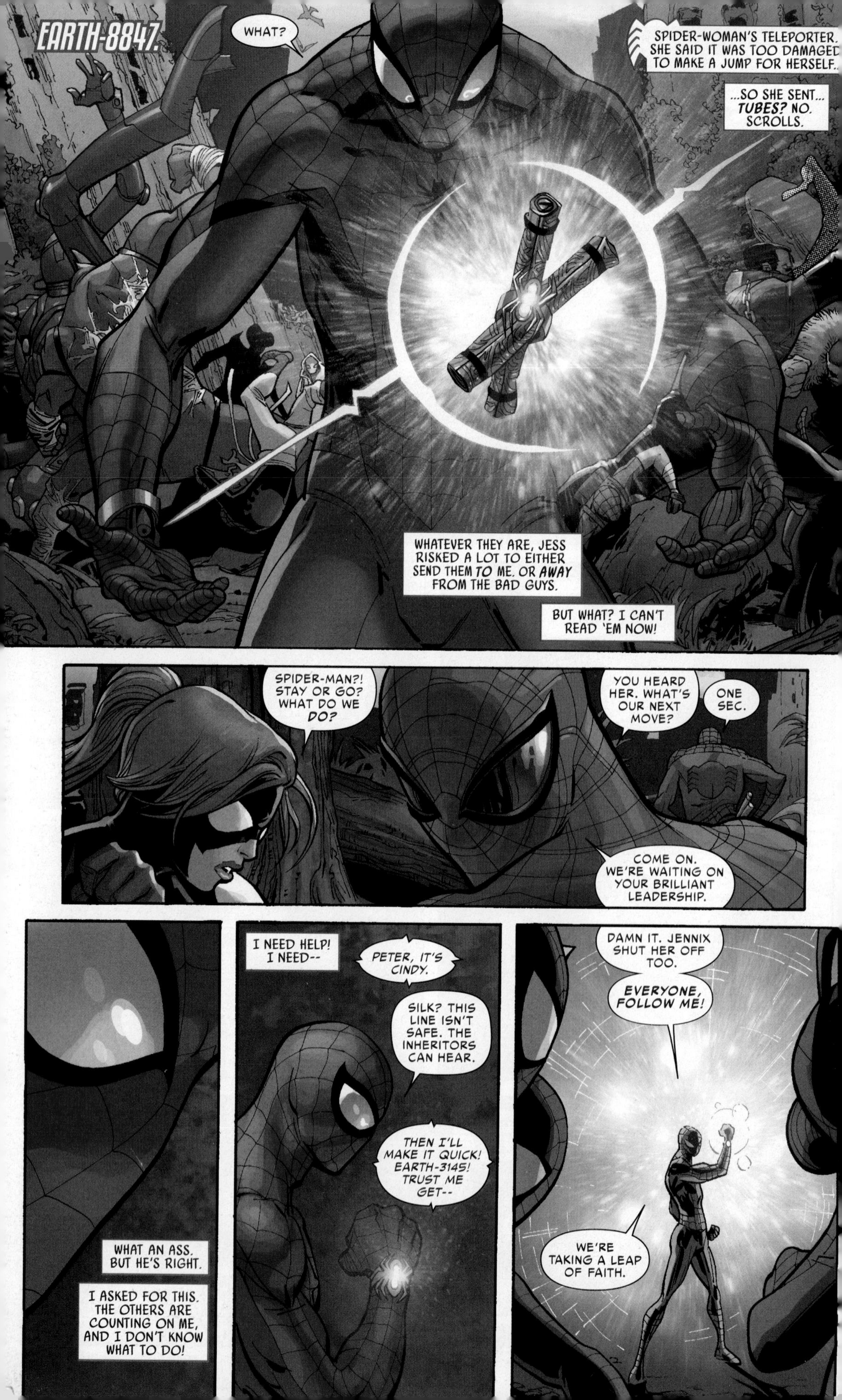
EARTH-8847.
WHAT?
SPIDER-WOMAN'S TELEPORTER. SHE SAID IT WAS TOO DAMAGED TO MAKE A JUMP FOR HERSELF.
...SO SHE SENT... TUBES? NO. SCROLLS.
WHATEVER THEY ARE, JESS RISKED A LOT TO EITHER SEND THEM TO ME. OR AWAY FROM THE BAD GUYS.
BUT WHAT? I CAN'T READ 'EM NOW!
SPIDER-MAN?! STAY OR GO? WHAT DO WE DO?
YOU HEARD HER. WHAT'S OUR NEXT MOVE?
ONE SEC.
COME ON. WE'RE WAITING ON YOUR BRILLIANT LEADERSHIP.
WHAT AN ASS. BUT HE'S RIGHT.
I ASKED FOR THIS. THE OTHERS ARE COUNTING ON ME, AND I DON'T KNOW WHAT TO DO!
I NEED HELP! I NEED--
PETER, IT'S CINDY.
SILK? THIS LINE ISN'T SAFE. THE INHERITORS CAN HEAR.
THEN I'LL MAKE IT QUICK! EARTH-3145! TRUST ME GET--
DAMN IT. JENNIX SHUT HER OFF TOO.
EVERYONE, FOLLOW ME!
WE'RE TAKING A LEAP OF FAITH.

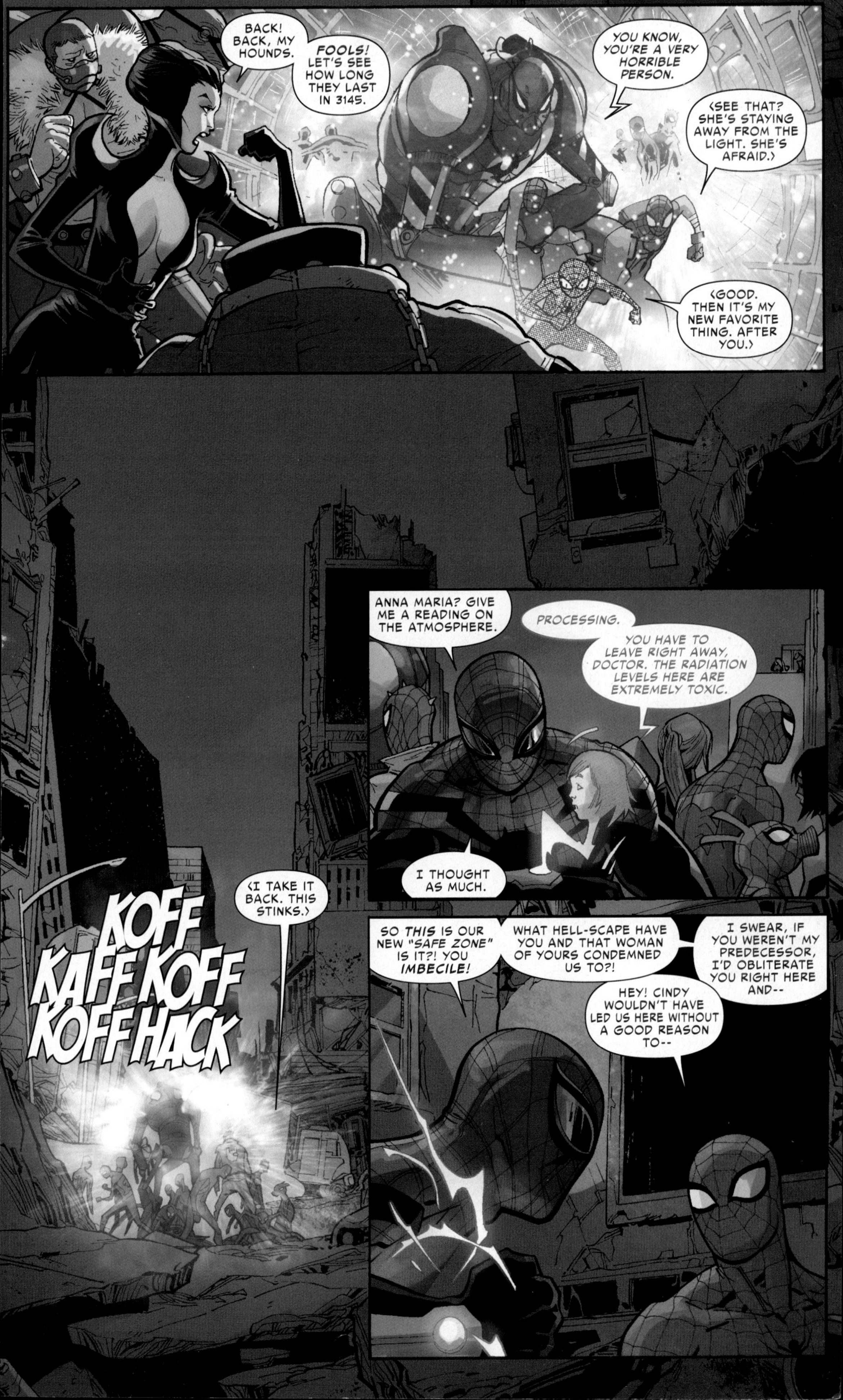
BACK! BACK, MY HOUNDS.
FOOLS! LET'S SEE HOW LONG THEY LAST IN 3145.
YOU KNOW, YOU'RE A VERY HORRIBLE PERSON.
‹SEE THAT? SHE'S STAYING AWAY FROM THE LIGHT. SHE'S AFRAID.›
‹GOOD. THEN IT'S MY NEW FAVORITE THING. AFTER YOU.›
KOFF KAFF KOFF KOFF HACK
‹I TAKE IT BACK. THIS STINKS.›
ANNA MARIA? GIVE ME A READING ON THE ATMOSPHERE.
PROCESSING.
YOU HAVE TO LEAVE RIGHT AWAY, DOCTOR. THE RADIATION LEVELS HERE ARE EXTREMELY TOXIC.
I THOUGHT AS MUCH.
SO THIS IS OUR NEW "SAFE ZONE" IS IT?! YOU IMBECILE!
WHAT HELL-SCAPE HAVE YOU AND THAT WOMAN OF YOURS CONDEMNED US TO?!
I SWEAR, IF YOU WEREN'T MY PREDECESSOR, I'D OBLITERATE YOU RIGHT HERE AND--
HEY! CINDY WOULDN'T HAVE LED US HERE WITHOUT A GOOD REASON TO--

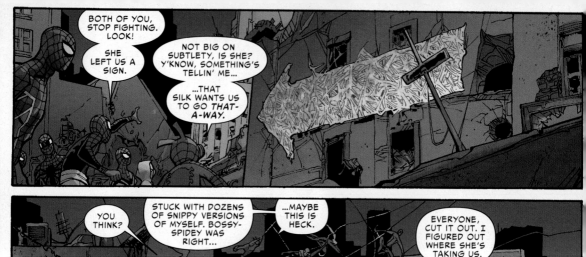

BOTH OF YOU, STOP FIGHTING. LOOK!

SHE LEFT US A SIGN.

NOT BIG ON SUBTLETY, IS SHE? Y'KNOW, SOMETHING'S TELLIN' ME...

...THAT SILK WANTS US TO GO THAT-A-WAY.

YOU THINK?

STUCK WITH DOZENS OF SNIPPY VERSIONS OF MYSELF. BOSSY-SPIDEY WAS RIGHT...

...MAYBE THIS IS HECK.

EVERYONE, CUT IT OUT. I FIGURED OUT WHERE SHE'S TAKING US.

SIMS TOWER.

AND IF IT'S ANYTHING LIKE THE SIMS TOWER FROM THE WORLD WHERE SILK AND I COME FROM...

A FALL-OUT SHELTER? THAT'S VERY CONVENIENT.

IT'S BETTER THAN THAT. EZEKIEL BUILT THESE TO HIDE US FROM THE INHERITORS.

AND IF THE CODE'S THE SAME IN EVERY DIMENSION...

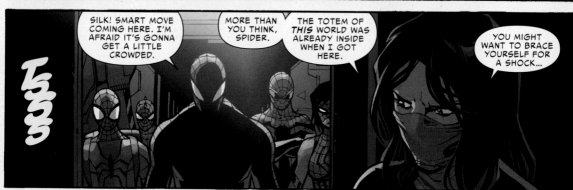

SILK! SMART MOVE COMING HERE. I'M AFRAID IT'S GONNA GET A LITTLE CROWDED.

MORE THAN YOU THINK, SPIDER.

THE TOTEM OF THIS WORLD WAS ALREADY INSIDE WHEN I GOT HERE.

YOU MIGHT WANT TO BRACE YOURSELF FOR A SHOCK...

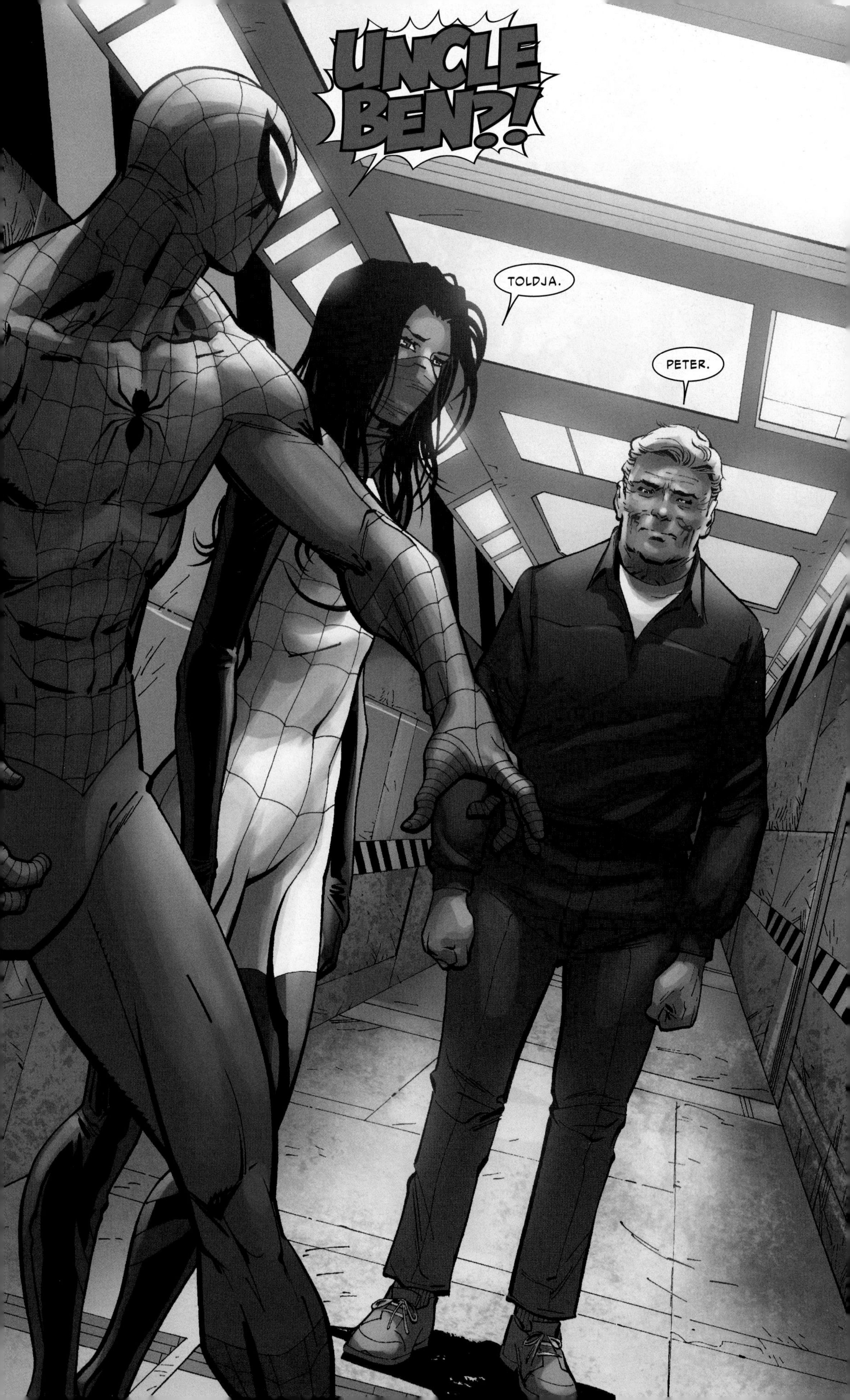
UNCLE BEN?!
TOLDJA.
PETER.

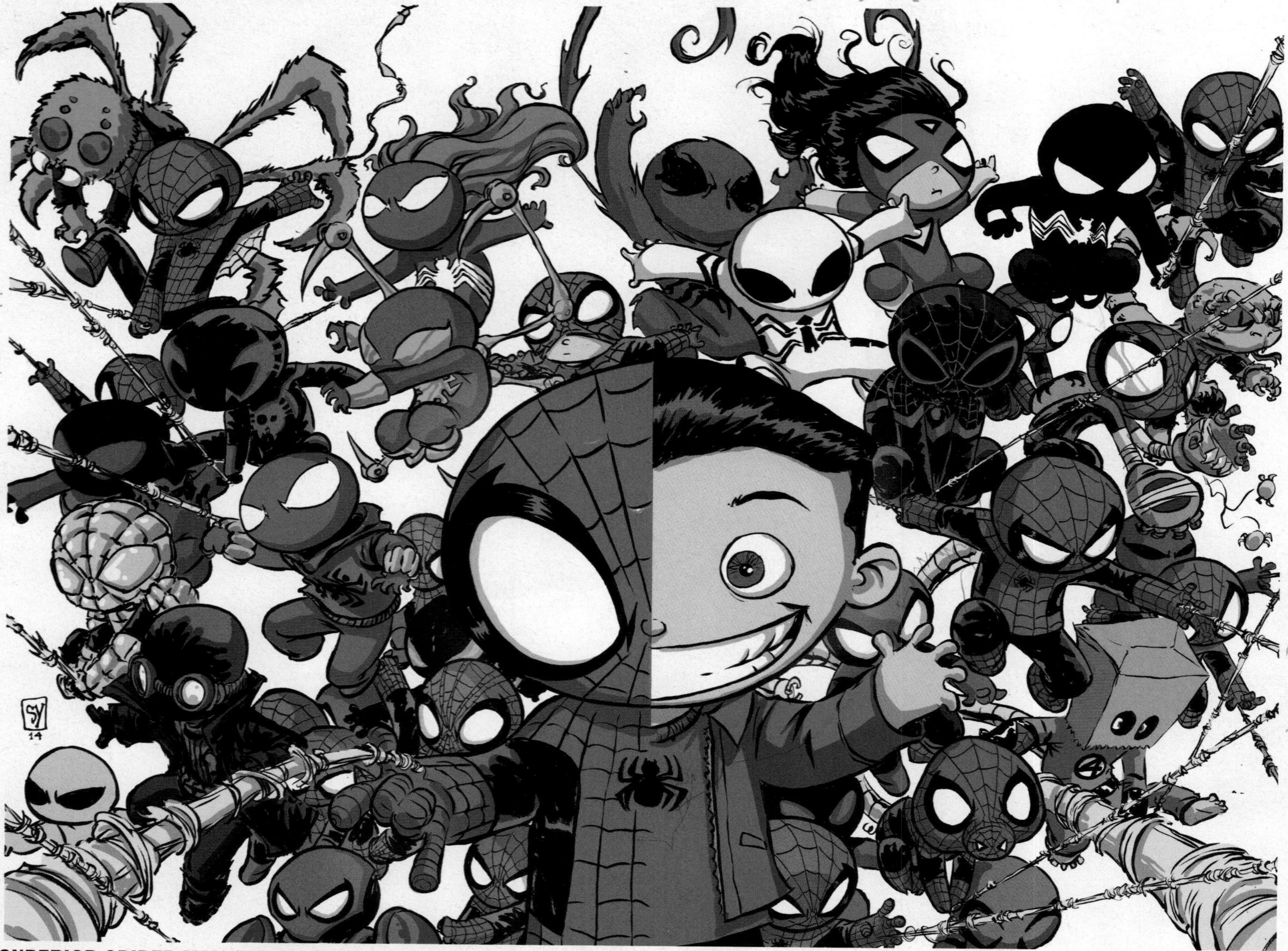
SY
14

SUPERIOR SPIDER-MAN #32 & AMAZING SPIDER-MAN #9 COMBINED VARIANTS
BY SKOTTIE YOUNG

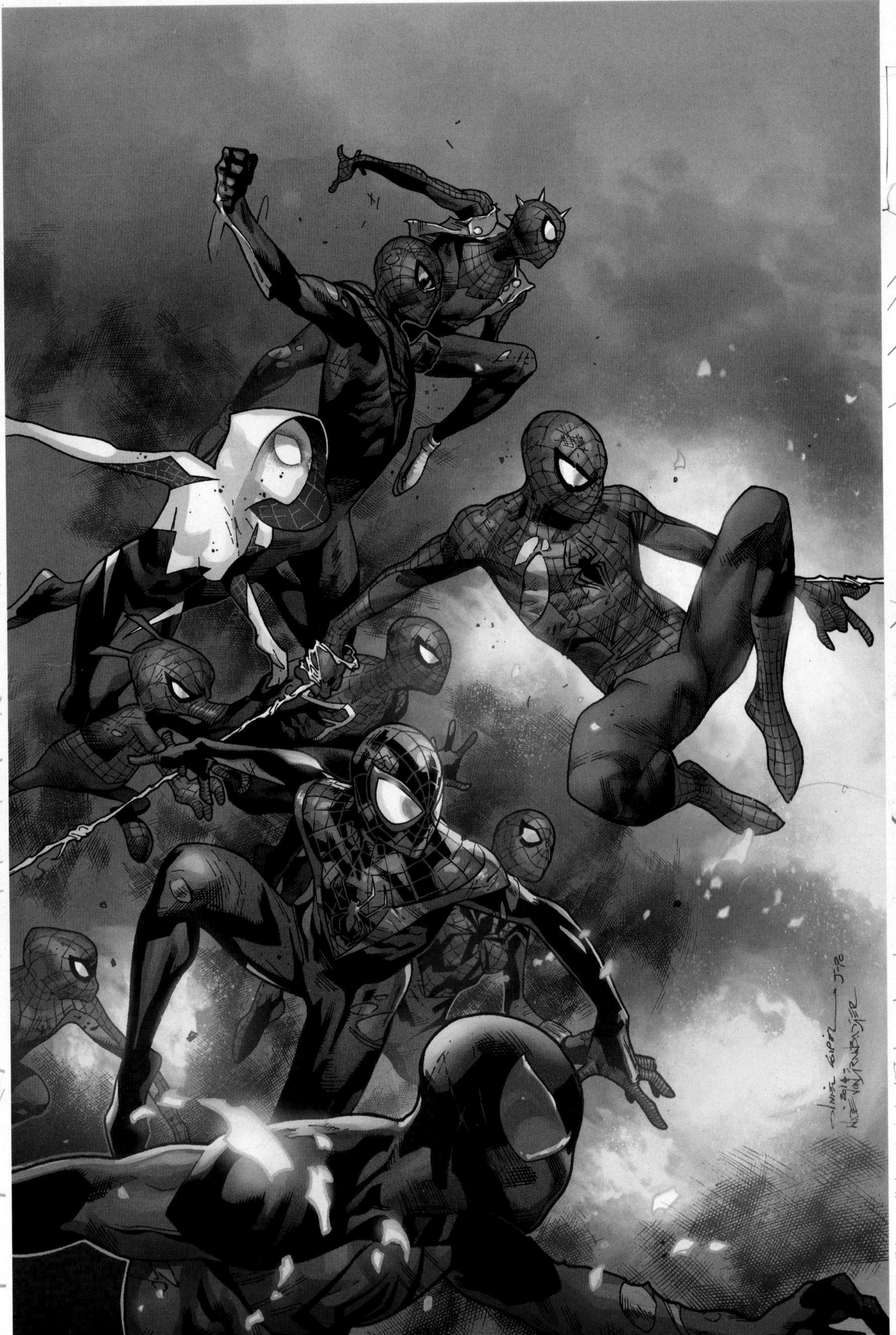

AMAZING SPIDER-MAN 13
SPIDER-VERSE, PART FIVE: SPIDER-MEN NO MORE

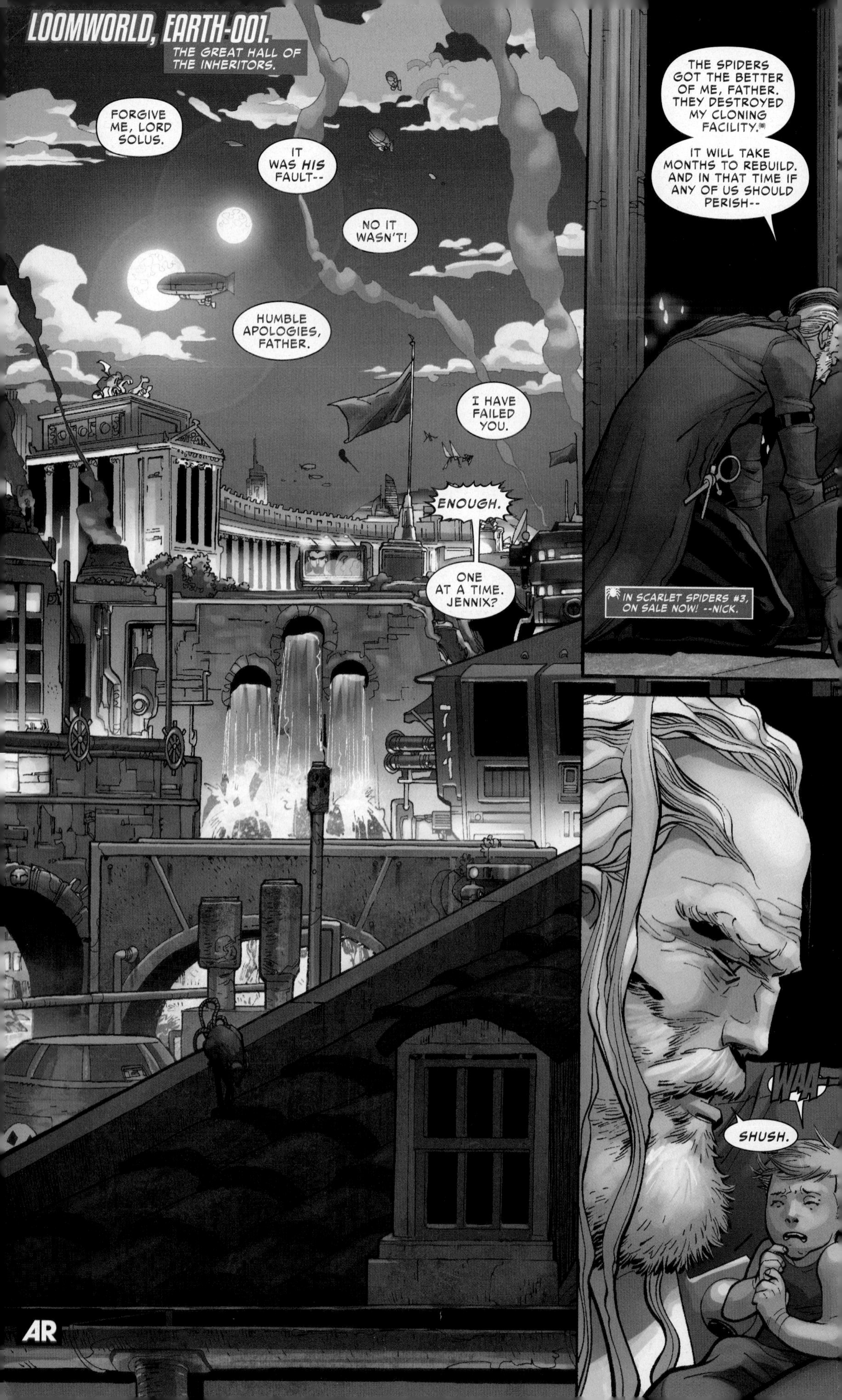
LOOMWORLD, EARTH-001.
THE GREAT HALL OF THE INHERITORS.
FORGIVE ME, LORD SOLUS.
IT WAS HIS FAULT--
NO IT WASN'T!
HUMBLE APOLOGIES, FATHER.
I HAVE FAILED YOU.
ENOUGH.
ONE AT A TIME. JENNIX?
THE SPIDERS GOT THE BETTER OF ME, FATHER. THEY DESTROYED MY CLONING FACILITY.*
IT WILL TAKE MONTHS TO REBUILD. AND IN THAT TIME IF ANY OF US SHOULD PERISH--
*IN SCARLET SPIDERS #3, ON SALE NOW! --NICK.
WAA
SHUSH.
AR

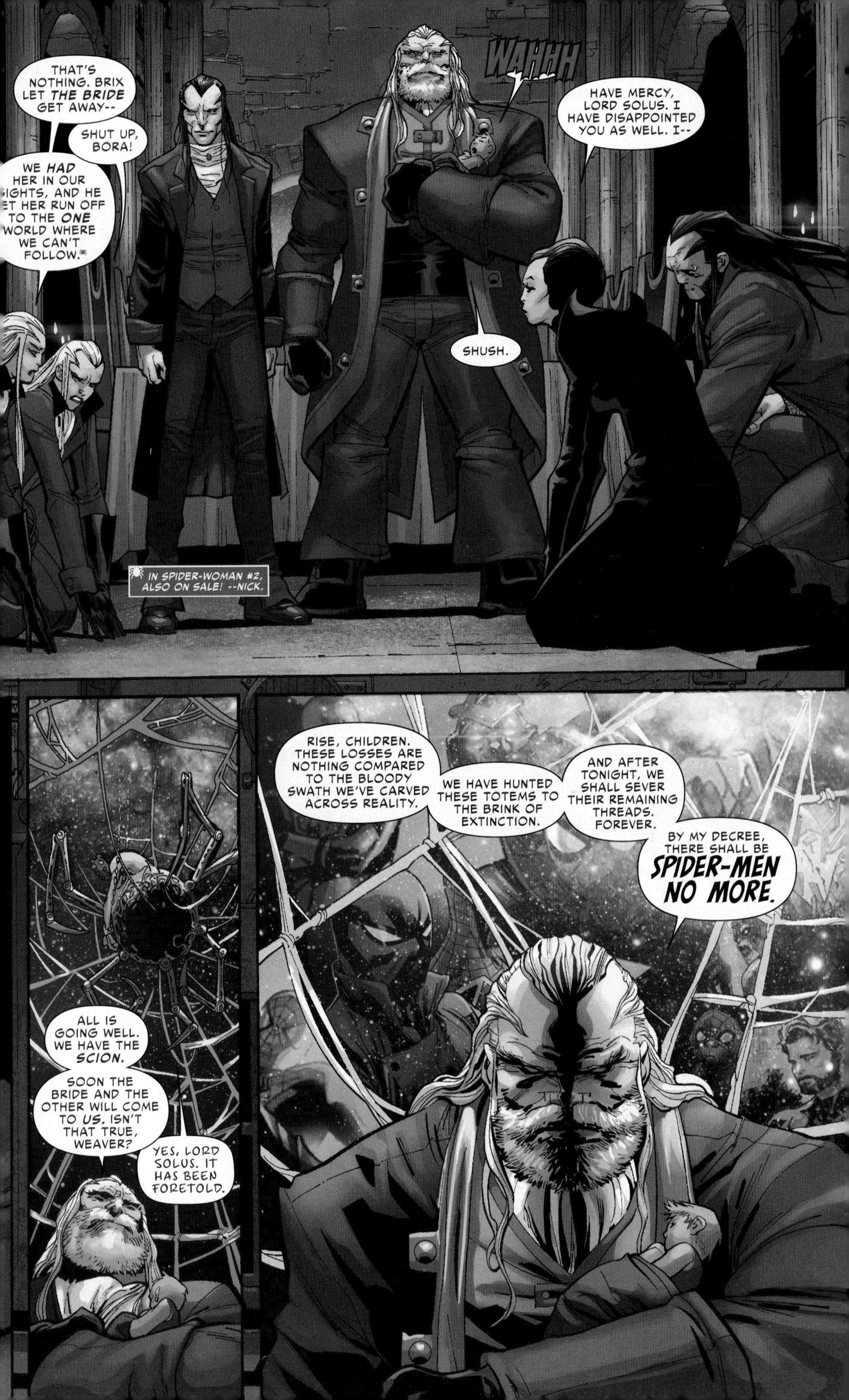
WAHHH
THAT'S NOTHING. BRIX LET THE BRIDE GET AWAY--
SHUT UP, BORA!
WE HAD HER IN OUR SIGHTS, AND HE LET HER RUN OFF TO THE ONE WORLD WHERE WE CAN'T FOLLOW.*
HAVE MERCY, LORD SOLUS. I HAVE DISAPPOINTED YOU AS WELL. I--
SHUSH.
*IN SPIDER-WOMAN #2, ALSO ON SALE! --NICK.
ALL IS GOING WELL. WE HAVE THE SCION.
SOON THE BRIDE AND THE OTHER WILL COME TO US. ISN'T THAT TRUE, WEAVER?
YES, LORD SOLUS. IT HAS BEEN FORETOLD.
RISE, CHILDREN. THESE LOSSES ARE NOTHING COMPARED TO THE BLOODY SWATH WE'VE CARVED ACROSS REALITY.
WE HAVE HUNTED THESE TOTEMS TO THE BRINK OF EXTINCTION.
AND AFTER TONIGHT, WE SHALL SEVER THEIR REMAINING THREADS. FOREVER.
BY MY DECREE, THERE SHALL BE SPIDER-MEN NO MORE.

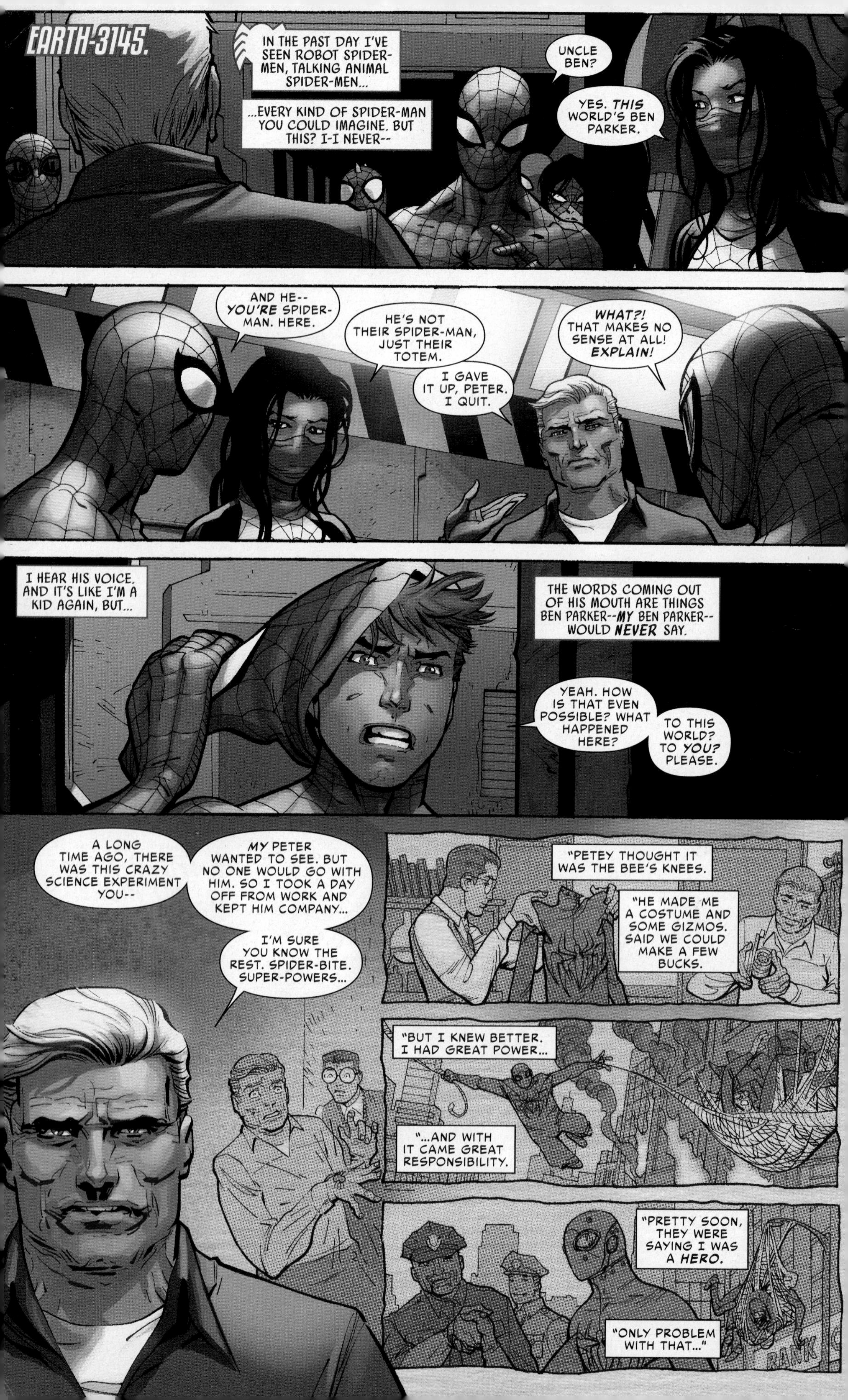
EARTH-3145.
IN THE PAST DAY I'VE SEEN ROBOT SPIDER-MEN, TALKING ANIMAL SPIDER-MEN...
...EVERY KIND OF SPIDER-MAN YOU COULD IMAGINE. BUT THIS? I-I NEVER--
UNCLE BEN?
YES. THIS WORLD'S BEN PARKER.
AND HE-- YOU'RE SPIDER-MAN. HERE.
HE'S NOT THEIR SPIDER-MAN, JUST THEIR TOTEM.
I GAVE IT UP, PETER. I QUIT.
WHAT?! THAT MAKES NO SENSE AT ALL! EXPLAIN!
I HEAR HIS VOICE. AND IT'S LIKE I'M A KID AGAIN, BUT...
THE WORDS COMING OUT OF HIS MOUTH ARE THINGS BEN PARKER--MY BEN PARKER--WOULD NEVER SAY.
YEAH. HOW IS THAT EVEN POSSIBLE? WHAT HAPPENED HERE?
TO THIS WORLD? TO YOU? PLEASE.
A LONG TIME AGO, THERE WAS THIS CRAZY SCIENCE EXPERIMENT YOU--
MY PETER WANTED TO SEE. BUT NO ONE WOULD GO WITH HIM. SO I TOOK A DAY OFF FROM WORK AND KEPT HIM COMPANY...
I'M SURE YOU KNOW THE REST. SPIDER-BITE. SUPER-POWERS...
"PETEY THOUGHT IT WAS THE BEE'S KNEES.
"HE MADE ME A COSTUME AND SOME GIZMOS. SAID WE COULD MAKE A FEW BUCKS.
"BUT I KNEW BETTER. I HAD GREAT POWER...
"...AND WITH IT CAME GREAT RESPONSIBILITY.
"PRETTY SOON, THEY WERE SAYING I WAS A HERO.
"ONLY PROBLEM WITH THAT..."

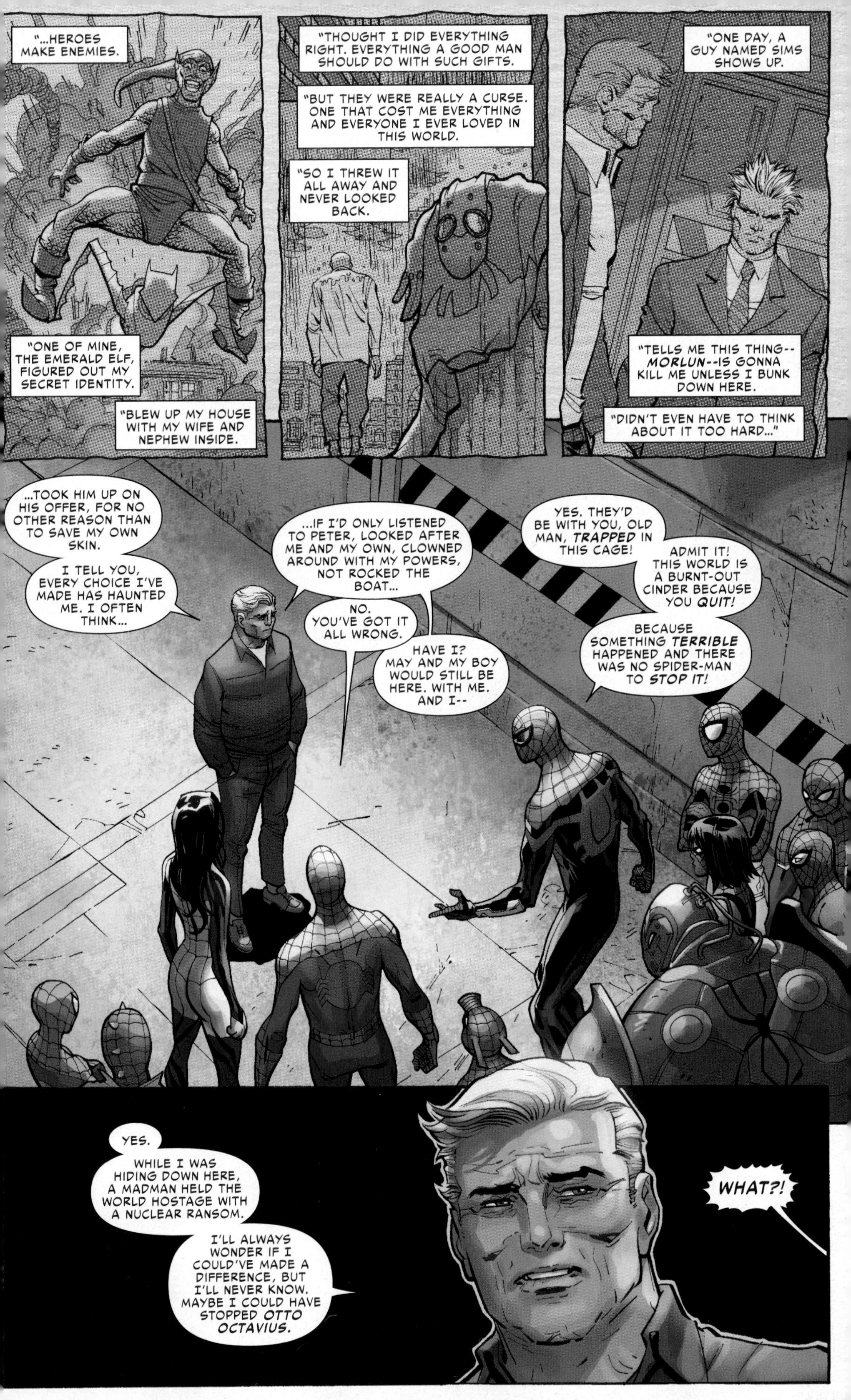
"...HEROES MAKE ENEMIES.
"ONE OF MINE, THE EMERALD ELF, FIGURED OUT MY SECRET IDENTITY.
"BLEW UP MY HOUSE WITH MY WIFE AND NEPHEW INSIDE.
"THOUGHT I DID EVERYTHING RIGHT. EVERYTHING A GOOD MAN SHOULD DO WITH SUCH GIFTS.
"BUT THEY WERE REALLY A CURSE. ONE THAT COST ME EVERYTHING AND EVERYONE I EVER LOVED IN THIS WORLD.
"SO I THREW IT ALL AWAY AND NEVER LOOKED BACK.
"ONE DAY, A GUY NAMED SIMS SHOWS UP.
"TELLS ME THIS THING-- MORLUN--IS GONNA KILL ME UNLESS I BUNK DOWN HERE.
"DIDN'T EVEN HAVE TO THINK ABOUT IT TOO HARD..."
...TOOK HIM UP ON HIS OFFER, FOR NO OTHER REASON THAN TO SAVE MY OWN SKIN.
I TELL YOU, EVERY CHOICE I'VE MADE HAS HAUNTED ME. I OFTEN THINK...
...IF I'D ONLY LISTENED TO PETER, LOOKED AFTER ME AND MY OWN, CLOWNED AROUND WITH MY POWERS, NOT ROCKED THE BOAT...
NO. YOU'VE GOT IT ALL WRONG.
HAVE I? MAY AND MY BOY WOULD STILL BE HERE. WITH ME. AND I--
YES. THEY'D BE WITH YOU, OLD MAN, TRAPPED IN THIS CAGE!
ADMIT IT! THIS WORLD IS A BURNT-OUT CINDER BECAUSE YOU QUIT!
BECAUSE SOMETHING TERRIBLE HAPPENED AND THERE WAS NO SPIDER-MAN TO STOP IT!
YES.
WHILE I WAS HIDING DOWN HERE, A MADMAN HELD THE WORLD HOSTAGE WITH A NUCLEAR RANSOM.
I'LL ALWAYS WONDER IF I COULD'VE MADE A DIFFERENCE, BUT I'LL NEVER KNOW. MAYBE I COULD HAVE STOPPED OTTO OCTAVIUS.
WHAT?!

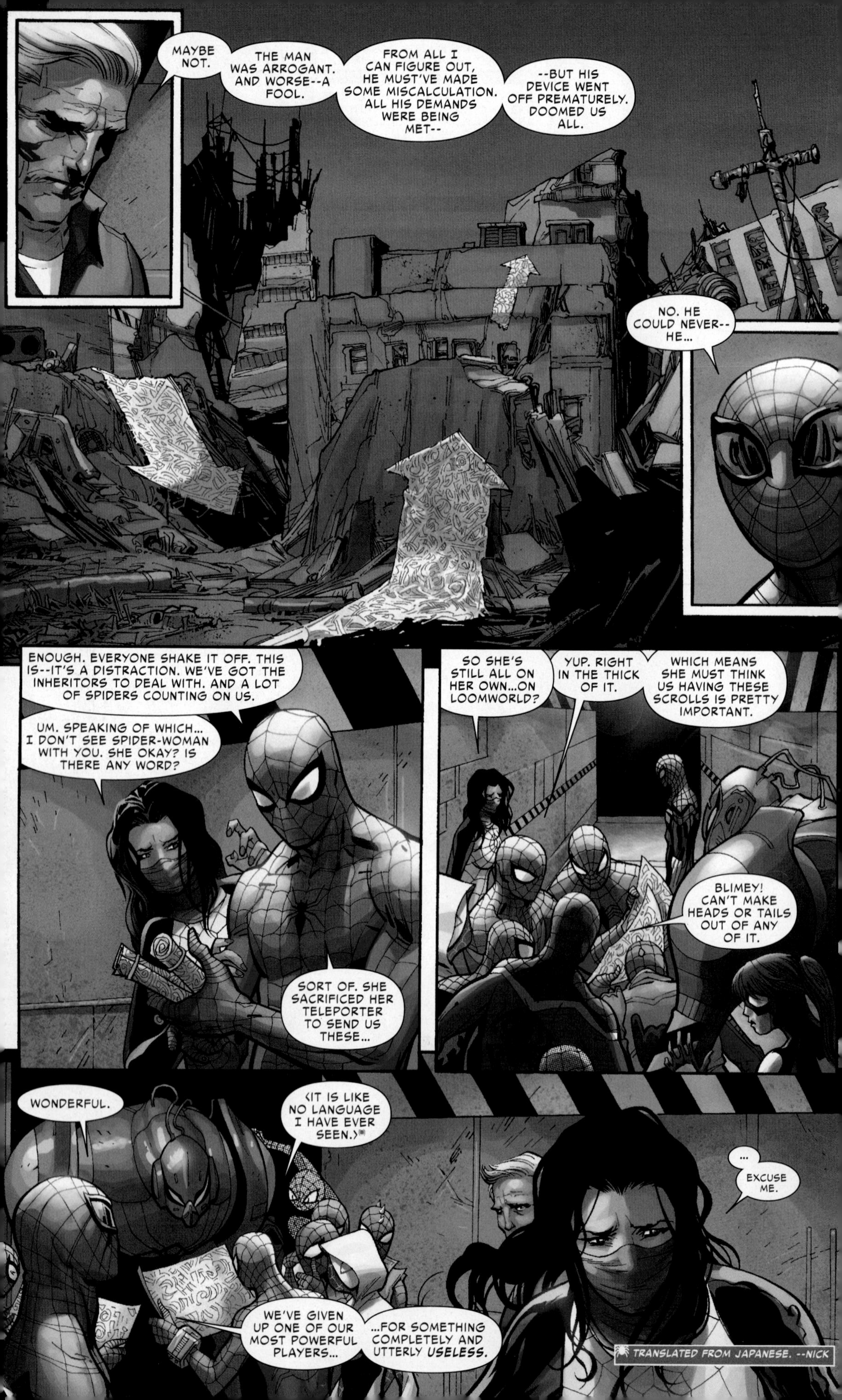
MAYBE NOT.
THE MAN WAS ARROGANT. AND WORSE--A FOOL.
FROM ALL I CAN FIGURE OUT, HE MUST'VE MADE SOME MISCALCULATION. ALL HIS DEMANDS WERE BEING MET--
--BUT HIS DEVICE WENT OFF PREMATURELY. DOOMED US ALL.
NO. HE COULD NEVER-- HE...
ENOUGH. EVERYONE SHAKE IT OFF. THIS IS--IT'S A DISTRACTION. WE'VE GOT THE INHERITORS TO DEAL WITH. AND A LOT OF SPIDERS COUNTING ON US.
UM. SPEAKING OF WHICH... I DON'T SEE SPIDER-WOMAN WITH YOU. SHE OKAY? IS THERE ANY WORD?
SORT OF. SHE SACRIFICED HER TELEPORTER TO SEND US THESE...
SO SHE'S STILL ALL ON HER OWN...ON LOOMWORLD?
YUP. RIGHT IN THE THICK OF IT.
WHICH MEANS SHE MUST THINK US HAVING THESE SCROLLS IS PRETTY IMPORTANT.
BLIMEY! CAN'T MAKE HEADS OR TAILS OUT OF ANY OF IT.
WONDERFUL.
<IT IS LIKE NO LANGUAGE I HAVE EVER SEEN.>*
WE'VE GIVEN UP ONE OF OUR MOST POWERFUL PLAYERS...
...FOR SOMETHING COMPLETELY AND UTTERLY *USELESS.*
... EXCUSE ME.
TRANSLATED FROM JAPANESE. --NICK

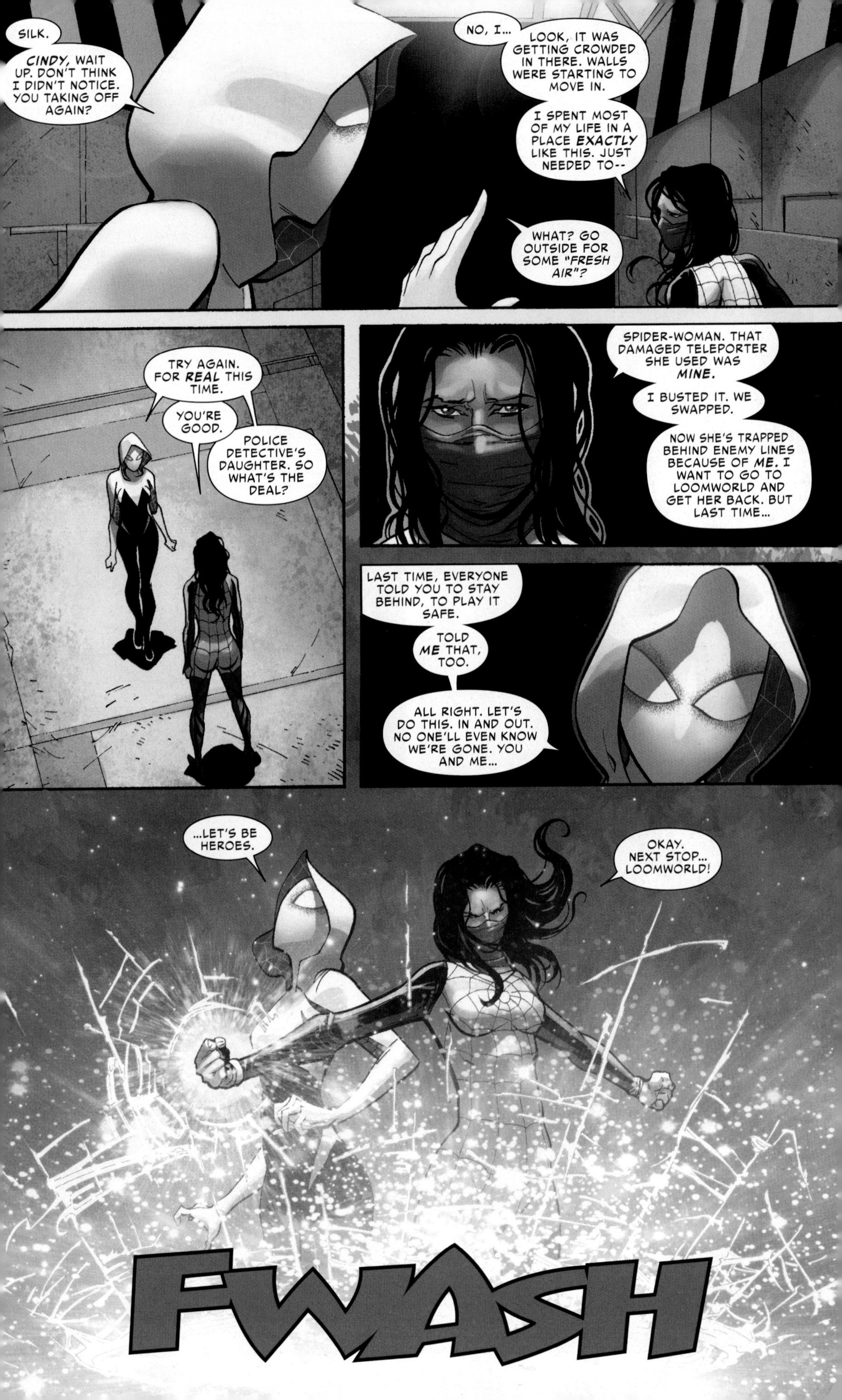

SILK.
CINDY, WAIT UP. DON'T THINK I DIDN'T NOTICE. YOU TAKING OFF AGAIN?
NO, I...
LOOK, IT WAS GETTING CROWDED IN THERE. WALLS WERE STARTING TO MOVE IN.
I SPENT MOST OF MY LIFE IN A PLACE *EXACTLY* LIKE THIS. JUST NEEDED TO--
WHAT? GO OUTSIDE FOR SOME *"FRESH AIR"?*
TRY AGAIN. FOR *REAL* THIS TIME.
YOU'RE GOOD.
POLICE DETECTIVE'S DAUGHTER. SO WHAT'S THE DEAL?
SPIDER-WOMAN. THAT DAMAGED TELEPORTER SHE USED WAS *MINE.*
I BUSTED IT. WE SWAPPED.
NOW SHE'S TRAPPED BEHIND ENEMY LINES BECAUSE OF *ME.* I WANT TO GO TO LOOMWORLD AND GET HER BACK. BUT LAST TIME...
LAST TIME, EVERYONE TOLD YOU TO STAY BEHIND, TO PLAY IT SAFE.
TOLD *ME* THAT, TOO.
ALL RIGHT. LET'S DO THIS. IN AND OUT. NO ONE'LL EVEN KNOW WE'RE GONE. YOU AND ME...
...LET'S BE HEROES.
OKAY. NEXT STOP... LOOMWORLD!
FWASH

HULLO. YOU ALL RIGHT?

OH. UM. NO. NOT REALLY.

WITH ALL THE GOINGS ON, HAVEN'T HAD A CHANCE.

NAME'S BILLY. BILLY BRADDOCK. SPIDER-UK. AND YOU ARE?

PAVITR PRABHAKAR. THE SPIDER-MAN OF MUMBAI.

I GUESS MY PROBLEM IS... HIM. PETER PARKER.

INDIA.

YES.

WHY SO DOWN, PAVITR? OUTSIDE OF THE FEARFUL ODDS AND MOST CERTAIN DOOM.

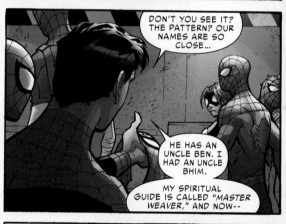

DON'T YOU SEE IT? THE PATTERN? OUR NAMES ARE SO CLOSE...

HE HAS AN UNCLE BEN. I HAD AN UNCLE BHIM.

MY SPIRITUAL GUIDE IS CALLED "MASTER WEAVER," AND NOW--

THERE ARE TOO MANY SIMILARITIES. I CANNOT ESCAPE IT. THAT FEELING...

...THAT HE IS THE REAL SPIDER-MAN. AND I AM SOME SORT OF ECHO. OR STRANGE REFLECTION.

AND EXPENDABLE.

I DON'T BELIEVE IT. NOT FOR A SECOND.

BACK HOME, I'M A MEMBER OF THE CAPTAIN BRITAIN CORPS. THERE ARE THOUSANDS OF US.

AND WHAT I'VE LEARNED IS THAT EACH MEMBER, FROM EACH WORLD, IS UNIQUE IN THEIR OWN WAY.

PAVITR, YOU ARE SPIDER-MAN. YOU'RE A HERO WHEREVER YOU ARE AND WHOEVER IS BY YOUR SIDE.

AND THAT OTHER FELLA? WHO'S TO SAY HE'S NOT A PALE REFLECTION OF YOU?

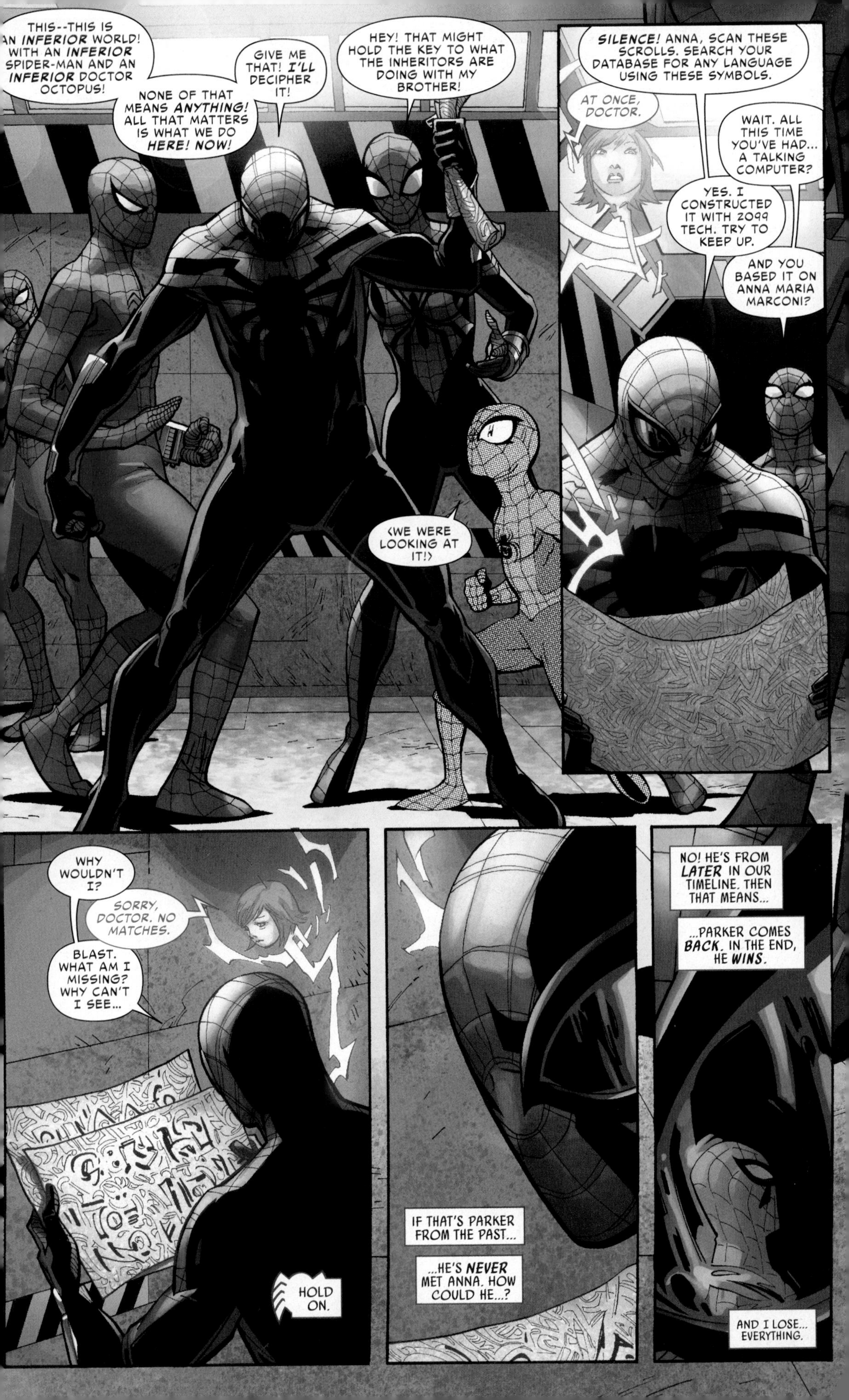
THIS--THIS IS AN INFERIOR WORLD! WITH AN INFERIOR SPIDER-MAN AND AN INFERIOR DOCTOR OCTOPUS!
NONE OF THAT MEANS ANYTHING! ALL THAT MATTERS IS WHAT WE DO HERE! NOW!
GIVE ME THAT! I'LL DECIPHER IT!
HEY! THAT MIGHT HOLD THE KEY TO WHAT THE INHERITORS ARE DOING WITH MY BROTHER!
<WE WERE LOOKING AT IT!>
SILENCE! ANNA, SCAN THESE SCROLLS. SEARCH YOUR DATABASE FOR ANY LANGUAGE USING THESE SYMBOLS.
AT ONCE, DOCTOR.
WAIT. ALL THIS TIME YOU'VE HAD... A TALKING COMPUTER?
YES. I CONSTRUCTED IT WITH 2099 TECH. TRY TO KEEP UP.
AND YOU BASED IT ON ANNA MARIA MARCONI?
WHY WOULDN'T I?
SORRY, DOCTOR. NO MATCHES.
BLAST. WHAT AM I MISSING? WHY CAN'T I SEE...
HOLD ON.
IF THAT'S PARKER FROM THE PAST...
...HE'S NEVER MET ANNA. HOW COULD HE...?
NO! HE'S FROM LATER IN OUR TIMELINE. THEN THAT MEANS...
...PARKER COMES BACK. IN THE END, HE WINS.
AND I LOSE... EVERYTHING.

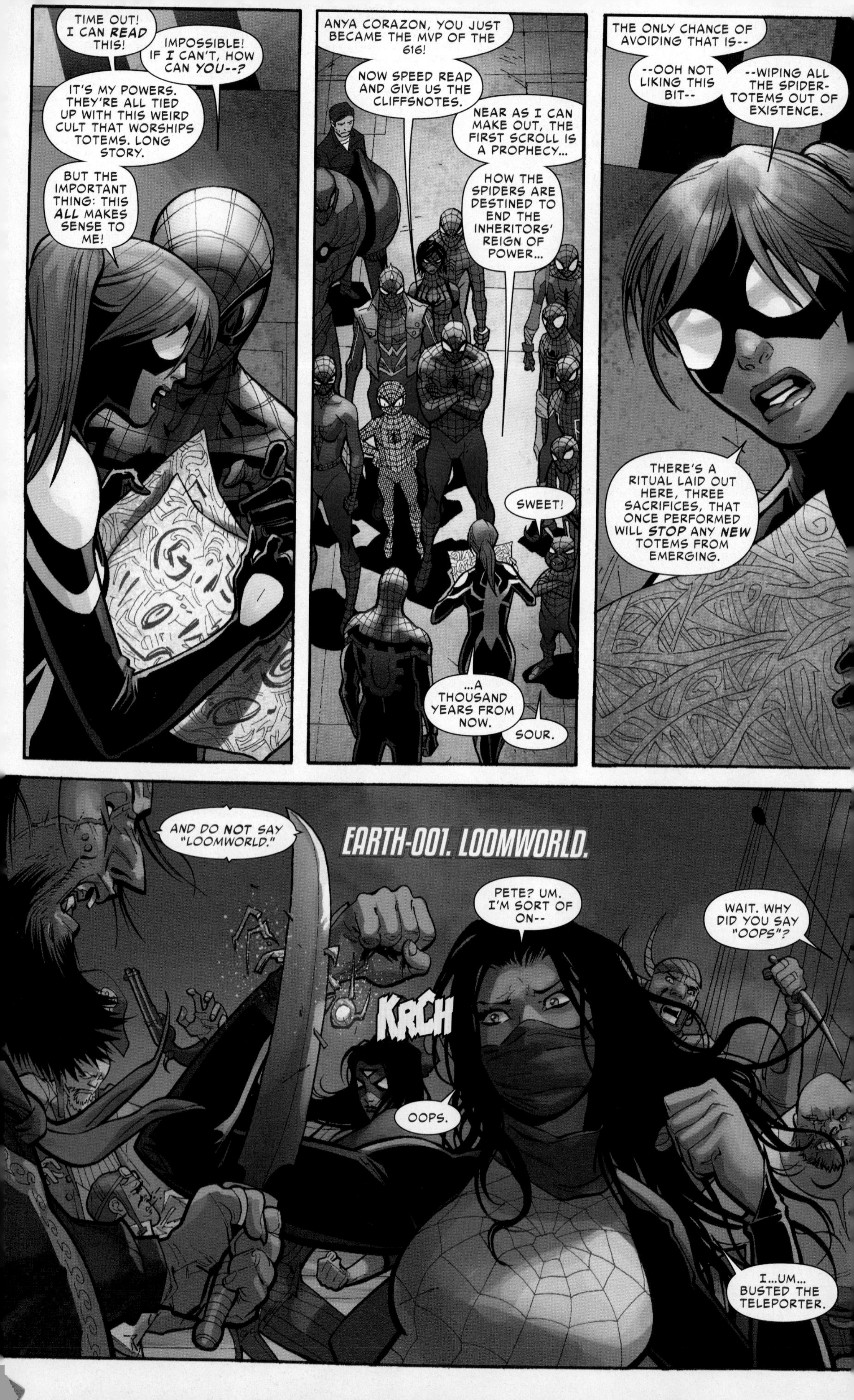
TIME OUT! I CAN READ THIS!
IMPOSSIBLE! IF I CAN'T, HOW CAN YOU--?
IT'S MY POWERS. THEY'RE ALL TIED UP WITH THIS WEIRD CULT THAT WORSHIPS TOTEMS. LONG STORY.
BUT THE IMPORTANT THING: THIS ALL MAKES SENSE TO ME!
ANYA CORAZON, YOU JUST BECAME THE MVP OF THE 616!
NOW SPEED READ AND GIVE US THE CLIFFSNOTES.
NEAR AS I CAN MAKE OUT, THE FIRST SCROLL IS A PROPHECY...
HOW THE SPIDERS ARE DESTINED TO END THE INHERITORS' REIGN OF POWER...
SWEET!
...A THOUSAND YEARS FROM NOW.
SOUR.
THE ONLY CHANCE OF AVOIDING THAT IS--
--OOH NOT LIKING THIS BIT--
--WIPING ALL THE SPIDER-TOTEMS OUT OF EXISTENCE.
THERE'S A RITUAL LAID OUT HERE, THREE SACRIFICES, THAT ONCE PERFORMED WILL STOP ANY NEW TOTEMS FROM EMERGING.
EARTH-001. LOOMWORLD.
AND DO NOT SAY "LOOMWORLD."
PETE? UM. I'M SORT OF ON--
WAIT. WHY DID YOU SAY "OOPS"?
KRCH
OOPS.
I...UM... BUSTED THE TELEPORTER.

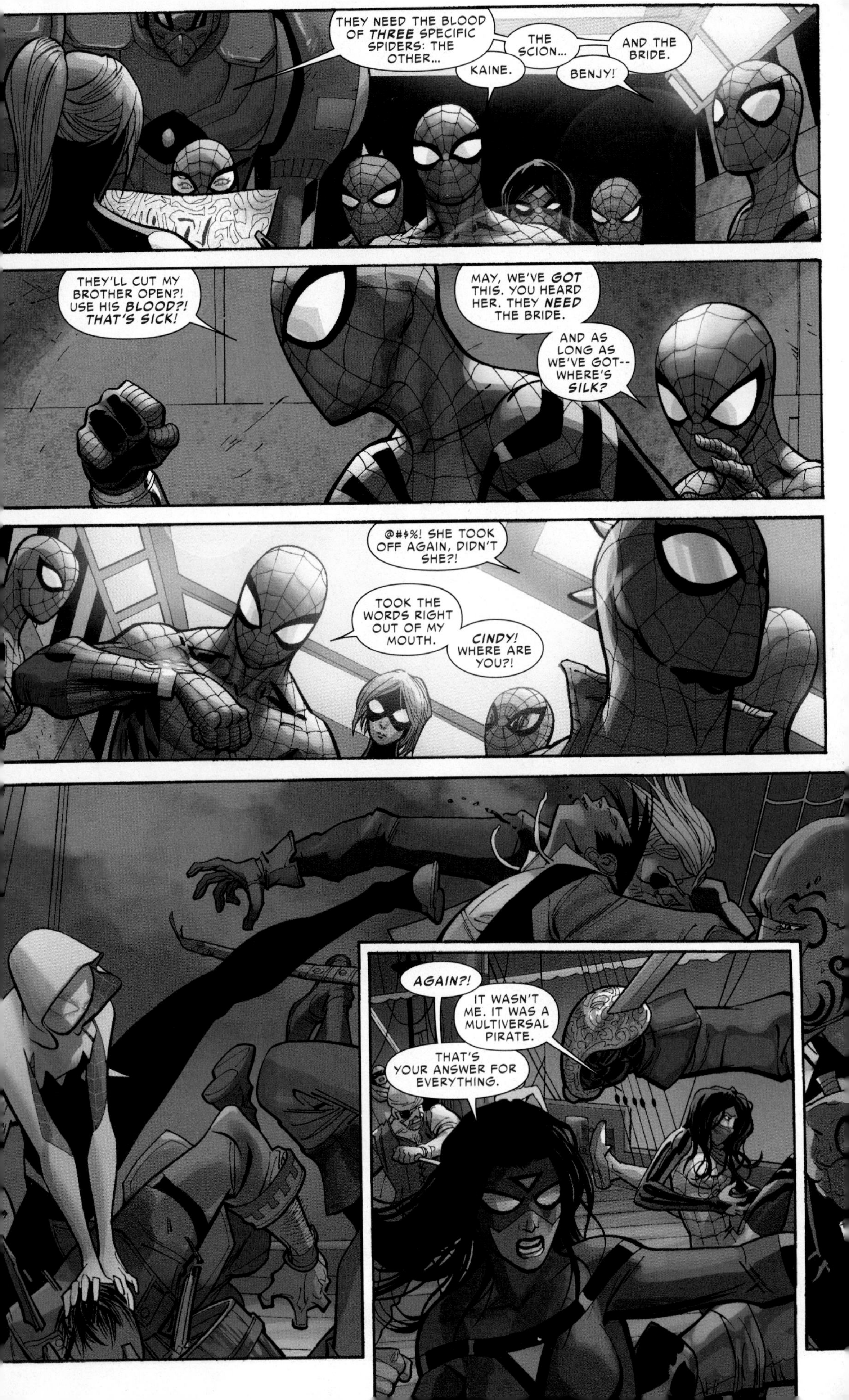
THEY NEED THE BLOOD OF THREE SPECIFIC SPIDERS: THE OTHER...
KAINE.
THE SCION...
BENJY!
AND THE BRIDE.
THEY'LL CUT MY BROTHER OPEN?! USE HIS BLOOD?! THAT'S SICK!
MAY, WE'VE GOT THIS. YOU HEARD HER. THEY NEED THE BRIDE.
AND AS LONG AS WE'VE GOT-- WHERE'S SILK?
@#$%! SHE TOOK OFF AGAIN, DIDN'T SHE?!
TOOK THE WORDS RIGHT OUT OF MY MOUTH.
CINDY! WHERE ARE YOU?!
AGAIN?!
IT WASN'T ME. IT WAS A MULTIVERSAL PIRATE.
THAT'S YOUR ANSWER FOR EVERYTHING.

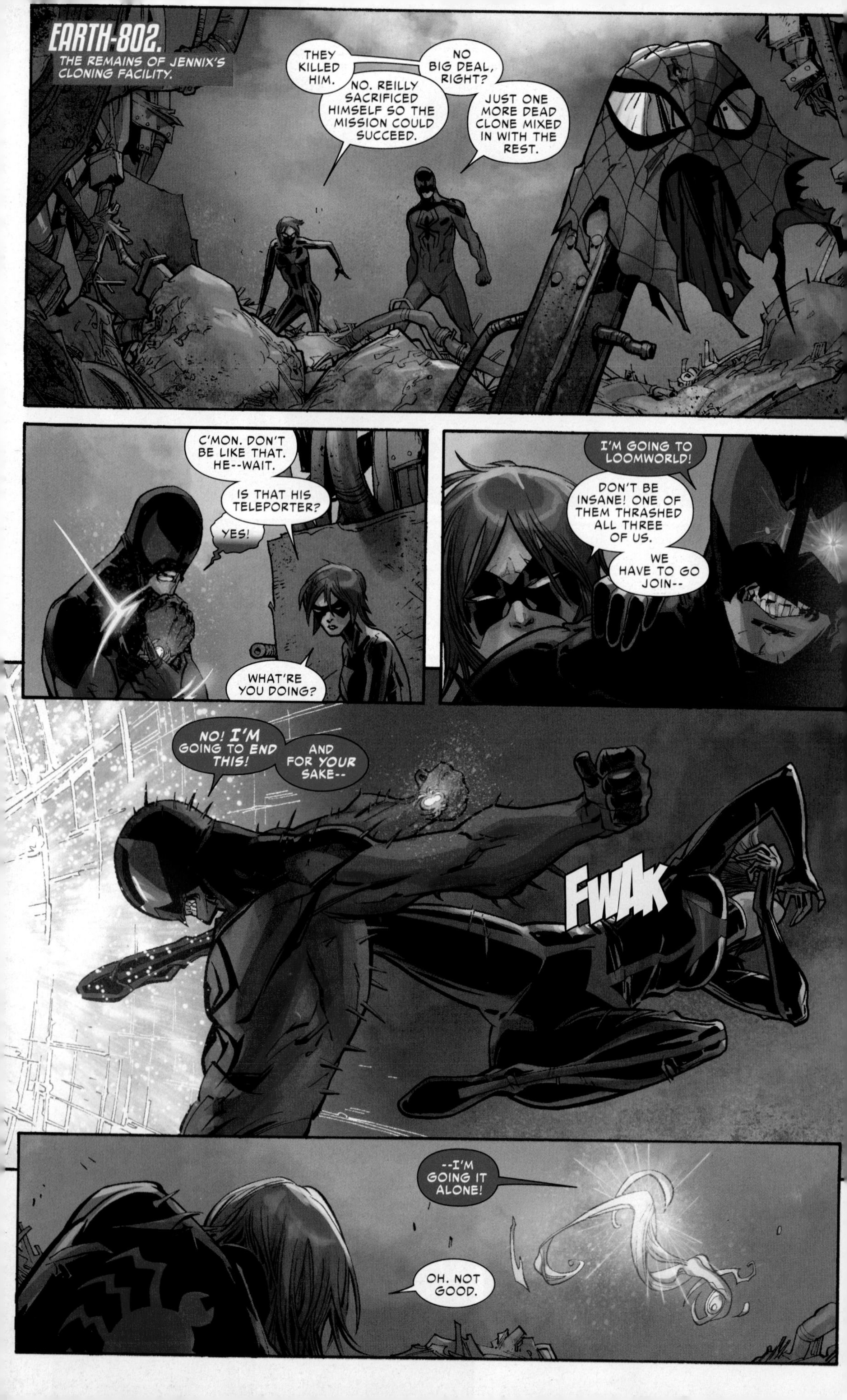
EARTH-802.
THE REMAINS OF JENNIX'S CLONING FACILITY.
THEY KILLED HIM.
NO BIG DEAL, RIGHT?
NO. REILLY SACRIFICED HIMSELF SO THE MISSION COULD SUCCEED.
JUST ONE MORE DEAD CLONE MIXED IN WITH THE REST.
C'MON. DON'T BE LIKE THAT. HE--WAIT.
IS THAT HIS TELEPORTER?
YES!
WHAT'RE YOU DOING?
I'M GOING TO LOOMWORLD!
DON'T BE INSANE! ONE OF THEM THRASHED ALL THREE OF US.
WE HAVE TO GO JOIN--
NO! I'M GOING TO END THIS!
AND FOR YOUR SAKE--
FWAK
--I'M GOING IT ALONE!
OH. NOT GOOD.

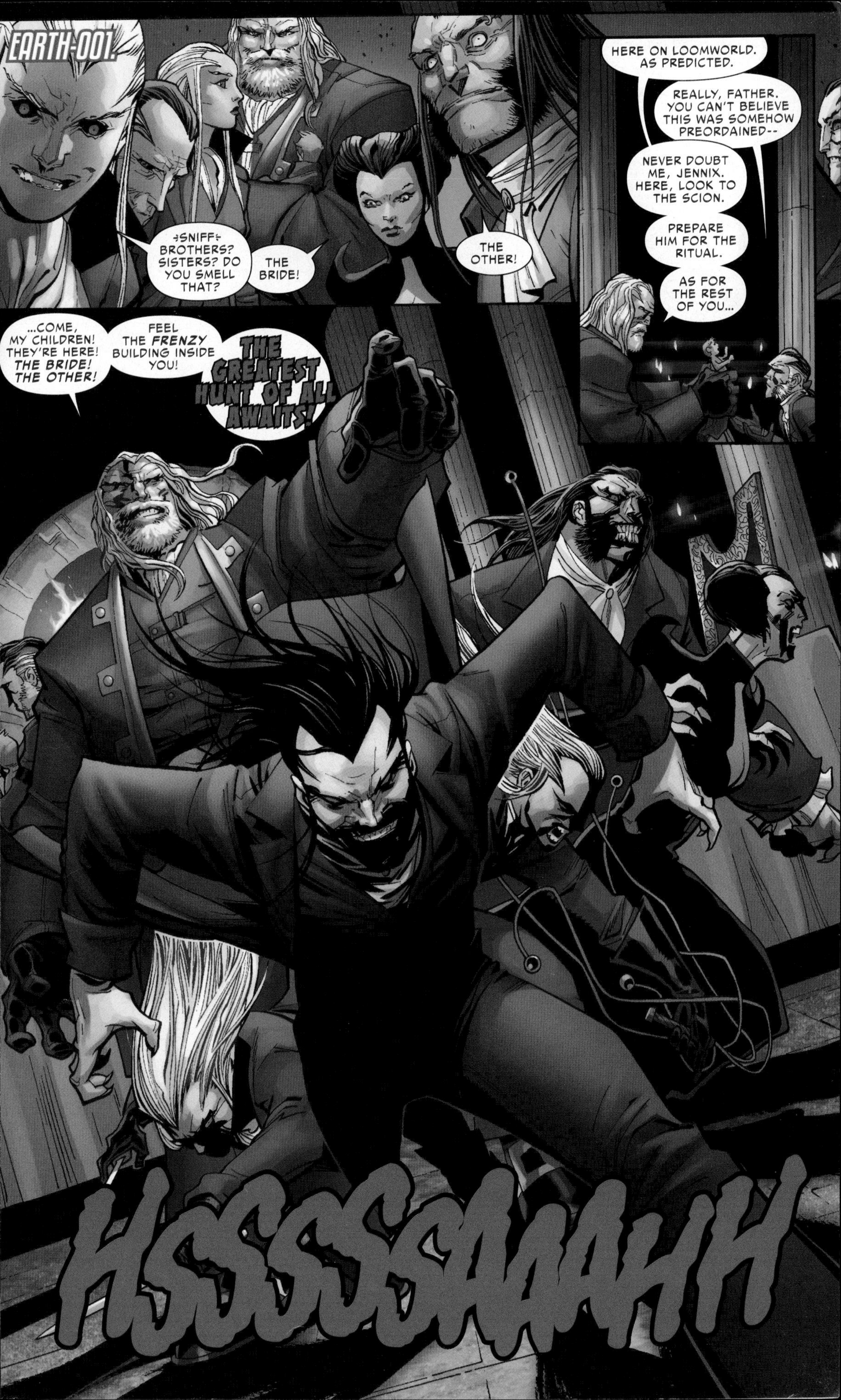
EARTH-001.
∻SNIFF∻ BROTHERS? SISTERS? DO YOU SMELL THAT?
THE BRIDE!
THE OTHER!
HERE ON LOOMWORLD. AS PREDICTED.
REALLY, FATHER. YOU CAN'T BELIEVE THIS WAS SOMEHOW PREORDAINED--
NEVER DOUBT ME, JENNIX. HERE, LOOK TO THE SCION.
PREPARE HIM FOR THE RITUAL.
AS FOR THE REST OF YOU...
...COME, MY CHILDREN! THEY'RE HERE! THE BRIDE! THE OTHER!
FEEL THE FRENZY BUILDING INSIDE YOU!
THE GREATEST HUNT OF ALL AWAITS!
HSSSSAAAHH

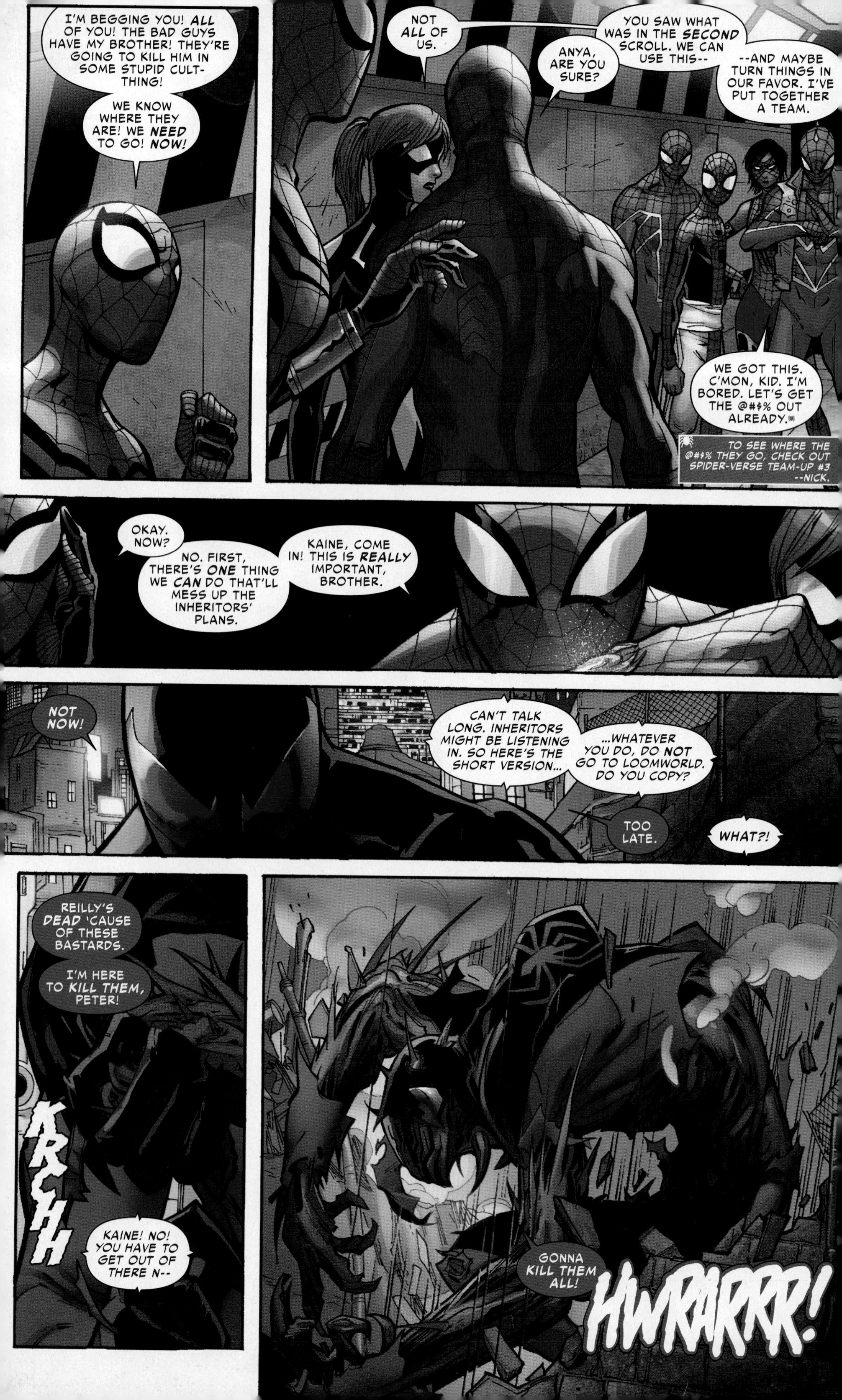
I'M BEGGING YOU! ALL OF YOU! THE BAD GUYS HAVE MY BROTHER! THEY'RE GOING TO KILL HIM IN SOME STUPID CULT-THING!
WE KNOW WHERE THEY ARE! WE NEED TO GO! NOW!
NOT ALL OF US.
ANYA, ARE YOU SURE?
YOU SAW WHAT WAS IN THE SECOND SCROLL. WE CAN USE THIS--
--AND MAYBE TURN THINGS IN OUR FAVOR. I'VE PUT TOGETHER A TEAM.
WE GOT THIS. C'MON, KID. I'M BORED. LET'S GET THE @#$% OUT ALREADY.
TO SEE WHERE THE @#$% THEY GO, CHECK OUT SPIDER-VERSE TEAM-UP #3 --NICK.
OKAY. NOW?
NO. FIRST, THERE'S ONE THING WE CAN DO THAT'LL MESS UP THE INHERITORS' PLANS.
KAINE, COME IN! THIS IS REALLY IMPORTANT, BROTHER.
NOT NOW!
CAN'T TALK LONG. INHERITORS MIGHT BE LISTENING IN. SO HERE'S THE SHORT VERSION...
...WHATEVER YOU DO, DO NOT GO TO LOOMWORLD. DO YOU COPY?
TOO LATE.
WHAT?!
REILLY'S DEAD 'CAUSE OF THESE BASTARDS.
I'M HERE TO KILL THEM, PETER!
KRCHH
KAINE! NO! YOU HAVE TO GET OUT OF THERE N--
GONNA KILL THEM ALL!
HWRARRR!

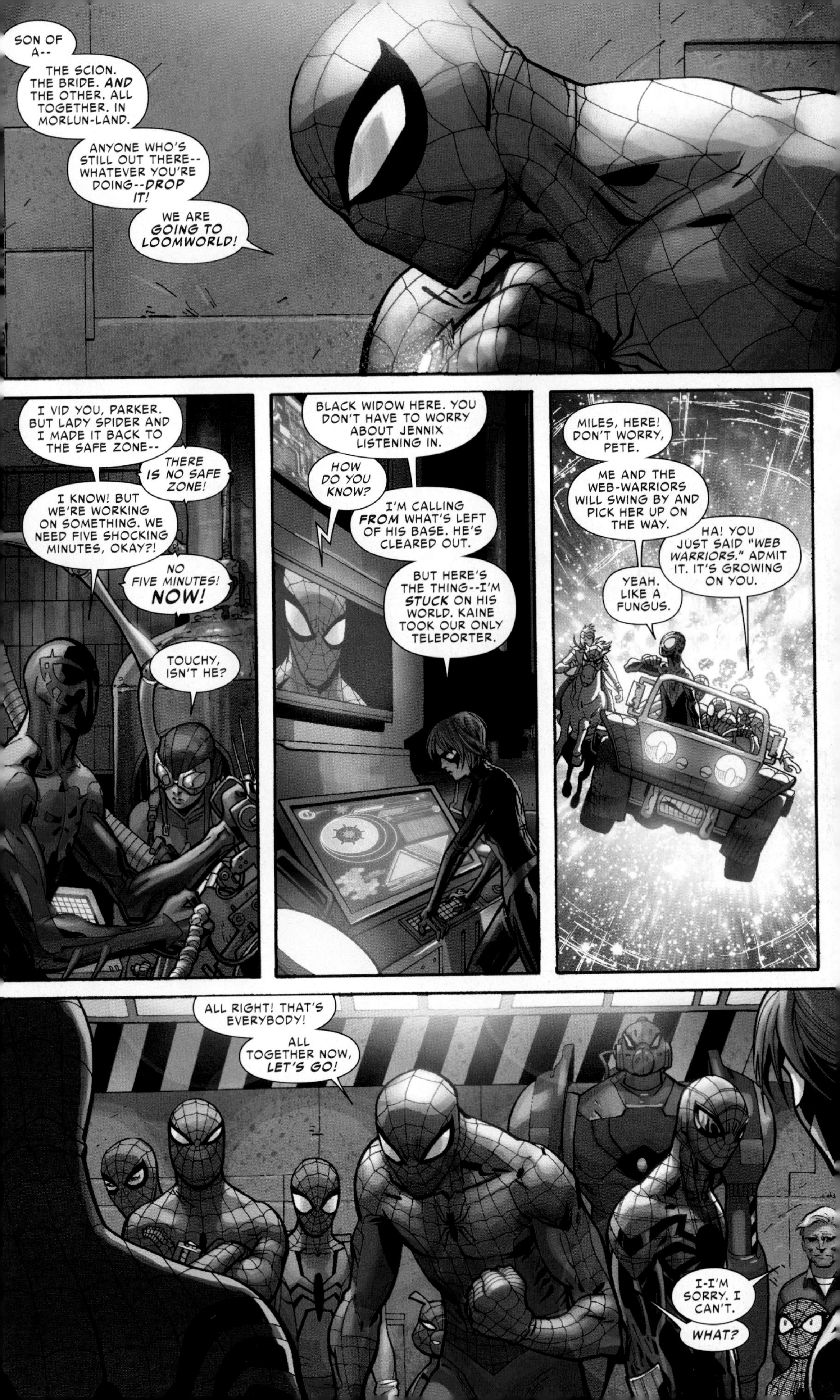
SON OF A--
THE SCION. THE BRIDE. AND THE OTHER. ALL TOGETHER. IN MORLUN-LAND.
ANYONE WHO'S STILL OUT THERE-- WHATEVER YOU'RE DOING--DROP IT!
WE ARE GOING TO LOOMWORLD!
I VID YOU, PARKER. BUT LADY SPIDER AND I MADE IT BACK TO THE SAFE ZONE--
THERE IS NO SAFE ZONE!
I KNOW! BUT WE'RE WORKING ON SOMETHING. WE NEED FIVE SHOCKING MINUTES, OKAY?!
NO FIVE MINUTES! NOW!
TOUCHY, ISN'T HE?
BLACK WIDOW HERE. YOU DON'T HAVE TO WORRY ABOUT JENNIX LISTENING IN.
HOW DO YOU KNOW?
I'M CALLING FROM WHAT'S LEFT OF HIS BASE. HE'S CLEARED OUT.
BUT HERE'S THE THING--I'M STUCK ON HIS WORLD. KAINE TOOK OUR ONLY TELEPORTER.
MILES, HERE! DON'T WORRY, PETE.
ME AND THE WEB-WARRIORS WILL SWING BY AND PICK HER UP ON THE WAY.
HA! YOU JUST SAID "WEB WARRIORS." ADMIT IT. IT'S GROWING ON YOU.
YEAH. LIKE A FUNGUS.
ALL RIGHT! THAT'S EVERYBODY!
ALL TOGETHER NOW, LET'S GO!
I-I'M SORRY. I CAN'T.
WHAT?

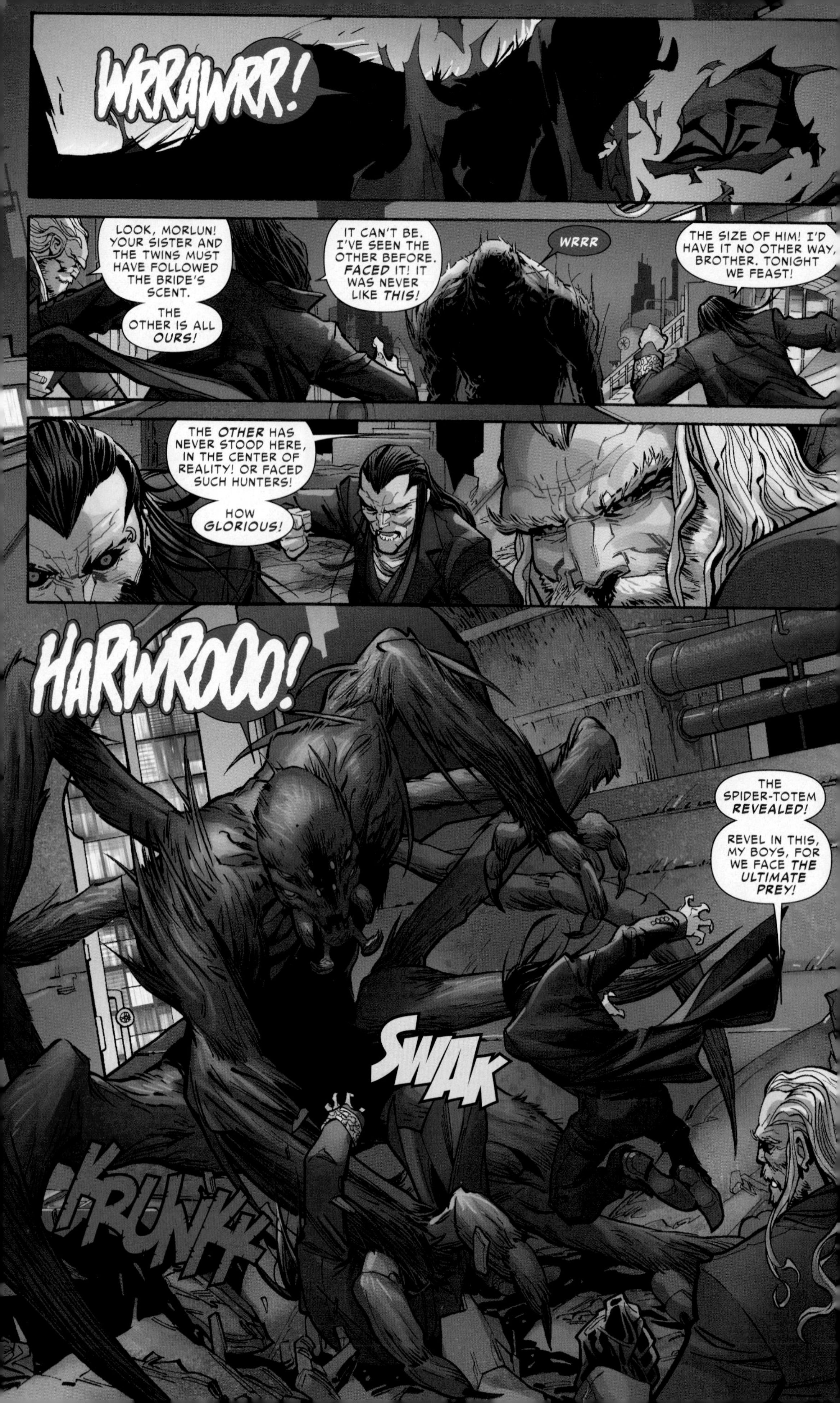
WRRAWRR!
LOOK, MORLUN! YOUR SISTER AND THE TWINS MUST HAVE FOLLOWED THE BRIDE'S SCENT.
THE OTHER IS ALL OURS!
IT CAN'T BE. I'VE SEEN THE OTHER BEFORE. FACED IT! IT WAS NEVER LIKE THIS!
WRRR
THE SIZE OF HIM! I'D HAVE IT NO OTHER WAY, BROTHER. TONIGHT WE FEAST!
THE OTHER HAS NEVER STOOD HERE, IN THE CENTER OF REALITY! OR FACED SUCH HUNTERS!
HOW GLORIOUS!
HARWROOO!
THE SPIDER-TOTEM REVEALED!
REVEL IN THIS, MY BOYS, FOR WE FACE THE ULTIMATE PREY!
SWAK
KRUNK

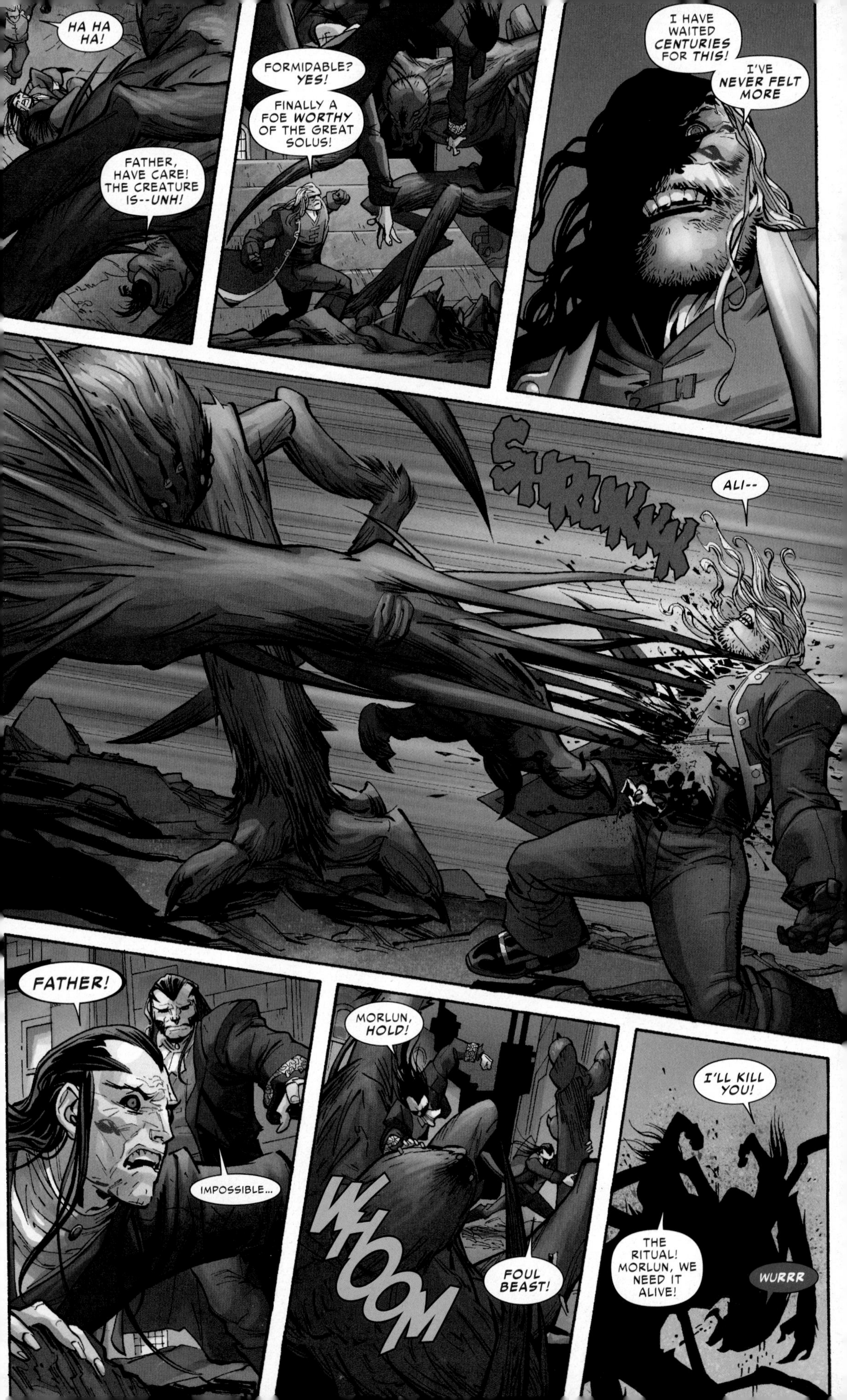
HA HA HA!
FATHER, HAVE CARE! THE CREATURE IS--UNH!
FORMIDABLE? YES!
FINALLY A FOE WORTHY OF THE GREAT SOLUS!
I HAVE WAITED CENTURIES FOR THIS!
I'VE NEVER FELT MORE
SHRUNKK
ALI--
FATHER!
IMPOSSIBLE...
MORLUN, HOLD!
WHOOM
FOUL BEAST!
I'LL KILL YOU!
THE RITUAL! MORLUN, WE NEED IT ALIVE!
WURRR

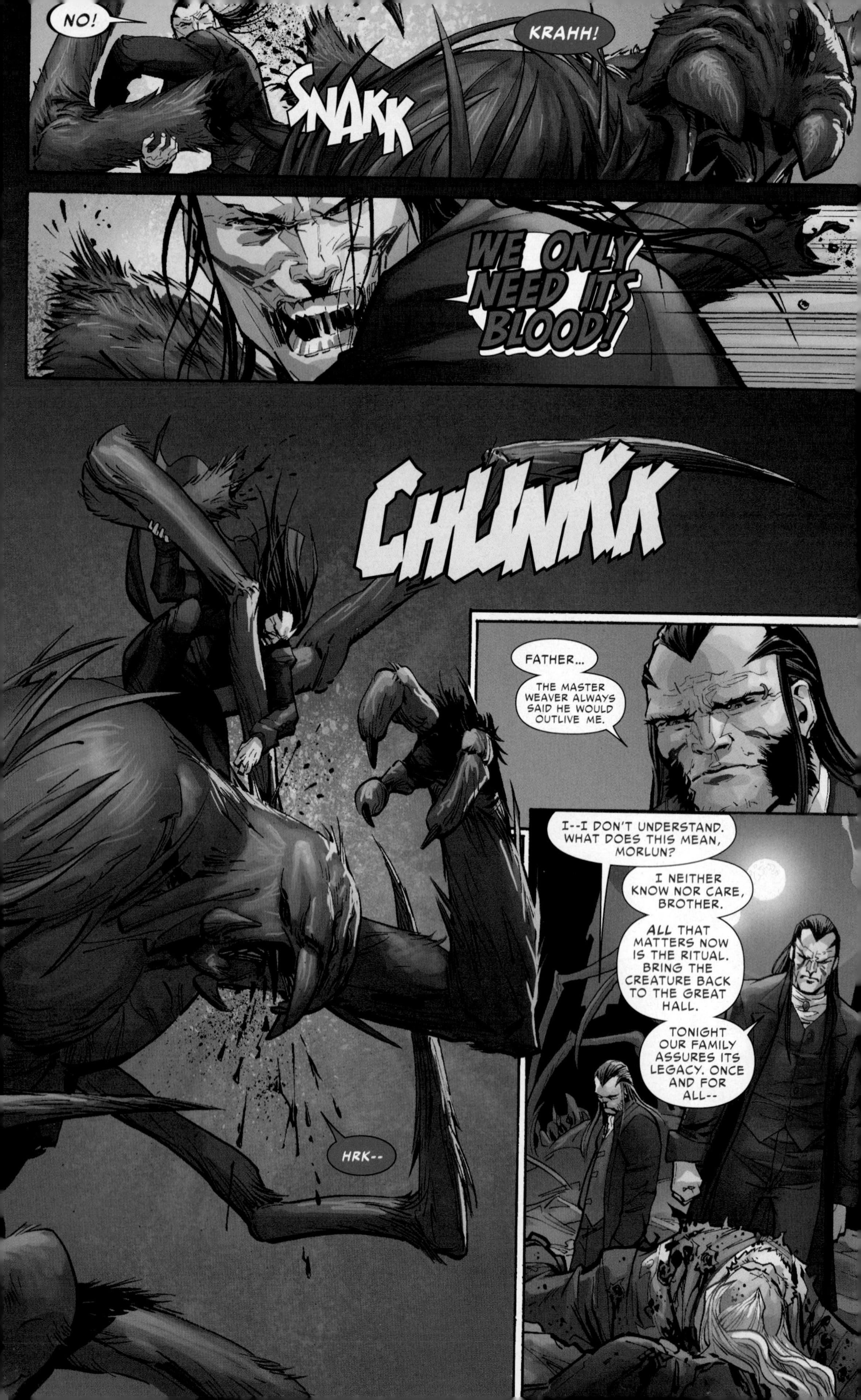
NO!
KRAHH!
SNAKK
WE ONLY NEED ITS BLOOD!
CHUNKK
HRK--
FATHER...
THE MASTER WEAVER ALWAYS SAID HE WOULD OUTLIVE ME.
I--I DON'T UNDERSTAND. WHAT DOES THIS MEAN, MORLUN?
I NEITHER KNOW NOR CARE, BROTHER.
ALL THAT MATTERS NOW IS THE RITUAL. BRING THE CREATURE BACK TO THE GREAT HALL.
TONIGHT OUR FAMILY ASSURES ITS LEGACY. ONCE AND FOR ALL--

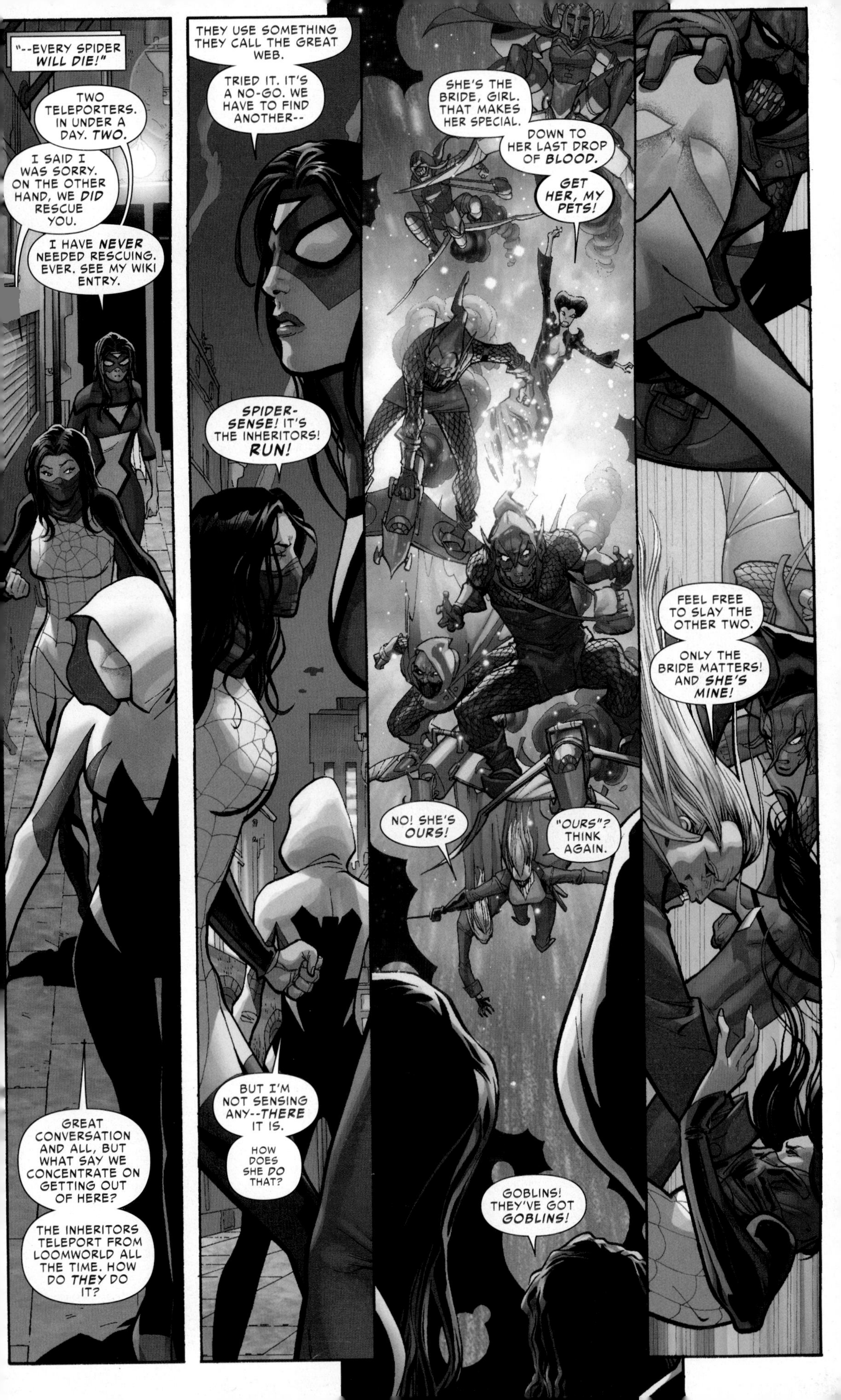

"--EVERY SPIDER WILL DIE!"
TWO TELEPORTERS. IN UNDER A DAY. TWO.
I SAID I WAS SORRY. ON THE OTHER HAND, WE DID RESCUE YOU.
I HAVE NEVER NEEDED RESCUING. EVER. SEE MY WIKI ENTRY.
GREAT CONVERSATION AND ALL, BUT WHAT SAY WE CONCENTRATE ON GETTING OUT OF HERE?
THE INHERITORS TELEPORT FROM LOOMWORLD ALL THE TIME. HOW DO THEY DO IT?
THEY USE SOMETHING THEY CALL THE GREAT WEB.
TRIED IT. IT'S A NO-GO. WE HAVE TO FIND ANOTHER--
SPIDER-SENSE! IT'S THE INHERITORS! RUN!
BUT I'M NOT SENSING ANY--THERE IT IS.
HOW DOES SHE DO THAT?
SHE'S THE BRIDE, GIRL. THAT MAKES HER SPECIAL.
DOWN TO HER LAST DROP OF BLOOD.
GET HER, MY PETS!
NO! SHE'S OURS!
"OURS"? THINK AGAIN.
GOBLINS! THEY'VE GOT GOBLINS!
FEEL FREE TO SLAY THE OTHER TWO.
ONLY THE BRIDE MATTERS! AND SHE'S MINE!

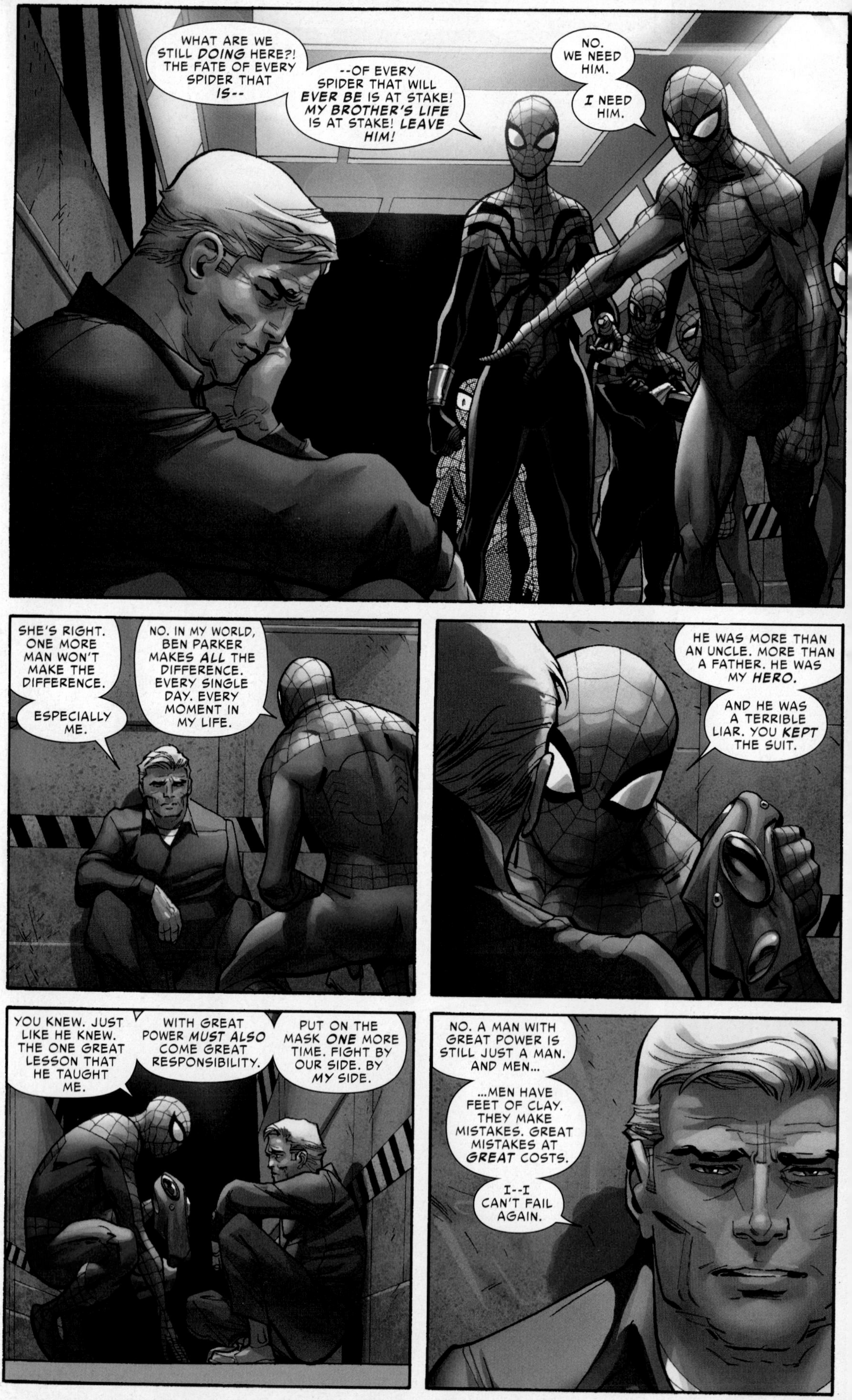
WHAT ARE WE STILL DOING HERE?! THE FATE OF EVERY SPIDER THAT IS--
--OF EVERY SPIDER THAT WILL EVER BE IS AT STAKE! MY BROTHER'S LIFE IS AT STAKE! LEAVE HIM!
NO. WE NEED HIM.
I NEED HIM.
SHE'S RIGHT. ONE MORE MAN WON'T MAKE THE DIFFERENCE.
ESPECIALLY ME.
NO. IN MY WORLD, BEN PARKER MAKES ALL THE DIFFERENCE. EVERY SINGLE DAY. EVERY MOMENT IN MY LIFE.
HE WAS MORE THAN AN UNCLE. MORE THAN A FATHER. HE WAS MY HERO.
AND HE WAS A TERRIBLE LIAR. YOU KEPT THE SUIT.
YOU KNEW. JUST LIKE HE KNEW. THE ONE GREAT LESSON THAT HE TAUGHT ME.
WITH GREAT POWER MUST ALSO COME GREAT RESPONSIBILITY.
PUT ON THE MASK ONE MORE TIME. FIGHT BY OUR SIDE. BY MY SIDE.
NO. A MAN WITH GREAT POWER IS STILL JUST A MAN. AND MEN...
...MEN HAVE FEET OF CLAY. THEY MAKE MISTAKES. GREAT MISTAKES AT GREAT COSTS.
I--I CAN'T FAIL AGAIN.

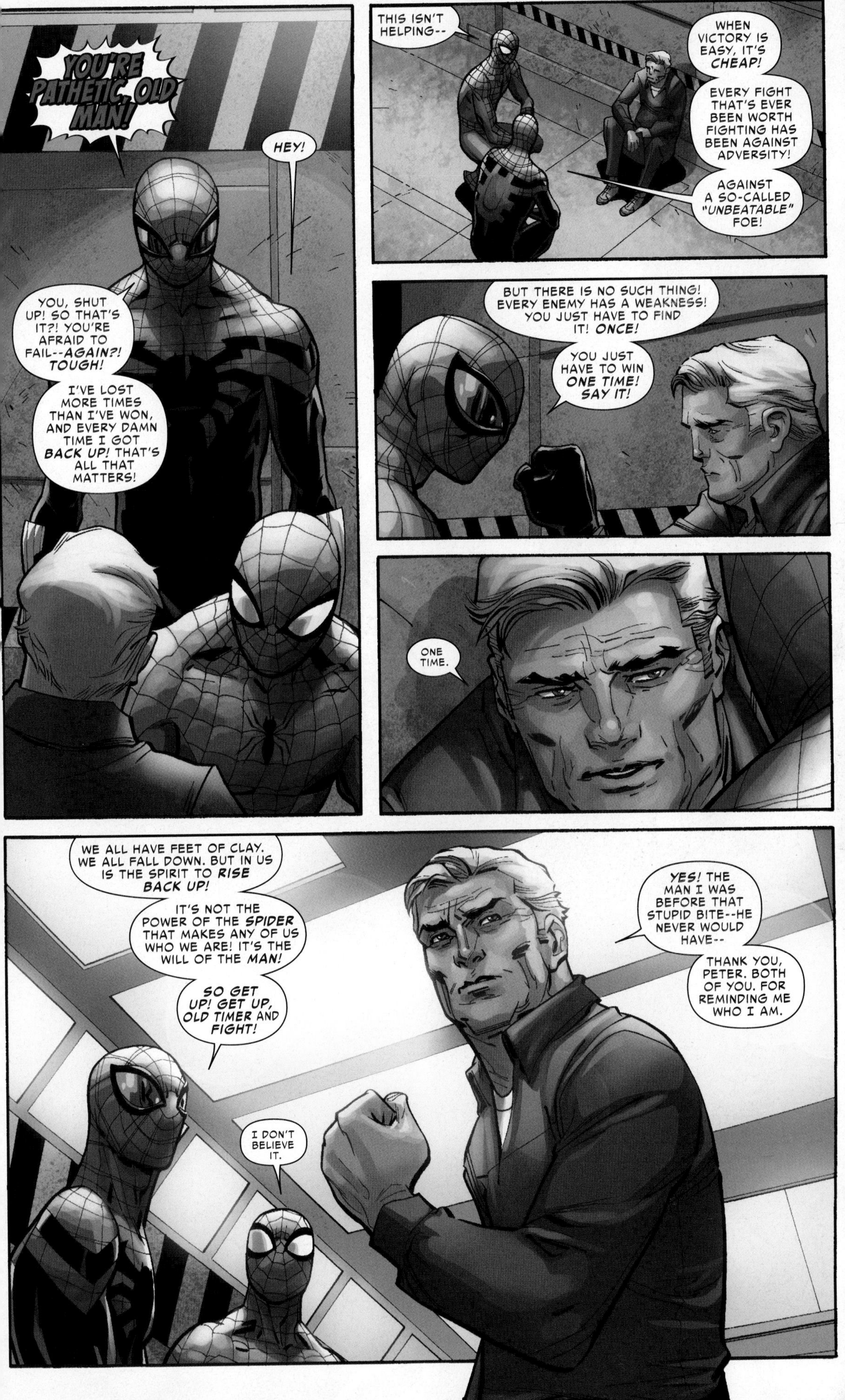
YOU'RE PATHETIC, OLD MAN!
HEY!
YOU, SHUT UP! SO THAT'S IT?! YOU'RE AFRAID TO FAIL--AGAIN?! TOUGH!
I'VE LOST MORE TIMES THAN I'VE WON, AND EVERY DAMN TIME I GOT BACK UP! THAT'S ALL THAT MATTERS!
THIS ISN'T HELPING--
WHEN VICTORY IS EASY, IT'S CHEAP!
EVERY FIGHT THAT'S EVER BEEN WORTH FIGHTING HAS BEEN AGAINST ADVERSITY!
AGAINST A SO-CALLED "UNBEATABLE" FOE!
BUT THERE IS NO SUCH THING! EVERY ENEMY HAS A WEAKNESS! YOU JUST HAVE TO FIND IT! ONCE!
YOU JUST HAVE TO WIN ONE TIME! SAY IT!
ONE TIME.
WE ALL HAVE FEET OF CLAY. WE ALL FALL DOWN. BUT IN US IS THE SPIRIT TO RISE BACK UP!
IT'S NOT THE POWER OF THE SPIDER THAT MAKES ANY OF US WHO WE ARE! IT'S THE WILL OF THE MAN!
SO GET UP! GET UP, OLD TIMER AND FIGHT!
I DON'T BELIEVE IT.
YES! THE MAN I WAS BEFORE THAT STUPID BITE--HE NEVER WOULD HAVE--
THANK YOU, PETER. BOTH OF YOU. FOR REMINDING ME WHO I AM.

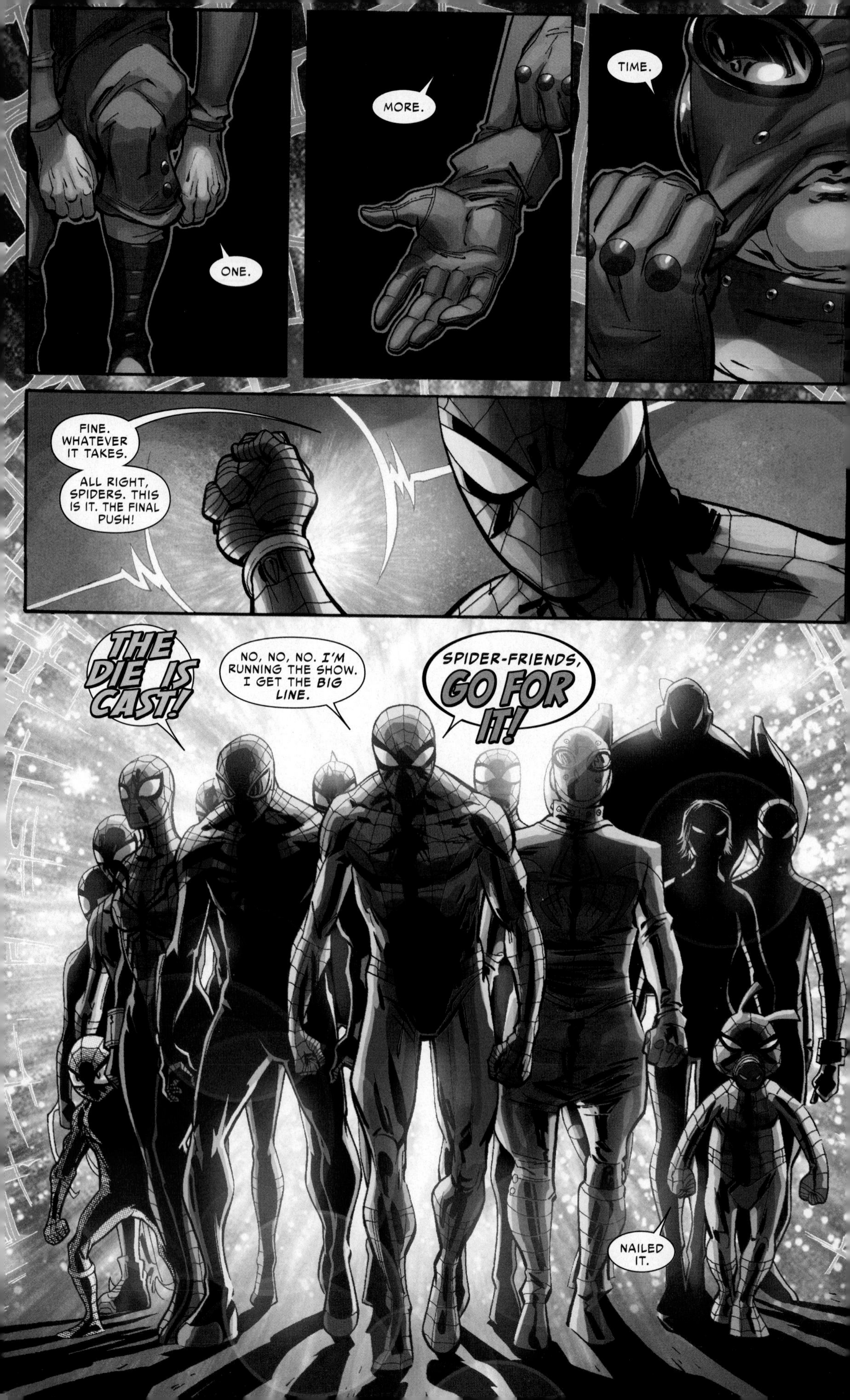
ONE.
MORE.
TIME.
FINE. WHATEVER IT TAKES.
ALL RIGHT, SPIDERS. THIS IS IT. THE FINAL PUSH!
THE DIE IS CAST!
NO, NO, NO. I'M RUNNING THE SHOW. I GET THE BIG LINE.
SPIDER-FRIENDS, GO FOR IT!
NAILED IT.

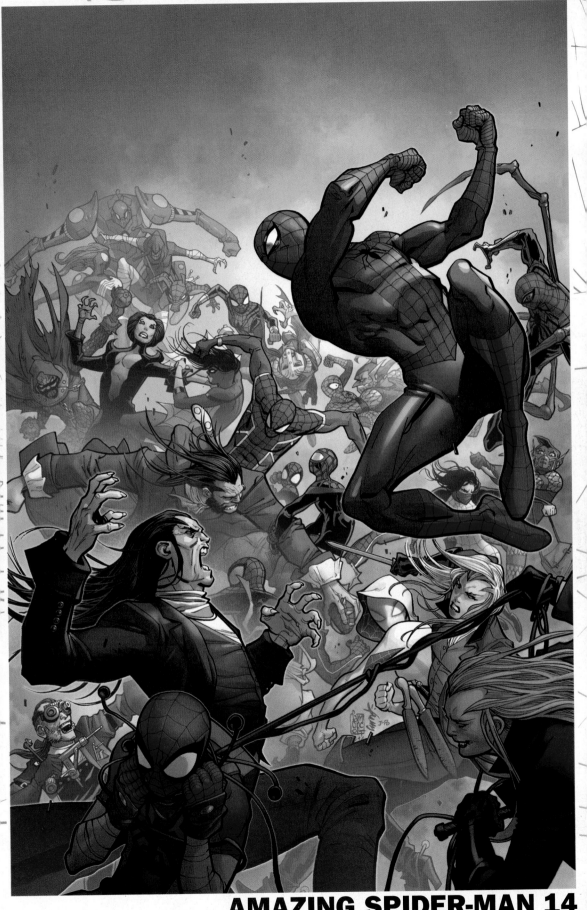

AMAZING SPIDER-MAN 14
SPIDER-VERSE, PART SIX: WEB WARRIORS

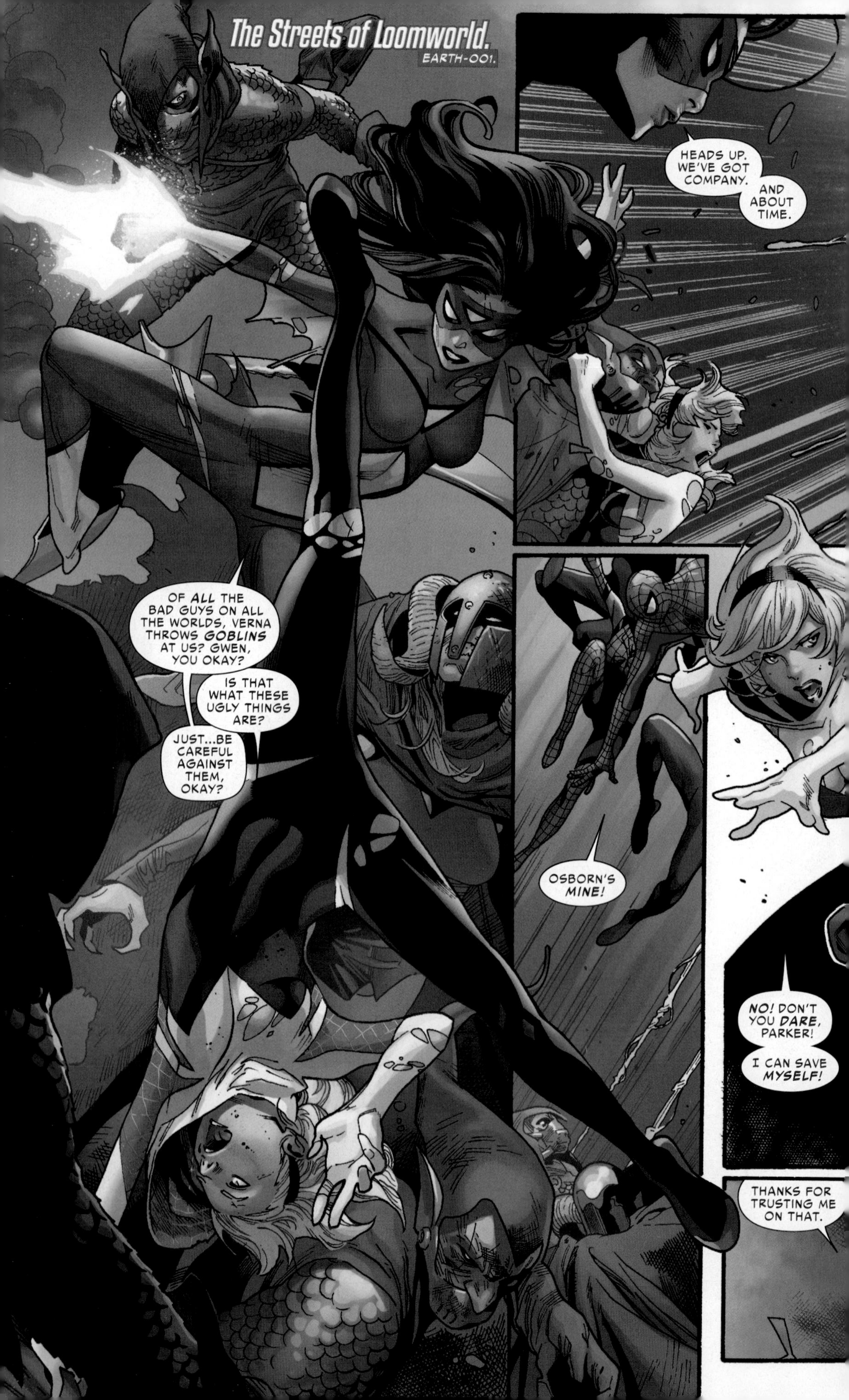
The Streets of Loomworld.
EARTH-001.
HEADS UP. WE'VE GOT COMPANY.
AND ABOUT TIME.
OF ALL THE BAD GUYS ON ALL THE WORLDS, VERNA THROWS GOBLINS AT US? GWEN, YOU OKAY?
IS THAT WHAT THESE UGLY THINGS ARE?
JUST...BE CAREFUL AGAINST THEM, OKAY?
OSBORN'S MINE!
NO! DON'T YOU DARE, PARKER!
I CAN SAVE MYSELF!
THANKS FOR TRUSTING ME ON THAT.

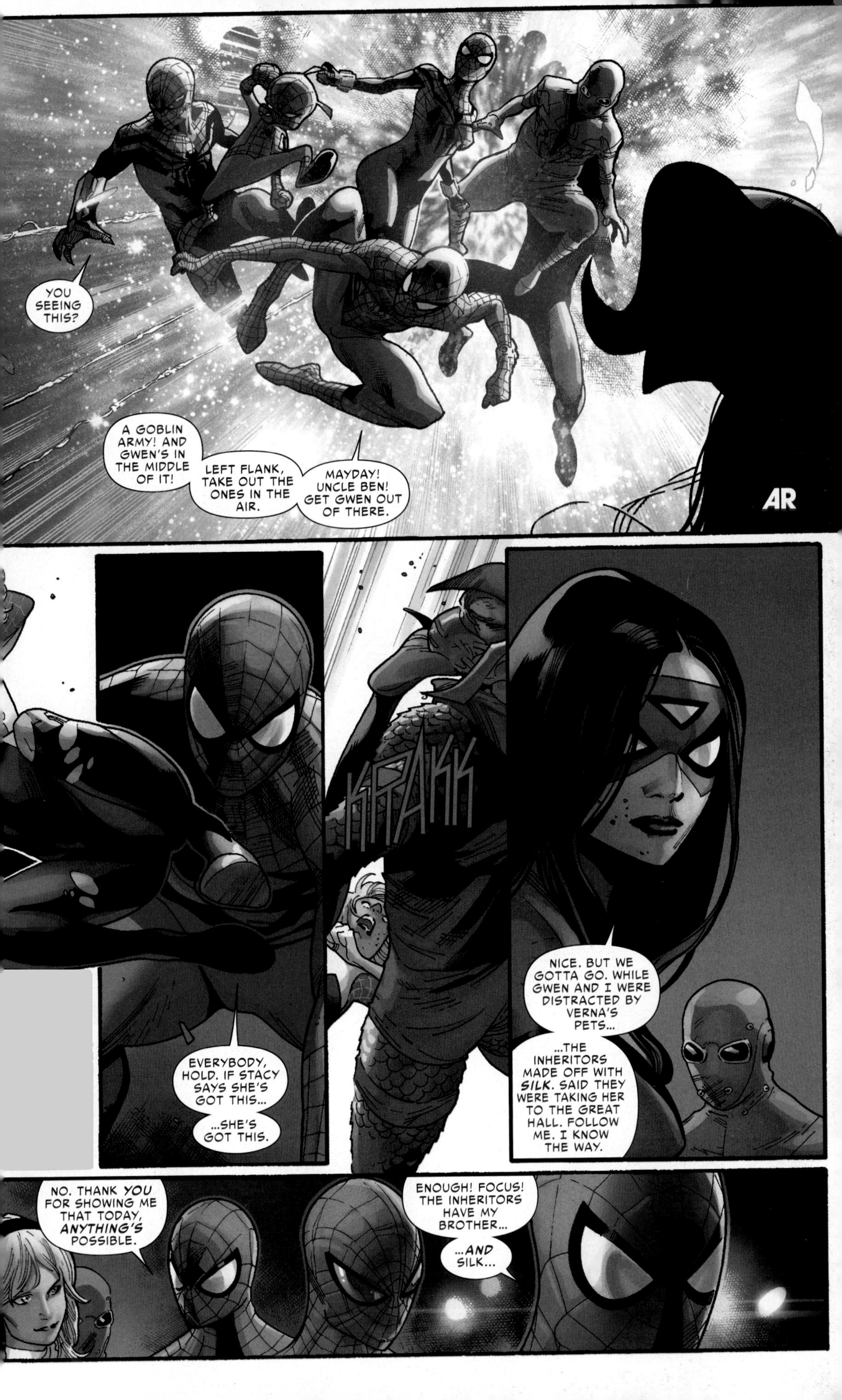

YOU SEEING THIS?
A GOBLIN ARMY! AND GWEN'S IN THE MIDDLE OF IT!
LEFT FLANK, TAKE OUT THE ONES IN THE AIR.
MAYDAY! UNCLE BEN! GET GWEN OUT OF THERE.
AR
KRAKK
EVERYBODY, HOLD. IF STACY SAYS SHE'S GOT THIS...
...SHE'S GOT THIS.
NICE. BUT WE GOTTA GO. WHILE GWEN AND I WERE DISTRACTED BY VERNA'S PETS...
...THE INHERITORS MADE OFF WITH SILK. SAID THEY WERE TAKING HER TO THE GREAT HALL. FOLLOW ME. I KNOW THE WAY.
NO. THANK YOU FOR SHOWING ME THAT TODAY, ANYTHING'S POSSIBLE.
ENOUGH! FOCUS! THE INHERITORS HAVE MY BROTHER...
...AND SILK...

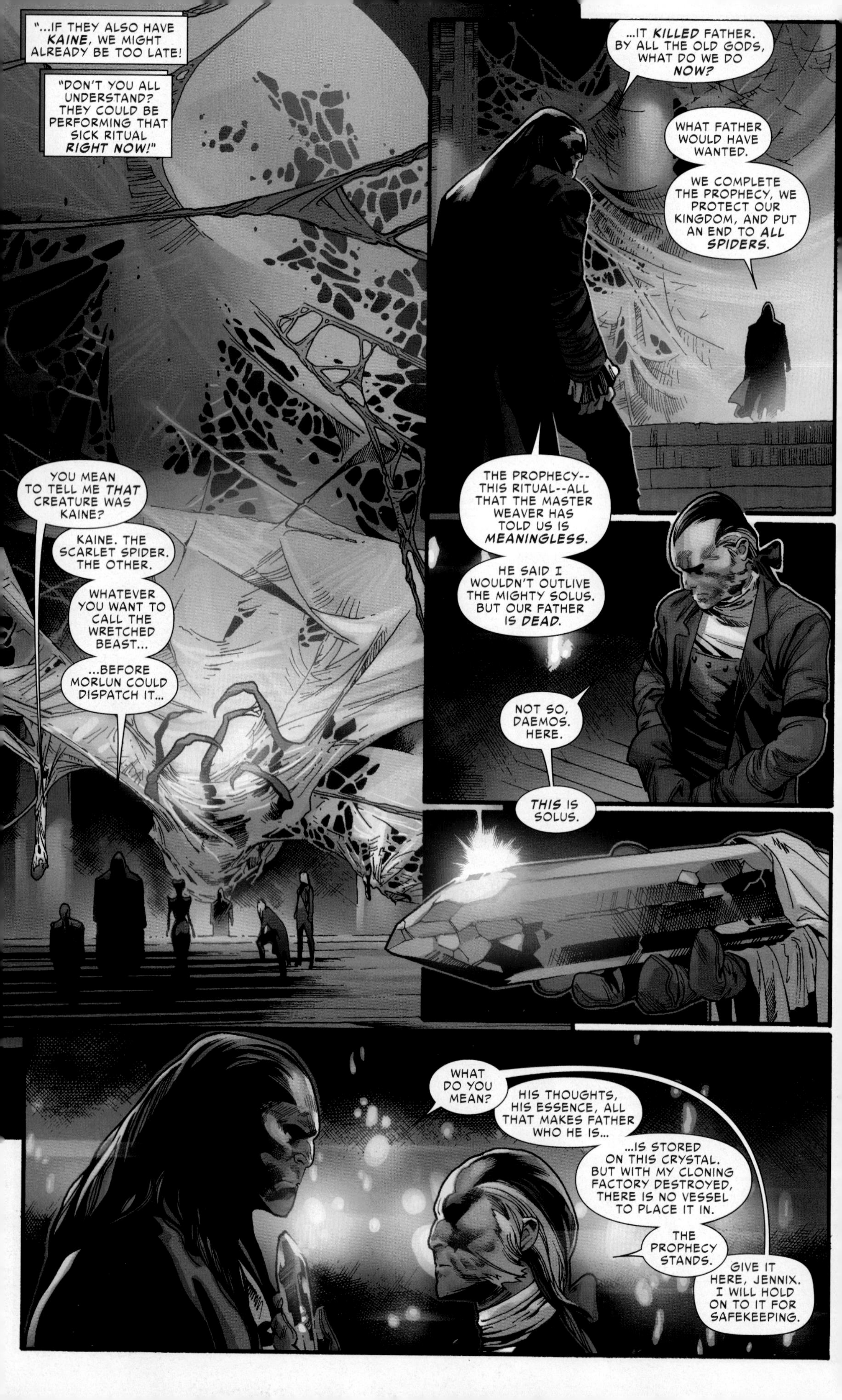
"...IF THEY ALSO HAVE KAINE, WE MIGHT ALREADY BE TOO LATE!
"DON'T YOU ALL UNDERSTAND? THEY COULD BE PERFORMING THAT SICK RITUAL RIGHT NOW!"
YOU MEAN TO TELL ME THAT CREATURE WAS KAINE?
KAINE. THE SCARLET SPIDER. THE OTHER.
WHATEVER YOU WANT TO CALL THE WRETCHED BEAST...
...BEFORE MORLUN COULD DISPATCH IT...
...IT KILLED FATHER. BY ALL THE OLD GODS, WHAT DO WE DO NOW?
WHAT FATHER WOULD HAVE WANTED.
WE COMPLETE THE PROPHECY, WE PROTECT OUR KINGDOM, AND PUT AN END TO ALL SPIDERS.
THE PROPHECY-- THIS RITUAL--ALL THAT THE MASTER WEAVER HAS TOLD US IS MEANINGLESS.
HE SAID I WOULDN'T OUTLIVE THE MIGHTY SOLUS. BUT OUR FATHER IS DEAD.
NOT SO, DAEMOS. HERE.
THIS IS SOLUS.
WHAT DO YOU MEAN?
HIS THOUGHTS, HIS ESSENCE, ALL THAT MAKES FATHER WHO HE IS...
...IS STORED ON THIS CRYSTAL. BUT WITH MY CLONING FACTORY DESTROYED, THERE IS NO VESSEL TO PLACE IT IN.
THE PROPHECY STANDS.
GIVE IT HERE, JENNIX. I WILL HOLD ON TO IT FOR SAFEKEEPING.

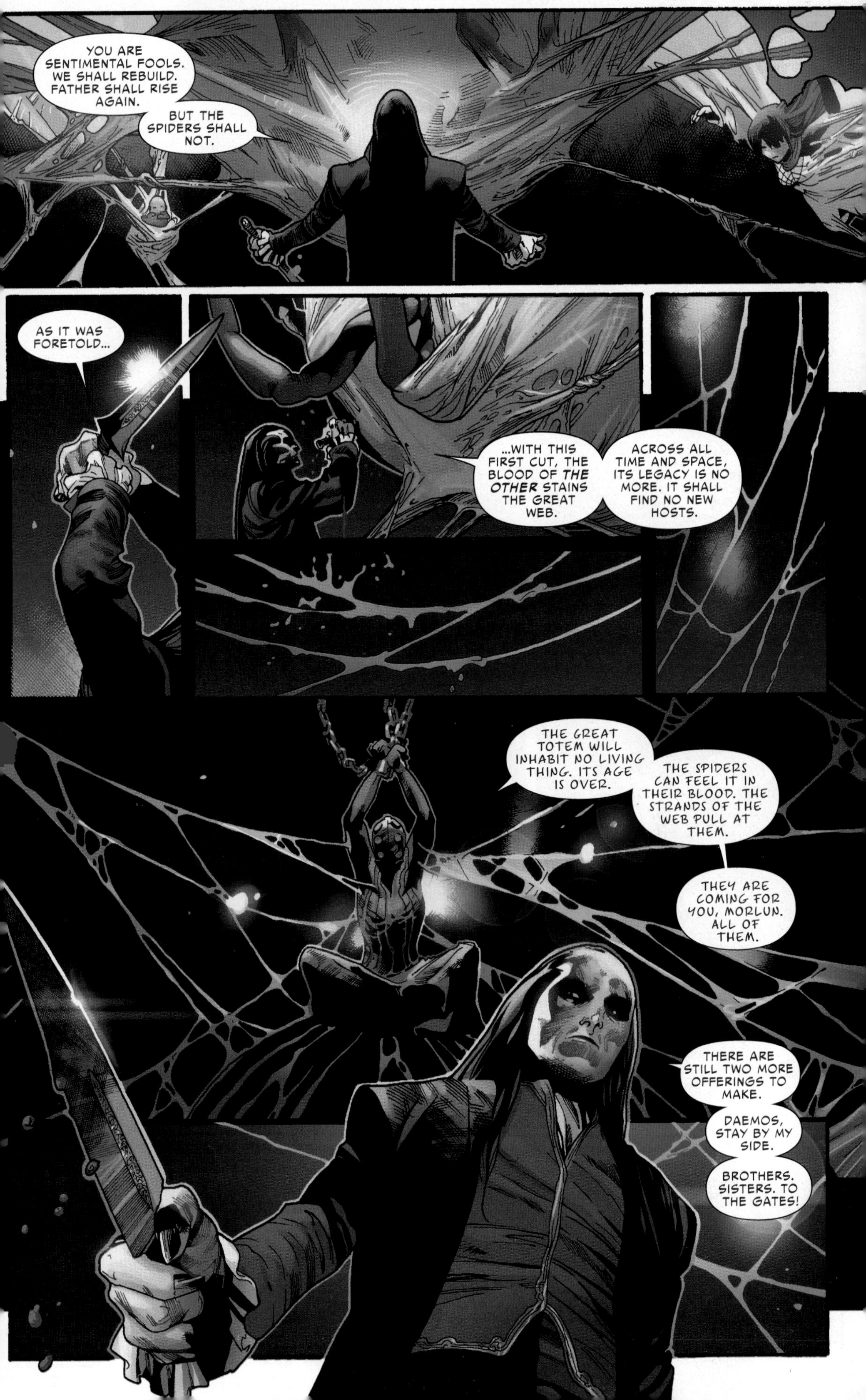

YOU ARE SENTIMENTAL FOOLS. WE SHALL REBUILD. FATHER SHALL RISE AGAIN.
BUT THE SPIDERS SHALL NOT.
AS IT WAS FORETOLD...
...WITH THIS FIRST CUT, THE BLOOD OF *THE OTHER* STAINS THE GREAT WEB.
ACROSS ALL TIME AND SPACE, ITS LEGACY IS NO MORE. IT SHALL FIND NO NEW HOSTS.
THE GREAT TOTEM WILL INHABIT NO LIVING THING. ITS AGE IS OVER.
THE SPIDERS CAN FEEL IT IN THEIR BLOOD. THE STRANDS OF THE WEB PULL AT THEM.
THEY ARE COMING FOR YOU, MORLUN. ALL OF THEM.
THERE ARE STILL TWO MORE OFFERINGS TO MAKE.
DAEMOS, STAY BY MY SIDE.
BROTHERS. SISTERS. TO THE GATES!

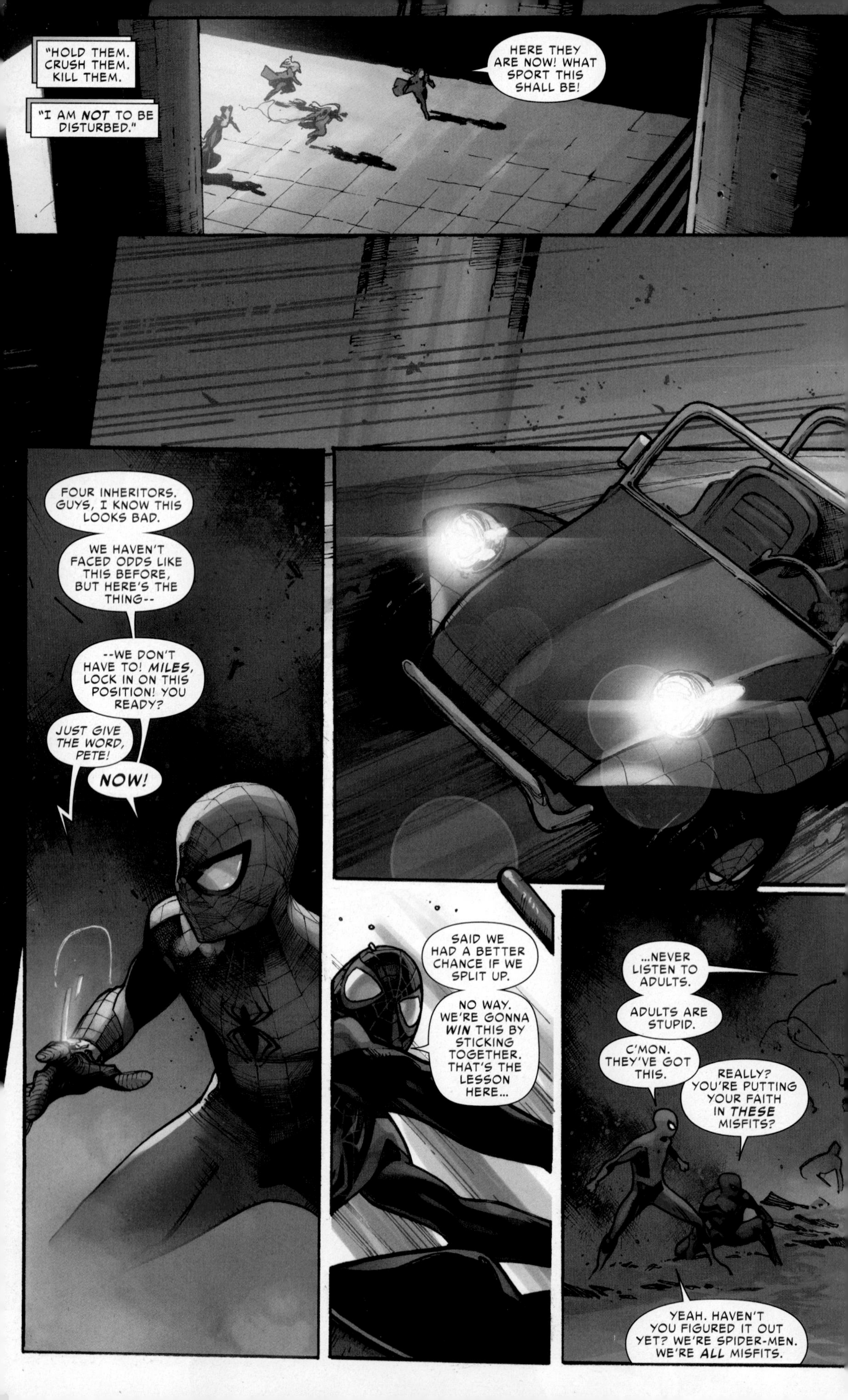
"HOLD THEM. CRUSH THEM. KILL THEM.
"I AM NOT TO BE DISTURBED."
HERE THEY ARE NOW! WHAT SPORT THIS SHALL BE!
FOUR INHERITORS. GUYS, I KNOW THIS LOOKS BAD.
WE HAVEN'T FACED ODDS LIKE THIS BEFORE, BUT HERE'S THE THING--
--WE DON'T HAVE TO! MILES, LOCK IN ON THIS POSITION! YOU READY?
JUST GIVE THE WORD, PETE!
NOW!
SAID WE HAD A BETTER CHANCE IF WE SPLIT UP.
NO WAY. WE'RE GONNA WIN THIS BY STICKING TOGETHER. THAT'S THE LESSON HERE...
...NEVER LISTEN TO ADULTS.
ADULTS ARE STUPID.
C'MON. THEY'VE GOT THIS.
REALLY? YOU'RE PUTTING YOUR FAITH IN THESE MISFITS?
YEAH. HAVEN'T YOU FIGURED IT OUT YET? WE'RE SPIDER-MEN. WE'RE ALL MISFITS.

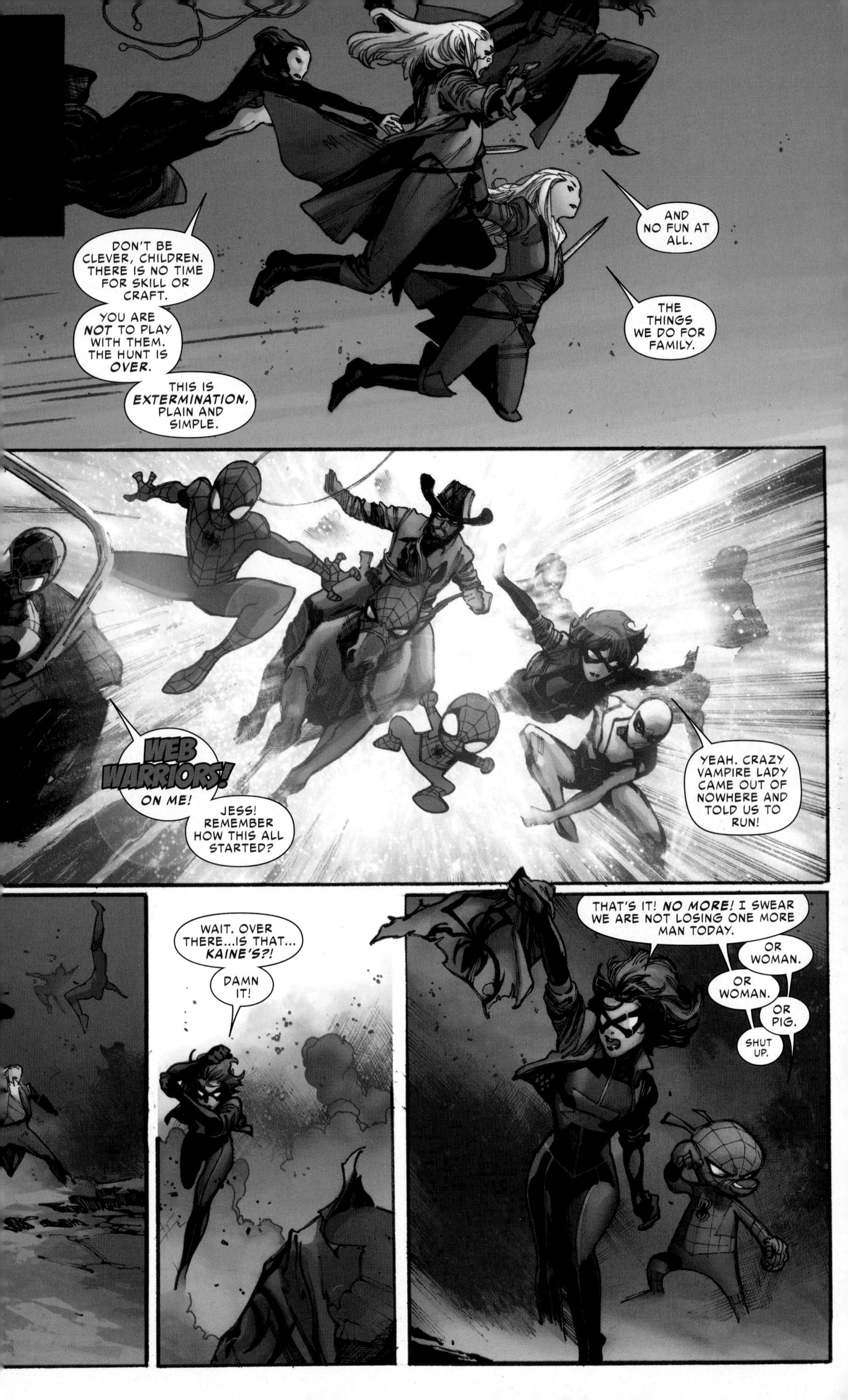

DON'T BE CLEVER, CHILDREN. THERE IS NO TIME FOR SKILL OR CRAFT.
YOU ARE NOT TO PLAY WITH THEM. THE HUNT IS OVER.
THIS IS EXTERMINATION, PLAIN AND SIMPLE.
AND NO FUN AT ALL.
THE THINGS WE DO FOR FAMILY.
WEB WARRIORS! ON ME!
JESS! REMEMBER HOW THIS ALL STARTED?
YEAH. CRAZY VAMPIRE LADY CAME OUT OF NOWHERE AND TOLD US TO RUN!
WAIT. OVER THERE...IS THAT... KAINE'S?!
DAMN IT!
THAT'S IT! NO MORE! I SWEAR WE ARE NOT LOSING ONE MORE MAN TODAY.
OR WOMAN.
OR WOMAN.
OR PIG.
SHUT UP.

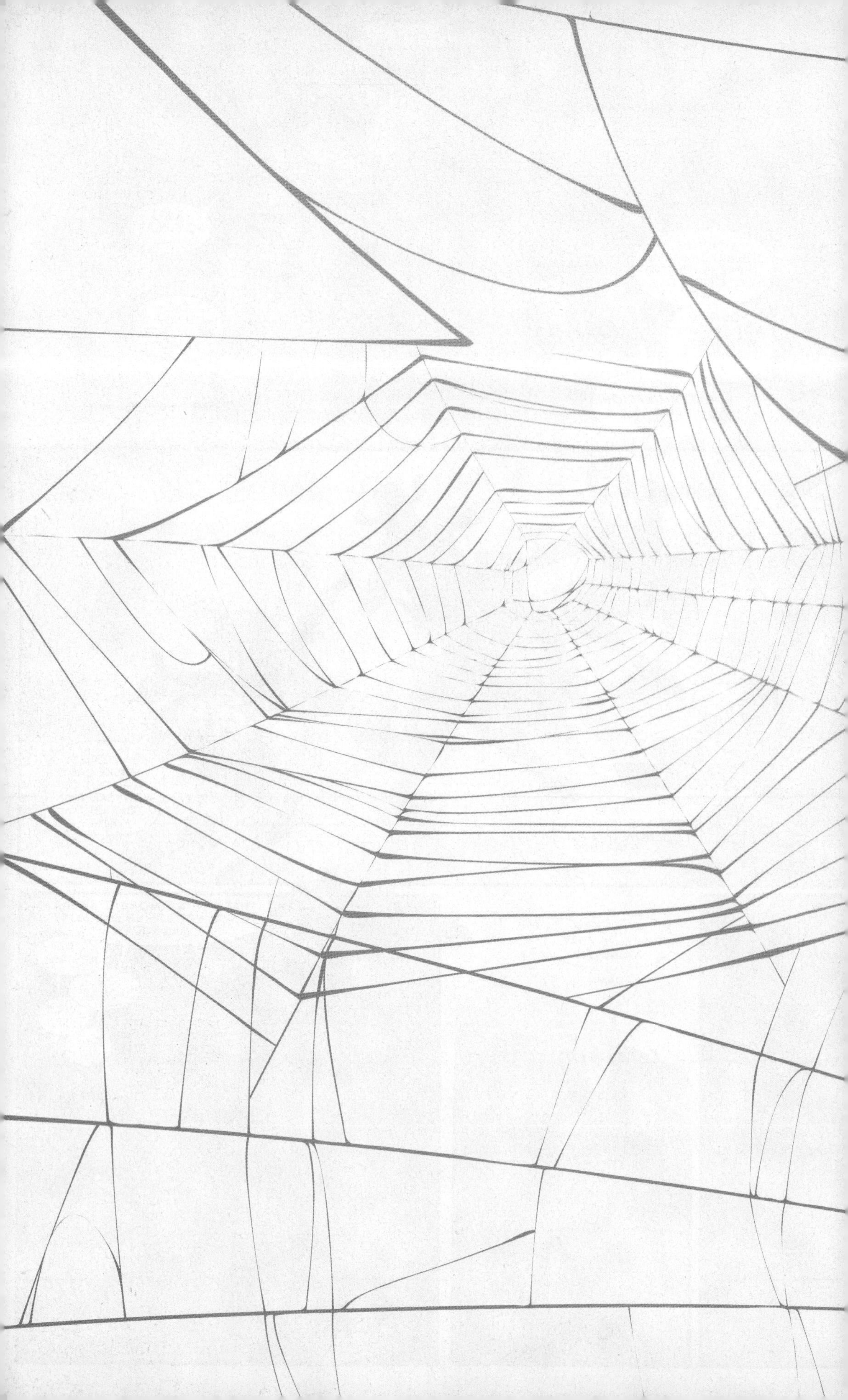

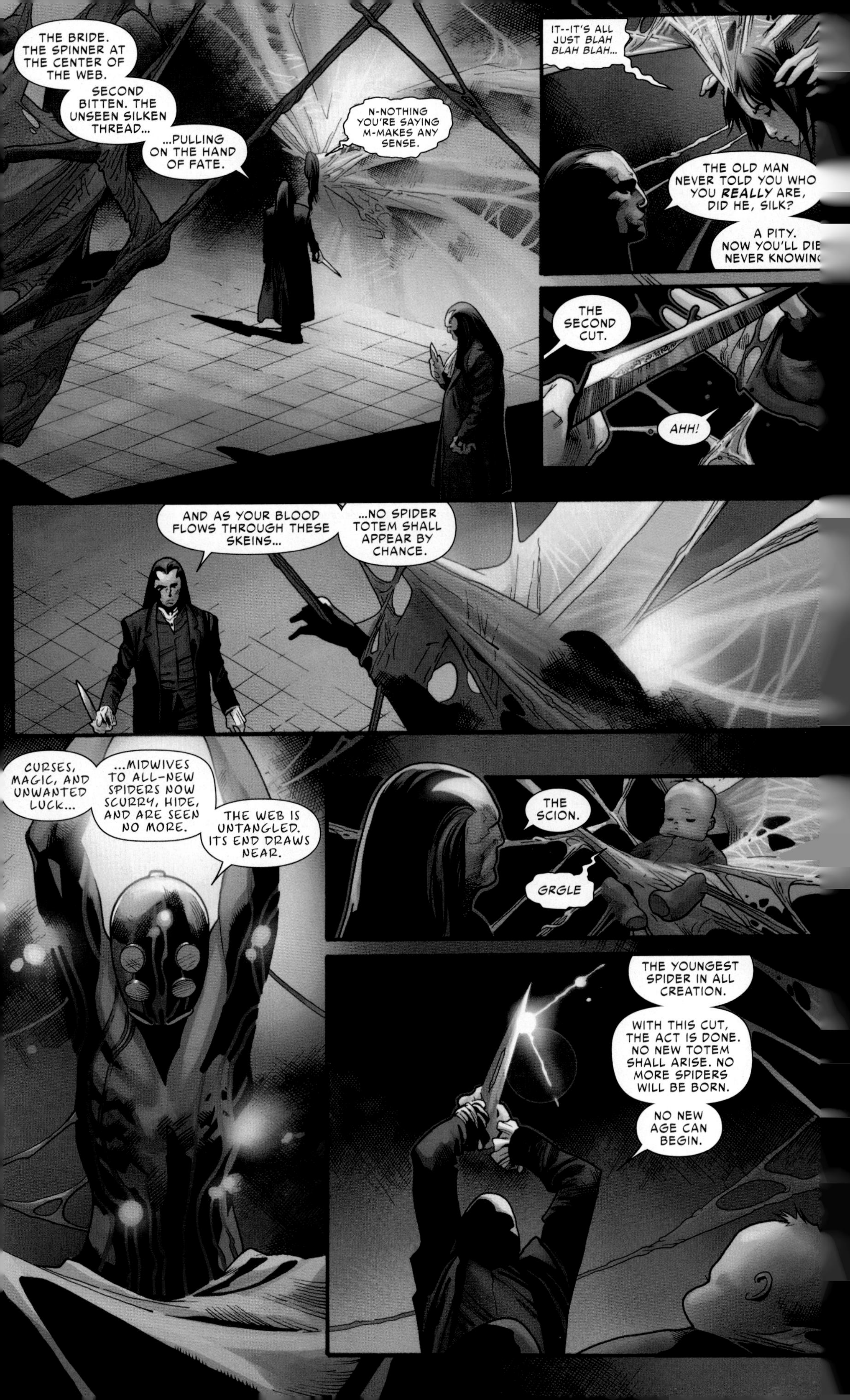
THE BRIDE. THE SPINNER AT THE CENTER OF THE WEB.
SECOND BITTEN. THE UNSEEN SILKEN THREAD...
...PULLING ON THE HAND OF FATE.
N-NOTHING YOU'RE SAYING M-MAKES ANY SENSE.
IT--IT'S ALL JUST BLAH BLAH BLAH...
THE OLD MAN NEVER TOLD YOU WHO YOU REALLY ARE, DID HE, SILK?
A PITY. NOW YOU'LL DIE NEVER KNOWING
THE SECOND CUT.
AHH!
AND AS YOUR BLOOD FLOWS THROUGH THESE SKEINS...
...NO SPIDER TOTEM SHALL APPEAR BY CHANCE.
CURSES, MAGIC, AND UNWANTED LUCK...
...MIDWIVES TO ALL-NEW SPIDERS NOW SCURRY, HIDE, AND ARE SEEN NO MORE.
THE WEB IS UNTANGLED. ITS END DRAWS NEAR.
THE SCION.
GRGLE
THE YOUNGEST SPIDER IN ALL CREATION.
WITH THIS CUT, THE ACT IS DONE. NO NEW TOTEM SHALL ARISE. NO MORE SPIDERS WILL BE BORN.
NO NEW AGE CAN BEGIN.

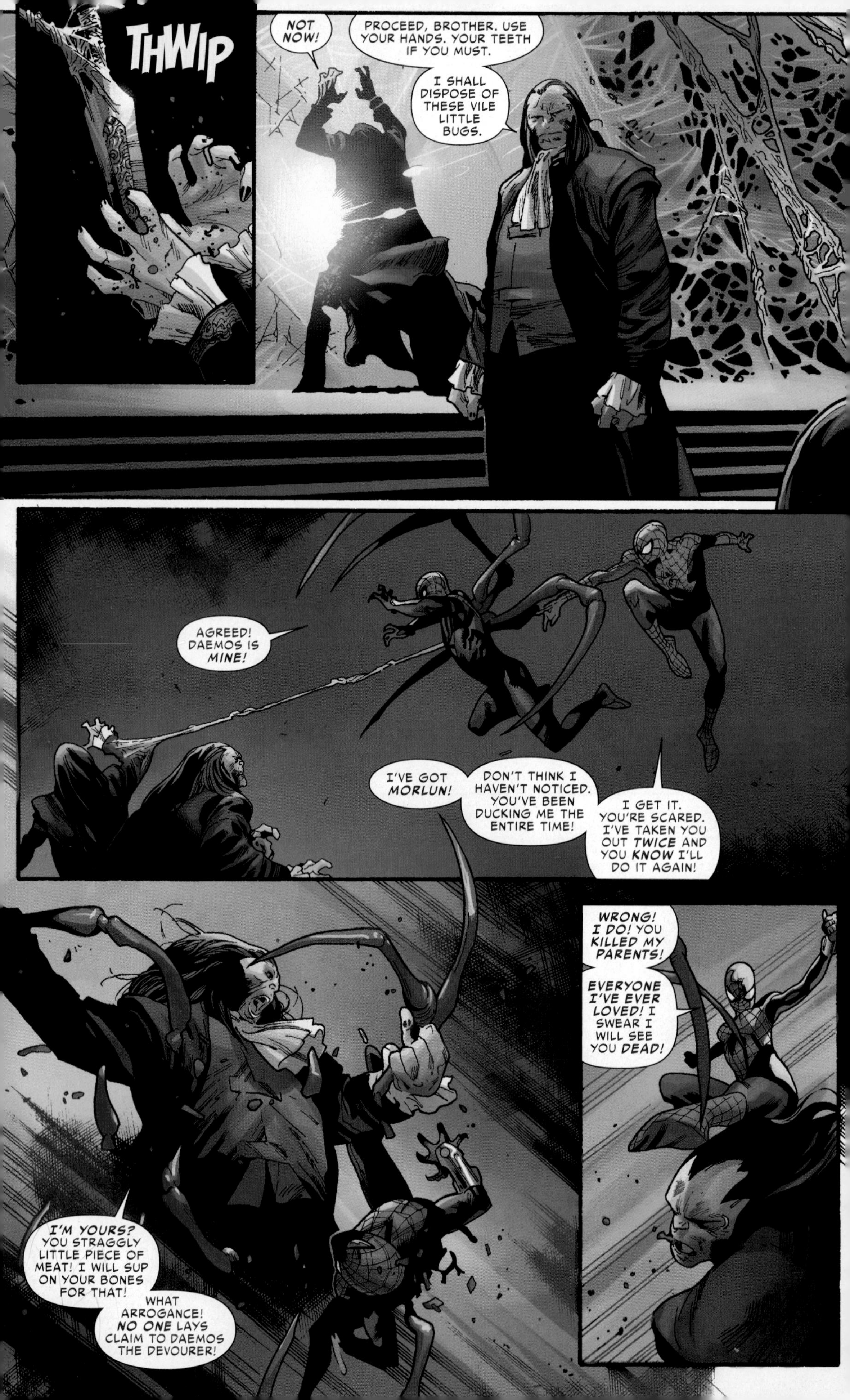
THWIP
NOT NOW!
PROCEED, BROTHER. USE YOUR HANDS. YOUR TEETH IF YOU MUST.
I SHALL DISPOSE OF THESE VILE LITTLE BUGS.
AGREED! DAEMOS IS MINE!
I'VE GOT MORLUN!
DON'T THINK I HAVEN'T NOTICED. YOU'VE BEEN DUCKING ME THE ENTIRE TIME!
I GET IT. YOU'RE SCARED. I'VE TAKEN YOU OUT TWICE AND YOU KNOW I'LL DO IT AGAIN!
WRONG! I DO! YOU KILLED MY PARENTS!
EVERYONE I'VE EVER LOVED! I SWEAR I WILL SEE YOU DEAD!
I'M YOURS? YOU STRAGGLY LITTLE PIECE OF MEAT! I WILL SUP ON YOUR BONES FOR THAT!
WHAT ARROGANCE! NO ONE LAYS CLAIM TO DAEMOS THE DEVOURER!

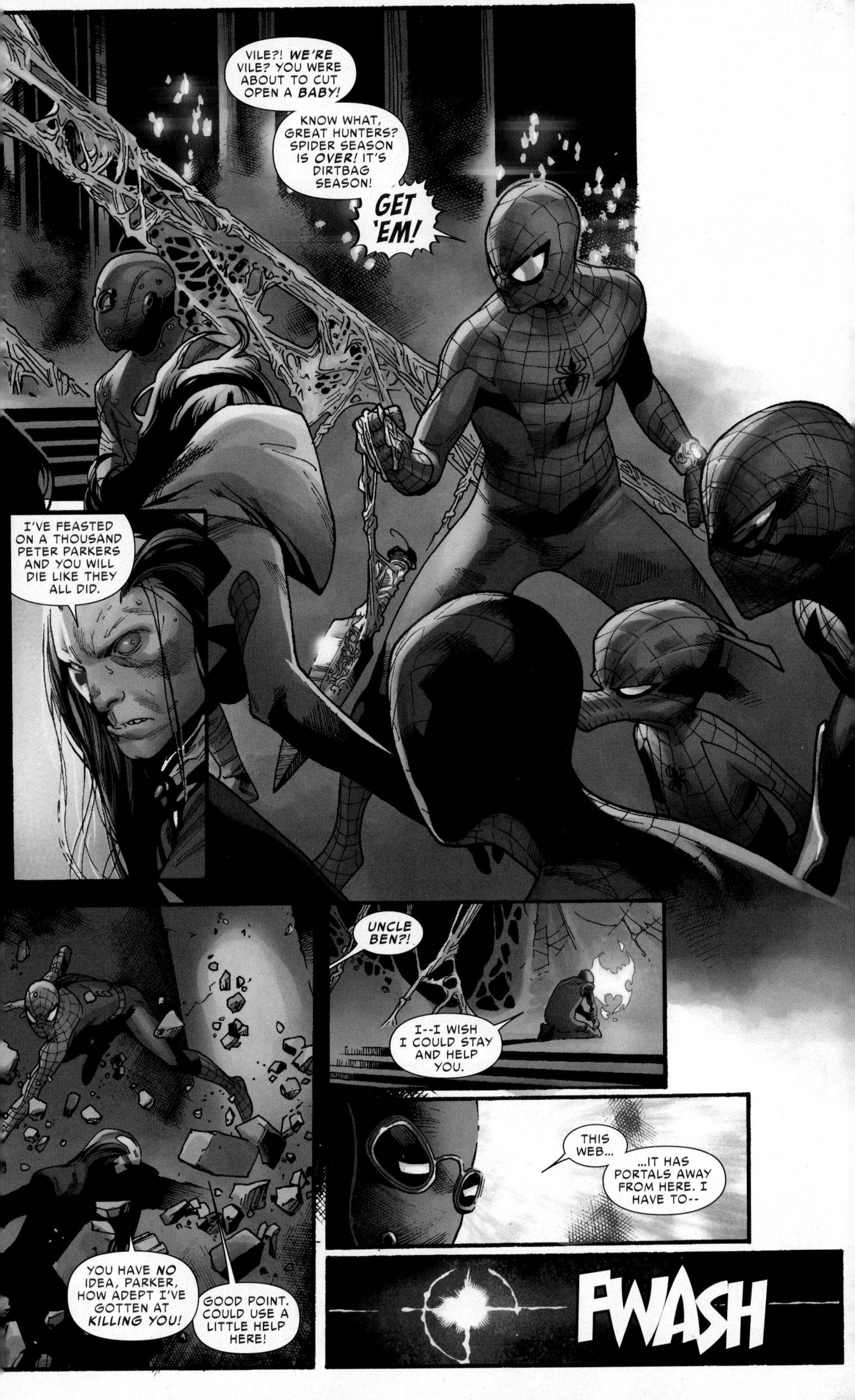
VILE?! WE'RE VILE? YOU WERE ABOUT TO CUT OPEN A BABY!
KNOW WHAT, GREAT HUNTERS? SPIDER SEASON IS OVER! IT'S DIRTBAG SEASON!
GET 'EM!
I'VE FEASTED ON A THOUSAND PETER PARKERS AND YOU WILL DIE LIKE THEY ALL DID.
YOU HAVE NO IDEA, PARKER, HOW ADEPT I'VE GOTTEN AT KILLING YOU!
GOOD POINT. COULD USE A LITTLE HELP HERE!
UNCLE BEN?!
I--I WISH I COULD STAY AND HELP YOU.
THIS WEB...
...IT HAS PORTALS AWAY FROM HERE. I HAVE TO--
FWASH

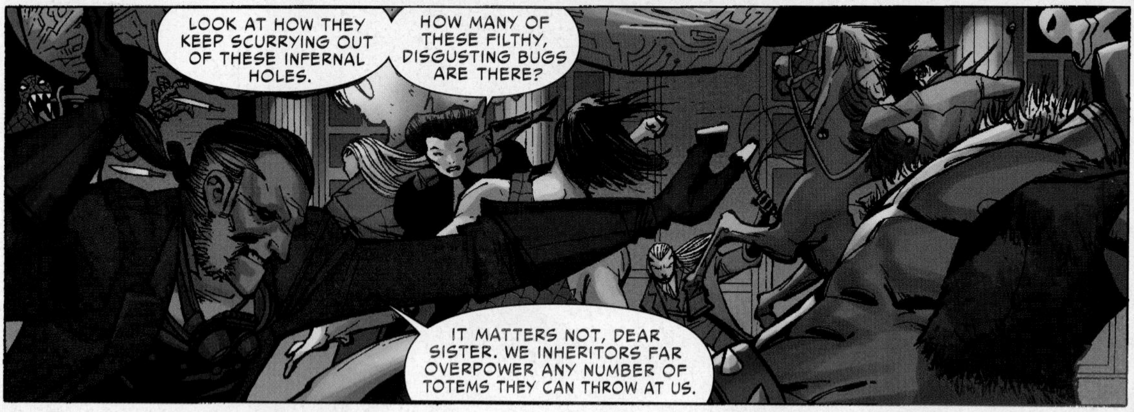
LOOK AT HOW THEY KEEP SCURRYING OUT OF THESE INFERNAL HOLES.
HOW MANY OF THESE FILTHY, DISGUSTING BUGS ARE THERE?
IT MATTERS NOT, DEAR SISTER. WE INHERITORS FAR OVERPOWER ANY NUMBER OF TOTEMS THEY CAN THROW AT US.

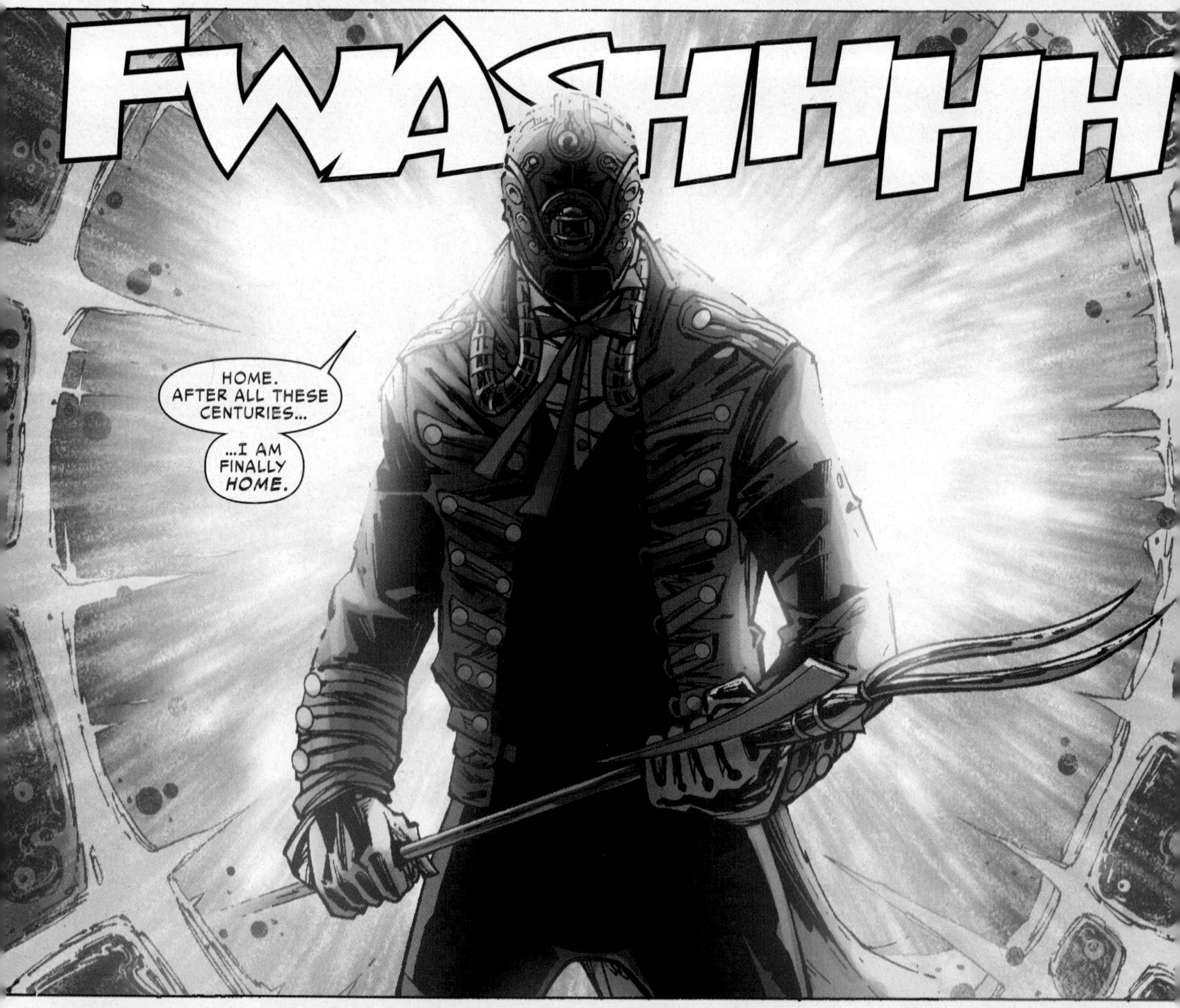
FWASHHHH
HOME. AFTER ALL THESE CENTURIES...
...I AM FINALLY *HOME*.

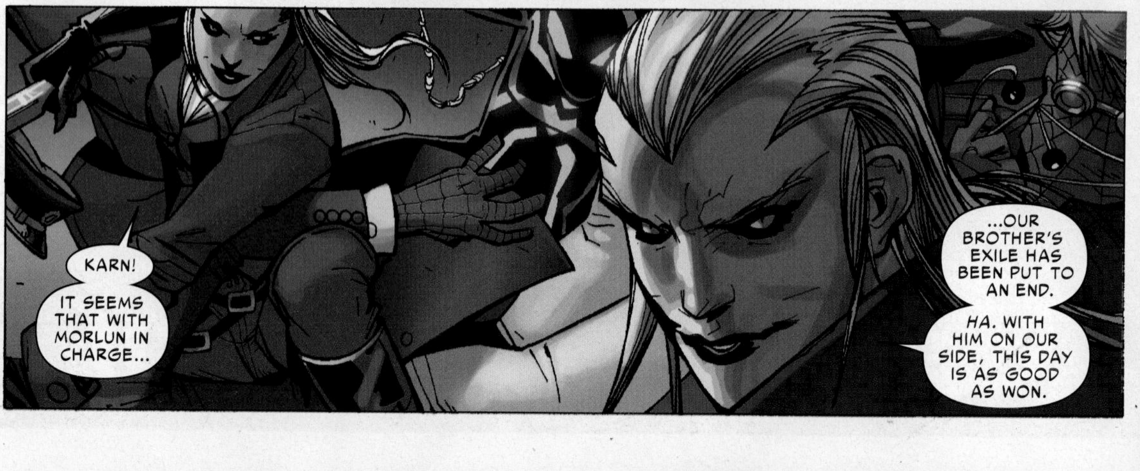
KARN!
IT SEEMS THAT WITH MORLUN IN CHARGE...
...OUR BROTHER'S EXILE HAS BEEN PUT TO AN END.
HA. WITH HIM ON OUR SIDE, THIS DAY IS AS GOOD AS WON.

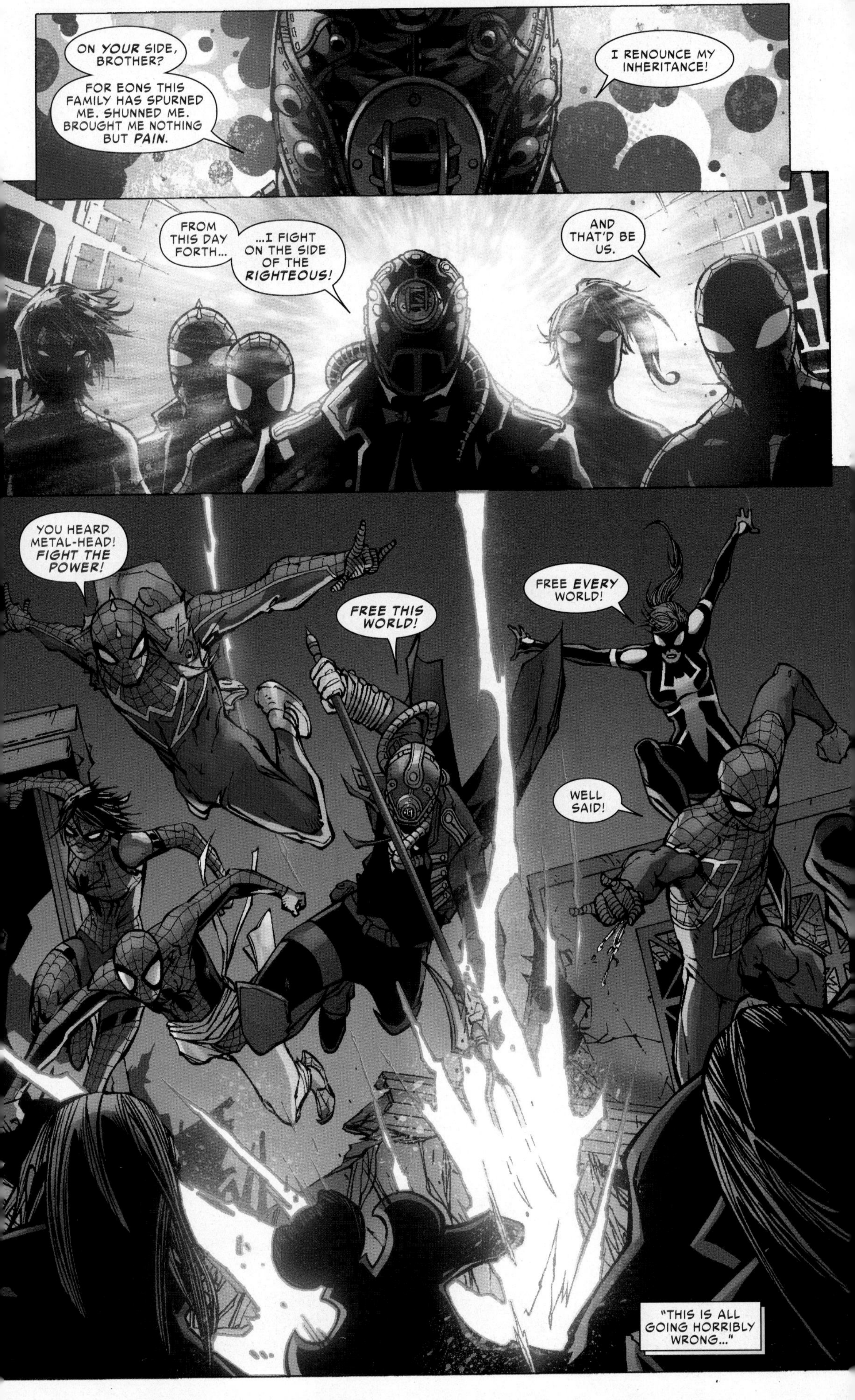
ON YOUR SIDE, BROTHER?
FOR EONS THIS FAMILY HAS SPURNED ME. SHUNNED ME. BROUGHT ME NOTHING BUT PAIN.
I RENOUNCE MY INHERITANCE!
FROM THIS DAY FORTH...
...I FIGHT ON THE SIDE OF THE RIGHTEOUS!
AND THAT'D BE US.
YOU HEARD METAL-HEAD! FIGHT THE POWER!
FREE THIS WORLD!
FREE EVERY WORLD!
WELL SAID!
"THIS IS ALL GOING HORRIBLY WRONG..."

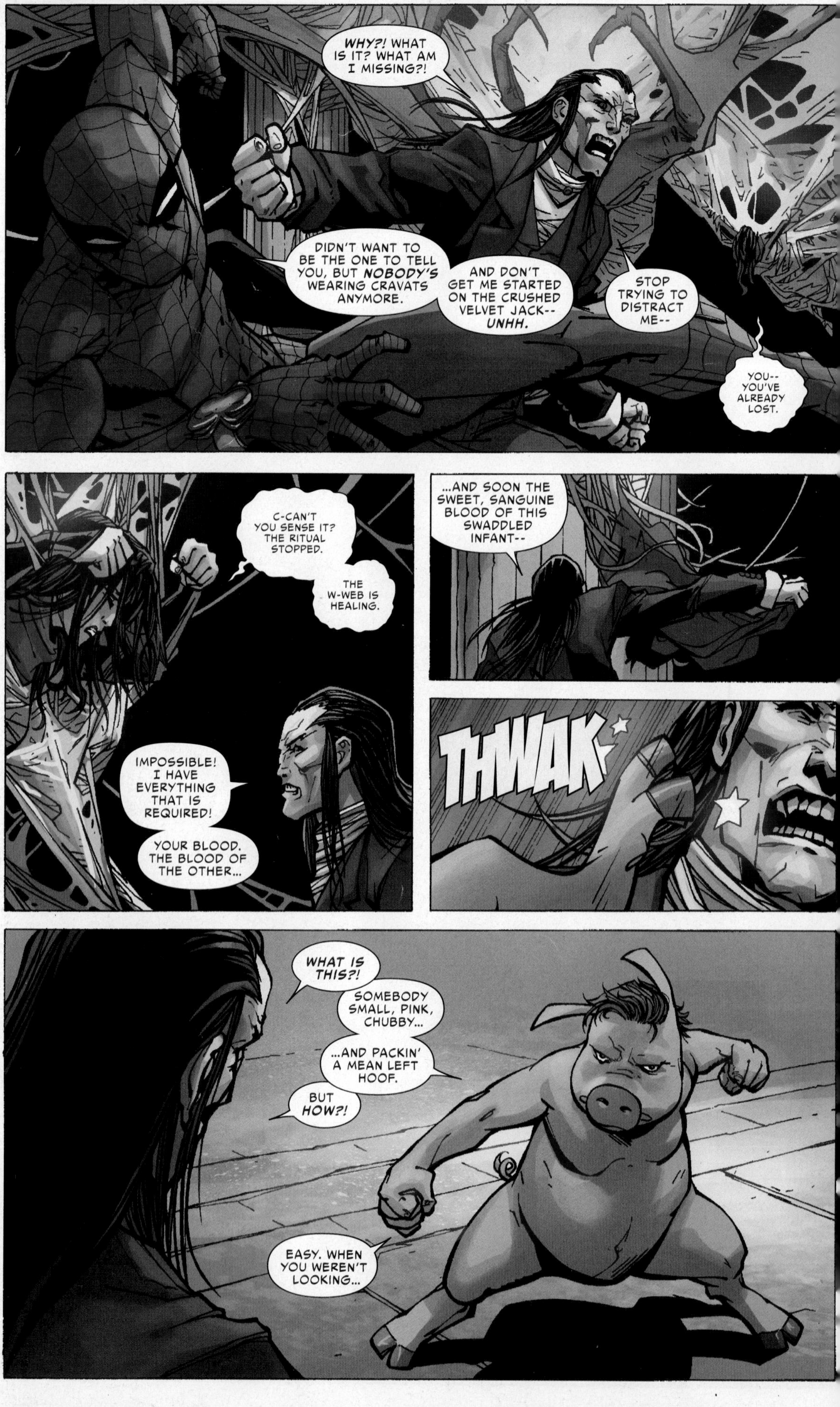

WHY?! WHAT IS IT? WHAT AM I MISSING?!
DIDN'T WANT TO BE THE ONE TO TELL YOU, BUT NOBODY'S WEARING CRAVATS ANYMORE.
AND DON'T GET ME STARTED ON THE CRUSHED VELVET JACK-- UNHH.
STOP TRYING TO DISTRACT ME--
YOU-- YOU'VE ALREADY LOST.
C-CAN'T YOU SENSE IT? THE RITUAL STOPPED.
THE W-WEB IS HEALING.
IMPOSSIBLE! I HAVE EVERYTHING THAT IS REQUIRED!
YOUR BLOOD. THE BLOOD OF THE OTHER...
...AND SOON THE SWEET, SANGUINE BLOOD OF THIS SWADDLED INFANT--
THWAK
WHAT IS THIS?!
SOMEBODY SMALL, PINK, CHUBBY...
...AND PACKIN' A MEAN LEFT HOOF.
BUT HOW?!
EASY. WHEN YOU WEREN'T LOOKING...

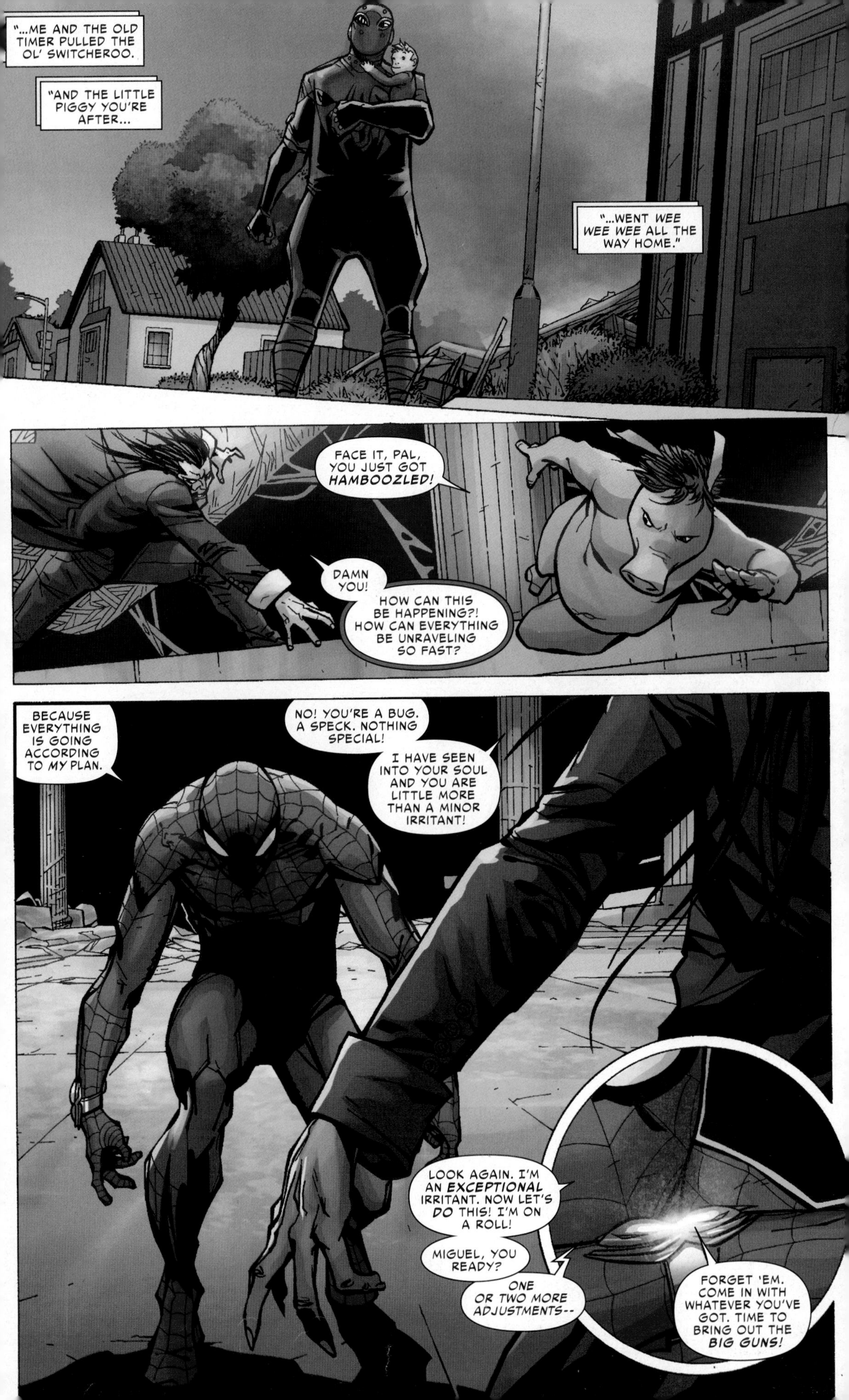
"...ME AND THE OLD TIMER PULLED THE OL' SWITCHEROO.
"AND THE LITTLE PIGGY YOU'RE AFTER...
"...WENT WEE WEE WEE ALL THE WAY HOME."
FACE IT, PAL, YOU JUST GOT HAMBOOZLED!
DAMN YOU!
HOW CAN THIS BE HAPPENING?! HOW CAN EVERYTHING BE UNRAVELING SO FAST?
BECAUSE EVERYTHING IS GOING ACCORDING TO MY PLAN.
NO! YOU'RE A BUG. A SPECK. NOTHING SPECIAL!
I HAVE SEEN INTO YOUR SOUL AND YOU ARE LITTLE MORE THAN A MINOR IRRITANT!
LOOK AGAIN. I'M AN EXCEPTIONAL IRRITANT. NOW LET'S DO THIS! I'M ON A ROLL!
MIGUEL, YOU READY?
ONE OR TWO MORE ADJUSTMENTS--
FORGET 'EM. COME IN WITH WHATEVER YOU'VE GOT. TIME TO BRING OUT THE BIG GUNS!

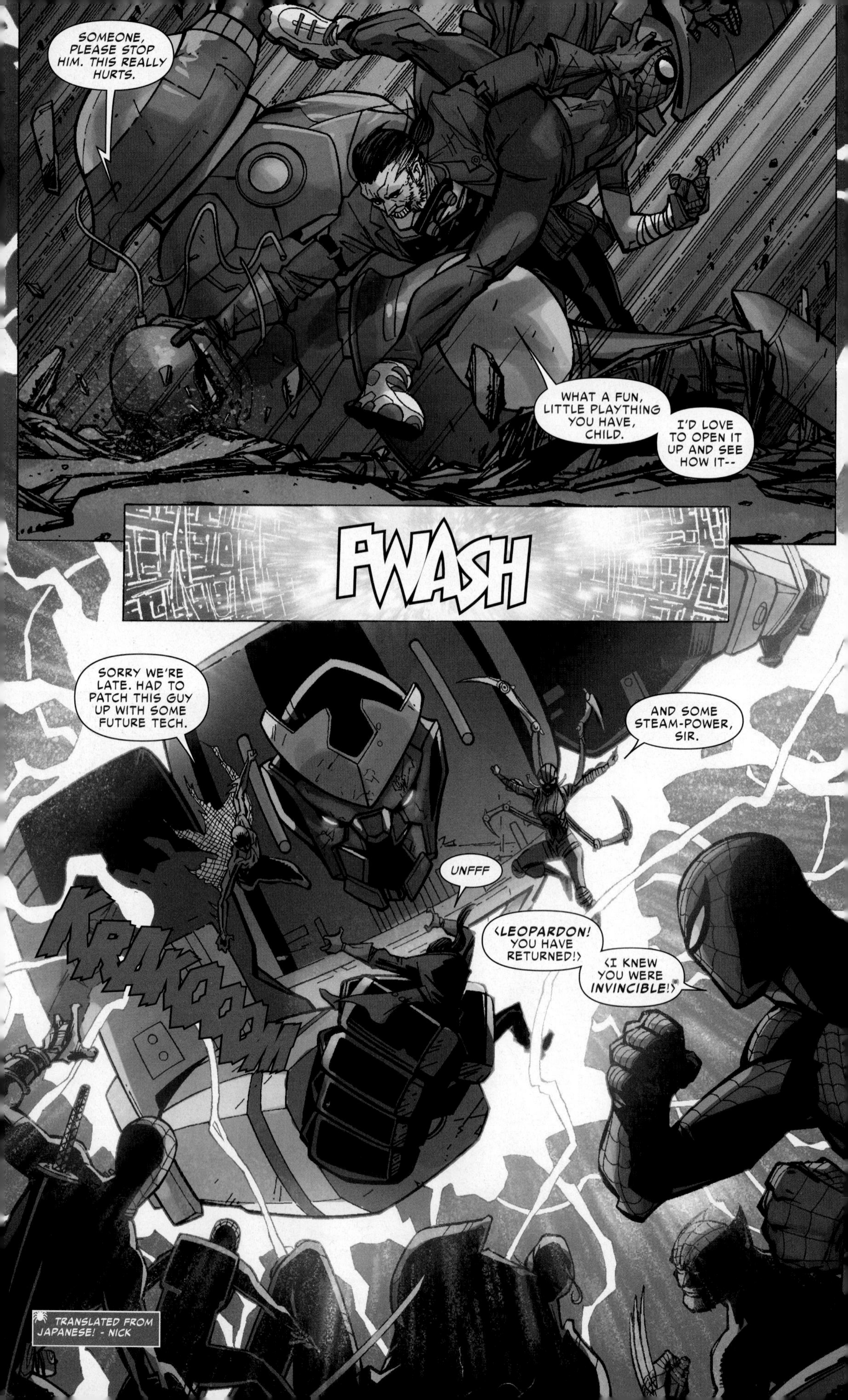
SOMEONE, PLEASE STOP HIM. THIS REALLY HURTS.
WHAT A FUN, LITTLE PLAYTHING YOU HAVE, CHILD.
I'D LOVE TO OPEN IT UP AND SEE HOW IT--
FWASH
SORRY WE'RE LATE. HAD TO PATCH THIS GUY UP WITH SOME FUTURE TECH.
AND SOME STEAM-POWER, SIR.
UNFFF
KRAKOOOM
‹LEOPARDON! YOU HAVE RETURNED!›
‹I KNEW YOU WERE INVINCIBLE!›
TRANSLATED FROM JAPANESE! - NICK

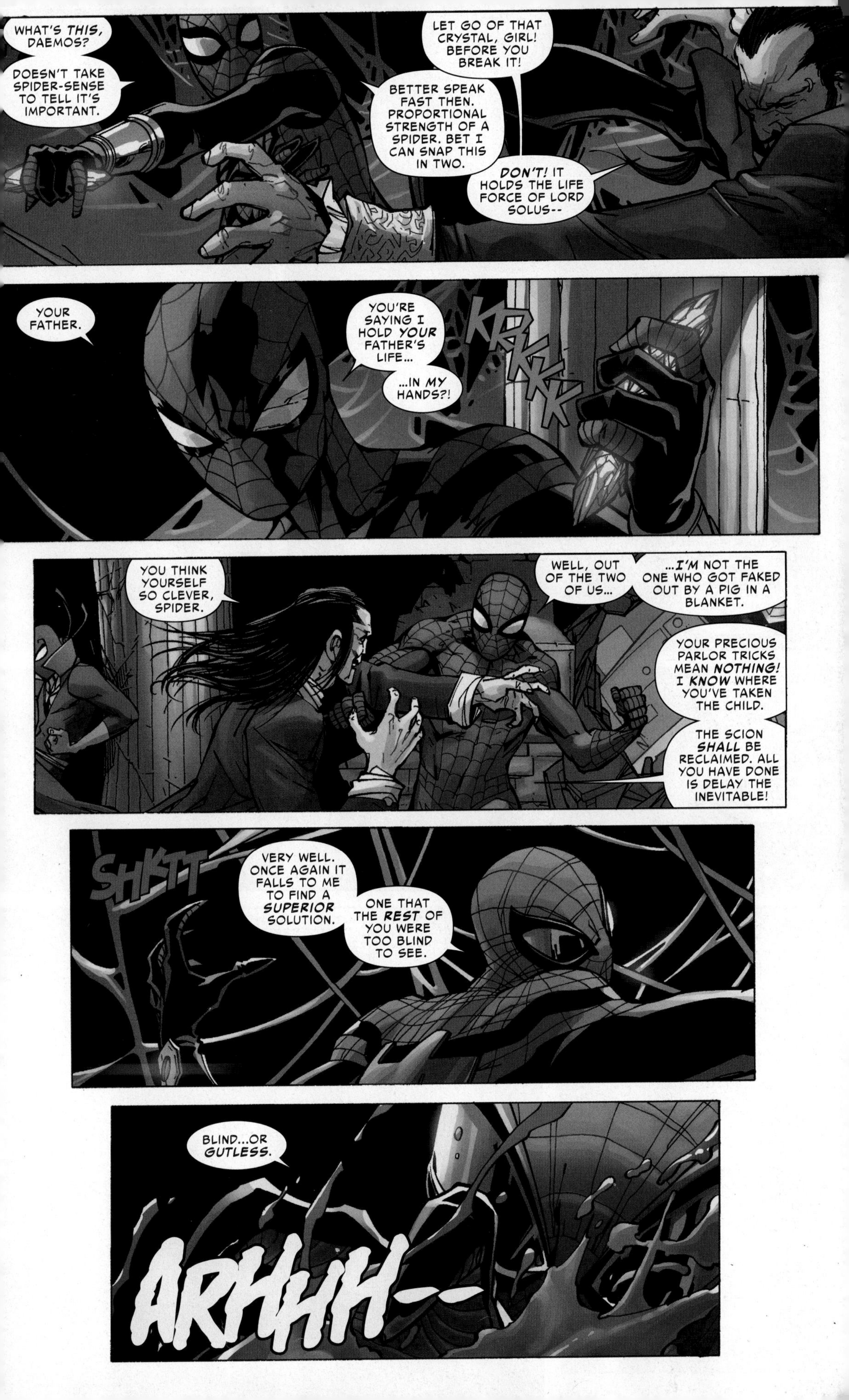
WHAT'S THIS, DAEMOS?
DOESN'T TAKE SPIDER-SENSE TO TELL IT'S IMPORTANT.
LET GO OF THAT CRYSTAL, GIRL! BEFORE YOU BREAK IT!
BETTER SPEAK FAST THEN. PROPORTIONAL STRENGTH OF A SPIDER. BET I CAN SNAP THIS IN TWO.
DON'T! IT HOLDS THE LIFE FORCE OF LORD SOLUS--
YOUR FATHER.
YOU'RE SAYING I HOLD YOUR FATHER'S LIFE...
...IN MY HANDS?!
KRKKKK
YOU THINK YOURSELF SO CLEVER, SPIDER.
WELL, OUT OF THE TWO OF US...
...I'M NOT THE ONE WHO GOT FAKED OUT BY A PIG IN A BLANKET.
YOUR PRECIOUS PARLOR TRICKS MEAN NOTHING! I KNOW WHERE YOU'VE TAKEN THE CHILD.
THE SCION SHALL BE RECLAIMED. ALL YOU HAVE DONE IS DELAY THE INEVITABLE!
SHKTT
VERY WELL. ONCE AGAIN IT FALLS TO ME TO FIND A SUPERIOR SOLUTION.
ONE THAT THE REST OF YOU WERE TOO BLIND TO SEE.
BLIND...OR GUTLESS.
ARHHH--

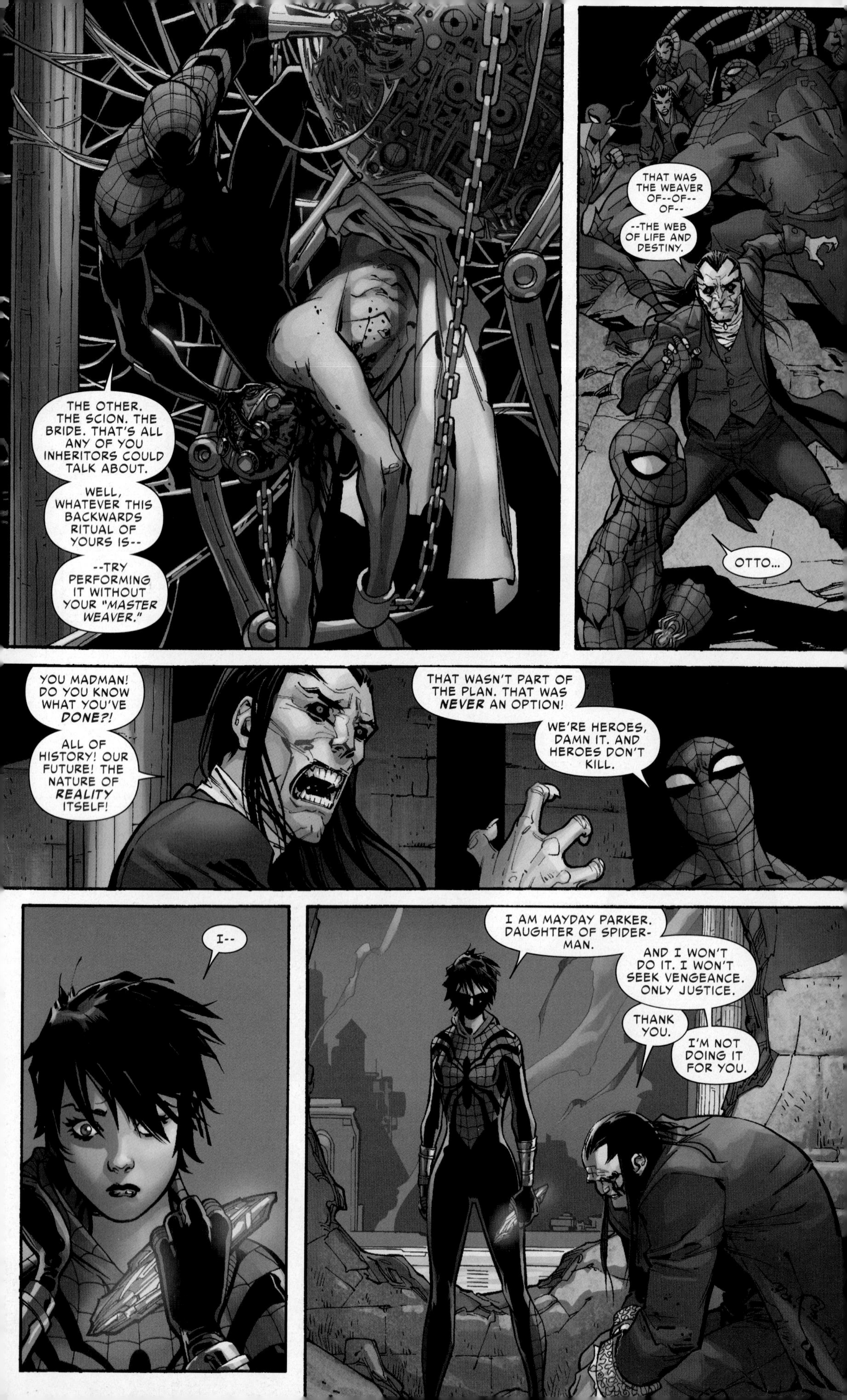
THE OTHER. THE SCION. THE BRIDE. THAT'S ALL ANY OF YOU INHERITORS COULD TALK ABOUT.
WELL, WHATEVER THIS BACKWARDS RITUAL OF YOURS IS--
--TRY PERFORMING IT WITHOUT YOUR "MASTER WEAVER."
THAT WAS THE WEAVER OF--OF--OF--
--THE WEB OF LIFE AND DESTINY.
OTTO...
YOU MADMAN! DO YOU KNOW WHAT YOU'VE DONE?!
ALL OF HISTORY! OUR FUTURE! THE NATURE OF REALITY ITSELF!
THAT WASN'T PART OF THE PLAN. THAT WAS NEVER AN OPTION!
WE'RE HEROES, DAMN IT. AND HEROES DON'T KILL.
I--
I AM MAYDAY PARKER. DAUGHTER OF SPIDER-MAN.
AND I WON'T DO IT. I WON'T SEEK VENGEANCE. ONLY JUSTICE.
THANK YOU.
I'M NOT DOING IT FOR YOU.

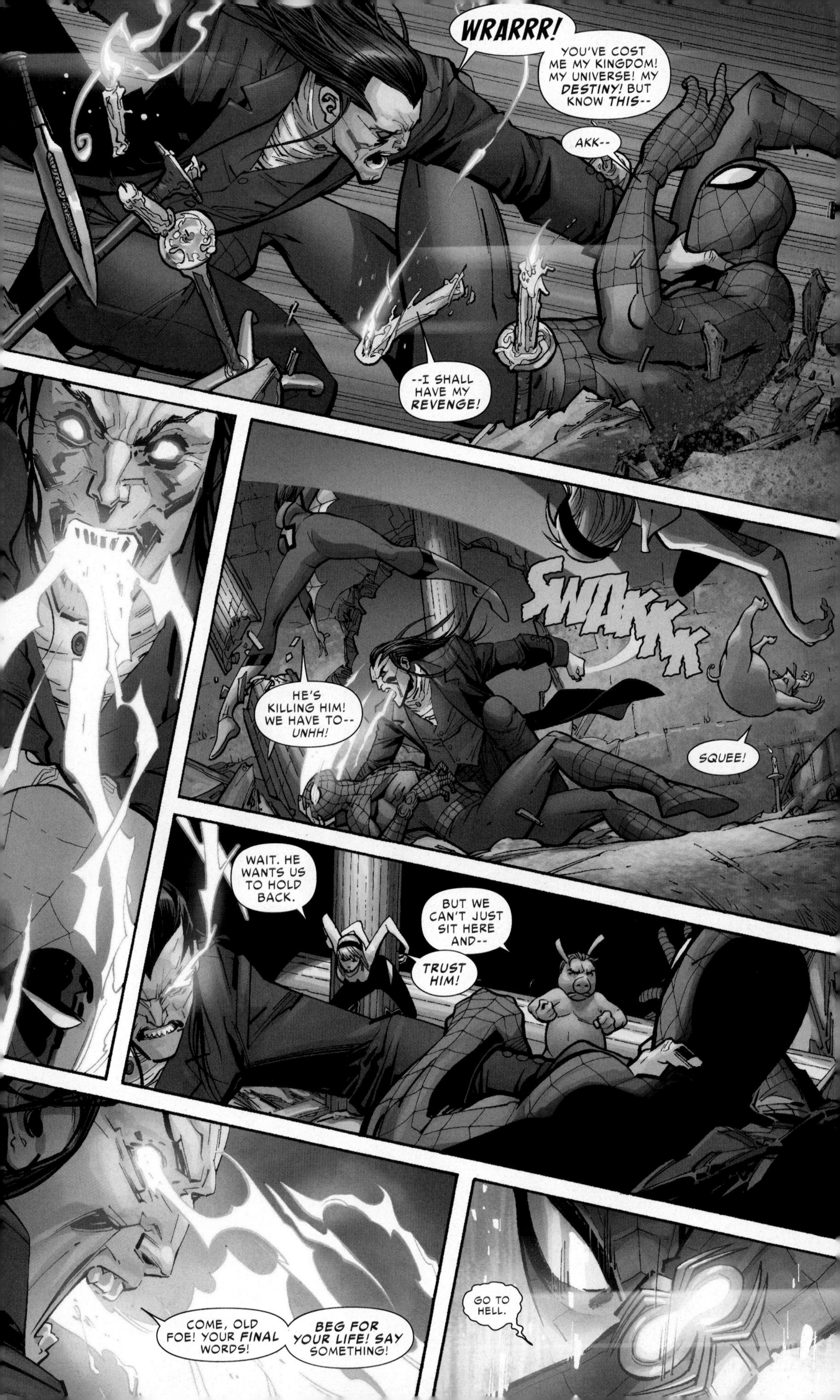
WRARRR!
YOU'VE COST ME MY KINGDOM! MY UNIVERSE! MY DESTINY! BUT KNOW THIS--
AKK--
--I SHALL HAVE MY REVENGE!
SWAKKK
HE'S KILLING HIM! WE HAVE TO-- UNHH!
SQUEE!
WAIT. HE WANTS US TO HOLD BACK.
BUT WE CAN'T JUST SIT HERE AND--
TRUST HIM!
COME, OLD FOE! YOUR FINAL WORDS!
BEG FOR YOUR LIFE! SAY SOMETHING!
GO TO HELL.

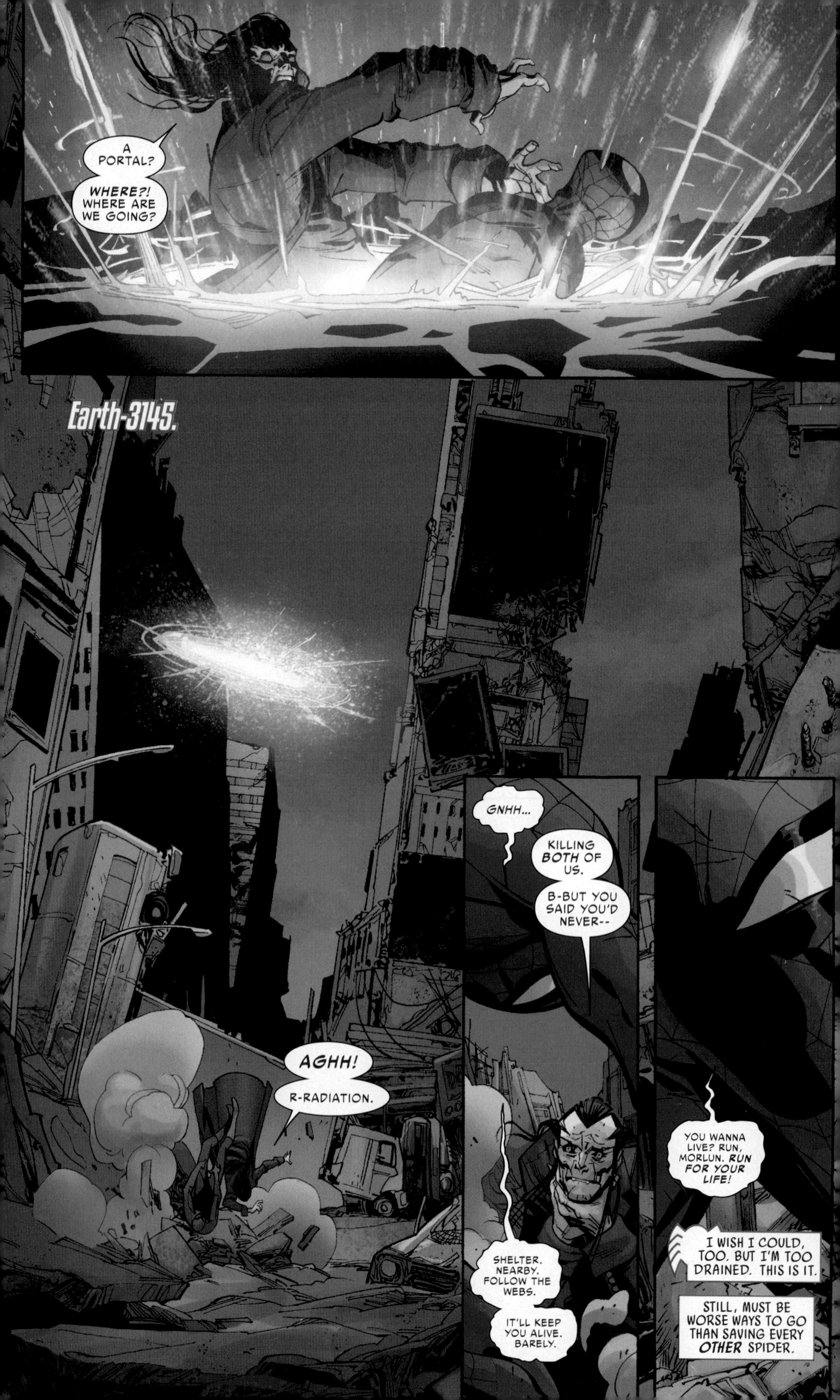

A PORTAL?
WHERE?! WHERE ARE WE GOING?
Earth-3145.
AGHH!
R-RADIATION.
GNHH...
KILLING BOTH OF US.
B-BUT YOU SAID YOU'D NEVER--
SHELTER. NEARBY. FOLLOW THE WEBS.
IT'LL KEEP YOU ALIVE. BARELY.
YOU WANNA LIVE? RUN, MORLUN. RUN FOR YOUR LIFE!
I WISH I COULD, TOO. BUT I'M TOO DRAINED. THIS IS IT.
STILL, MUST BE WORSE WAYS TO GO THAN SAVING EVERY OTHER SPIDER.

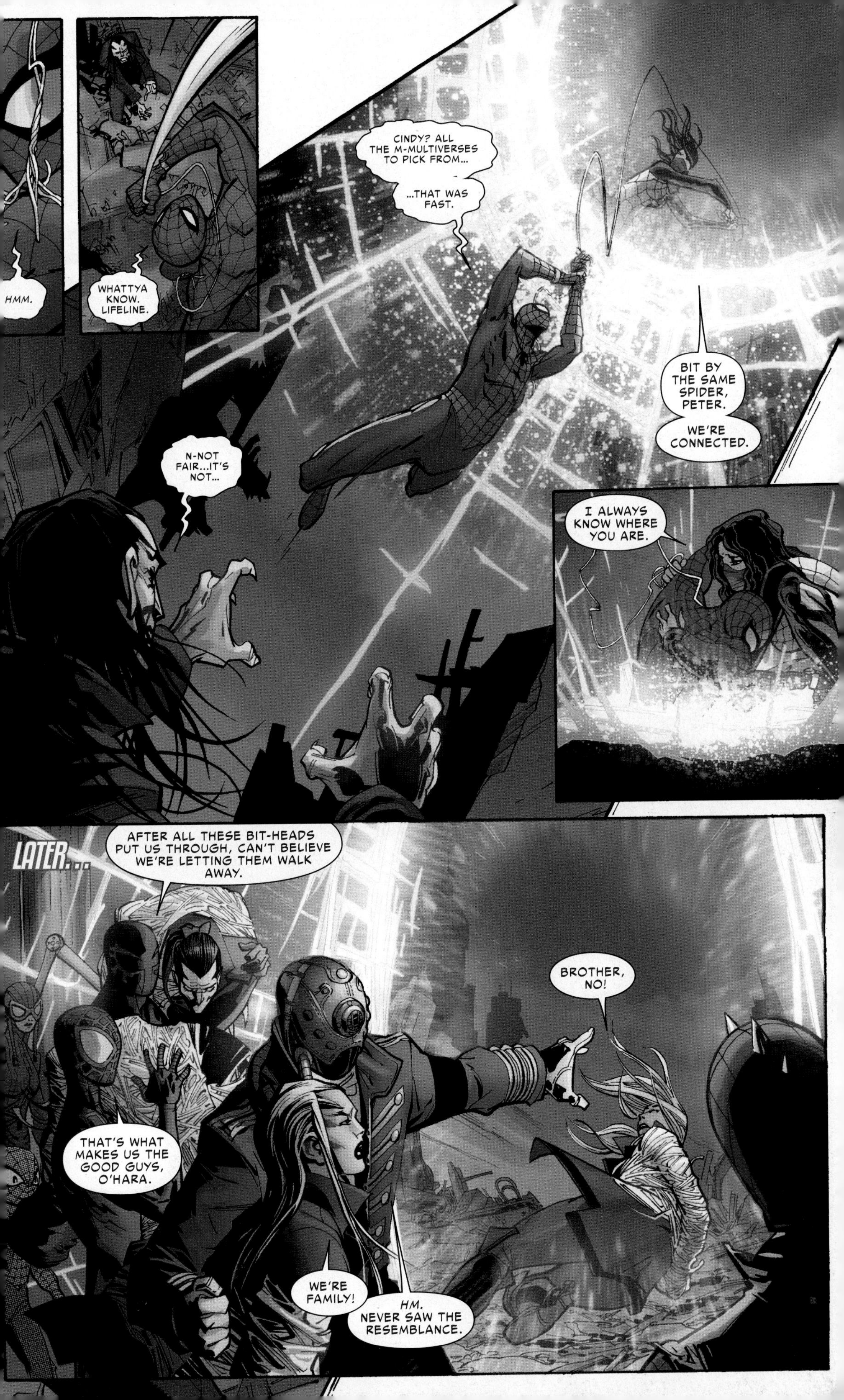
HMM.
WHATTYA KNOW. LIFELINE.
CINDY? ALL THE M-MULTIVERSES TO PICK FROM...
...THAT WAS FAST.
BIT BY THE SAME SPIDER, PETER.
WE'RE CONNECTED.
N-NOT FAIR...IT'S NOT...
I ALWAYS KNOW WHERE YOU ARE.
LATER...
AFTER ALL THESE BIT-HEADS PUT US THROUGH, CAN'T BELIEVE WE'RE LETTING THEM WALK AWAY.
THAT'S WHAT MAKES US THE GOOD GUYS, O'HARA.
BROTHER, NO!
WE'RE FAMILY!
HM. NEVER SAW THE RESEMBLANCE.

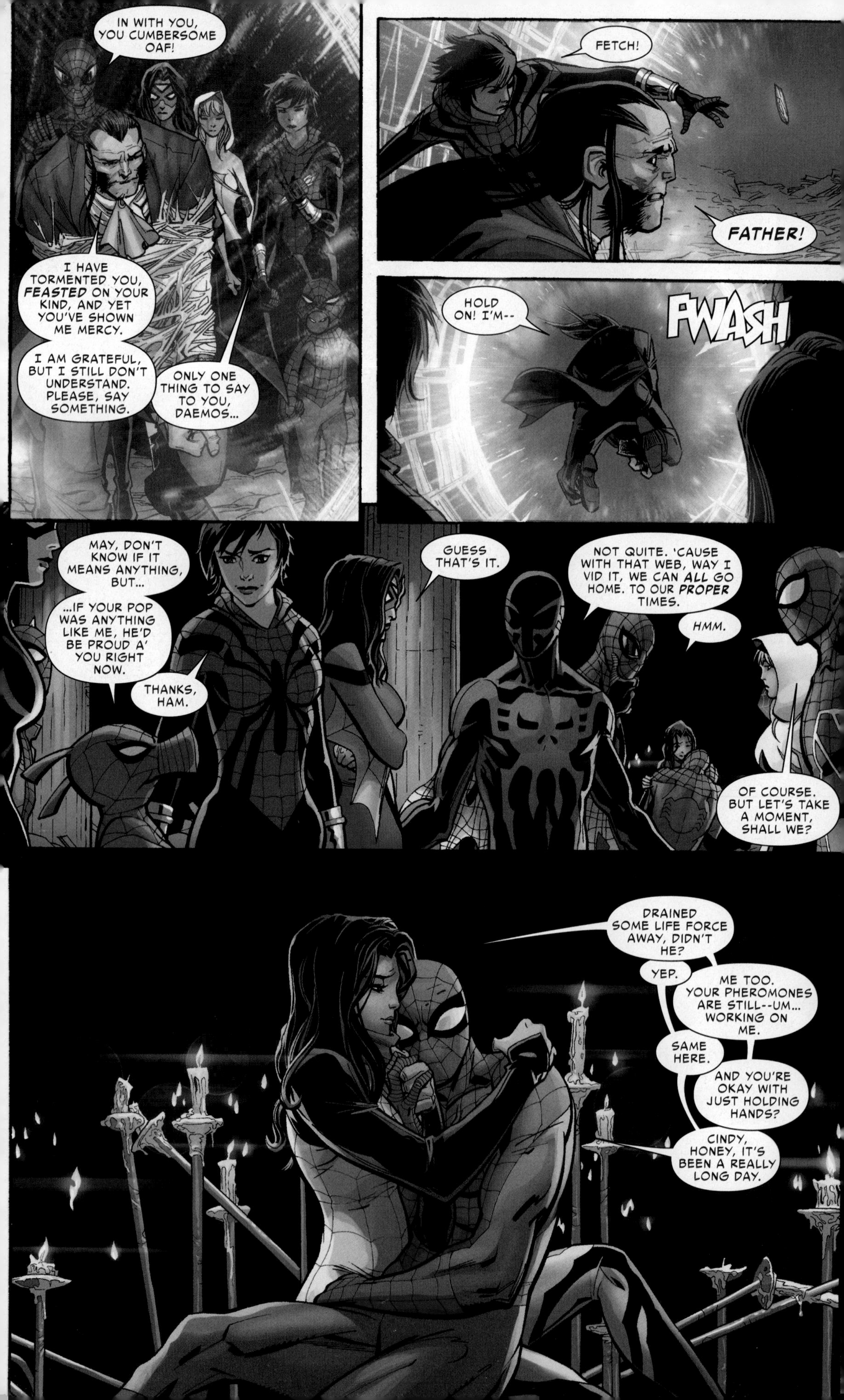
IN WITH YOU, YOU CUMBERSOME OAF!
I HAVE TORMENTED YOU, FEASTED ON YOUR KIND, AND YET YOU'VE SHOWN ME MERCY.
I AM GRATEFUL, BUT I STILL DON'T UNDERSTAND. PLEASE, SAY SOMETHING.
ONLY ONE THING TO SAY TO YOU, DAEMOS...
FETCH!
FATHER!
HOLD ON! I'M--
FWASH
MAY, DON'T KNOW IF IT MEANS ANYTHING, BUT...
...IF YOUR POP WAS ANYTHING LIKE ME, HE'D BE PROUD A' YOU RIGHT NOW.
THANKS, HAM.
GUESS THAT'S IT.
NOT QUITE. 'CAUSE WITH THAT WEB, WAY I VID IT, WE CAN ALL GO HOME. TO OUR PROPER TIMES.
HMM.
OF COURSE. BUT LET'S TAKE A MOMENT, SHALL WE?
DRAINED SOME LIFE FORCE AWAY, DIDN'T HE?
YEP.
ME TOO. YOUR PHEROMONES ARE STILL--UM... WORKING ON ME.
SAME HERE.
AND YOU'RE OKAY WITH JUST HOLDING HANDS?
CINDY, HONEY, IT'S BEEN A REALLY LONG DAY.

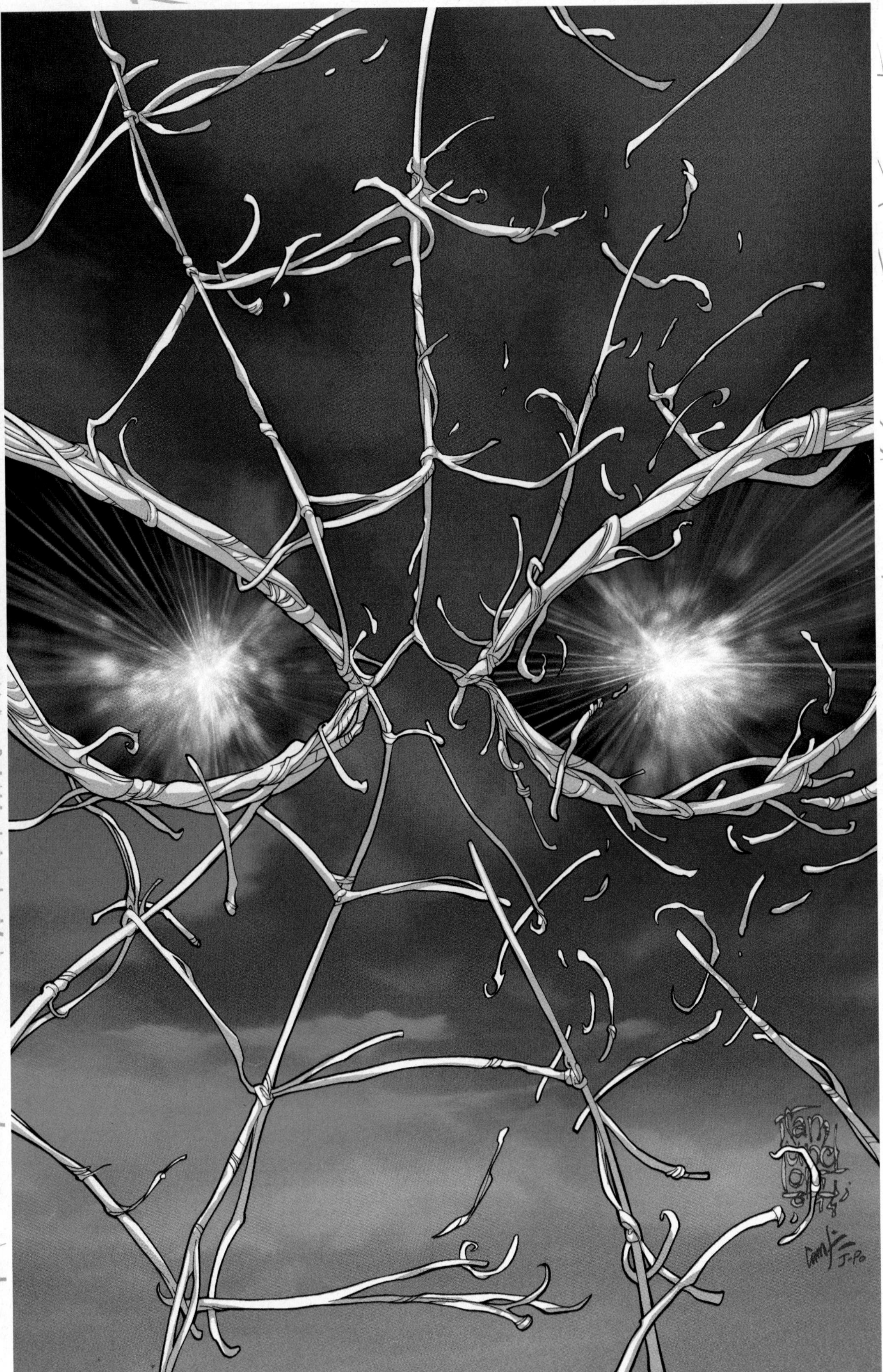

AMAZING SPIDER-MAN 15
SPIDER-VERSE EPILOGUE

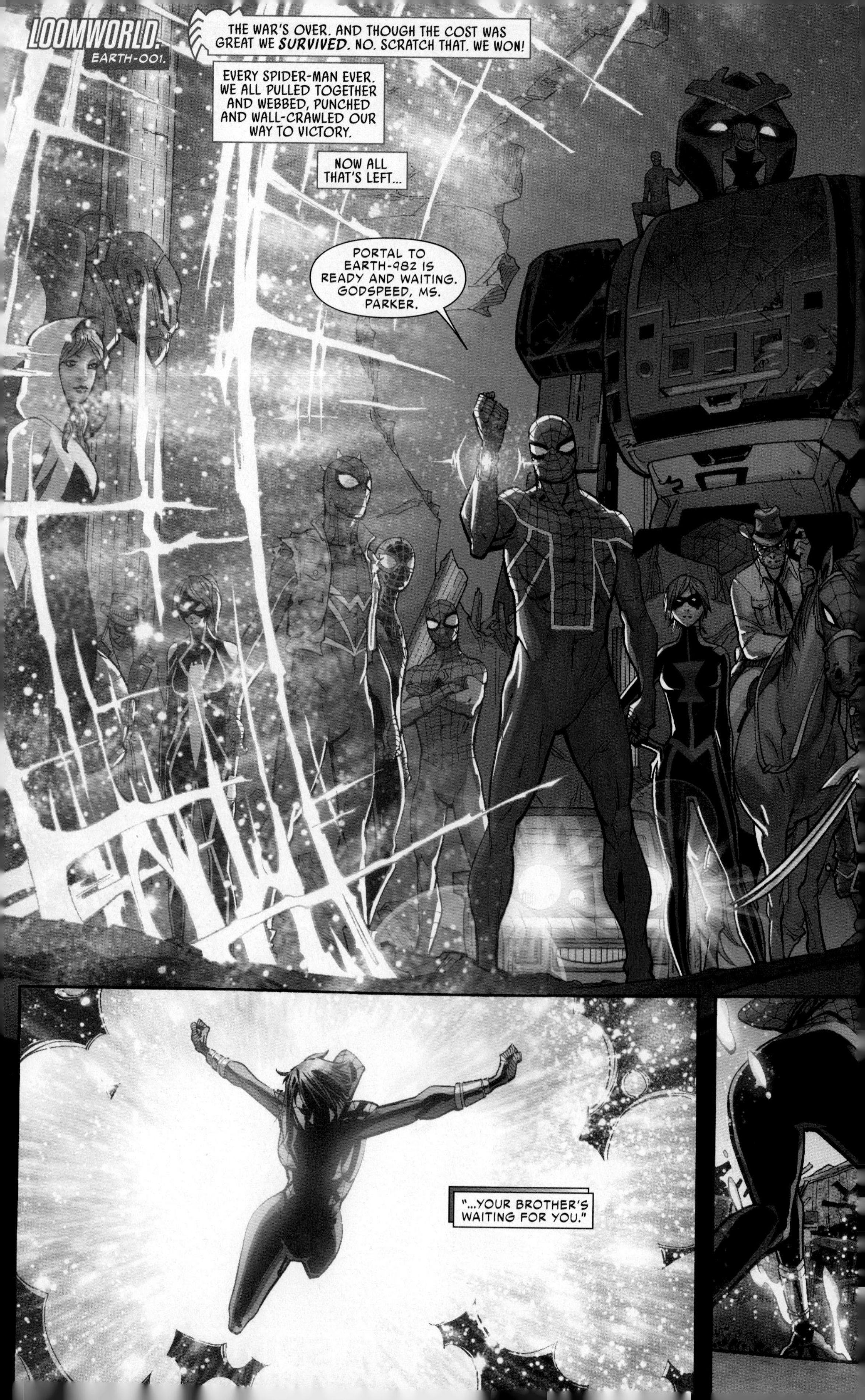
LOOMWORLD.
EARTH-001.
THE WAR'S OVER. AND THOUGH THE COST WAS GREAT WE SURVIVED. NO. SCRATCH THAT. WE WON!
EVERY SPIDER-MAN EVER. WE ALL PULLED TOGETHER AND WEBBED, PUNCHED AND WALL-CRAWLED OUR WAY TO VICTORY.
NOW ALL THAT'S LEFT...
PORTAL TO EARTH-982 IS READY AND WAITING. GODSPEED, MS. PARKER.
"...YOUR BROTHER'S WAITING FOR YOU."

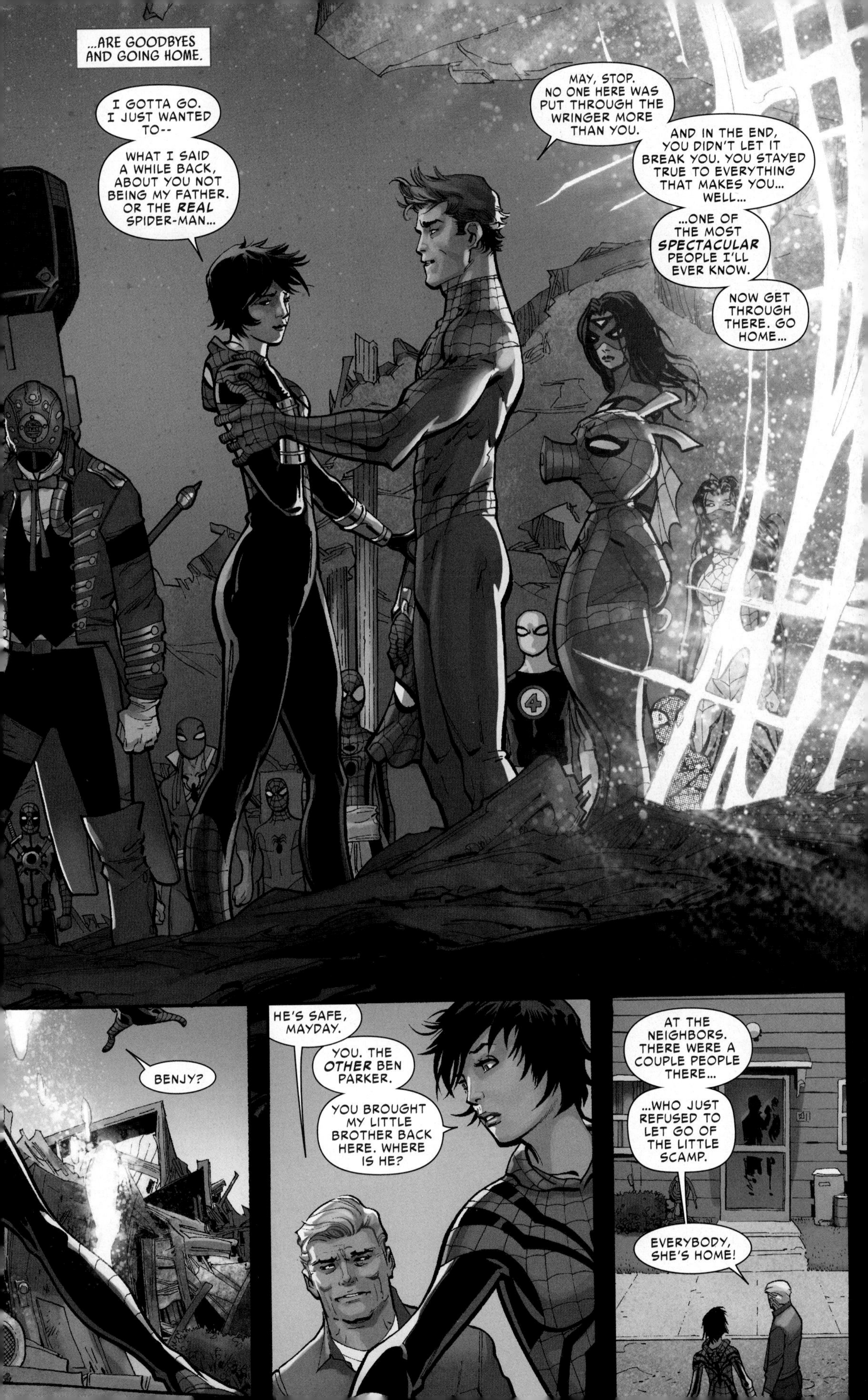
...ARE GOODBYES AND GOING HOME.
I GOTTA GO. I JUST WANTED TO--
WHAT I SAID A WHILE BACK, ABOUT YOU NOT BEING MY FATHER. OR THE REAL SPIDER-MAN...
MAY, STOP. NO ONE HERE WAS PUT THROUGH THE WRINGER MORE THAN YOU.
AND IN THE END, YOU DIDN'T LET IT BREAK YOU. YOU STAYED TRUE TO EVERYTHING THAT MAKES YOU... WELL...
...ONE OF THE MOST SPECTACULAR PEOPLE I'LL EVER KNOW.
NOW GET THROUGH THERE. GO HOME...
BENJY?
HE'S SAFE, MAYDAY.
YOU. THE OTHER BEN PARKER.
YOU BROUGHT MY LITTLE BROTHER BACK HERE. WHERE IS HE?
AT THE NEIGHBORS. THERE WERE A COUPLE PEOPLE THERE...
...WHO JUST REFUSED TO LET GO OF THE LITTLE SCAMP.
EVERYBODY, SHE'S HOME!

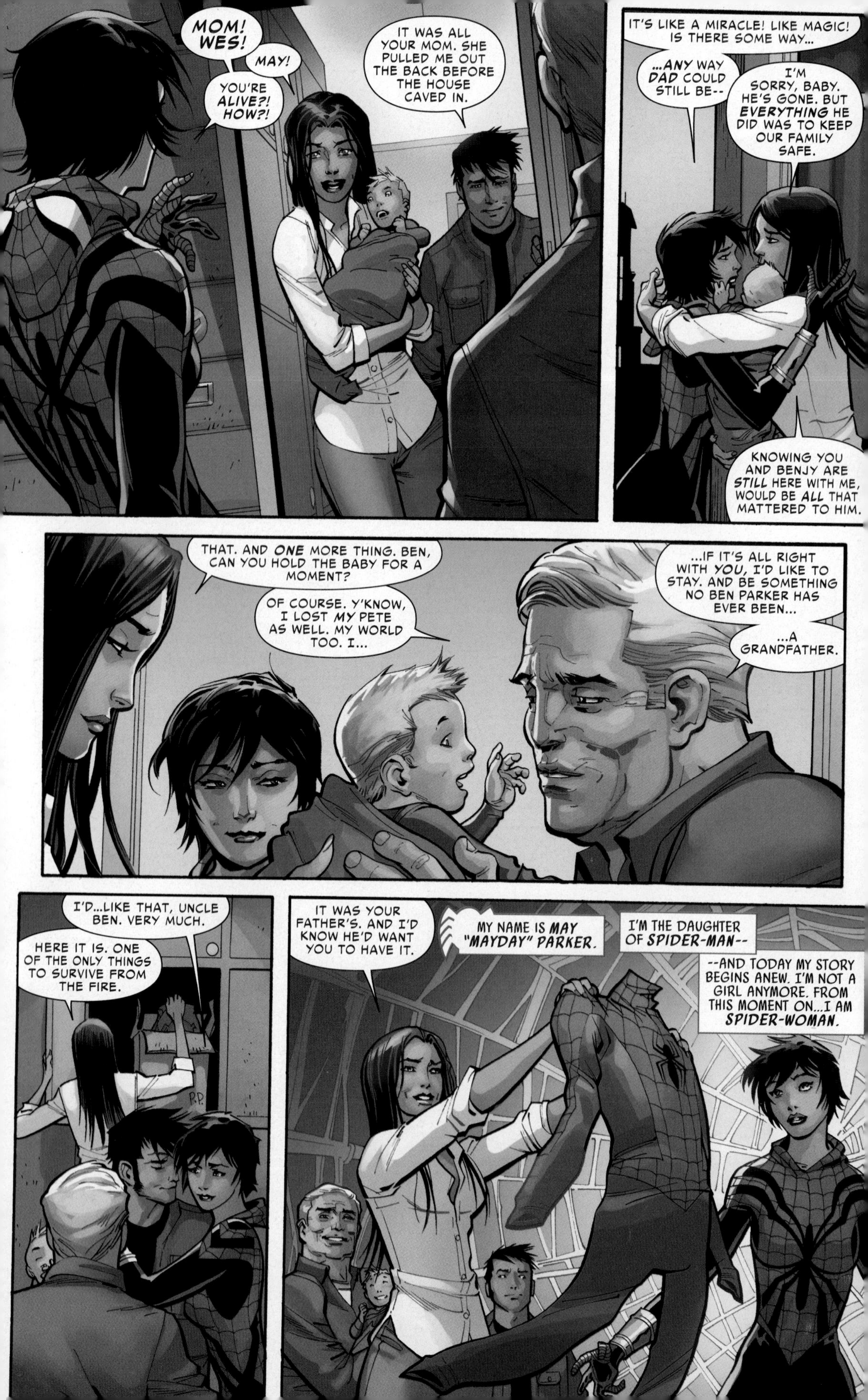
MOM! WES!
MAY!
YOU'RE ALIVE?! HOW?!
IT WAS ALL YOUR MOM. SHE PULLED ME OUT THE BACK BEFORE THE HOUSE CAVED IN.
IT'S LIKE A MIRACLE! LIKE MAGIC! IS THERE SOME WAY...
...ANY WAY DAD COULD STILL BE--
I'M SORRY, BABY. HE'S GONE. BUT EVERYTHING HE DID WAS TO KEEP OUR FAMILY SAFE.
KNOWING YOU AND BENJY ARE STILL HERE WITH ME, WOULD BE ALL THAT MATTERED TO HIM.
THAT. AND ONE MORE THING. BEN, CAN YOU HOLD THE BABY FOR A MOMENT?
OF COURSE. Y'KNOW, I LOST MY PETE AS WELL. MY WORLD TOO. I...
...IF IT'S ALL RIGHT WITH YOU, I'D LIKE TO STAY. AND BE SOMETHING NO BEN PARKER HAS EVER BEEN...
...A GRANDFATHER.
I'D...LIKE THAT, UNCLE BEN. VERY MUCH.
HERE IT IS. ONE OF THE ONLY THINGS TO SURVIVE FROM THE FIRE.
IT WAS YOUR FATHER'S. AND I'D KNOW HE'D WANT YOU TO HAVE IT.
MY NAME IS MAY "MAYDAY" PARKER.
I'M THE DAUGHTER OF SPIDER-MAN--
--AND TODAY MY STORY BEGINS ANEW. I'M NOT A GIRL ANYMORE. FROM THIS MOMENT ON...I AM SPIDER-WOMAN.

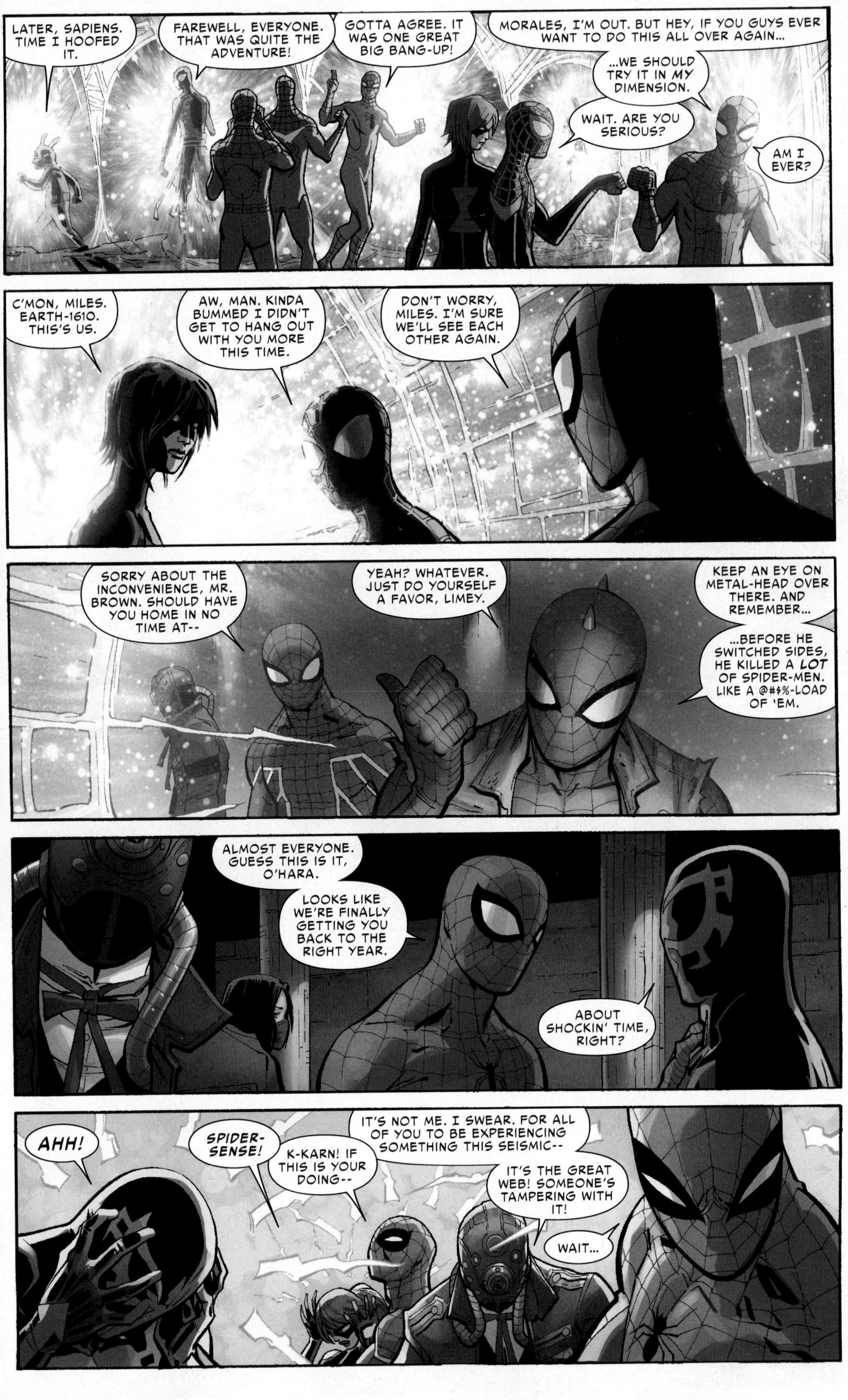
LATER, SAPIENS. TIME I HOOFED IT.
FAREWELL, EVERYONE. THAT WAS QUITE THE ADVENTURE!
GOTTA AGREE. IT WAS ONE GREAT BIG BANG-UP!
MORALES, I'M OUT. BUT HEY, IF YOU GUYS EVER WANT TO DO THIS ALL OVER AGAIN...
...WE SHOULD TRY IT IN MY DIMENSION.
WAIT. ARE YOU SERIOUS?
AM I EVER?
C'MON, MILES. EARTH-1610. THIS'S US.
AW, MAN. KINDA BUMMED I DIDN'T GET TO HANG OUT WITH YOU MORE THIS TIME.
DON'T WORRY, MILES. I'M SURE WE'LL SEE EACH OTHER AGAIN.
SORRY ABOUT THE INCONVENIENCE, MR. BROWN. SHOULD HAVE YOU HOME IN NO TIME AT--
YEAH? WHATEVER. JUST DO YOURSELF A FAVOR, LIMEY.
KEEP AN EYE ON METAL-HEAD OVER THERE. AND REMEMBER...
...BEFORE HE SWITCHED SIDES, HE KILLED A LOT OF SPIDER-MEN. LIKE A @#$%-LOAD OF 'EM.
ALMOST EVERYONE. GUESS THIS IS IT, O'HARA.
LOOKS LIKE WE'RE FINALLY GETTING YOU BACK TO THE RIGHT YEAR.
ABOUT SHOCKIN' TIME, RIGHT?
AHH!
SPIDER-SENSE!
K-KARN! IF THIS IS YOUR DOING--
IT'S NOT ME. I SWEAR. FOR ALL OF YOU TO BE EXPERIENCING SOMETHING THIS SEISMIC--
IT'S THE GREAT WEB! SOMEONE'S TAMPERING WITH IT!
WAIT...

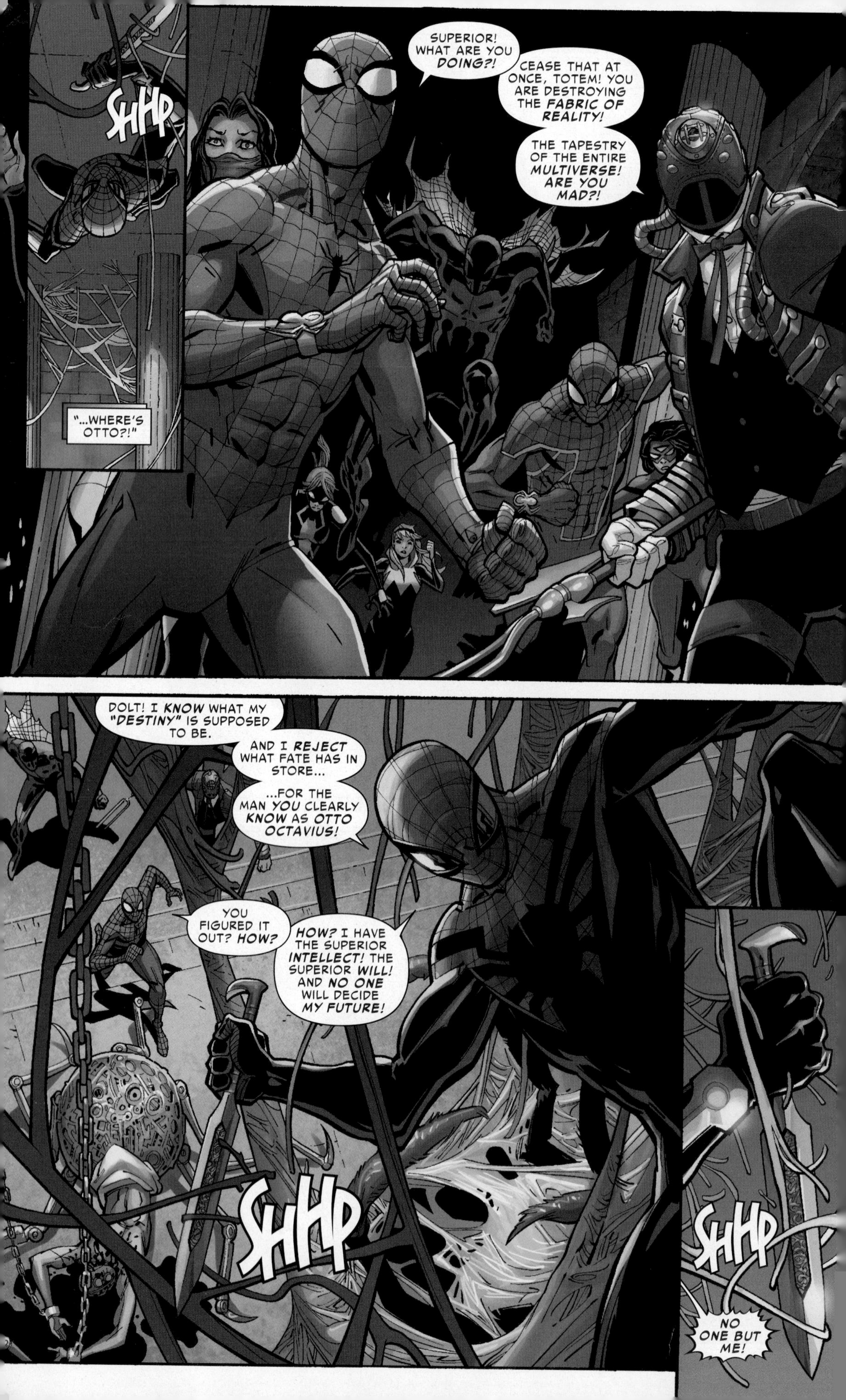
SHHP
"...WHERE'S OTTO?!"
SUPERIOR! WHAT ARE YOU DOING?!
CEASE THAT AT ONCE, TOTEM! YOU ARE DESTROYING THE FABRIC OF REALITY!
THE TAPESTRY OF THE ENTIRE MULTIVERSE! ARE YOU MAD?!
DOLT! I KNOW WHAT MY "DESTINY" IS SUPPOSED TO BE.
AND I REJECT WHAT FATE HAS IN STORE...
...FOR THE MAN YOU CLEARLY KNOW AS OTTO OCTAVIUS!
YOU FIGURED IT OUT? HOW?
HOW? I HAVE THE SUPERIOR INTELLECT! THE SUPERIOR WILL! AND NO ONE WILL DECIDE MY FUTURE!
SHHP
SHHP
NO ONE BUT ME!

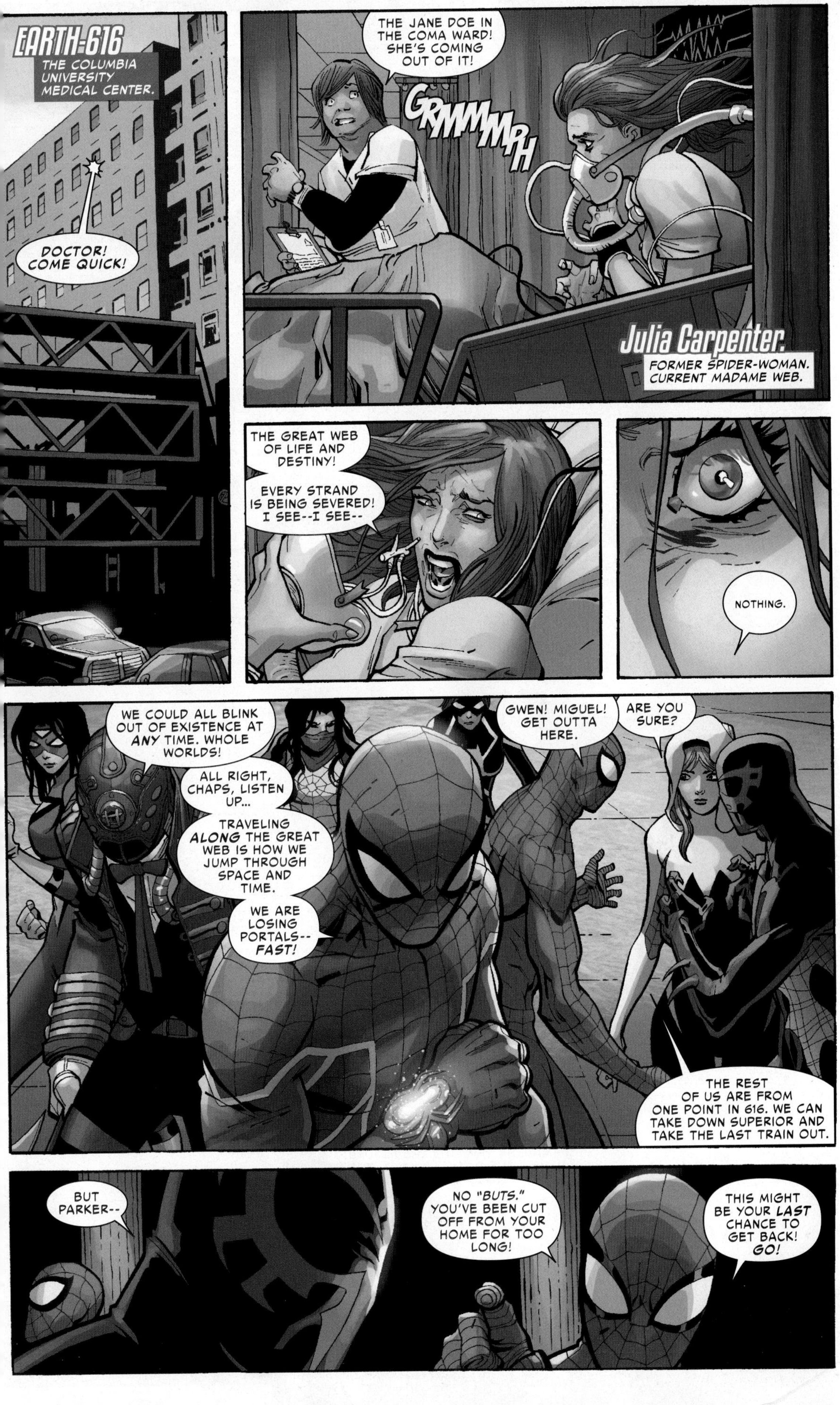
EARTH-616
THE COLUMBIA UNIVERSITY MEDICAL CENTER.
DOCTOR! COME QUICK!
THE JANE DOE IN THE COMA WARD! SHE'S COMING OUT OF IT!
GRMMMMRPH
Julia Carpenter.
FORMER SPIDER-WOMAN. CURRENT MADAME WEB.
THE GREAT WEB OF LIFE AND DESTINY!
EVERY STRAND IS BEING SEVERED! I SEE--I SEE--
NOTHING.
WE COULD ALL BLINK OUT OF EXISTENCE AT ANY TIME. WHOLE WORLDS!
ALL RIGHT, CHAPS, LISTEN UP...
TRAVELING ALONG THE GREAT WEB IS HOW WE JUMP THROUGH SPACE AND TIME.
WE ARE LOSING PORTALS-- FAST!
GWEN! MIGUEL! GET OUTTA HERE.
ARE YOU SURE?
THE REST OF US ARE FROM ONE POINT IN 616. WE CAN TAKE DOWN SUPERIOR AND TAKE THE LAST TRAIN OUT.
BUT PARKER--
NO "BUTS." YOU'VE BEEN CUT OFF FROM YOUR HOME FOR TOO LONG!
THIS MIGHT BE YOUR LAST CHANCE TO GET BACK! GO!

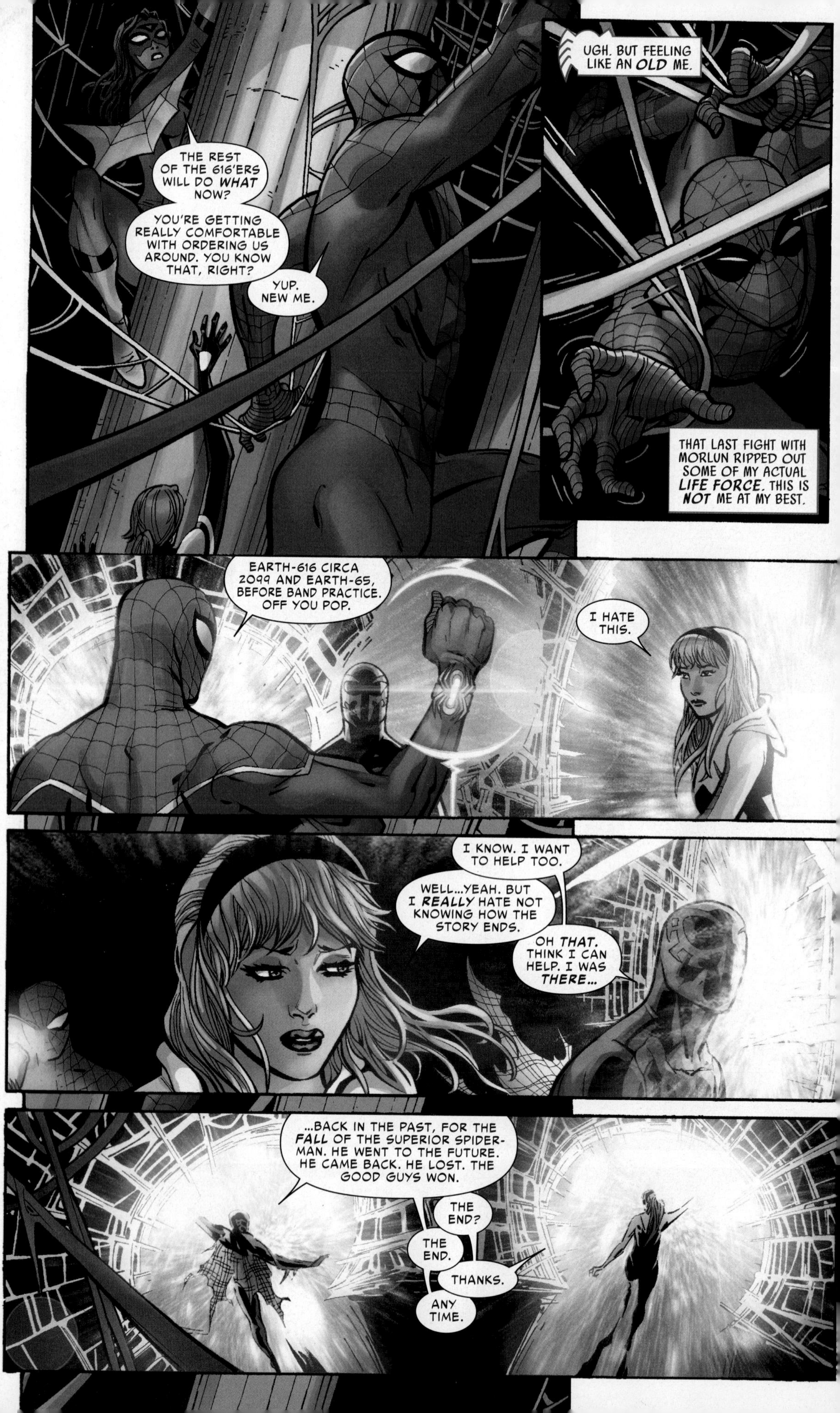
THE REST OF THE 616'ERS WILL DO WHAT NOW?
YOU'RE GETTING REALLY COMFORTABLE WITH ORDERING US AROUND. YOU KNOW THAT, RIGHT?
YUP. NEW ME.
UGH. BUT FEELING LIKE AN OLD ME.
THAT LAST FIGHT WITH MORLUN RIPPED OUT SOME OF MY ACTUAL LIFE FORCE. THIS IS NOT ME AT MY BEST.
EARTH-616 CIRCA 2099 AND EARTH-65, BEFORE BAND PRACTICE. OFF YOU POP.
I HATE THIS.
I KNOW. I WANT TO HELP TOO.
WELL...YEAH. BUT I REALLY HATE NOT KNOWING HOW THE STORY ENDS.
OH THAT. THINK I CAN HELP. I WAS THERE...
...BACK IN THE PAST, FOR THE FALL OF THE SUPERIOR SPIDER-MAN. HE WENT TO THE FUTURE. HE CAME BACK. HE LOST. THE GOOD GUYS WON.
THE END?
THE END.
THANKS.
ANY TIME.

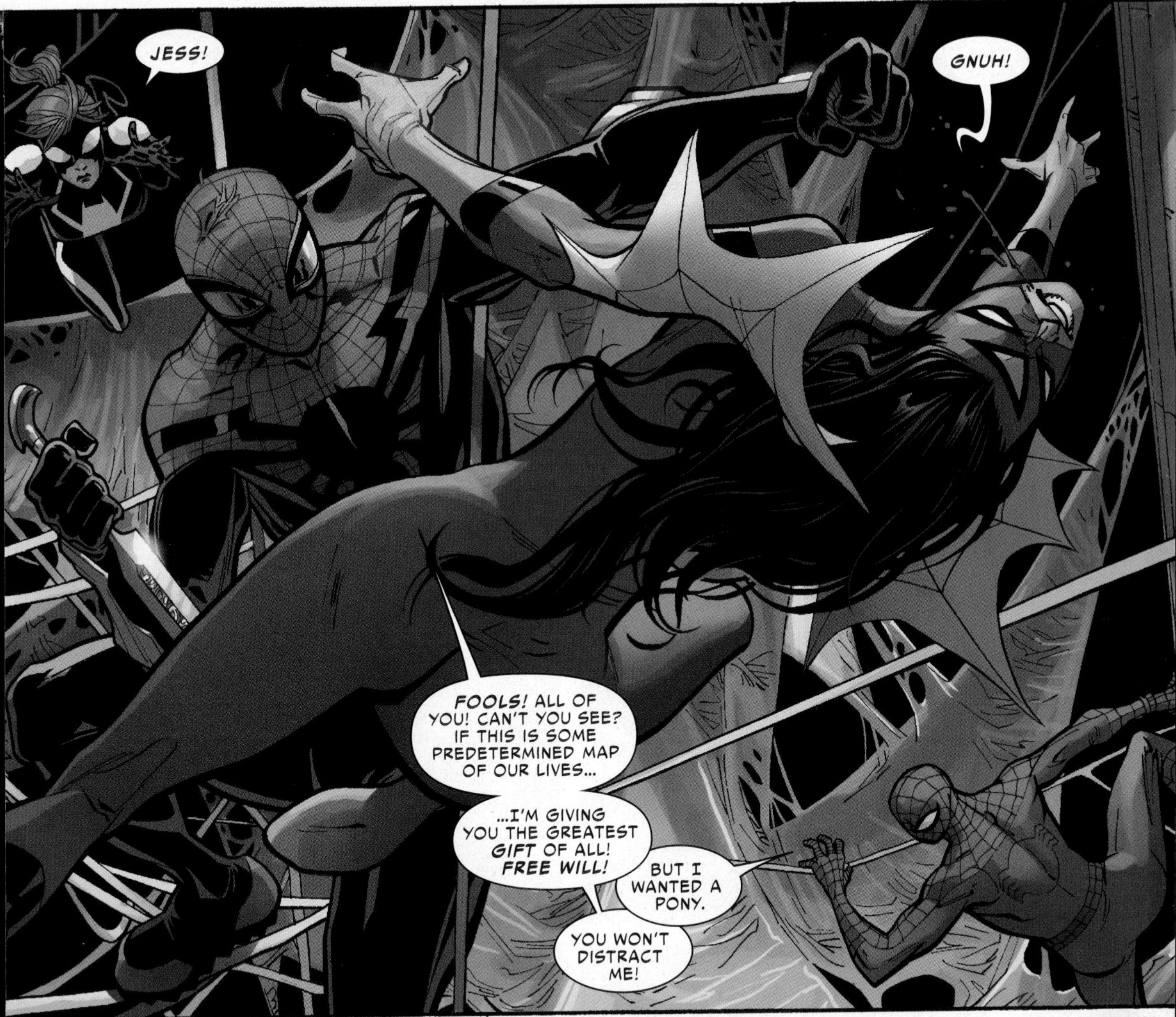
JESS!
GNUH!
FOOLS! ALL OF YOU! CAN'T YOU SEE? IF THIS IS SOME PREDETERMINED MAP OF OUR LIVES...
...I'M GIVING YOU THE GREATEST GIFT OF ALL! FREE WILL!
BUT I WANTED A PONY.
YOU WON'T DISTRACT ME!
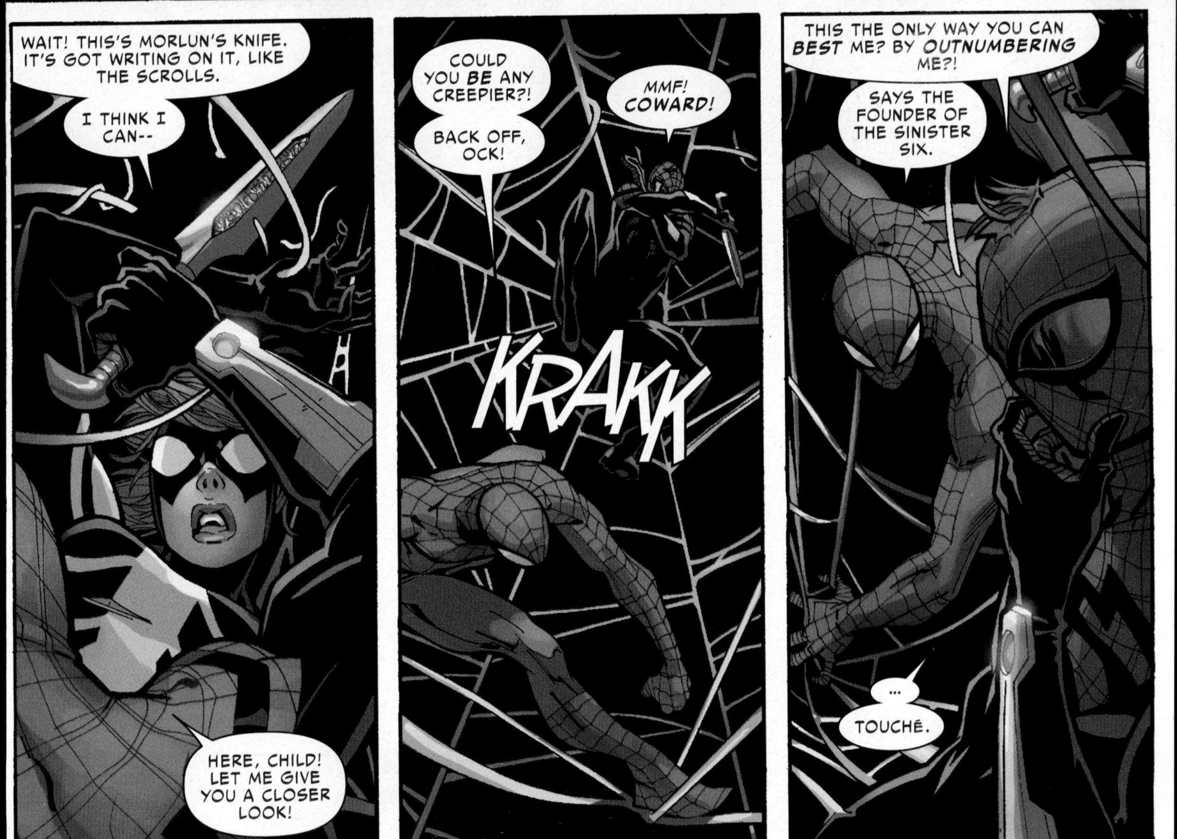
WAIT! THIS'S MORLUN'S KNIFE. IT'S GOT WRITING ON IT, LIKE THE SCROLLS.
I THINK I CAN--
HERE, CHILD! LET ME GIVE YOU A CLOSER LOOK!
COULD YOU BE ANY CREEPIER?!
BACK OFF, OCK!
MMF! COWARD!
KRAKK
THIS THE ONLY WAY YOU CAN BEST ME? BY OUTNUMBERING ME?!
SAYS THE FOUNDER OF THE SINISTER SIX.
...
TOUCHÉ.

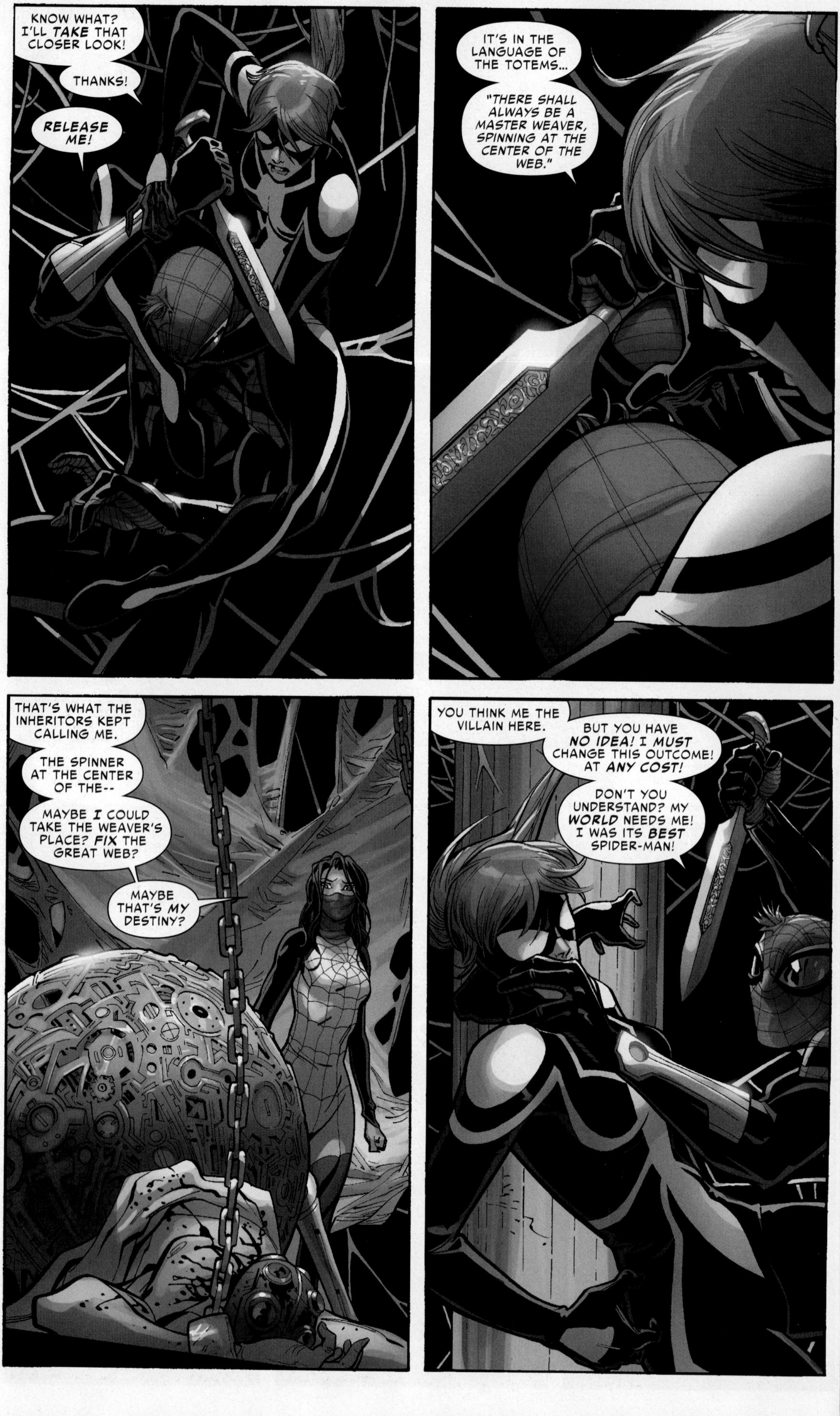
KNOW WHAT? I'LL *TAKE* THAT CLOSER LOOK!
THANKS!
RELEASE ME!
IT'S IN THE LANGUAGE OF THE TOTEMS...
"THERE SHALL ALWAYS BE A MASTER WEAVER, SPINNING AT THE CENTER OF THE WEB."
THAT'S WHAT THE INHERITORS KEPT CALLING ME.
THE SPINNER AT THE CENTER OF THE--
MAYBE *I* COULD TAKE THE WEAVER'S PLACE? *FIX* THE GREAT WEB?
MAYBE THAT'S *MY* DESTINY?
YOU THINK ME THE VILLAIN HERE.
BUT YOU HAVE *NO IDEA! I MUST* CHANGE THIS OUTCOME! AT *ANY COST!*
DON'T YOU UNDERSTAND? MY *WORLD* NEEDS ME! I WAS ITS *BEST* SPIDER-MAN!

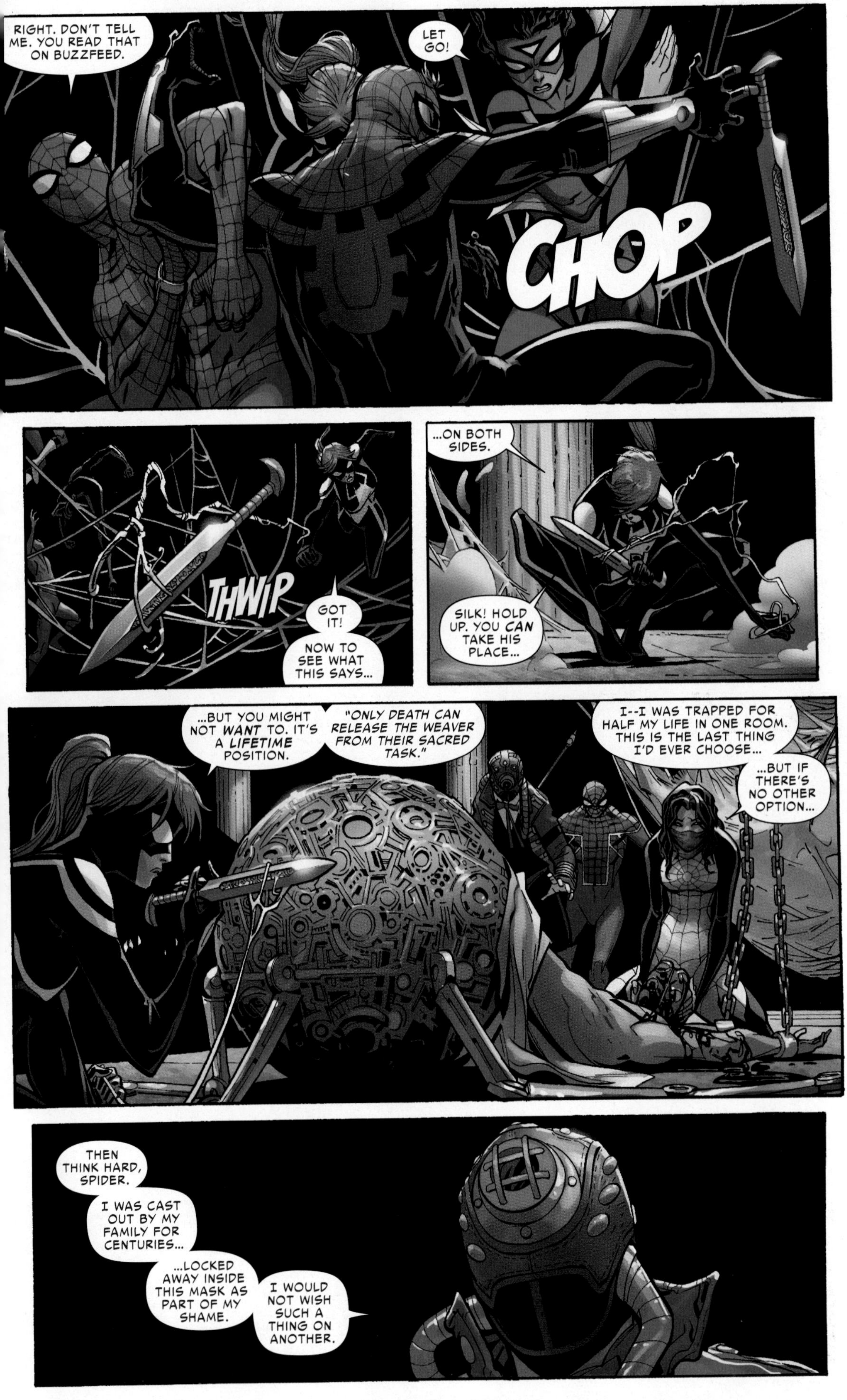
RIGHT. DON'T TELL ME. YOU READ THAT ON BUZZFEED.
LET GO!
CHOP
THWIP
GOT IT!
NOW TO SEE WHAT THIS SAYS...
...ON BOTH SIDES.
SILK! HOLD UP. YOU CAN TAKE HIS PLACE...
...BUT YOU MIGHT NOT WANT TO. IT'S A LIFETIME POSITION.
"ONLY DEATH CAN RELEASE THE WEAVER FROM THEIR SACRED TASK."
I--I WAS TRAPPED FOR HALF MY LIFE IN ONE ROOM. THIS IS THE LAST THING I'D EVER CHOOSE...
...BUT IF THERE'S NO OTHER OPTION...
THEN THINK HARD, SPIDER.
I WAS CAST OUT BY MY FAMILY FOR CENTURIES...
...LOCKED AWAY INSIDE THIS MASK AS PART OF MY SHAME.
I WOULD NOT WISH SUCH A THING ON ANOTHER.

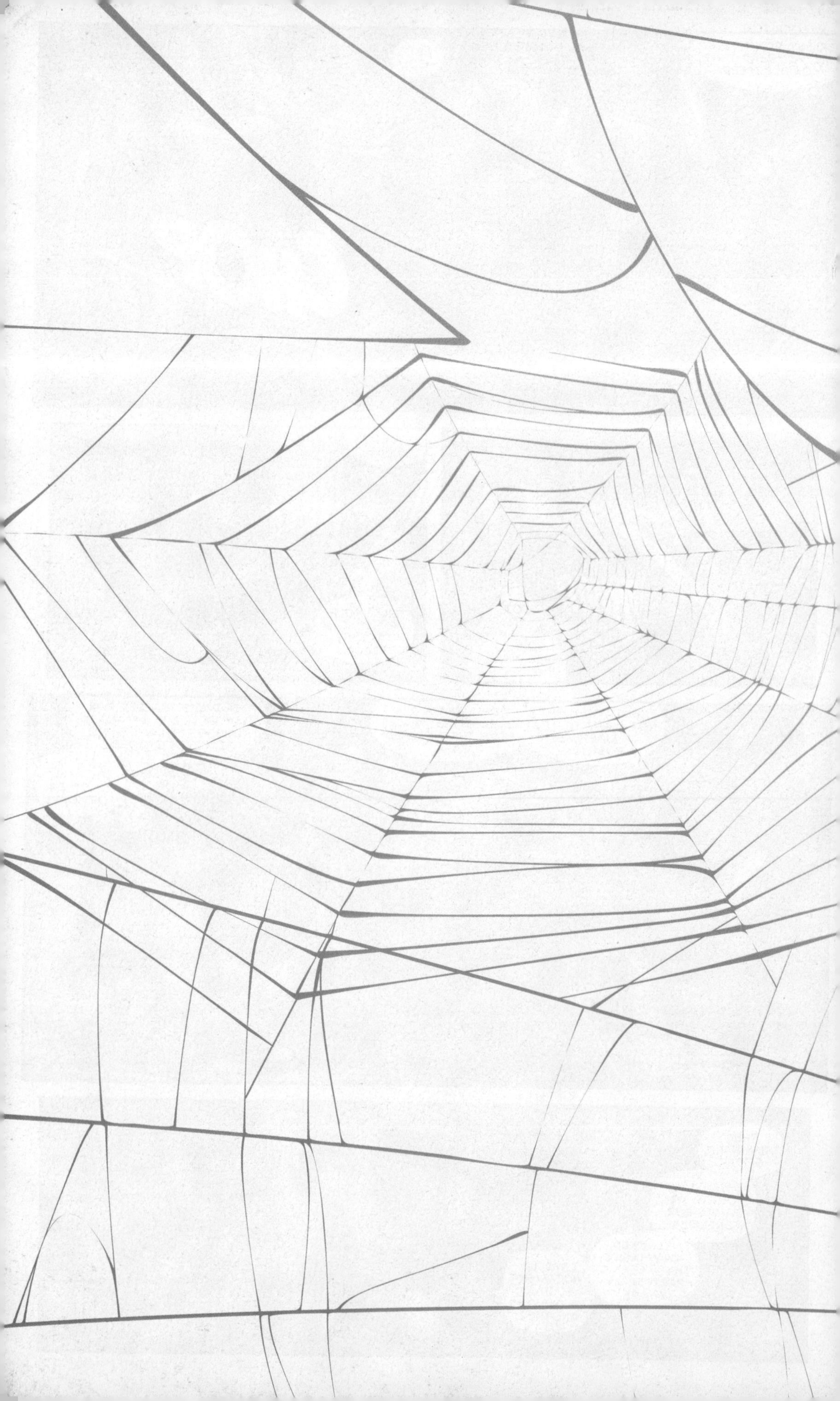

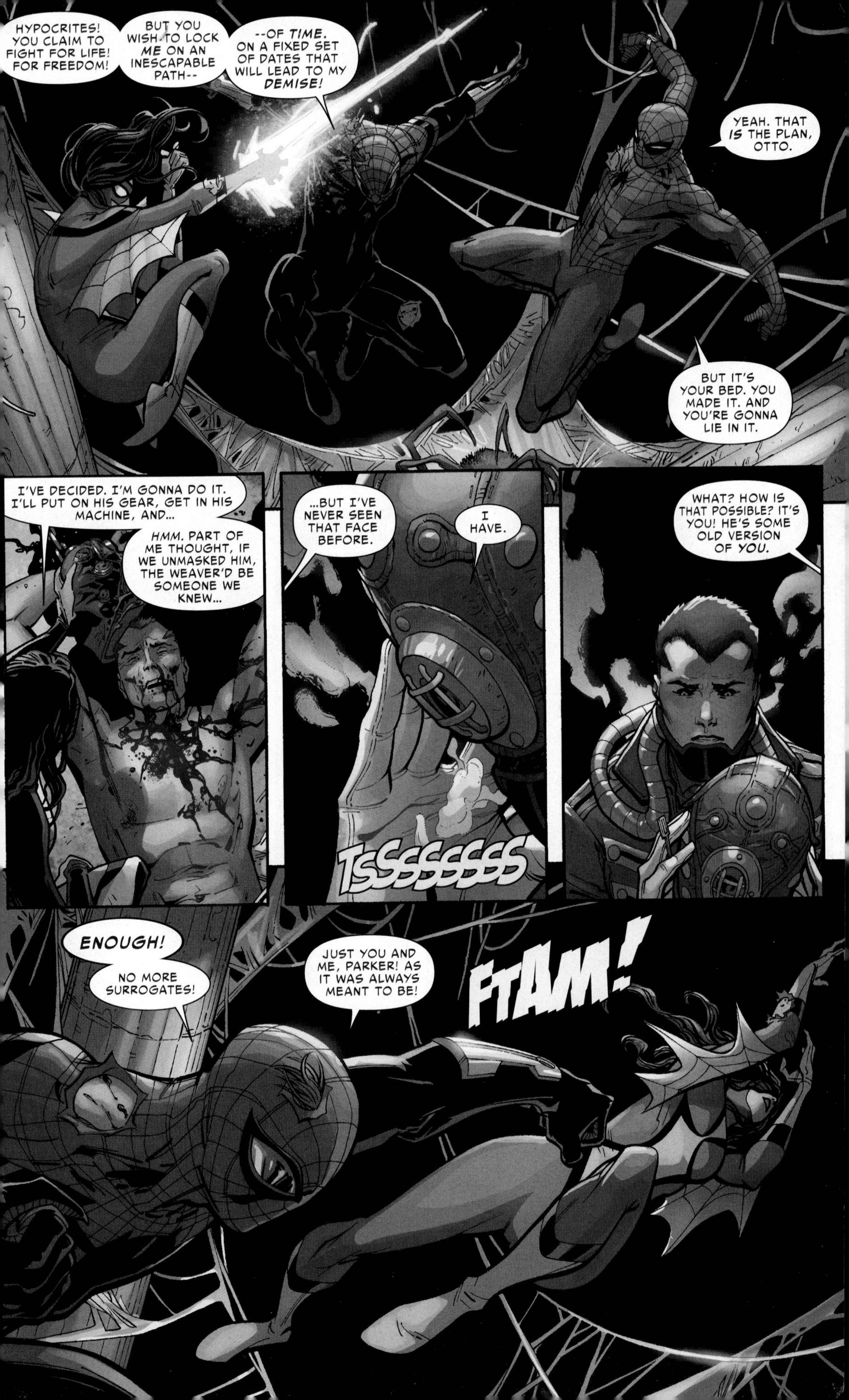
HYPOCRITES! YOU CLAIM TO FIGHT FOR LIFE! FOR FREEDOM!
BUT YOU WISH TO LOCK *ME* ON AN INESCAPABLE PATH--
--OF *TIME*. ON A FIXED SET OF DATES THAT WILL LEAD TO MY *DEMISE!*
YEAH. THAT *IS* THE PLAN, OTTO.
BUT IT'S YOUR BED. YOU MADE IT. AND YOU'RE GONNA LIE IN IT.
I'VE DECIDED. I'M GONNA DO IT. I'LL PUT ON HIS GEAR, GET IN HIS MACHINE, AND...
HMM. PART OF ME THOUGHT, IF WE UNMASKED HIM, THE WEAVER'D BE SOMEONE WE KNEW...
...BUT I'VE NEVER SEEN THAT FACE BEFORE.
I HAVE.
TSSSSSSSS
WHAT? HOW IS THAT POSSIBLE? IT'S YOU! HE'S SOME OLD VERSION OF *YOU*.
ENOUGH!
NO MORE SURROGATES!
JUST YOU AND ME, PARKER! AS IT WAS ALWAYS MEANT TO BE!
FTAM!

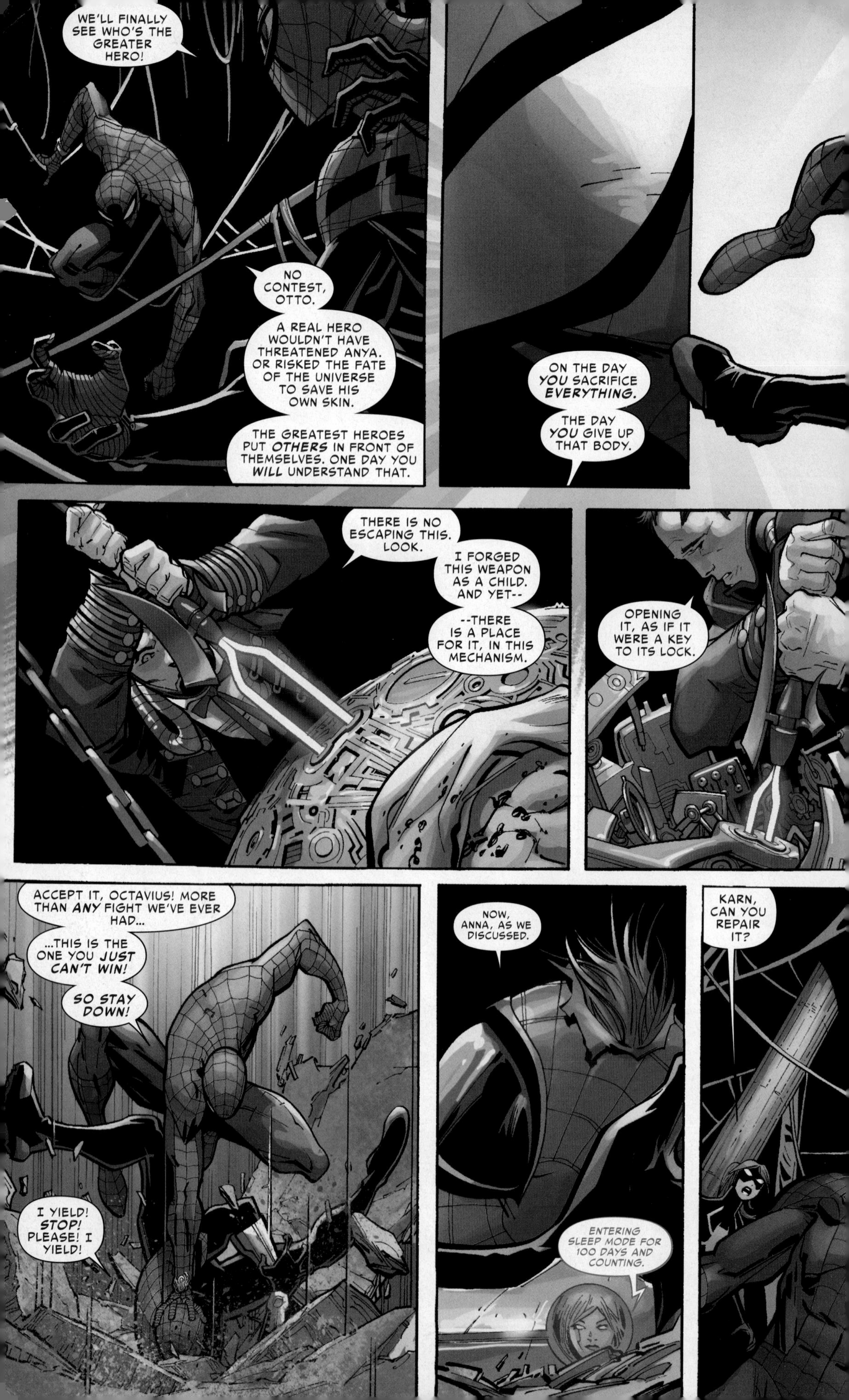
WE'LL FINALLY SEE WHO'S THE GREATER HERO!
NO CONTEST, OTTO.
A REAL HERO WOULDN'T HAVE THREATENED ANYA. OR RISKED THE FATE OF THE UNIVERSE TO SAVE HIS OWN SKIN.
THE GREATEST HEROES PUT OTHERS IN FRONT OF THEMSELVES. ONE DAY YOU WILL UNDERSTAND THAT.
ON THE DAY YOU SACRIFICE EVERYTHING.
THE DAY YOU GIVE UP THAT BODY.
THERE IS NO ESCAPING THIS. LOOK.
I FORGED THIS WEAPON AS A CHILD. AND YET--
--THERE IS A PLACE FOR IT, IN THIS MECHANISM.
OPENING IT, AS IF IT WERE A KEY TO ITS LOCK.
ACCEPT IT, OCTAVIUS! MORE THAN ANY FIGHT WE'VE EVER HAD...
...THIS IS THE ONE YOU JUST CAN'T WIN!
SO STAY DOWN!
I YIELD! STOP! PLEASE! I YIELD!
NOW, ANNA, AS WE DISCUSSED.
ENTERING SLEEP MODE FOR 100 DAYS AND COUNTING.
KARN, CAN YOU REPAIR IT?

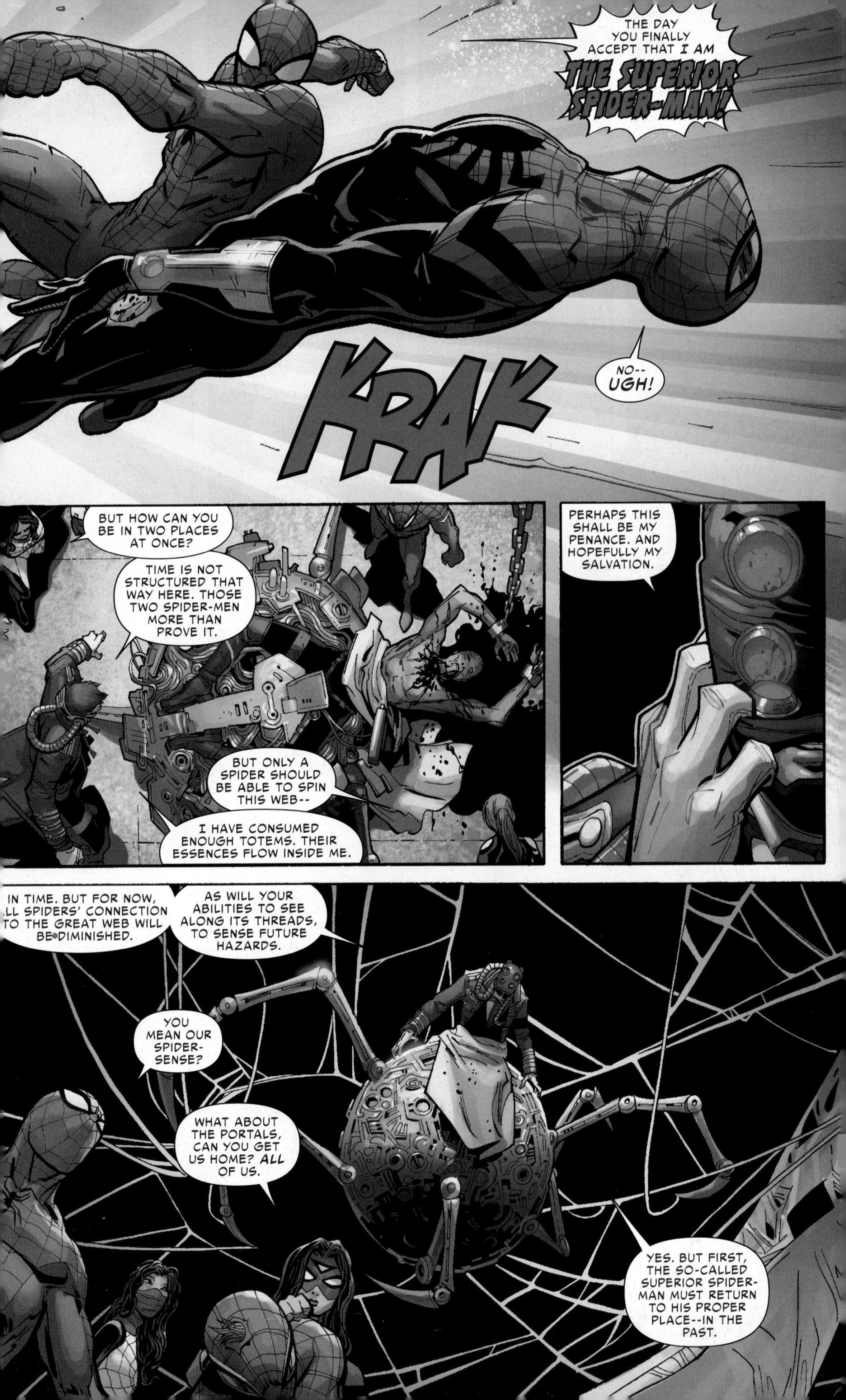
THE DAY YOU FINALLY ACCEPT THAT I AM THE SUPERIOR SPIDER-MAN!
KRAK
NO-- UGH!
BUT HOW CAN YOU BE IN TWO PLACES AT ONCE?
TIME IS NOT STRUCTURED THAT WAY HERE. THOSE TWO SPIDER-MEN MORE THAN PROVE IT.
BUT ONLY A SPIDER SHOULD BE ABLE TO SPIN THIS WEB--
I HAVE CONSUMED ENOUGH TOTEMS. THEIR ESSENCES FLOW INSIDE ME.
PERHAPS THIS SHALL BE MY PENANCE. AND HOPEFULLY MY SALVATION.
IN TIME. BUT FOR NOW, LL SPIDERS' CONNECTION TO THE GREAT WEB WILL BE DIMINISHED.
AS WILL YOUR ABILITIES TO SEE ALONG ITS THREADS, TO SENSE FUTURE HAZARDS.
YOU MEAN OUR SPIDER-SENSE?
WHAT ABOUT THE PORTALS, CAN YOU GET US HOME? ALL OF US.
YES. BUT FIRST, THE SO-CALLED SUPERIOR SPIDER-MAN MUST RETURN TO HIS PROPER PLACE--IN THE PAST.

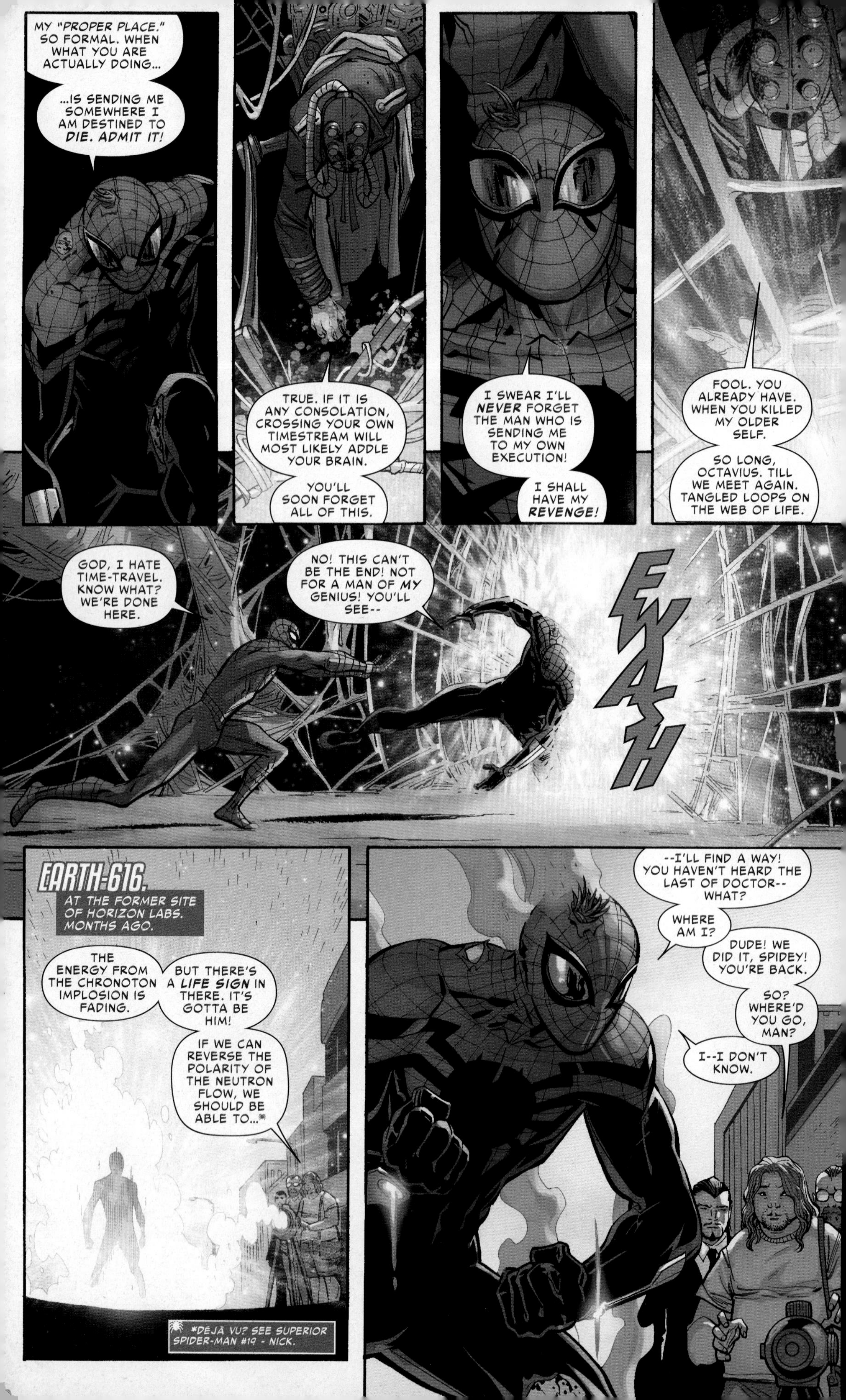

MY "PROPER PLACE." SO FORMAL. WHEN WHAT YOU ARE ACTUALLY DOING...
...IS SENDING ME SOMEWHERE I AM DESTINED TO DIE. ADMIT IT!
TRUE. IF IT IS ANY CONSOLATION, CROSSING YOUR OWN TIMESTREAM WILL MOST LIKELY ADDLE YOUR BRAIN.
YOU'LL SOON FORGET ALL OF THIS.
I SWEAR I'LL NEVER FORGET THE MAN WHO IS SENDING ME TO MY OWN EXECUTION!
I SHALL HAVE MY REVENGE!
FOOL. YOU ALREADY HAVE. WHEN YOU KILLED MY OLDER SELF.
SO LONG, OCTAVIUS. TILL WE MEET AGAIN. TANGLED LOOPS ON THE WEB OF LIFE.
GOD, I HATE TIME-TRAVEL. KNOW WHAT? WE'RE DONE HERE.
NO! THIS CAN'T BE THE END! NOT FOR A MAN OF MY GENIUS! YOU'LL SEE--
FWASH
EARTH-616.
AT THE FORMER SITE OF HORIZON LABS. MONTHS AGO.
THE ENERGY FROM THE CHRONOTON IMPLOSION IS FADING.
BUT THERE'S A LIFE SIGN IN THERE. IT'S GOTTA BE HIM!
IF WE CAN REVERSE THE POLARITY OF THE NEUTRON FLOW, WE SHOULD BE ABLE TO...*
*DÉJÀ VU? SEE SUPERIOR SPIDER-MAN #19 - NICK.
--I'LL FIND A WAY! YOU HAVEN'T HEARD THE LAST OF DOCTOR-- WHAT?
WHERE AM I?
DUDE! WE DID IT, SPIDEY! YOU'RE BACK.
SO? WHERE'D YOU GO, MAN?
I--I DON'T KNOW.

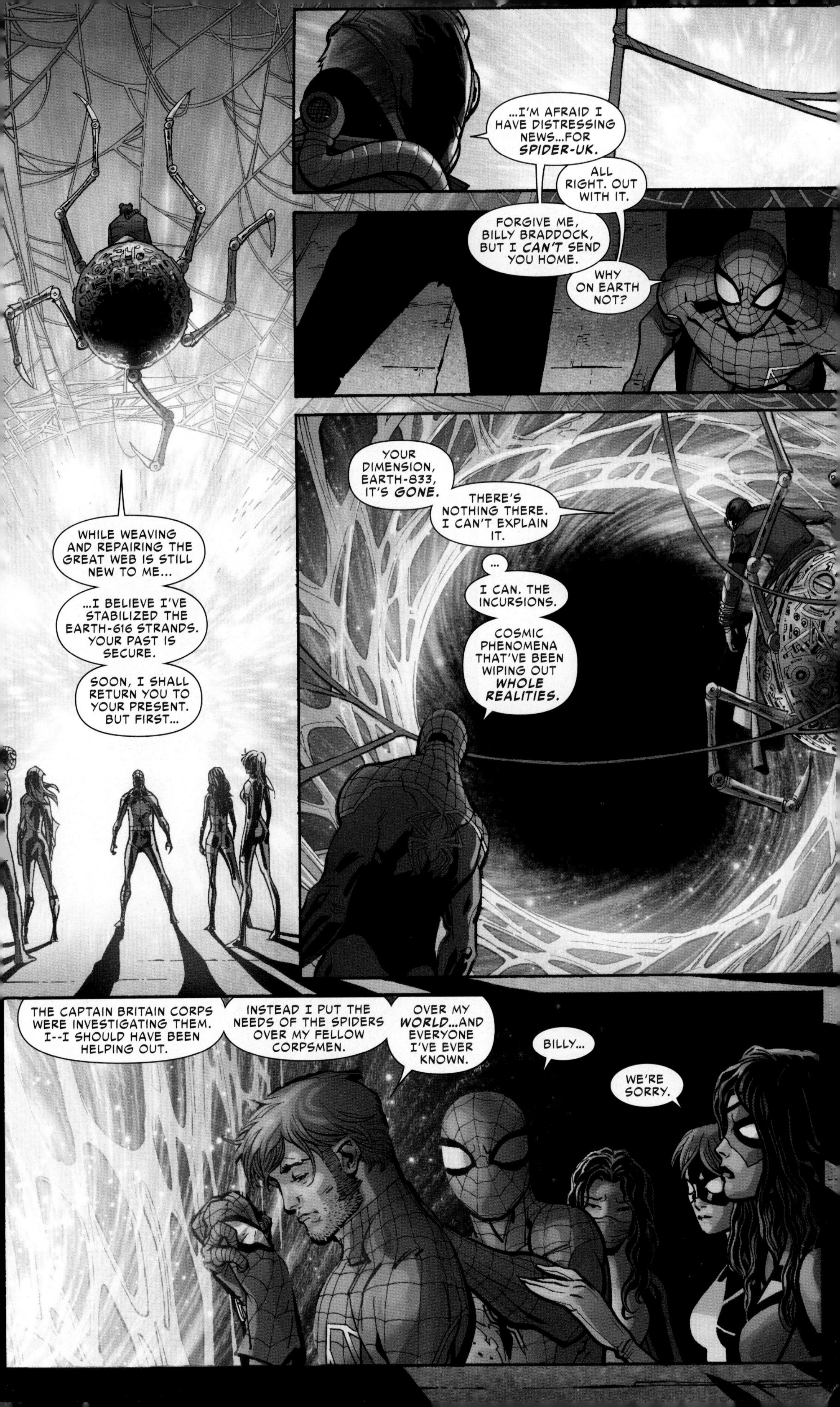
...I'M AFRAID I HAVE DISTRESSING NEWS...FOR SPIDER-UK.
ALL RIGHT. OUT WITH IT.
FORGIVE ME, BILLY BRADDOCK, BUT I CAN'T SEND YOU HOME.
WHY ON EARTH NOT?
WHILE WEAVING AND REPAIRING THE GREAT WEB IS STILL NEW TO ME...
...I BELIEVE I'VE STABILIZED THE EARTH-616 STRANDS. YOUR PAST IS SECURE.
SOON, I SHALL RETURN YOU TO YOUR PRESENT. BUT FIRST...
YOUR DIMENSION, EARTH-833, IT'S GONE.
THERE'S NOTHING THERE. I CAN'T EXPLAIN IT.
...
I CAN. THE INCURSIONS.
COSMIC PHENOMENA THAT'VE BEEN WIPING OUT WHOLE REALITIES.
THE CAPTAIN BRITAIN CORPS WERE INVESTIGATING THEM. I--I SHOULD HAVE BEEN HELPING OUT.
INSTEAD I PUT THE NEEDS OF THE SPIDERS OVER MY FELLOW CORPSMEN.
OVER MY WORLD...AND EVERYONE I'VE EVER KNOWN.
BILLY...
WE'RE SORRY.

I KNOW IT DOESN'T COMPARE, BUT WITHOUT *YOU* BRINGING US ALL TOGETHER...

...WE SPIDERS WOULDN'T HAVE STOOD A CHANCE AGAINST THE INHERITORS.

THANKS, MATE.

SPEAKING OF THE BIG BAD GUYS...

...WE'RE SURE THAT RADIOACTIVE WORLD CAN HOLD 'EM?

AND *NOT*... Y'KNOW...*KILL* THEM? I MEAN, DON'T THEY NEED TO EAT SPIDER TOTEMS TO LIVE?

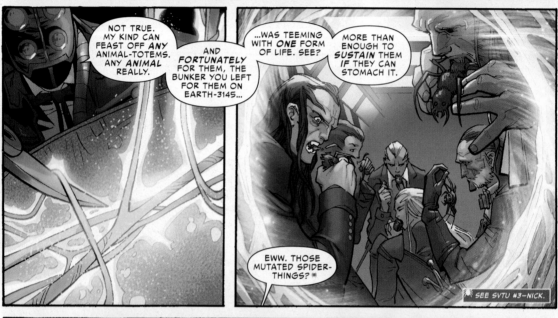

NOT TRUE. MY KIND CAN FEAST OFF *ANY* ANIMAL-TOTEMS. ANY *ANIMAL* REALLY.

AND *FORTUNATELY* FOR THEM, THE BUNKER YOU LEFT FOR THEM ON EARTH-3145...

...WAS TEEMING WITH *ONE* FORM OF LIFE. SEE?

MORE THAN ENOUGH TO *SUSTAIN* THEM IF THEY CAN STOMACH IT.

EWW. THOSE MUTATED SPIDER-THINGS?

SEE SVTU #3—NICK.

GOOD. IT'S MORE THAN THEY DESERVE.

WE LOST A LOT OF GOOD SPIDER-MEN BECAUSE OF THEM.

INCLUDING MY FRIEND, MY BROTHER, KAINE.

HE DESERVED BETTER THAN TO GO OUT LIKE...*THAT.*

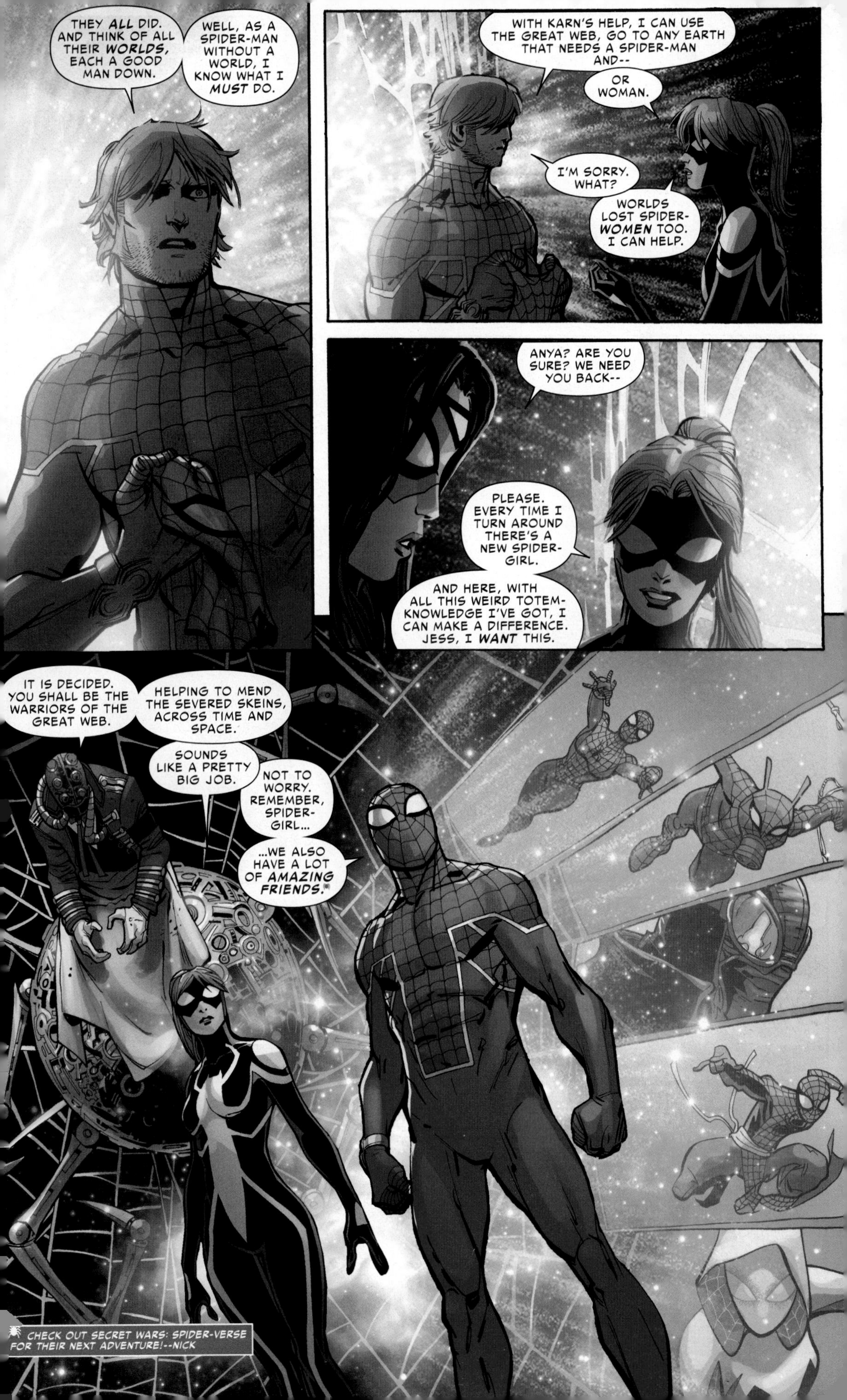
THEY ALL DID. AND THINK OF ALL THEIR WORLDS, EACH A GOOD MAN DOWN.
WELL, AS A SPIDER-MAN WITHOUT A WORLD, I KNOW WHAT I MUST DO.
WITH KARN'S HELP, I CAN USE THE GREAT WEB, GO TO ANY EARTH THAT NEEDS A SPIDER-MAN AND--
OR WOMAN.
I'M SORRY. WHAT?
WORLDS LOST SPIDER-WOMEN TOO. I CAN HELP.
ANYA? ARE YOU SURE? WE NEED YOU BACK--
PLEASE. EVERY TIME I TURN AROUND THERE'S A NEW SPIDER-GIRL.
AND HERE, WITH ALL THIS WEIRD TOTEM-KNOWLEDGE I'VE GOT, I CAN MAKE A DIFFERENCE. JESS, I WANT THIS.
IT IS DECIDED. YOU SHALL BE THE WARRIORS OF THE GREAT WEB.
HELPING TO MEND THE SEVERED SKEINS, ACROSS TIME AND SPACE.
SOUNDS LIKE A PRETTY BIG JOB.
NOT TO WORRY. REMEMBER, SPIDER-GIRL...
...WE ALSO HAVE A LOT OF AMAZING FRIENDS.
CHECK OUT SECRET WARS: SPIDER-VERSE FOR THEIR NEXT ADVENTURE!--NICK

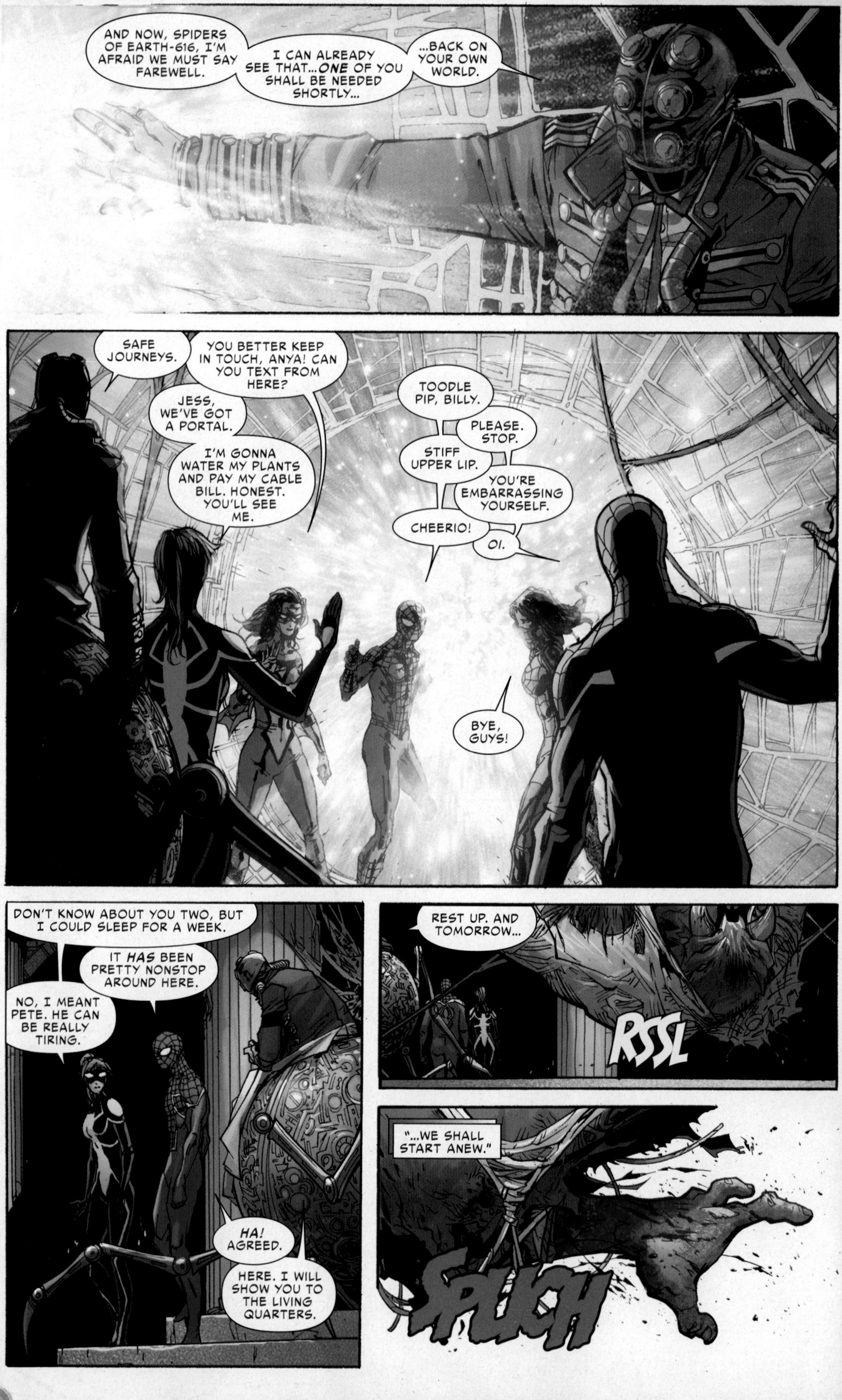
AND NOW, SPIDERS OF EARTH-616, I'M AFRAID WE MUST SAY FAREWELL.
I CAN ALREADY SEE THAT...ONE OF YOU SHALL BE NEEDED SHORTLY...
...BACK ON YOUR OWN WORLD.
SAFE JOURNEYS.
YOU BETTER KEEP IN TOUCH, ANYA! CAN YOU TEXT FROM HERE?
JESS, WE'VE GOT A PORTAL.
I'M GONNA WATER MY PLANTS AND PAY MY CABLE BILL. HONEST. YOU'LL SEE ME.
TOODLE PIP, BILLY.
PLEASE. STOP.
STIFF UPPER LIP.
YOU'RE EMBARRASSING YOURSELF.
CHEERIO!
OI.
BYE, GUYS!
DON'T KNOW ABOUT YOU TWO, BUT I COULD SLEEP FOR A WEEK.
IT HAS BEEN PRETTY NONSTOP AROUND HERE.
NO, I MEANT PETE. HE CAN BE REALLY TIRING.
HA! AGREED.
HERE. I WILL SHOW YOU TO THE LIVING QUARTERS.
REST UP. AND TOMORROW...
RSSL
"...WE SHALL START ANEW."
SPLUCH

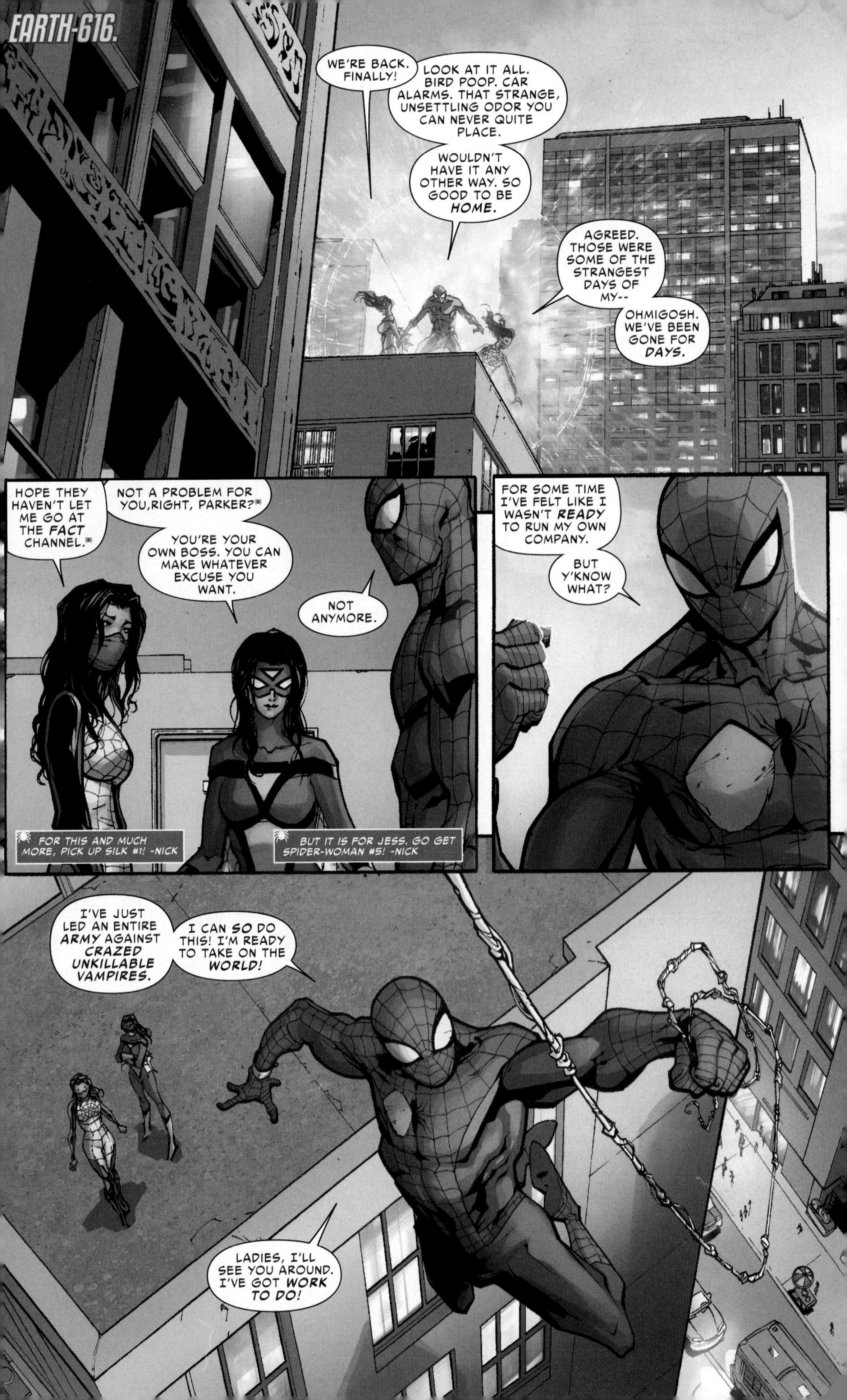
EARTH-616.
WE'RE BACK. FINALLY!
LOOK AT IT ALL. BIRD POOP. CAR ALARMS. THAT STRANGE, UNSETTLING ODOR YOU CAN NEVER QUITE PLACE.
WOULDN'T HAVE IT ANY OTHER WAY. SO GOOD TO BE HOME.
AGREED. THOSE WERE SOME OF THE STRANGEST DAYS OF MY--
OHMIGOSH. WE'VE BEEN GONE FOR DAYS.
HOPE THEY HAVEN'T LET ME GO AT THE FACT CHANNEL.
NOT A PROBLEM FOR YOU,RIGHT, PARKER?
YOU'RE YOUR OWN BOSS. YOU CAN MAKE WHATEVER EXCUSE YOU WANT.
NOT ANYMORE.
FOR THIS AND MUCH MORE, PICK UP SILK #1! -NICK
BUT IT IS FOR JESS. GO GET SPIDER-WOMAN #5! -NICK
FOR SOME TIME I'VE FELT LIKE I WASN'T READY TO RUN MY OWN COMPANY.
BUT Y'KNOW WHAT?
I'VE JUST LED AN ENTIRE ARMY AGAINST CRAZED UNKILLABLE VAMPIRES.
I CAN SO DO THIS! I'M READY TO TAKE ON THE WORLD!
LADIES, I'LL SEE YOU AROUND. I'VE GOT WORK TO DO!

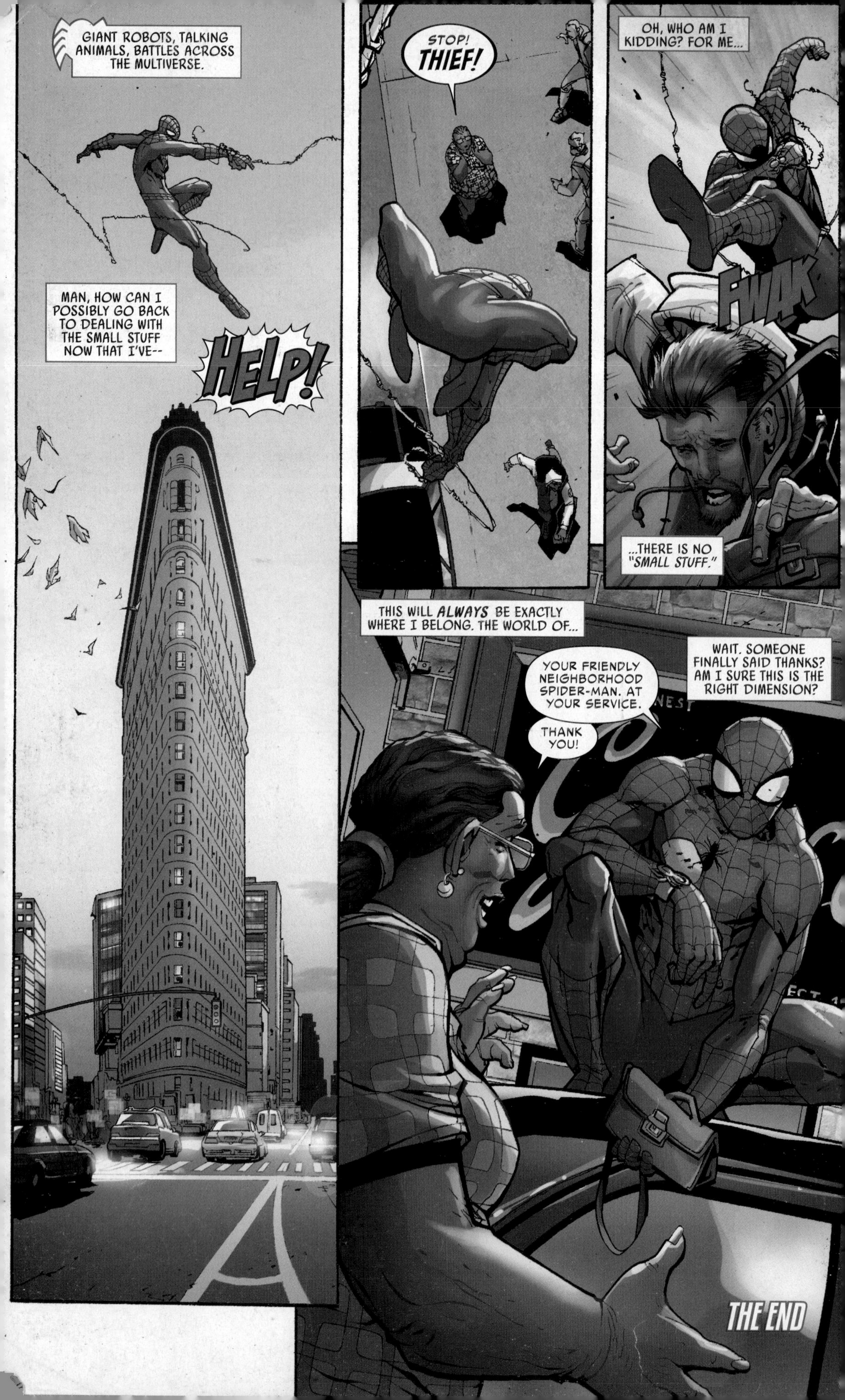
GIANT ROBOTS, TALKING ANIMALS, BATTLES ACROSS THE MULTIVERSE.
MAN, HOW CAN I POSSIBLY GO BACK TO DEALING WITH THE SMALL STUFF NOW THAT I'VE--
HELP!
STOP! THIEF!
OH, WHO AM I KIDDING? FOR ME...
FWAK
...THERE IS NO "SMALL STUFF."
THIS WILL ALWAYS BE EXACTLY WHERE I BELONG. THE WORLD OF...
YOUR FRIENDLY NEIGHBORHOOD SPIDER-MAN. AT YOUR SERVICE.
THANK YOU!
WAIT. SOMEONE FINALLY SAID THANKS? AM I SURE THIS IS THE RIGHT DIMENSION?
THE END